LGBT Psychology and Mental Health

Recent Titles in Practical and Applied Psychology

The Powerful Bond between People and Pets: Our Boundless Connections to
Companion Animals
P. Elizabeth Anderson

Sexual Enslavement of Girls and Women Worldwide
Andrea Parrot and Nina Cummings

The Global Muslim Community at a Crossroads: Understanding Religious
Beliefs, Practices, and Infighting to End the Conflict
Abdul Basit, Editor

Living in an Environmentally Traumatized World: Healing Ourselves and Our
Planet
Darlyne G. Nemeth, Robert B. Hamilton, and Judy Kuriansky, Editors

The Psychology of Black Boys and Adolescents
Kirkland Vaughans and Warren Spielberg, Editors

Lucid Dreaming: New Perspectives on Consciousness in Sleep
Ryan Hurd and Kelly Bulkeley, Editors

The Myth of Black Anti-Intellectualism: A True Psychology of African American Students
Kevin O. Cokley

Borderline Personality Disorder: New Perspectives on a Stigmatizing and Over-
used Diagnosis
Jacqueline Simon Gunn and Brent Potter

Ecopsychology: Advances from the Intersection of Psychology and Environmental Protection
*Darlyne G. Nemeth, Set Editor, with Robert B. Hamilton and Judy Kuriansky, Vol-
ume Editors*

Weapons of Mass Psychological Destruction and the People Who Use Them
Larry C. James and Terry L. Oroszi, Editors

The Psychosocial Aspects of a Deadly Epidemic: What Ebola Has Taught Us
about Holistic Healing
Judy Kuriansky, PhD, Editor

LGBT Psychology and Mental Health
Emerging Research and Advances

Richard Ruth and Erik Santacruz,
Editors

Practical and Applied Psychology
Judy Kuriansky, Series Editor

 PRAEGER™

An Imprint of ABC-CLIO, LLC
Santa Barbara, California • Denver, Colorado

Library of Congress Cataloging-in-Publication Data

Names: Ruth, Richard, editor. | Santacruz, Erik, editor.
Title: LGBT psychology and mental health : emerging research and advances / Richard Ruth and
  Erik Santacruz, editors.
Description: Santa Barbara, California : Praeger, [2017] | Series: Practical and applied
  psychology | Includes bibliographical references and index.
Identifiers: LCCN 2017026566 (print) | LCCN 2017045823 (ebook) | ISBN 9781440843389
  (ebook) | ISBN 9781440843372 (hardcopy : alk. paper)
Subjects: LCSH: Sexual minorities—Mental health. | Sexual minorities—Psychology.
Classification: LCC RC451.4.G39 (ebook) | LCC RC451.4.G39 L48 2017 (print) |
  DDC 362.196/89008664—dc23
LC record available at https://lccn.loc.gov/2017026566

ISBN: 978–1–4408–4337–2 (print)
     978–1–4408–4338–9 (ebook)

21 20 19 18 17   1 2 3 4 5

This book is also available as an eBook.

Praeger
An Imprint of ABC-CLIO, LLC

ABC-CLIO, LLC
130 Cremona Drive, P.O. Box 1911
Santa Barbara, California 93116-1911
www.abc-clio.com

This book is printed on acid-free paper ∞

Manufactured in the United States of America

Contents

Series Foreword

When I first met the coeditor of this book, Erik Santacruz, he was my student in a graduate class in "Human Intimacy and Sexuality" at Teachers College, Columbia University. When he explained his class project about "barebacking"—unprotected sex risking HIV/AIDS that was still persisting—I immediately thought that this paper needed to be published and in a new book presenting many current issues in the LGBT field. I encouraged him continually to do this, and now I am thrilled and proud that he teamed with another of his graduate professors, Richard Ruth, to do so. Together they have collected chapter contributors with varied and interesting views that add richness to professional and personal perspectives in the field.

My commitment to highlighting new developments in this field stems back decades, when, as a young researcher in depression and schizophrenia, my team at Columbia Psychiatric Institute first became involved in the sexuality field at the request of Masters and Johnson ("the grandparents of sex therapy") to evaluate their treatment. That led to my being invited on the team defining the sexuality criteria in the American Psychiatric Association's then-*Diagnostic and Statistical Manual*'s third edition, mired in debates about homosexuality as a disease and now, decades later, freed from pathological models. Also in those early days—way before Caitlyn Jenner's ever-so-public gender transition—I was asked by a surgeon performing sex-reassignment surgery to evaluate patients' emotional stability (when in fact several candidates were too at risk for major depression) and subsequently developed holistic treatment plans, as my and others' research and clinical practice evolved into new approaches to identity and behavior.

As a journalist, I have watched the public evolve. Madonna kissed Britney Spears on MTV, and Katy Perry sang "I Kissed a Girl." Now, the *Modern Family* TV show has popular gay characters. A student at my alma mater, Smith College, insisted on being called "It." After so many distress calls over decades to my radio talk show, youth questioning their choice of partners welcomed the chapter in my *Generation Sex* book, "Guys Who Like Guys Who Like Girls Who Do Girls Who Do Guys Like They're Girls . . .," which addressed behavior now considered normal. And at the talkback I did after a play, *Last Sunday in June,* audiences noticed that gay relationships face similar jealousies and devotions as heterosexual ones.

This book is important to so many public and professional groups, as the chapters present new perspectives and models about the LGBT community, especially important today in our political and social media climate. Chapter contributors introduce us to many terms some may find new or unfamiliar, such as "sexual nonconformity," "cisgender," and "intersectionality" (an important term related to diversity) and even LGBTIQQA+—an acronym I have taught in my classes. As the authors themselves conclude, that there is still so much more to explore, I wonder what letters can be added to that acronym, as more insights come to light in this important field.

Judy Kuriansky, PhD
Series Editor, Practical and Applied Psychology

1

Introduction: Why This Book and What You Can Expect

Richard Ruth and Erik Santacruz

WHY THIS BOOK?

LGBT psychology affirms that coming out is a lifelong process, but one with key inflection points (Gonsiorek & Rudolph, 1991; Reynolds & Hanjorgiris, 2000; Rivers & Gordon, 2010). The same can be said for LGBT psychology and LGBT mental health more broadly. It is now more than 50 years since Hooker's seminal research affirmed that gayness and lesbianism are psychologically healthy (Hooker, 1993); some of our founding thinkers and pioneer clinicians are no longer with us (Isay, 1997, 2010). Our grounding texts include several now in extensively revised versions (Bieschke, Perez, & DeBord, 2007; Clarke, Ellis, Peel, & Riggs, 2010; Garnets & Kimmel, 2003; Greene & Croom, 2000), and new collections of groundbreaking theory and science emerge regularly (Glassgold & Drescher, 2014; Lewis & Marshall, 2011; Patterson & D'Augelli, 2012; Singh & dickey, 2016). A January 31, 2016, Google Scholar search for publications on LGBT psychology yielded more than 744,000 results, a number that will certainly grow by the time you read this. The American Psychological Association (APA) now has guidelines for LGB and trans and gender-nonconforming practice (American Psychological Association, 2011, 2015) that represent the collective values, will, and vision of the profession.

So it seems fair to agree that LGBT psychology "came out" long ago and has become a vibrant, diverse field in its own right. But that development brings with it challenges of its own.

Definitional Challenges

Our field does not have consensual, operationalized definitions of who lesbian, gay, bisexual, transgender, and gender-nonconforming people are. We know, from work that builds on Kinsey's early research, that sexual orientation lies on a spectrum, likely with more lying in the middle than at either end

(Haslam, 1997; Savin-Williams, 2014). At times, research has been criticized for conflating sexual orientation and gender identity/expression in its frameworks and methods (Bohan, 1996; Chrisler & McCreary, 2010; Diamond, 2002; Parent, DeBlaere, & Moradi, 2013), and clinical work has been criticized for assuming uniform pathways of development in LGBT lives that do not capture, or mischaracterize, the diversity within our communities (Fassinger & Arseneau, 2007). As space for LGBT people to shape their identities in self-determined ways evolves, rapidly, some within our communities reject older labels, referring to identify as "queer," for example, and want psychologists' work to respect their subjective realities (van Anders, 2015).

Who Sets the Agenda?

LGBT communities are composed of often quite choosy consumers. We can, and should, be picky about the research in which we choose to participate and the clinical services we seek. As authors in this volume will make clear, from multiple perspectives and in multiple ways, research that does not start out by seeking community input and that is not shaped on a template of community priorities, concerns, and sensibilities, and clinical work that is not developed through collaborative understandings and relationships with LGBT clients and patients, is at risk of going off course and potentially causing harm. We succeed when collaborative agenda setting is part of our work (Garnets & D'Augelli, 2005; Harper, Jamil, & Wilson, 2007; Herek & Garnets, 2007; Wheeler, 2003).

This is not to in any way dismiss the difficulty of such undertakings. It takes years of training to develop the sophisticated competencies funders and consumers of, and audiences for, psychological research and psychological services now have every right to expect. Perhaps in part as a result, it can be more difficult than it formerly was to enlist communities in the development of research agendas and practice frameworks. There is more that has to be taken into account and held in mind. Oppressed LGBT communities, struggling with basic issues of safety and survival, may not see the need for psychological research, preventive interventions based on psychological science, or psychological service models that feel alien to community norms (Harper & Schneider, 2003). That said, although it can be hard for psychologists to convey the concepts and methods that shape our work to nonpsychologist audiences, it is what our communities demand, and it is what our field now holds as its consensually shared values (APA, 2011, 2015).

Intersectionality

As Wallace and Santacruz point out, with clarity, conviction, and systematic scholarly scaffolding in their contributions to this volume, and other contributors to this book reinforce, LGBT psychology has, too often in its history, narrowed its focus and scope to white, economically privileged LGBT psychology. As so often has happened in the history of psychology, a recognition of this bias and skew, and its serious, deleterious, and disempowering impact—on the direction and reception of LGBT psychology and on the lives of racial/ethnic minority and economically oppressed LGBT people—has been necessary but not sufficient. Still today, too much of LGBT psychology's theory, research, and clinical practice does not address intersectional realities that demand to be addressed.

However, the hegemonic influence of an LGBT psychology oblivious to the salience of race, ethnicity, gender, gender expression, including nonbinary gender expression, (dis)ability, and social class is over. A particular point of pride for us is that many of the contributors to this volume (and both its editors) are racial/ethnic minority psychologists and colleagues from related professions. Other contributors are committed, battle-tested allies of marginalized sectors within the LGBT population. We think, speak, and write here in voices shaped by our experience in the communities we come from and inhabit. Our hope is that our readers will trace the influence of this grounding in within-LGBT diversity in the thinking and approaches they will find in this volume.

Who Is the Audience?

An earlier generation of LGBT psychological research and clinical practice has been criticized as oriented toward proving to heterosexual, mainstream audiences that being LGBT was not a pathology, clarifying distinctions between LGBT and other populations, and showing how concepts and methods developed for heterosexual and cisgender populations might be extended to LGBT populations (Harper & Schneider, 2003; Herek, 2010).

Increasingly, however, LGBT psychology is defining its agenda as working within, by, and for LGBT communities. Following in directions racial/ethnic minority and women psychologists have taken, LGBT psychology as a field is becoming less interested in explaining LGBT psychological realities to non-LGBT audiences and more interested in providing servant leadership to our own LGBT communities. Several writers in this volume extend the critique of earlier psychological work and operate within this newer perspective.

Methodological Challenges

A full discussion of the complex issues in considering what methodological approaches are best suited to study LGBT realities and what clinical methods are best suited to help LGBT people goes beyond the scope of these introductory comments but is at the heart, in many ways, of the contributions in this volume. We start with a few observations.

While there is huge potential in Internet and Web-based research, there are also cautions, including, relevant to our focus here, that methods that privilege technological facilitation have the potential to conclude that advantaged sectors of LGBT communities represent the only LGBT realities that need considering (Birnbaum, 2004; Reips, 2002), a flaw that hampered early HIV/AIDS research as well (Parker, 2001). LGBT populations tend to be less advantaged than cisgender/heterosexual populations (Badgett, Durso, & Schneebaum, 2013); not all in our communities have ready technological access.

Increasingly, qualitative methods, on their own or as part of mixed methods approaches, are seen as key to understanding intersectional LGBT experience (Johnson & Martínez Guzmán, 2013; Warner, 2004). Psychology's preference for the rigor that operationalized variables and quantitative methods can bring runs the risk of measuring variables that do not reflect what is relevant to LGBT persons (Morin, 1977).

Particularities of Tensions between Theory, Research, and Practice

Disjunctures in perspectives and ideas between clinicians and researchers are pervasive and often corrosive in psychology. Psychological scientists often view clinicians as other than scientists and as not grounded in empirical imperatives. Clinicians often view psychological research as less relevant to day-to-day clinical realities than researchers are prone to think. The kaleidoscopic variations in scientist/practitioner differences in psychology are often dizzying—they include clinicians who push for empirically validated treatments and stake claims on what is and is not empirical and scientists who embrace psychodynamic, or systemic, or postmodern paradigms of science, for example.

These differences are as present in LGBT psychology as in any other part of the field, but perhaps with a twist: Similar to what used to happen in gay bars (Lewin & Leap, 2002), there can be a kind of social leveling—LGBT psychology often celebrates being a place where many different kinds of psychologists meet and interact more freely than they do elsewhere, something we hope you will see demonstrated in this volume.

Queer theory (Sullivan, 2003), increasingly its own intellectual discipline, simultaneously draws from, critiques, and challenges LGBT psychology. As a result, LGBT psychologists face a choice between when we do best to stay within our own silos and when our work is served by engaging with other perspectives from both within and outside psychology.

You likely will not find any of these tensions definitively resolved in this book. Rather, our hope is that you will find interesting takes and creative ideas about how they play out and can evolve in productive ways.

* * * * *

Before going into how this book aims to enter into and contribute to this evolution in LGBT psychology, it is important for us, as editors, to situate ourselves, an important point LGBT psychology takes from its roots in feminist contributions to psychological thinking and methods (Fine, 1992), which emphasizes that the personal is political (Hanisch, 2005/1969) and that that has important implications for psychological conceptualizations and methods and makes the case that being explicit about one's subjective point of departure is not just permitted, but perhaps even necessary in all psychological work.

RICHARD RUTH

It's different today, but, in my growing up years, the gay desires I began to discover in myself from a young age were definitely cause for ostracism, if not, at times, violent attack. Childhood was not safe. Adolescence was a bit more hopeful, because the turbulence of the 1960s offered a different sense of possibility.

I began my graduate training in clinical psychology in 1972. My undergraduate training, partly in the United States and partly in Latin America, had given me a rich grounding in psychology, but not psychology in a U.S. idiom. I did not really know the history or the definitional state at the time of clinical psychology, as a discipline and a field in the United States. What I knew was that I wanted to help people, as a therapist, and I assumed that my program would, as it were, teach me my trade. I naively, and incorrectly, assumed that my graduate program would immerse me in depth in psychological science (I was wrong there; the coverage was *lite*; I valued my exposure to social psychology but had to develop my continuing interest in other areas of psychological science on my own) and meld scientific and clinical training with the new, transformative discoveries of the women's movement, the ethnic liberation movements, and the broad currents of social change afoot at the time.

I could say I began my training as an out gay man, in those heady days not so long after Stonewall, and that would be true, but, in retrospect, only partially true. At no point did my graduate program create space or support for me to integrate elements of my personal gay identity with my emerging professional socialization. When I first came out to a supervisor, he calmly—averting eye contact, pipe in hand—told me that, no, I was not gay. How does one respond to that?

My classmates were more tolerant, and none was explicitly homophobic; but my instructors made virtually no mention of gayness as a topic of inquiry, much less something one might expect to work with in clinical practice. This was of a piece with their reluctance to include anything related to race, ethnicity, gender, or class in our curriculum and their tendency to become annoyed if any of us tried to raise such issues for discussion. As a gay man who was also proud of my working-class background and bicultural identity, I smoldered. And, being practical, I focused on trying to survive.

Thus, when I began seeing LGBT patients, at my first job, I was happy, but on my own. I brought generic clinical skills and personal instincts I trusted but little science, validated clinical methods, or supervisory scaffolding to the work. From what I have gathered from talking with other LGBT psychologists of my generation—with few exceptions, that is how it was.

When I think back, it seems it was such a short time—in subjective time, at least—between the springing up of the gay liberation movement, as we called it at the time, and the coming of HIV/AIDS. But, in that time, I saw, at the community mental health centers where I worked, gay men, lesbian women, bisexual patients, and LGB couples. These patients approached our work together anxious I would pathologize them and therefore wary in a way for which, having begun to get to know our field, I could not fault them; but they also came in need.

I was proud to find myself rising to the occasion to help meet their mental health needs—affirming their identities, their desires, their hopes, and their sense that possibilities for fuller, richer, less burdened lives were rapidly emerging. I mostly did not tell my supervisors or administrators what was happening behind closed doors. It did not yet feel possible, much less safe. I began seeing my first transgender patients; when they came to our clinic and no one else seemed interested in seeing them, I gladly stepped forward. I have been actively involved as an ally of transgender and gender-nonconforming communities ever since. It is a matter of paying back a debt—it was, after all, transgender people who first took up the battle at Stonewall.

One thing about me, I have a deep and abiding love for the big tent of psychology, and I always love to learn new things. After graduate school, I did postgraduate trainings in psychoanalysis, family systems therapy, and neuropsychology. While, once again, I did not encounter LGBT mentors or role models in any of my postgraduate experiences, I at least found a stance that went beyond tolerance to affirmation, encouragement, and support. I felt more able to begin talking, in supervisions and seminars, about some of my experiences working with LGBT patients, what I was learning from them, and how it fit with or challenged what we were learning in these advanced clinical trainings.

Then came HIV/AIDS—in its first years, when, as clinicians, what we could offer was so painfully limited. I joined the ranks of my colleagues who stepped onto the front lines, taking care of patients, in my case in a hospital and to a lesser extent in my practice. Patients, and friends, died in large numbers; I could be by their side, and offer what comfort and support I could, while trying to hold myself together at a time when a week with a single funeral was a gentle week.

Fast forward. For the next two decades, I worked in community mental health and in private clinical practice. While I had research skills and interests, I saw less possibility for myself in that sector of psychology—while I knew that, at least, there were LGBT patients who wanted to see me, I never personally encountered any researchers who were LGBT-affirmative. That is not to say they were not out there—you will read from some of them in this volume—but just to describe my personal experience and trajectory.

I began teaching part-time and publishing some qualitative research and clinical and theoretical work but—shaped by my early professional experience—saw little chance and found little motivation to connect with active currents in organized LGBT psychology. Partly, that was because what I read and heard, in the moments a busy clinical life permitted, mostly had to do with more advantaged communities than the one I came from and the ones I served. More of my clinical work takes place in Spanish than in English and always has.

I began to get more of a sense of the richness in the emergence of LGBT psychology as a field when I began becoming active in the APA. I joined Division 44, the Society for the Psychological Study of Lesbian, Gay, Bisexual and Transgender Issues, and began eagerly soaking up its presentations and publications. I was appointed to committees and then to leadership positions in my home APA division, Division 39 (Psychoanalysis), and made it a priority to bring LGBT perspectives and concerns to our work. It was easier to do by this point; others had proceeded me, and joined me, in doing so.

Life evolves. I now divide my time between clinical practice; teaching, supervising, and doing research in a PsyD program; and teaching in an interdisciplinary LGBT Health Policy and Practice graduate certificate program (about which you will hear more in this volume).

My LGBT graduate students have an experience very different from the one that shaped me. They can take focused coursework, find LGBT content infused in most if not all their courses, see LGBT patients and get good supervision on their work with members of our communities from the earliest points in their training, have out gay mentors and role models eager to work with them, and research topics of relevance and interest to our communities, with support from experienced faculty.

I do not hold out my experience as representative of gay men, or even of gay psychologists, or as equipping me for depth of conversance with all the areas of LGBT psychology that will be explored in this volume. But, in the rich, evolving productivity and innovation of LGBT psychology today, I feel proud to be part of a community of professionals engaged with, and respected for, serving our communities, in scientific, clinical, and theoretical dimensions of service. Now, I am part of the first generation of *legally married* gay psychologists. I get to be an old married guy, and to help the upcoming generation of LGBT mental health professionals. I go out and do great things.

ERIK SANTACRUZ

I grew up extremely poor, which meant that my family did not have access to health insurance or healthcare services. This led to an upbringing where I was in constant fear of illness. Simply stated, getting sick was not an option. I also grew up in a family environment that fully embraced our Mexican culture.

Growing up poor and Mexican in Southern California meant that illness would be cured by the local *curandero* (i.e., medicine person) or within our family, using a remedies passed down from previous generations. At times, these Mexican home remedies worked, and they returned balance to the body. More often than not, however, these concoctions tasted awful, and I was skeptical of their effects, if any. I am reminded of the time my mother boiled lime leaves into a tea for me to drink to cure my first hangover. To this day, I am not sure if it was a real remedy or a Mexican mother's gentle way of demonstrating her disapproval of my first experimentation with drinking alcohol—the tea was awful! It had quite an impact on my taste buds and my stomach. Needless to say, it took a few years before I ever touched an alcoholic beverage again.

My Mexican identity argues that these remedies are relatively effective. However, my mainstream U.S. identity argues that many of these remedies are not sufficient to treat the multiplicity of illnesses that plague ethnic, low-income communities. Thus, at an early age, my experience as an impoverished Mexican American served as an inspiration to help my community heal.

My early trajectory was not pointed toward college. The school system I attended was underfunded, which meant that the scant resources available were allocated to students considered to be the most promising.

I was placed on a vocational career track. I will never forget the day, as a freshman in high school, when I was handed a booklet and told to pick my vocational career. At 13, I was to make a decision that would influence the rest of my life. As I flipped through the pages, nothing seemed appealing to me until I stumbled upon a page with bolded words that read "Health Careers Choices." As I kept reading, I was promised the possibility of becoming a medical assistant. I reasoned that this track would satisfy my mother's desire to see me making a living without *quebrandome la espalda* ("breaking my back"). Perhaps most importantly, as I read about the possibility of becoming a medical assistant, I was reminded of the poor health in which many members of my community, including my immediate family, found themselves. On the periphery of my mind, I envisioned becoming a medical assistant as my opportunity to help my community heal.

I devoted afternoons throughout my junior and senior years in high school to taking the courses necessary to become a medical assistant. In addition, I opted to take additional courses; I was told that doing so would allow me to become licensed, which would translate into a higher hourly wage.

These additional courses changed my trajectory. I would be blessed with the opportunity to train under Mrs. Helen Fey, a registered nurse turned health educator. Mrs. Fey, a warm Filipina woman, was small in stature, but she exuded endless strength. As a required assignment, she asked that we write a paper on an illness of choice.

During this period, I was in the initial stages of exploring my sexual identity as a gay man. This was a time when gay men who frequented gay venues were constantly bombarded with public health messages suggesting that we were very likely to contract HIV. Growing up poor teaches the ability to make the most out of every situation. What I now understand to be fear-based health-education campaigns inspired me to write my paper on HIV.

Writing my first major academic assignment on HIV went from a paper exploring the illness at a biological level to a paper that explored the biopsychosocial intricacies that sustain HIV disease. I learned that HIV not only continues to be an epidemic of massive proportions but also that it impacts both Black and Latino communities at exceedingly disproportionate rates.

Perhaps most importantly, for the first time in my high school career, someone gave me positive reinforcement. When Mrs. Fey returned my paper, she gently pulled me aside, looked me in the eyes, and informed me that medical assisting was not for me. She urged me to enroll in the local community college. Mrs. Fey was one of the first individuals to boldly proclaim I could be anything I wanted to be.

My first semester at the community college was a success, in part, due to the awareness and confidence Mrs. Fey had instilled in me and to my newly discovered passion to study HIV in a broader behavioral health context. With this in mind, I pursued a major in sociology and transferred to the University of California at Berkeley, where my studies focused on the sociology of health and illness.

My undergraduate honors thesis, "Sex without Barriers," explored the Internet culture of men who have unprotected sex with men, colloquially known as "barebackers." I found that, by defining barebacking as only involving lack of use of a condom, previous researchers implicitly reduced this phenomenon to a physical act of sex; consequently, the solutions proposed to reduce the transmission of HIV and sexually transmitted infections (STIs) were overly simplistic. My research demonstrated that barebacking is much more than condom-less sex and that the health community must consider the importance of the psychosocial complexities that sustain this phenomenon. I learned how contextual factors intersect with the multiple identities we hold to create health outcomes. For the first time, I learned how my identity as a Mexican American, low-income, gay male predisposed me, and the larger community, to HIV—and I decided to do something about it.

I enrolled in the Department of Health Education, in the Health and Behavior Program, at Teachers College, Columbia University, where I ultimately earned an EdD in health education.

Columbia University was the ideal setting for my research training. Not only did it give me a solid foundation in HIV, human sexuality, and adolescent/adult instruction, but it also provided me with critical theoretical background. I was taught that safer-sex instruction is most effective when it meets people where they are and when it is free of negative value judgments toward any types of sexual practices.

I was given the opportunity to engage in research projects that utilized the minority stress model to capture how young gay men of color perceive, respond to, and cope with oppression and discrimination as they navigate online social networking spaces. I had the opportunity to train under professors whose early work has revolutionized our understanding of HIV. In particular, Professor Barbara Wallace, a licensed clinical psychologist and the first African American female to attain tenure at Teachers College, became an important figure in my life. Her influence led me to take elective courses in the Department of Clinical and Counseling Psychology, where I met clinical psychologist, radio host, and media commentator Dr. Judy Kuriansky, and renowned sex therapist and author Dr. Ruth Westheimer—two figures who also became instrumental in my developing career. With their unrelenting guidance, these women helped me discover the power and potential of the psychological perspective on health and behavior. In particular, via their teaching and mentorship, I learned that LGBT youth are emerging as a community with unique experiences that can not only serve to empower them but also have the potential to disrupt their sense of self, as they are often targets of violent and vicious oppression enacted both within and outside their racial/ethnic communities. I therefore developed a desire to augment my doctoral training in health education with training in clinical psychology that would permit me to be not only a researcher and scholar but also a practicing clinician and psychological consultant working with LGBT communities of color.

Thus, my trajectory took another turn, leading to training in clinical psychology at The George Washington University, under the supervision of my mentor and colleague, Professor Richard Ruth. While this book has grown out of our ongoing collaboration, its origins can be traced to an invitation to produce this volume from Dr. Judy Kuriansky, as I concluded my training at Columbia University. In an essential way, her invitation to help produce this volume is a marker of her deep and positive influence on me. Development at important moments is a product of the influence of key individuals; I want to acknowledge Dr. Kuriansky's important influence on me, with great gratitude.

Now, as a health educator and as a psychologist-in-training, I continue to address the HIV epidemic, via psychoeducation and psychotherapy as well as through research. My clinical interests have expanded to include the broader range of illnesses the broader LGBT community experiences, especially LGBT people of color.

Finding a voice and an identity is perhaps one of the greatest challenges an LGBT individual can face. This is especially true for those of us who embrace intersectional identities. My current clinical work with LGBT-identified children, adolescents, and young adults now complements my academic training. Like the contributions in this book, my own trajectory brings together voices of past and present pioneers with my own lived experiences. I embrace the challenge and the opportunity of working together with others to positively influence the mental health outcomes of the future LGBT generation.

WHAT TO EXPECT IN THIS BOOK

The traditional approach to compiling an edited volume in an area of psychology is to attempt to map the terrain, in all of its relevant dimensions, and try to arrive at some kind of an authoritative take on the state of the subfield. That has not been our approach to this volume. Rather, our goal has been to assemble emerging contributors to LGBT psychology with important things to say and facilitate them presenting their ideas in their own "voices." LGBT psychology is now too vast, and evolving too rapidly, for the traditional approach to be viable, in our view at least.

This relates to another key point: Some have questioned whether there is such a thing as an LGBT community, at least a cohesive or unified one (Weiss, 2004); whether the differences between lesbian, gay, and bisexual people, whose sexual orientation is key to their identity, and transgender and gender-nonconforming people, whose gender and gender expression help define their psychological realities, have something in common besides shared enemies; or whether these are all increasingly outdated, and oppressive, categories, and emerging queer realities (Yount, 2009) should be psychology's focus.

We do not take a stand on this issue, nor is it our aspiration to do so. Rather, what we take great pride in offering the readers of this volume is a collection of voices from the clinical and scientific front lines. We invite you to engage with the ideas presented here and use them as a stimulus to formulate your own thoughts and action plans.

REFERENCES

American Psychological Association. (2011). *Guidelines for psychotherapy with lesbian, gay, & bisexual clients.* Developed by the APA Division 44 committee on lesbian, gay, and bisexual concerns joint task force on guidelines for working with lesbian, gay, and bisexual clients. Retrieved from http://www.apa.org/pi/lgbt/resources/guidelines.aspx

American Psychological Association. (2015). *Guidelines for psychological practice with transgender and gender non-conforming people.* Washington, DC: APA. Retrieved from https://www.apa.org/practice/guidelines/transgender.pdf

Badgett, M. V., Durso, L. E., & Schneebaum, A. (2013). *New patterns of poverty in the lesbian, gay, and bisexual community.* Retrieved from https://escholarship.org/uc/item/8dq9d947

Bieschke, K. J., Perez, R. M., & DeBord, K. A. (Eds.). (2007). *Handbook of counseling and psychotherapy with lesbian, gay, and bisexual clients* (2nd ed.). Washington, DC: American Psychological Association.

Birnbaum, M. H. (2004). Human research and data collection via the Internet. *Annual Review of Psychology, 55,* 803–832.

Bohan, J. S. (1996). *Psychology and sexual orientation: Coming to terms*. New York, NY: Routledge.

Chrisler, J. C., & McCreary, D. R. (2010). *Handbook of gender research in psychology* (Vol. 1). New York, NY: Springer.

Clarke, V., Ellis, S. J., Peel, E., & Riggs, D. W. (2010). *Lesbian, gay, bisexual, trans & queer psychology: An introduction*. New York, NY: Cambridge University Press.

Diamond, M. (2002). Sex and gender are different: Sexual identity and gender identity are different. *Clinical Child Psychology and Psychiatry, 7*, 320–334.

Fassinger, R. E., & Arseneau, J. R. (2007). "I'd rather get wet than be under that umbrella": Differentiating the experiences and identities of lesbian, gay, bisexual, and transgender people. In K. J. Bieschke, R. M. Perez, & K. A. DeBord (Eds.), *Handbook of counseling and psychotherapy with lesbian, gay, bisexual, and transgender clients* (2nd ed., pp. 19–49). Washington, DC: APA Books.

Fine, M. (1992). *Disruptive voices: The possibilities of feminist research*. Ann Arbor, MI: University of Michigan Press.

Garnets, L. D., & Kimmel, D. C. (Eds.). (2003). *Psychological perspectives on lesbian, gay, and bisexual experiences* (2nd ed.). New York, NY: Columbia University Press.

Glassgold, J. M., & Drescher, J. (Eds.). (2014). *Activism and LGBT psychology*. New York, NY: Routledge.

Gonsiorek, J. C., & Rudolph, J. R. (1991). Homosexual identity: Coming out and other developmental events. In J. C. Gonsiorek & J. D. Weinrich (Eds.), *Homosexuality: Research implications for public policy* (pp. 161–176). Thousand Oaks, CA: Sage.

Greene, B., & Croom, G. L. (Eds.). (2000). *Education, research, and practice in lesbian, gay, bisexual, and transgendered psychology: A resource manual*. Thousand Oaks, CA: Sage.

Hanisch, C. (2005/1969). The personal is political. Retrieved May 1, 2015, from http://www.carolhanisch.org/CHwritings/PIP.html. Originally published in *Liberation*, pp. 76–78.

Harper, G. W., Jamil, O. B., & Wilson, B. D. (2007). Collaborative community-based research as activism: Giving voice and hope to lesbian, gay, and bisexual youth. *Journal of Gay & Lesbian Psychotherapy, 11*, 99–119.

Harper, G. W., & Schneider, M. (2003). Oppression and discrimination among lesbian, gay, bisexual, and transgendered people and communities: A challenge for community psychology. *American Journal of Community Psychology, 31*, 243–252.

Haslam, N. (1997). Evidence that male sexual orientation is a matter of degree. *Journal of Personality and Social Psychology, 73*, 862.

Herek, G. M. (2010). Sexual orientation differences as deficits: Science and stigma in the history of American psychology. *Perspectives on Psychological Science, 5*, 693–699.

Herek, G. M., & Garnets, L. D. (2007). Sexual orientation and mental health. *Annual Review of Clinical Psychology, 3*, 353–375.

Hooker, E. (1993). Reflections of a 40-year exploration: A scientific view on homosexuality. *American Psychologist, 48*, 450–453.

Isay, R. A. (1997). *Becoming gay: The journey to self-acceptance*. New York, NY: Macmillan.

Isay, R. A. (2010). *Being homosexual: Gay men and their development*. New York, NY: Vintage.

Johnson, K., & Martínez Guzmán, A. (2013). Rethinking concepts in participatory action research and their potential for social transformation: Post-structuralist informed methodological reflections from LGBT and Trans-Collective projects. *Journal of Community & Applied Social Psychology, 23*, 405–419.

Lewin, E, & Leap, W. L. (Eds.). (2002). *Out in theory: The emergence of lesbian and gay anthropology*. Chicago, IL: University of Illinois Press.

Lewis, M. K., & Marshall, I. (2011). *LGBT psychology: Research perspectives and people of African descent*. New York, NY: Springer.

Morin, S. F. (1977). Heterosexual bias in psychological research on lesbianism and male homosexuality. *American Psychologist, 32*, 629–637.

Parent, M. C., DeBlaere, C., & Moradi, B. (2013). Approaches to research on intersectionality: Perspectives on gender, LGBT, and racial/ethnic identities. *Sex Roles, 68*, 639–645.

Parker, R. (2001). Sexuality, culture, and power in HIV/AIDS research. *Annual Review of Anthropology, 30*, 163–179.

Patterson, C. J., & D'Augelli, A. R. (Eds.). (2012). *Handbook of psychology and sexual orientation*. New York, NY: Oxford University Press.

Reips, U. D. (2002). Internet-based psychological experimenting: Five dos and five don'ts. *Social Science Computer Review, 20*, 241–249.

Reynolds, A. L, & Hanjorgiris, W. F. (2000). Coming out: Lesbian, gay, and bisexual identity development. In R. M. Perez, K. A. DeBord, & K. J. Bieschke (Eds.), *Handbook of counseling and psychotherapy with lesbian, gay, and bisexual clients* (pp. 35–55). Washington, DC: American Psychological Association.

Rivers, I., & Gordon, K. (2010). "Coming out," context and reason: First disclosure of sexual orientation and its consequences. *Psychology & Sexuality, 1*, 21–33.

Savin-Williams, R. C. (2014). An exploratory study of the categorical versus spectrum nature of sexual orientation. *Journal of Sex Research, 51*, 446–453.

Singh, A. A., & dickey, l. m. (Eds.). (2016). *Affirmative counseling and psychological practice with transgender and gender nonconforming clients*. Washington, DC: APA Books.

Sullivan, N. (2003). *A critical introduction to queer theory*. New York, NY: New York University Press.

van Anders, S. M. (2015). Beyond sexual orientation: Integrating gender/sex and diverse sexualities via sexual configurations theory. *Archives of Sexual Behavior, 44*, 1177–1213.

Warner, D. N. (2004). Towards a queer research methodology. *Qualitative Research in Psychology, 1*, 321–337.

Weiss, J. T. (2004). GL vs. BT: The archaeology of biphobia and transphobia within the US gay and lesbian community. *Journal of Bisexuality, 3*, 25–55.

Wheeler, D. P. (2003). Methodological issues in conducting community-based health and social services research among urban Black and African American LGBT populations. *Journal of Gay & Lesbian Social Services, 15*, 65–78.

Yount, P. (2009). *Denying queer realities: Scripting the normative homo* (Doctoral dissertation). Johnson City: East Tennessee State University.

2

New Developments in LGBT Development: What's New and What's (Still) True

Stephen L. Forssell

Psychology has been interested in same-sex-oriented and gender variant individuals for well over 125 years. Developmental theories of homosexuality and transgenderism have swung from the severely pathological to the normative and touched on all points in between. The science of same-sex attraction and gender identity development has progressed significantly as we have come to better understand the biological and genetic underpinnings of gender and erotic and romantic attraction. Cultural norms around LGBT people, their relationships, and their place in society have changed in tandem.

The purpose of this chapter is to examine the latest developments in LGBT development, and to identify the newest findings about LGBT identity and mental health and place them in the context of prevailing science and current societal norms. We will first review the history of theories about development and get up to speed with the latest in sexual orientation and gender identity measurement approaches. Then, we will inventory the state of knowledge about key milestones in the healthy development of LGBT identity at each of four developmental stages: toddlerhood and early childhood; adolescence; young and mid-adulthood; and later adulthood and old age. At each milestone we will review established knowledge and look into emerging trends and controversies and reflect on some key policy issues along the way.

A few notes before we get started: We will be discussing findings that apply for the most part in North America, Europe, and parts of Latin America. In contrast with the West, the environment for LGBT people in many areas of Africa and Asia is becoming ever more repressive (Bailey et al., 2016). Second, we will use the convenient but imprecise shorthand of "LGBT" to refer to nonheterosexual and noncisgender people, recognizing that many prefer other terms. For brevity's sake we will also interchangeably use sexual orientation and "SO" as well as gender identity and "GI," often combining them to "SOGI." Lastly, we will occasionally employ the oft used term "sexual minority" to describe the broader population of LGBT and queer-identified people, acknowledging that to some the term engenders a "lesser than" status.

CH-CH-CH-CHANGES ...

What are the latest developments in development? What is different about growing into an L, G, B, or T identity now as opposed to five or 10 years ago? Before we examine each of the four developmental stages, we will review the history and current status of developmental theories of sexual orientation and gender identity development and related measurement approaches.

DEVELOPMENTAL THEORIES

Beginning with von Richard Kraft-Ebbing's *Psychopathia Sexualis* in 1886, psychology has concerned itself with the nature and etiology of same-sex behavior and attraction. Decidedly pathological in nature at first, models of same-sex orientation have gradually morphed from a disease model into models that incorporate a normative framing for nonheterosexual orientation.

The nature and nurture camps have eternally battled for etiological legitimacy. Is homosexuality learned or genetically bestowed? Is it the result of "(bad) parenting" or "(bad) genes"? In current times, nature-driven arguments about same-sex orientation are generally associated with more accepting societal views ("they are just born that way"), whereas nurture-based arguments tend to be associated with more negative views ("sexual orientation is a choice, and homosexuality is the wrong choice"; Bailey et al., 2016). But this association has not always been the case. The eugenics movement of the 1920s and 1930s, for instance, particularly in Nazi Germany, viewed homosexuality as both a genetic and an inferior trait (Grau & Shoppmann, 2013). Prevailing explanations for the causes of homosexuality have vacillated from Krafft-Ebbing's (2013/1886) "loathsome disease" framing, to Freud's early notion of inadequate negotiation of the phallic stage, to early genetic determinism (Galton, 1883; Rushton, 1990), to Skinnerian behaviorist notions of learned behavior (Weinberg & Bell, 1972) or culturally constructed gender (the "John/Joan" case; see Colapinto, 2000), back to genetic determinism (the "gay gene," see Hamer, Hu, Magnuson, Hu, & Pattatucci, 1993), to a culturally embedded fluidity of women's sexual orientation (Diamond, 2012; Farr, Diamond, & Boker, 2014), to a flurry of research that demonstrates a biologic and genetic link to orientation (Bailey & Pillard, 1995; LeVay, 1996, 2011). Our best current understanding of the nature of SO is that it is primarily genetically and biologically driven, but that society and culture influence the degree to which and the way in which it is expressed or suppressed (Bailey et al., 2016).

Etiology notwithstanding, our focus will be on the health of LGBT persons. We are concerned here with framing same-sex attractions and noncisgender identities as a part of a normally occurring range of possible outcomes as opposed to inherently maladaptive ones. Alfred Kinsey went a long way toward normalizing same-sex behavior with his studies of sexual behavior in the human male (Kinsey, Pomeroy, & Martin, 1998/1948) and female (Kinsey, Pomeroy, Martin, & Gebhard, 1998/1953). More than anything, the volumes by Kinsey and colleagues made it clear that homosexual behavior was neither rare nor limited to urban areas or gay ghettos.

The earliest empirical evidence for the normal functioning of same-sex-oriented persons came with Evelyn Hooker's (1957) study comparing gay men in Los Angeles with a matched group of heterosexual men. The two groups were indistinguishable from each other as far as psychological adjustment went. But it took an act of civil disobedience combined with considerable political will more than 15 years later to have homosexuality officially bumped from the list of sexual disorders in the *Diagnostic and Statistical Manual of Mental Disorders* (DSM; Bayer, 1981; Drescher, 2015).

Since the American Psychiatric Association made that leap in 1973, models of normative same-sex orientation identity have emerged (e.g., Cass, 1979; Coleman, 1982; Troiden, 1988). They each involve moving through various stages typified by increased self-awareness, increased acceptance starting with the self and extending to family, peers, and society, and greater connectivity to a broader community. Arguably the most enduring among them has been Vivienne Cass's (1979, 1984, 2016) model of homosexual identity development. It has come under some criticism (Kenneady & Oswalt, 2014) but has persisted in part because of its relative flexibility and sensitivity to social context. The usefulness of these stage models reminds us that developing LGB people have to adapt over time to a world in which their status is neither the dominant nor necessarily the accepted one and that they must negotiate this difference and successfully form an integrated identity despite these challenges in order to mature in a healthy manner.

DEFINING AND MEASURING SEXUAL ORIENTATION AND GENDER IDENTITY

Why collect data on SOGI? To sexologists, mental health professionals, and public health researchers, SOGI data is integral to their work. But until recently, these efforts have largely been niche endeavors within LGBT mental health or HIV/AIDS epidemiological perspectives.

The "mainstreaming" of LGBT health is a recent phenomenon. Starting roughly with the publication by the Institute of Medicine (IOM) of *The Health of Lesbian, Gay, Bisexual, and Transgender People* (2011), the broader medical profession has turned its attention to the importance of the LGBT population. The IOM document was critical in crystallizing the effort to address the health of LGBT people in medical and mental health training and improve care delivery across the board. Progressive policies enacted since in the federal government during the Obama administration (HHS, 2012) and training programs developed for medical and mental health professionals, such as the one at The George Washington University, have further propelled this trend. Recognizing the value of SOGI data, presently collected in 12 different federal surveys and studies, an interagency work group recently released a public commentary on the importance of valid SOGI data collection (Federal Interagency Working Group on Improving Measurement of Sexual Orientation and Gender Identity in Federal Surveys, 2016).

The first issue we need to address if we are to seriously conduct or evaluate research or clinical work in this area is quite basic: How does one validly measure SO and GI? Past research has commonly used categorical labels to capture SO: heterosexual/straight, homosexual/lesbian, homosexual/gay, or bisexual, with the occasional checkbox for "other." The 7-point Kinsey Scale (Kinsey, Pomeroy, & Martin, 1998/1948) gives us a means of capturing degrees of attraction to same- and other-sex persons that a categorical model does not. SO is also commonly measured in three separate domains—identity, attraction, and behavior—which often but do not always overlap.

Three topics of interest for SO measurement have emerged recently. One is the rise of *alternative labels* to the more commonly used "lesbian," "gay," and "bisexual." A significant minority of nonheterosexual people prefers the use of other labels that better capture their experience of sexuality and gender and, more to the point, reject traditional ones because they are seen as laden with too much cultural baggage and stereotyped imagery (Fassinger & Arseneau, 2007). Galupo, Mitchell, and Davis (2015) surveyed 448 sexual minority adults ages 18–62 and found that, in addition to the 40 percent who identified as LGB, significant numbers identified primarily as queer (15.6%) and pansexual (15.6%). "Queer" is a term, once decidedly pejorative, that has been reclaimed and repurposed as an umbrella term for "not heterosexual" (or "not cisgender"). "Pansexual" is another term commonly used to denote a sexual or romantic attraction to potentially any individual, regardless of gender or gender identity. A smaller number identified as fluid (1.8%), asexual (1.3%), and other (2.7%). These alternative terms are better able to capture a fluidity of sexual orientation that is excluded by traditional verbiage.

This leads us directly to a second recent issue in SO measurement—an apparent rise in *sexual orientation fluidity*. In the recent past, works by Diamond (2005) and others have documented fluidity in girls and women's SO, noting they are more likely than boys and men to change the labels they apply to their orientations—to and from lesbian, bisexual, and heterosexual—perhaps more than once. Boys' and men's SO development, on the other hand, had been viewed as more unidirectional and abrupt, as a kind of flipping of a switch—from straight to gay; from straight to bisexual; or from straight to bisexual to gay, and not changing from there. More recently, however, there is a body of evidence emerging that suggests that orientation fluidity extends to boys and men (Galupo et al., 2015; Katz-Wise, 2014; Katz-Wise & Hyde, 2015).

The third shift is in our *understanding of gender identity*. In the same way that measurement of orientation has changed, gender identity measurement has also recently had to adapt to account for similarly nonbinary, fluid, and label-defying possibilities. The term "transgender" itself has taken on an umbrella-type role, acting as a catchall for all manners of noncisgender identities and expressions. The notion of transgender is itself by definition a developmental phenomenon—something about a person's gender changes. The "traditional" notion of transgender conserves the gender identity dichotomy of male and female. "Transsexuals" were persons transitioning from a biological male to female, or from female to male, through hormonal and surgical procedures intended to right their bodies with their felt identities. More recently, the possibility of adopting a nonbinary gender identity has emerged culturally, and the gender nonbinary is receiving attention in the scientific literature. Persons rejecting the gender binary have opted to use labels such as genderqueer, gender-fluid, agender, pangender, polygender, or simply nongender or nonbinary (Katz-Wise, Reisner, Hughto, & Keo-Meier, 2016; Richards et al., 2016). Gender nonbinary organizations (e.g., nonbinary.org) and blogs have sprung up in communities and on the Internet in tandem.

From a measurement standpoint, this poses some challenges. The traditional approach is to use a forced-choice gender identity measurement item that lists the range of most likely options for how one currently identifies, for example, female, male, transgender female, transgender male, nonbinary, perhaps more, with an "other" box to capture alternatives.

More recently, a two-stage question has come into favor. The first inquires about *present gender identity*: female, male, transgender female, transgender male, gender queer/nonbinary, a "different gender" category (with a fill-in "other" box), and "something else." The second question asks about the *sex assigned at birth*: male, female, or decline to answer (National LGBT Health Education Center, 2015). Note that sex assigned at birth does not capture the .1 –.2 percent of intersex births where biological sex is indeterminate (Meyer-Bahlburg, 2005), as birth certificates force a male-female dichotomy. That notwithstanding, the two-stage approach is better able to capture the experience and developmental shift in both identity and biology that could be lost with the "single frame" snapshot of current identity and is considered the best practice in gender identity measurement (Cahill, Baker, Deutsch, Keatley, & Makadon, 2016; Conron, Landers, Reisner, & Sell, 2014).

Two other recent advances in the way we scientifically explore SOGI development have revolutionized the study of the LGBT population. The *minority stress model* (Meyer, 2003) has provided a tremendously useful framework for understanding the independent and significant impact of stigma on LGBT people. Sexual minorities are frequent targets of harassment and bullying, starting in childhood and adolescence. They also receive negative messages from society and their culture about homosexuality, bisexuality, and transgenderism. The minority stress model has helped us tease out covarying and confounding factors that independently (but not entirely) explain negative physical and mental health disparities for LGBT adolescents. This model has helped us empirically establish that being a sexual minority in and of itself, independent of other factors, conveys stress that negatively impacts health.

In concert with the minority stress model is the undeniable importance of *intersectionality* or understanding the interconnected nature of race, class, gender, sexual orientation, and other identities and their complex relationship with systems of discrimination. Although intersectionality has been a guiding principal in sociological and civil rights literature since the late 1980s, it has only relatively recently been a focus of new research and clinical approaches for the LGBT population.

DEVELOPMENTAL STAGES

Like any developmental phenomenon, SO and GI development occurs over the life span. In this section we will review the state of knowledge regarding four developmental stages: toddlerhood and early childhood, adolescence, early- to mid-adulthood, and later adulthood and old age, including emerging findings, current trends, and a few festering controversies.

Toddlerhood and Childhood

Studying sexual minority development during early childhood might once have been thought of as taboo or pointless. Humans, however, experience sexual thoughts and feelings well before puberty (Okami, Olmstead, & Abramson, 1997). Although we usually think of the critical developmental stage for sexual orientation and gender identity as adolescence, an emerging LGB or T identity has roots in early school- and even preschool-age children.

There are a number of reasons why these issues are more salient in early childhood now than in the past. The Internet age and the widespread availability of other media content (television, video games), for better and for worse, have made voluminous amounts of information about LGBT culture readily available to teens, tweens, and upper elementary school-age children. Many have regular access to computers, smartphones, and social media where this information—and much misinformation—is amply available. Issues that come to a head for LGBT youth during the middle school and high school years, such as bullying, harassment, and social ostracism, now get their start earlier (Fite et al., 2013).

The most observable aspect of toddlerhood and early childhood with relevance to SOGI is gender nonconformity or, as we will refer to it here, gender variance. Research at least as far back as the mid-1980s links gender variant behavior in young children to future same-sex orientation. Green's (1985) so-called sissy boy study found that over two-thirds of a group of 44 clinically referred feminine-acting boys ages 3.5–11 identified as bisexual or homosexual at follow-up during adolescence or early adulthood. Subsequent studies have added support for this link between early gender variant behavior and eventual same-sex orientation, both for boys and girls. Rieger, Linsenmeier, Gygax, and Bailey (2008), for instance, collected early childhood videos of LGB and straight participants and showed them to blind coders, who reliably labeled pre-homosexual children as more gender nonconforming than pre-heterosexual children.

Since the removal of homosexuality from the DSM in 1973, LGB youth developmental models have focused on trajectories of normative and healthy development. Although controversial when it was first proposed, with the debut of *DSM-5* (2013), transgender individuals, too, are no longer classifiable as having "gender identity disorder." Instead, the diagnosis of "gender dysphoria" (GD) came into use, placing the emphasis on the disconnection between individuals' experienced gender identity and their physical bodies rather than on pathology.

Emerging Trends, New Research, and Controversies

One recent trend both in the clinical literature and in society at large is toward opening up space for freer and more divergent gender expression in young children. Research on parents' experience with their gender variant children has shown that some parents grow to accept and support their children's difference rather than to reject or try to change their behavior (Hill & Menvielle, 2009). In concert with these attitudinal shifts on the part of parents, support groups for parents, such as Gender Spectrum (genderspectrum.org), have begun to appear. There is evidence to support that these are positive developments. In a comparative study of clinics for gender variant children, Hill, Menvielle, Sica, and Johnson (2010) found that children referred to an affirming intervention program displayed lower levels of pathology than those being seen at other similar, but nonaffirming, gender clinics. In tandem, clinicians have turned their focus toward developing variance-positive interventions and helping encourage support for parents of gender variant children (Menvielle & Hill, 2010).

A related but controversial topic involves pre-transgender children entering puberty (Lament, 2015). Hormones and hormone blockers have powerful effects on the developing bodies of children as well as on their social and psychosexual development (Fernández, Guerra, Díaz, Garcia-Vega, & Álvarez-Diaz, 2015). Over the past few decades, clinical use of hormone blockers to "hit the pause button" on puberty has become salient as self-identified transgender children develop cognitively and their parents and physicians wrestle with the question of whether the child's gender identity will ultimately end up as something other than the one assigned at birth. If a cross gender identity is eventually embraced, the question then becomes when and if to administer body-altering hormones and other procedures to masculinize or feminize the body.

The crux of the controversy is that, although many gender variant young children who persistently claim a transgender identity meet criteria for GD, only a small percentage of young children with a GD diagnosis will carry their transgender identity into adolescence (Wallien & Cohen-Kettenis, 2008). A greater percentage of children with a GD diagnosis in adolescence (but still not all) will identify as transgender in adulthood (Zucker, 2008). However, Ehrensaft (2011), among others, endorses greater openness to use of puberty-blocking hormones in early adolescents who desire them after a rigorous professional consultation process. This is important in that earlier hormonal intervention can lead to better eventual surgical outcomes for children who identify as transgender in adulthood.

The World Professional Association for Transgender Health's (WPATH) *Standards of Care* recommends a staged, gradual process of hormonal treatment, moving from fully reversible to partially reversible therapies starting in adolescence, prior to irreversible surgical interventions (WPATH, 2011). The American Psychiatric Association left the door open for appropriate treatment aimed at resolving the dysphoria in preadolescent youth (Byne et al., 2012). It is also worth noting that many who identify as transgender in adulthood and ultimately transition do not report having had symptoms of GD as children (Lawrence, 2010). Therefore, gender variant behavior in early childhood is not the whole story on transgender identity development.

Adolescence

With homosexuality gone from the official list of mental disorders, research into the healthy development of sexual minority adolescents began in earnest in the early 1990s. What quickly emerged was the finding that LGBT youth were at higher risk for a host of behavioral and mental health problems, including depression (Bradford, Ryan, & Rothblum, 1994), substance use (Shifrin & Solis, 1992), and prostitution (Tremble, 1993), among others. Connections between these outcomes and antecedent victimization and stigmatizing of sexual minority youth were explored from early on as well (Mallon, 1994; Pilkington & D'Augelli, 1995).

Despite increased acceptance of LGBT persons in recent years, stigma, discrimination, and harassment have persisted. The 2013 GLSEN survey (Kosciw,

Greytak, Palmer, & Boesen, 2014) of 7,898 LGBT students between ages 13 and 21 in the United States found that nearly three-quarters (74.1%) had been verbally harassed because of their sexual orientation, more than a fourth (27.2%) often or frequently. More than half (55.2%) were verbally harassed at school due to gender expression.

A recently completed study from the National Center for Transgender Equality (NCTE; James et al., 2016) surveyed the largest sample of exclusively transgender people to date (*N* = 27,715). They found that 54 percent of those who expressed a transgender identity or were perceived as transgender in grades K–12 reported harassment, 24 percent reported physical assault, 17 percent left a K–12 school because of mistreatment, and six percent were expelled. College and vocational school students experienced mistreatment as well, with 24 percent experiencing verbal, physical, or sexual harassment (James et al., 2016).

Continued research into the consequences of victimization has yielded more of the same. Consistent with the minority stress model, being a victim of harassment and discrimination due to LGBT status has been found to be associated with negative psychosocial adjustment in numerous studies since 2000 (e.g., D'Augelli, Grossman, & Starks, 2006; Friedman, Koeske, Silvestre, Korr, & Sites, 2006; Toomey, Card, & Casper, 2014). Many studies have shown LGBT youth are at elevated risk for depression (e.g., Bruce, Harper, & Bauermeister, 2015; Burns, Ryan, Garofalo, Newcomb, & Mustanski, 2015), anxiety (e.g., Grant et al., 2014; Marshal et al., 2012), and suicidal ideation and suicide attempts (e.g., Bostwick et al., 2014; Mustanski & Liu, 2013). LGBT youth are also more likely than their heterosexual counterparts to engage in unhealthy behaviors, including smoking and alcohol and other substance abuse (e.g., Cabaj, 2015; Harawa et al., 2008; Huebner, Thoma, & Neilands, 2015). Furthermore, LGBT youth are at higher risk for HIV/AIDS and other sexually transmitted infections (Centers for Disease Control [CDC], 2016) and for homelessness (e.g., Keuroghlian, Shtasel, & Bassuk, 2014; Rosario, Schrimshaw, & Hunter, 2012; Wilson & Kastanis, 2015).

Other research has revealed mental health differences among diverse LGBT youth populations. Bisexual youth have been found to be more vulnerable to lower well-being than gay and lesbian youth, for instance (Shilo & Savaya, 2012). Shilo and Savaya (2012) also found that it appears transgender youth have significantly more negative outcomes than cisgender heterosexual and LGB youth. A study of 106 female-to-male and 74 male-to-female youth patients in a community mental health setting found that transgender youth were at a two- to threefold increased risk of depression, anxiety disorder, suicidal ideation, suicide attempt, and self-harm and had received more in- and outpatient mental health referrals than their cisgender peers (Reisner et al., 2015). Other work has shown transgender youth to have higher rates of depression, anxiety, and suicidal behaviors than their cisgender LGB counterparts (Clements-Nolle, Marx, &

Katz, 2006; Grossman & D'Augelli, 2007). Interestingly, some evidence suggests that gay male adolescents are more at risk for negative psychological adjustment on factors such as depression, guilt, shame, and negative self-esteem than older gay men (Bybee, Sullivan, Zielonka, & Moes, 2009).

A number of recent studies have noted intersectional effects of race and gender among LGBT youth. Bostwick et al. (2014), for instance, examined a number of mental health outcomes, including feelings of sadness, suicidal thoughts, and self-harm, in a large sample of sexual minority youth. Compared with white youth, Asian and Black sexual minority youth had lower risk for some of these negative mental health outcomes, but Native American, Latino, and multiracial youth had greater risk. Female sexual minority youth showed greater risk on most health outcome measures compared with male youth (Bostwick et al., 2014). In a separate study, Black sexual minority youth were less likely to be diagnosed with a lifetime major depressive episode than white youth (Burns et al., 2015).

Emerging Trends, New Research, and Controversies
Coming Out

"Coming out," or the process of disclosing a same-sex orientation to others, is one of the most studied aspects of sexual orientation development (Cohen & Savin-Williams, 2012). The coming out process for transgender people has started to gain attention in the empirical literature as well (Bockting & Coleman, 2016; James et al., 2016).

The environment for coming out as LBG or T has been changing rapidly, mostly for the better (Pew Research, 2013). In contrast with older cohorts, LGBT youth coming of age now have more access to information about the nature of their identities through the Internet, and they now find legal marriage across the country; more welcoming and supportive employers; healthcare systems and providers tending to the needs of LGBT patients; expanding legal protections for LGBT people in many states; and same-age and adult LGBT role models in popular culture and throughout their communities as peers, neighbors, teachers, and elected officials. All of that said, these gains are incomplete, as rights and protections are still lacking for LGB and especially transgender individuals in employment, housing, and public accommodations (Lambda Legal, 2016).

The existence of supporting environments, and a culture that—even if not entirely accepting—has LGBT on the radar, has encouraged more openness on the part of young LGBT people. There is a developing body of evidence that LGB youth are coming out earlier than ever before and openly expressing their identities in social media and other contexts. Compared with older age cohorts who came out to others well into their 20s, LGB persons who were 18–24 years of age in late 2003 and early 2004 reported coming out prior to age 17 on average

(Grov, Bimbi, Nanín, & Parsons, 2006). Additional studies comparing age cohorts (Drasin et al., 2008; Dunlap, 2016) found similar trends. Anecdotal accounts show even younger ages, with children as young as 12 and 13 coming out not just to their families but to their peers and schoolmates as well (Denizet-Lewis, 2009). It is important to note that the above studies were conducted with non-probability convenience samples and that more rigorous methods are needed to confirm this trend.

The environment for transgender coming out is also different now from what it was only a few short years ago. With the highly public coming out of Caitlyn Jenner in 2015, and the visibility of transgender actors such as Laverne Cox and characters in popular culture and entertainment (*Transparent*, *Orange Is the New Black*), gender identity and transgender issues are on the tips of the tongues of the American populace as never before. Retrospective data from the NCTE study (James et al., 2016) reveal that the majority of respondents (60%) reported feeling that their gender was different from the one assigned at birth prior to age 11. Another 21 percent started to think of themselves as transgender when they were 15 or younger.

However, coming out to others as transgender happened much later. Only 15 percent started to tell others they were transgender prior to age 16. The available evidence also suggests that. although transgender individuals may be self-identifying at earlier ages than in the past, they are doing so later than their cisgender LGB peers (Makadon, Mayer, Potter, & Goldhammer, 2015), and more rigorous study with non-convenience samples is needed.

The Complexity of Coming Out

It has long been understood that coming out is not a singular event but rather is a process that unfolds over time. While the end result of coming out is generally seen as positive and resulting in healthier identity development and lower pathology rates, disruption and uncertainty during the process can cause ill effects, as is clear from the research cited earlier in this chapter on depression, anxiety, and other psychological distress. Sex differences in the trajectory of coming out have been so widely noted in the literature (e.g., Savin-Williams & Ream, 2003) that noted researchers have dedicated large parts of their careers to exploring gender-specific characteristics of coming out for boys (e.g., Savin-Williams, 2016) and girls (Diamond, 2006).

Recent work has revealed some of the other complexities of the coming out process. Watson, Wheldon, and Russell (2015) examined youth in varying states of outness with family, friends, and people at school. They found that those who were out to some people but not to others showed lower academic achievement and experienced more harassment than youth who were out to everyone or out to nobody. Watson et al. (2015) posited that managing dual identities as "out" and "not out" simultaneously drove this finding.

In a separate study examining fluidity in the coming out process, Everett (2015) found that the process of changing toward a more same-sex orientation was correlated with increased depressive symptoms but not with changes toward a more opposite-sex orientation. Negative impacts were also greatest for those who identified as heterosexual at baseline or had not indicated previous same-sex romantic attractions or relationships.

Social Media and the Internet

Social media is a relatively recent phenomenon in our culture. We are only beginning to grasp its effect on developing sexual minority youth. That said, there is now a growing cohort of adolescents who have never known life without Facebook, Instagram, and Twitter.

Social media hold potential for both positive and negative impacts. On the positive side, the Internet and social media have provided LGBT youth more opportunities for access to essential information about themselves, their communities, and their health and to meet and interact with peers, find a supportive community, and counteract geographic or emotional isolation. Through a series of semi-structured interviews with 33 LGBT youth about their coming out experiences, Fox and Ralston (2016) found that social media served as a learning platform for LGBT youths' identity-formation process, including using social media as a source of information about LGBT issues and learning about social roles and as a context for experimenting with romantic and sexual relationships. Craig, McInroy, McCready, DiCesare, and Pettaway (2015) found that sexual minority youth who were frequent users of social media reported that their online experiences offered what they perceived to be safe spaces for information sharing and building community support. Along the same lines, Varjas, Meyers, Kiperman, and Howard (2013) found that LGB youth felt technology provided supports that they might not otherwise have had, and many reported using technology to come out.

But social media can be a double-edged sword. The Internet age has opened up new avenues for misinformation, harassment, and bullying and has made it easier for youth and adults alike to be exposed to pervasive negative attitudes about LGBT people (Cooper & Blumenfeld, 2012; Varjas et al., 2013). In the social media age, one's friends can literally be counted on Facebook and other platforms, providing the opportunity for comparison, judging, and humiliation. "Cyberbullying" has become an ongoing concern for schools, parents, and youth alike. It can be carried out with relative ease through text messages, e-mail, social media platforms (e.g., Facebook), cell phones, and chat rooms. In a sample of 264 Canadian students in seventh through ninth grades, Li (2006) found that nearly half were bullying victims, and about a fourth had been cyberbullied. In their qualitative semi-structured interviews with 15- to 18-year-old LGB participants, Varjas et al. (2013) documented personal narratives of cyberbullying experiences and reported that 11 of their 18 participants thought sexual orientation was a common reason for cyberbullying. With social media's reach continuing to grow, social media will certainly continue to be a focal point of research for many years to come.

Conversion Therapy

Another still-current and pressing topic in LGBT mental health is the practice of conversion or reparative therapy. These individual therapies and group counseling programs, often clergy- or religious layperson-based, purport to convert gay, lesbian, and bisexual people to heterosexuality.

The clinical and research literature could not be clearer that these attempts are both ineffective and can have severe negative effects on persons subjected to these practices. These include loss of sexual desire, increased depression, increased suicide risk, and anxiety (Beckstead & Morrow, 2004; Haldeman, 2012; Shidlo & Schroeder, 2002). The religiously based flagship program Exodus International shut down a few years ago, acknowledging the ineffectiveness and harm of their approaches (Payne, 2013).

But others persist. Of great concern to mental health professionals is conversion therapy's continued use with unwilling LGBT adolescents (Hein & Matthews, 2010).

The focus of many health advocates has shifted to a policy effort to have laws changed in states to ban the practice of conversion therapy, primarily with minors who are not capable of legally refusing these therapies. As of the writing, only five states plus the District of Columbia have laws that prohibit parents or others from forcing minor children into such programs or therapies.

It's Getting Better? Resilience in LGBT Adolescents

In 2011, syndicated columnist Dan Savage launched a website called It Gets Better (http://www.itgetsbetter.org/), aimed at counteracting suicide and giving voice to LGBT youth who have experienced bullying, discrimination, violence, and suicidal thoughts, with the hope it would inspire LGBT young people to persevere and keep a positive outlook on their futures. The website became wildly popular and talked about in mainstream media.

Asakura and Craig (2014) conducted a qualitative study to explore the resilience that the It Gets Better project hoped to encourage. The authors analyzed videos posted on the site and concluded that life did not necessarily get better for the 21 youth who posted the videos analyzed. However, they did discover some pathways that could lead to resilience in LGBT youth.

Birkett, Newcomb, and Mustanski (2015) followed up on this question. Using a longitudinal approach, they found that—yes—it gets better for LGBT youth, sort of. In their racially and ethnically diverse sample of 231 youth, both psychological distress and victimization decreased as the youth phased into late adolescence and adulthood. Support from parents, peers, and significant others was associated with decreased psychological distress. However, victimization varied among the youth. For those for whom victimization was highest, psychological distress remained high.

These studies are reflective of a broader trend toward a research focus on youth resilience (Meyer, 2015). With a sample of 232 primarily African American LGBT youth ages 16–20, McConnell, Birkett, and Mustanski (2015) found that combinations of different types of support sources were related to better mental health outcomes, with family support especially relevant. Roe (2015) used semi-structured interviews with 18 youth to examine LGBT adolescent experiences of support from peers and how youths' school experiences shaped their peer interactions. Roe (2015) found that, although the youth in her study feared judgment from non-LGBT peers, and not all peers were supportive, LGBT youth still thought peers were an important source of emotional and functional support.

Interventions: Counteracting Stigma and Discrimination

Turning research about resilience into realized change for LGBT youth is the mission of intervention efforts. The body of research reviewed in this chapter gives us a framework for understanding the many factors that contribute to negative outcomes, and this understanding can be used to develop interventions to mitigate them and to promote efficacious approaches to reducing stigma and harassment and helping sexual minority youth survive and thrive. Researchers, clinicians, and interventionists alike have turned their attention to establishing best clinical practices and developing effective interventions and clinical strategies to help reduce these disparities (Forssell, Gamache, & Dwan, 2017).

There are two ways to attack the problem of stigma and discrimination. One involves working with the youth who are the targets of stigma and discrimination. The other is to target those who are the source of the harassment. Focusing on reducing victimization involves working with people in the lives of LGBT youth as much as with the youth themselves. This means reaching out to affect the attitudes of peers, family members, teachers, religious leaders, and others in the community. Home-based intervention programs, such as the Family Acceptance Project (https://familyproject.sfsu.edu/overview), target the parents and family members of LGBT youth. Unaccepting parents are often motivated by positive intent—they want their children to be happy; however, they fear that living as openly LGBT will result in an unhappy life. The Family Acceptance Project's approach is to help parents understand that rejecting behaviors ultimately result in unhappy children.

Gay-straight alliances, or GSAs, are student-run clubs that try to build support for LGBT students and unity with straight peers. They have thrived in

U.S. schools recently (GSA Network, 2017). Greytak, Kosciw, and Boesen (2013) examined school resources for LGBT students and found that GSAs, supportive educators, and LGBT-inclusive curricula were related to lower levels of victimization. The benefits to transgender students were even stronger than for cisgender LGB students. Poteat, Sinclair, DiGiovanni, Koenig, and Russell (2013) also found that schools with GSAs experienced lower suicide rates for students overall, with the highest benefit in reduced suicidality for LGBT youth in the schools studied.

Early/Middle Adulthood: Partnering, Parenting, and Parting

As LGBT youth become LGBT adults, their status as marginalized individuals follows them into adulthood and can negatively impact their opportunities for employment, living arrangements, and other aspects of day-to-day life—as well as their mental health. Legal and institutional obstacles to equal rights and adequate healthcare accompany the cultural obstacles. As of October, 2016, 28 states allowed discrimination against LGBT persons in employment, housing, and public accommodations; three additional states permit transgender discrimination in the same domains (Equality Federation, 2016). Only 19 states plus the District of Columbia have laws offering protections based on both sexual orientation and gender identity. A few states have moved to enact ordinances specifically requiring people to only use bathrooms that are consistent with their birth-assigned genders. At the writing, 51 percent of LGBT Americans can be fired from a job, denied housing, or refused service at businesses or governmental entities as a function of where they live (Equality Federation, 2016).

Workplace Discrimination, Harassment, and Wage Disparities

These negative social and legal realities are no doubt contributors to workplace discrimination and income disparities between LGB and heterosexual adults and between transgender and cisgender adults. In a 2011 report, the Williams Institute, an independent public policy center at UCLA Law School, summarized the state of the research on workplace environment for LGBT people (Sears & Mallory, 2011). They found that 27 percent of LGB people had experienced some form of discrimination based on SO in the previous five years, and seven percent had lost a job. Among those out about their SO at work, this number was higher, with 38 percent experiencing at least one form of discrimination in the same five-year period (Sears & Mallory, 2011). The NCTE study (James et al., 2016) found that 30 percent of transgender respondents who had held a job in the previous year had been fired, denied a promotion, or had experienced some other form of mistreatment at work because of their gender identity or expression, and 77 percent had hidden their gender identity or delayed transition or taken other steps to avoid mistreatment at work.

The commonly held stereotype that those with same-sex partners, gay men in particular, who are wealthier and have more disposable income than heterosexuals is not supported by data. Several studies have found between 11 and 27 percent lower income for gay and bisexual men as compared with heterosexual men (Allegretto & Arthur, 2001; Black, Gates, Sanders, & Taylor, 2000; Sears & Mallory, 2011).

For lesbians, however, the trend was the reverse. Black et al. (2000) found that lesbian women earned 20–34 percent more than heterosexual women.

The data on transgender individuals suggest they experience wage disparities and unemployment at higher rates than cisgender people. Participants in the NCTE study (James et al., 2016) were unemployed at a rate three times the national average and were more than twice as likely to live in poverty (29% vs. 14%) and three times more likely to have a household income of less than $10,000 per year (12% vs. 4%) than the general population.

Mental Health

Although LGBT adults are generally mentally healthy and function well in society (Cochran & Mays, 2006; Herek & Garnets, 2007), the stigma and discrimination that are so salient for LGBT adolescents unfortunately persist into adulthood, though the contexts change somewhat. Given the disparities and discrimination that have been reviewed in this section, both social and institutional, it is perhaps not surprising that LGB adults have been found to experience elevated levels of anxiety and mood disorders, specifically depression, in one study both over the 12 months prior to the time of the study and over their lifetimes, compared to heterosexual adults. Rates for suicidal ideation and behavior appear higher as well (IOM, 2011).

The trend emerging for transgender people mirrors what has been found in the LGB population—higher rates of depression, anxiety, and suicidal ideation. The NCTE study provided dramatic data about the mental health, behavioral health, and experiences with the healthcare system for trans-identified people (James et al., 2016). The study found that 39 percent of respondents were experiencing serious psychological distress at the time of the study (vs. 5% of the general population) and that 40 percent had attempted suicide at some point in their lives (as compared with 4.6% of the general population). Respondents also had over three times the national average rate of HIV infection, with racial minority transgender women the most adversely affected. Respondents also reported high rates of illicit drug use, marijuana consumption, and nonmedical prescription use. Respondents' experiences with healthcare providers were also highly negative, with 28 percent reporting having postponed medical care due to discrimination and 48 percent unable to afford care. Additionally, 19 percent said they were refused care due to their transgender or gender-nonconforming status, 28 percent reported they had been harassed in medical settings, and two percent reported they had been victims of violence in doctors' offices (James et al., 2016).

The good news that arose from the NCTE study findings was that, like LGB youth, transgender adults experienced better outcomes when their families were supportive and accepting. Trans people with accepting families were less likely to report psychological distress, attempt suicide, use alcohol and drugs, and experience homelessness, and they were more likely to report overall good health than those with nonaccepting families (James et al., 2016).

Couple Functioning and Parenting

We now have 30+ years of empirical research to draw upon about the functioning of LGB people in couple relationships and as parents. The overwhelming preponderance of evidence shows that, despite societal disadvantages, institutional and legal barriers, and persisting discrimination, same-sex couples function very well in committed relationships and are more similar to opposite-sex couples than they are different (Kurdek, 2005). The qualities of their relationships and levels of satisfaction are similar to opposite-sex couples and are generally positive (Kurdek, 2001). Same-sex couples and heterosexual couples experience conflict at similar rates and about similar issues—primarily finances—but same-sex couples appear better at negotiating conflict and staying positive in conflict situations (Gottman et al., 2003; Kurdek, 2004). Relationship stability showed differences in early research, with same-sex relationships showing lesser stability, but the same data also suggested that the status of legal marriage was a driving factor in relationship stability, as cohabiting heterosexual couples' break-up rates were similar to those of unmarried same-sex partners (Blumstein & Schwartz, 1983).

The body of evidence is similarly strong that LGB couples who parent function similarly to heterosexual couples who parent. Children raised in same-sex-parented families do not demonstrate confusion over gender (Anderssen, Amlie, & Ytteroy, 2002; Golombok, Spencer, & Rutter, 1983; Gottman, 1990). They do not display different rates of gender atypical play or adjustment problems (Farr, Forssell, & Patterson, 2010a). Parents of these children also function well, not differing from their heterosexual counterparts on parental discipline, parenting stress, relationship satisfaction (Farr et al., 2010a), or sexual satisfaction (Farr, Forssell, & Patterson, 2010b).

Emerging Trends, New Research, and Controversies
Marriage

Perhaps the most significant social change for LGBT adults in the past few years has been access to the institution of legal marriage. By late 2009, only five states had legalized same-sex marriage. By early 2015 that count had jumped to

36 states plus the District of Columbia. With the *Obergefell* Supreme Court ruling in June, 2015, full legal marriage was available in all 50 states and the District of Columbia. The impact of this rapid shift has become of interest to health professionals, who have considered whether access to legal marriage would result in a healthier LGBT population and whether the formal commitment to marriage would affect same-sex couple longevity and relationship quality.

Prior to the availability of same-sex marriage in the United States, break-up rates for same-sex partners were higher than for heterosexual partners. Both Blumstein and Schwartz (1983) and Kurdek (1998, 2004) found that heterosexual married couples were less likely to dissolve than gay male and lesbian cohabiting couples. As the availability of formalized and legal commitments in the form of civil unions, domestic partnerships, and full marriage increased, however, the relationship-bolstering impact started to become apparent. Whitton, Kuryluk, and Khaddouma (2015) found that same-sex partnered adults in legally formalized unions showed greater stability and higher relationship satisfaction than those in socially (but not legally) formalized or nonformalized relationships. Using a nationally representative sample of over 3,000 participants, Rosenfeld (2014) found that marriage leveled the playing field for same-sex partners' relationship stability. Relationship dissolution rates for legally married same-sex partners have been lower than those for unmarried partners and have not differed from those of heterosexual married couples.

Access to marriage also seems to have a protective effect on the physical and mental health of LGBT people. Using a large nationally representative data set, Hatzenbuehler, McLaughlin, Keyes, and Hasin (2010) found that, in states that instituted same-sex marriage bans during the 2004 and 2005 election cycles, psychiatric disorders increased for LGB people, where there was no similar increase for heterosexual people or in states where such bans were not implemented. In a separate study, Hatzenbuehler et al. (2012) found that, in the 12 months after same-sex marriage went into effect in Massachusetts, there was a significant decrease in medical and mental healthcare visits for gay men in the state. Riggle, Wickham, Rostosky, Rothblum, and Balsam (2016) found that people in civil same-sex marriages reported more support from their partners. They also found that those living in states with legal same-sex marriage were more comfortable with themselves and engaged in less concealment of their LGB identities.

As the marriages that were created after the 2015 *Obergefell* ruling mature and evolve, there will no doubt be additional research to follow and the opportunity to observe these relationships longitudinally in the context of full marriage equality throughout the country. But the evidence to date suggests that the formal institution of marriage, now available to people of all sexual orientations, promotes relationship longevity, better quality relationships, comfort with an LGB identity, and better health outcomes.

Minority Stress Research

The minority stress model has been used as a basis for investigating and better understanding LGBT adult development and health disparities in deeper and more complex ways than had been explored in the past. Researchers have sought to document and investigate these effects of LGBT minority stress in numerous studies on a broad, societal scale and in studies specific to LGBT young adults. We will touch on just a few here whose work is garnering attention.

Hatzenbuehler (2014) was among the first to use methodologies to quantify how minority stress has been institutionalized in broad, macrosocial forms. He found that structural stigma is a risk indicator for both mental and physical health problems in LGB populations.

Eldahan et al. (2016) examined the impact of minority stress in a population of 371 gay and bisexual men in New York City. They employed a daily diary approach, asking participants to record their daily experiences of minority stress and their affect over a 30-day period. Consistent with the model, minority stress predicted higher levels of negative and anxious affect and lower levels of positive affect, suggesting a link between minority stress and mood and anxiety disorder symptoms.

Looking deeper into the complexity of LGB identities, Kuyper and Bos (2016) examined health behaviors and mental health in a group of 528 Dutch young adults who self-identified as "mostly heterosexual" and as gay or lesbian. They found that participants who identified as "mostly heterosexual" showed higher levels of psychological distress, suicidality, drug use, and smoking than lesbian and gay young adults. Those who identified as mostly heterosexual were also more likely to report higher levels of internalized negativity about same-sex attraction, were less open about their orientations to family, were less involved in the LGB community, and had fewer LGB friends than those who identified as lesbian and gay. This finding suggests that minority stress might vary within LGB populations and is consistent with previous research reflecting more negative outcomes for bisexually identified people.

Later Adulthood and Old Age

LGBT elders have long been an understudied segment of the community. Much of the established research on LGBT people in their later years reflects cohort effects of generations that matured at times when homosexuality was viewed more negatively (IOM, 2011). For LGBT persons now in their late 70s and older, laws against homosexual behavior were often actively enforced, and stigma around homosexuality was far more prevalent than it is now; consequently, very few LGB people were out of the closet in the 1950s and 1960s. Gender issues were poorly understood, so many transgender people lived in a combination of confusion, secrecy, and fear. For that cohort, the gay liberation movement that started with the Stonewall gay rights rebellion came well into their adult years.

A slightly younger cohort, now in their late 50s and 60s, experienced Stonewall as early adolescents and young adults. They also endured the advent of the AIDS crisis in their prime adult years. Life with the stigma of AIDS and the loss that came with it are characteristics that demarcate this age group.

Some middle adult to late adult LGBT persons have been able to make connections with a gay community that only started to coalesce well after their personal coming of age. Others are less connected to or feel less comfortable with younger LGBT people who have come of age in more accepting times.

Research has also shown that older LGBT adults are less likely to have life partners as supports and more likely to experience isolation and a lack of effective support networks (Barker, Herdt, & de Vries, 2006; MetLife, 2006; Shippy, Cantor, & Brennan, 2004). Many experience stigma and discrimination not only from their same-aged peers but also from workers in facilities charged with their care and protection (Hurd, 2015). Very few retirement communities and nursing facilities are proactively LGBT-positive, so much abuse goes unchallenged (Hurd, 2015; Miller, 2016). Older LGBT people are less likely to be out to family and are often placed in retirement and nursing facilities by relatives who are either insensitive to or unaware of their LGBT status.

What little research is available suggests that LGBT elders report high rates of lifetime experiences with stigma, discrimination, and violence (Hurd, 2015; IOM, 2011). A survey from Justice in Aging of LGBT adults living in long-term care settings found that a majority believed they would face discrimination from housing staff if they were open about their orientations (Cohens, 2015). The report captured hundreds of stories of problems LGBT seniors have encountered with housing staff, ranging from harassment to refusals to provide basic services or care.

Concurrent with this discrimination, and in line with the minority stress model, older lesbians and gay men appear to have higher levels of mental and behavioral health problems, including anxiety disorders, depression and other mood disorders, suicidality, and tobacco and alcohol use (IOM, 2011; Shippy et al., 2004; Valanis et al., 2000). The mental health concerns of bisexual and transgender elders are much less studied, but the available data suggest that they, too, have elevated rates of these same problems (IOM, 2011).

As the battle against HIV/AIDS has progressed and as survival rates have improved, more HIV+ men and women are living longer, many entering old age. Promoting resilience and psychological well-being is critical for this group. But many have lost partners and friends, experienced elevated rates of depression as a result, and find themselves navigating losses complicated by a lack of social networks (Cahill & Valadez, 2013; High et al., 2012; Mavandadi, Zanjani, Ten Have, & Oslin, 2009).

New HIV infections are a concern for LGBT elders. When elder LGB part-ners pass away, some return to dating underestimating their personal risk for HIV. This should not be a surprise given that HIV prevention messages target younger-aged men who have sex with men (MSM).

Emerging Trends and Controversies

A 2015 position statement from the American Geriatrics Society makes clear that the needs of LGBT older adults are still largely unmet (Hurd, 2015). The statement cites recent data that found that more than 50 percent of LGB and 70 percent of transgender elders had experienced discrimination in a healthcare setting at the hands of their providers, including refusal of care and overt deroga-tory statements (Lambda Legal, 2010). Among other points, the position state-ment advocates that SO, GI, and gender expression should be included in patient nondiscrimination policies; that visitation policies should grant equal access for same-sex and transgender couples; that such policies should allow equal access to support persons whom elders designate even if these persons may not become legal family members; and that increased training in the health of LGBT elders for caseworkers should become available.

The good news is that recent research is both finding evidence of elder LGBT resilience and emerging pursuit of best practices for sustaining resilience in LGBT senior populations (Grossman, 2006). With resilience as a framework for investigation, Fredriksen-Goldsen, Kim, Shiu, Goldsen, and Emlet (2015) used a cross-sectional methodology to investigate the relationship between physical and mental health–related quality of life variables in a sample of more than 2,500 LGBT adults ages 50 and older. While controlling for age and other relevant variables, they found that physical and mental health was negatively impacted by discrimination and chronic health conditions. Health was posi-tively associated with social support, social network size, physical and leisure activities, lack of substance use, employment, and income. Discrimination was particularly salient for the older participants in the study.

The nonprofit group SAGE (Services and Advocacy for Lesbian, Gay and Bisexual Elders; http://www.sageusa.org/) offers national programs to support LGBT elders across the country, including consumer resources, employment, housing, and social and emotional support. Trainings for elder care workers on the issues and needs of LGBT persons are being developed and made available (e.g., lgbtagingcenter.org) to improve care for aging LGBT persons.

CONCLUSION

Years of study of LGBT people have offered us much insight into the factors that contribute to positive LGBT mental health and identity development. Recent advances in theory, such as intersectionality and the minority stress model, and new approaches for measuring the diversity within the constantly changing and evolving LGBT community enable us to better understand the complexities of mental health and development of those with varied sexual orientations and gender identities at all points along the developmental age spectrum.

REFERENCES

Allegretto, S. A., & Arthur, M. M. (2001). An empirical analysis of homosexual/heterosexual male earnings differentials: Unmarried and unequal? *ILR Review*, *54*, 631–646.

Anderssen, N., Amlie, C., & Ytteroy, E. A. (2002). Outcomes for children with lesbian or gay parents: A review of studies from 1978 to 2000. *Scandinavian Journal of Psychology*, *43*, 335–351.

Asakura, K., & Craig, S. L. (2014). "It Gets Better" . . . but how? Exploring resilience development in the accounts of LGBTQ adults. *Journal of Human Behavior in the Social Environment*, *24*(3), 253–266. doi:10.1080/10911359.2013.808971

Badgett, M. L. (1995). The wage effects of sexual orientation discrimination. *ILR Review*, *48*, 726–739.

Bailey, J. M., & Pillard, R. C. (1995). Genetics of human sexual orientation. *Annual Review of Sex Research*, *VI*, 126–150.

Bailey, J. M., Vasey, P. L., Diamond, L. M., Breedlove, S. M., Vilain, E., & Epprecht, M. (2016). Sexual orientation, controversy, and science. *Psychological Science in the Public Interest*, *17*(2), 45–101. doi:10.1177/1529100616637616

Barker, J. C., Herdt, G., & de Vries, B. (2006). Social support in the lives of lesbians and gay men at midlife and later. *Sexuality Research & Social Policy: A Journal of the NSRC*, *3*(2), 1–23.

Bayer, R. (1981). *Homosexuality and American psychiatry: The politics of diagnosis*. New York, NY: Basic Books.

Beckstead, A. L., & Morrow, S. L. (2004). Mormon clients' experiences of conversion therapy: The need for a new treatment approach. *The Counseling Psychologist*, *32*(5), 651–690. doi:10.1177/0011000004267555

Birkett, M., Newcomb, M. E., & Mustanski, B. (2015). Does it get better? A longitudinal analysis of psychological distress and victimization in lesbian, gay, bisexual, transgender, and questioning youth. *Journal of Adolescent Health*, *56*(3), 280–285. doi:10.1016/j.jadohealth.2014.10.275

Black, D., Gates, G., Sanders, S., & Taylor, L. (2000). Demographics of the gay and lesbian population in the United States: Evidence from available systematic data. *Demography*, *37*, 139–154.

Blumstein, P., & Schwartz, P. (1983). *American couples*. Retrieved June 25, 2017, from http://www.popline.org/node/411150

Bockting, W., & Coleman, E. (2016). Developmental stages of the transgender coming-out process: Toward an integrated identity. In R. Ettner, S. Monstrey, E. Coleman, R. Ettner, S. Monstrey, & E. Coleman (Eds.), *Principles of transgender medicine and surgery* (pp. 137–158). New York, NY: Routledge/Taylor & Francis Group.

Bostwick, W. B., Meyer, I., Aranda, F., Russell, S., Hughes, T., Birkett, M., & Mustanski, B. (2014). Mental health and suicidality among racially/ethnically diverse sexual minority youths. *American Journal of Public Health*, *104*, 1129–1136.

Bradford, J., Ryan, C., & Rothblum, E. D. (1994). National Lesbian Health Care Survey: Implications for mental health care. *Journal of Consulting and Clinical Psychology*, 62(2), 228–242. doi:10.1037/0022-006X.62.2.228

Bruce, D., Harper, G. W., & Bauermeister, J. A. (2015). Minority stress, positive identity development, and depressive symptoms: Implications for resilience among sexual minority male youth. *Psychology of Sexual Orientation and Gender Diversity*, 2(3), 287–296.

Burns, M. N., Ryan, D. T., Garofalo, R., Newcomb, M. E., & Mustanski, B. (2015). Mental health disorders in young urban sexual minority men. *Journal of Adolescent Health*, 56, 52–58.

Bybee, J. A., Sullivan, E. L., Zielonka, E., & Moes, E. (2009). Are gay men in worse mental health than heterosexual men? The role of age, shame and guilt, and coming-out. *Journal of Adult Development*, 16(3), 144–154. doi:10.1007/s10804-009-9059-x

Byne, W., Bradley, S. J., Coleman, E., Eyler, A. E., Green, R., Menvielle, E. J., ... Tompkins, D. A. (2012). Report of the American Psychiatric Association task force on treatment of gender identity disorder. *Archives of Sexual Behavior*, 41(4), 759–796. doi:10.1007/s10508-012-9975-x

Cabaj, R. P. (2015). Substance use issues among gay, bisexual, and transgender people. In M. Galanter, H. D. Kleber, K. T. Brady, M. Galanter, H. D. Kleber, & K. T. Brady (Eds.), *The American Psychiatric Publishing textbook of substance abuse treatment* (5th ed., pp. 707–721). Arlington, VA: American Psychiatric Publishing, Inc.

Cahill, S., & Valadez, R. (2013). Growing older with HIV/AIDS: New public health challenges. *American Journal of Public Health*, 103(3), 7–15.

Cahill, S. R., Baker, K., Deutsch, M. B., Keatley, J., & Makadon, H. J. (2016, April 3). Inclusion of sexual orientation and gender identity in Stage 3 meaningful use guidelines: A huge step forward for LGBT health. *LGBT Health*, 3(2), 100–102. doi:10.1089/lgbt.2015.0136

Cass, V. C. (1979). Homosexuality identity formation: A theoretical model. *Journal of Homosexuality*, 4, 219–235.

Cass, V. C. (1984). Homosexual identity formation: Testing a theoretical model. *Journal of Sex Research*, 20(2), 143–167. doi:10.1080/00224498409551214

Cass, V. C. (2016). A quick guide to the Cass Theory of Lesbian & Gay Identity Formation. Self-published.

Centers for Disease Control (CDC). (2016). http://www.cdc.gov/hiv/group/age/youth/

Clements-Nolle, K., Marx, R., & Katz, M. (2006). Attempted suicide among transgender persons: The influence of gender-based discrimination and victimization. *Journal of Homosexuality*, 51(3), 53–69. doi:10.1300/J082v51n03_04

Cochran, S. D., & Mays, V. M. (2006). Estimating prevalence of mental and substance-using disorders among lesbians and gay men from existing national health data. In A. M. Omoto & H. S. Kurtzman (Eds.), *Sexual orientation and mental health: Examining identity and development in lesbian, gay, and bisexual people* (pp. 143–165). Washington, DC: American Psychological Association.

Cohen, K. M., & Savin-Williams, R. C. (2012). Coming out to self and others: Developmental milestones. In P. Levounis, J. Drescher, M. E. Barber, P. Levounis, J. Drescher, & M. E. Barber (Eds.), *The LGBT casebook* (pp. 17–33). Arlington, VA: American Psychiatric Publishing, Inc.

Cohens, K. (2015, June 30). LGBT older adults in long-term care facilities: Stories from the field. Retrieved from http://www.justiceinaging.org/lgbt-older-adults-in-long-term-care-facilities-stories-from-the-field-2/

Colapinto, J. (2000). *As nature made him: The boy who was raised as a girl.* New York, NY: Harper Collins.

Coleman, E. (1982). Developmental stages of the coming out process. *Journal of Homosexuality, 7*(2/3), 31–43.

Conron, K. J., Landers, S. J., Reisner, S. L., & Sell, R. L. (2014). Sex and gender in the US Health Surveillance System: A call to action. *American Journal of Public Health, 104*(6), 970–976. doi:10.2105/ajph.2013.301831

Cooper, R. M., & Blumenfeld, W. J. (2012). Responses to cyberbullying: A descriptive analysis of the frequency of and impact on LGBT and allied youth. *Journal of LGBT Youth, 9*(2), 153–177. doi:10.1080/19361653.2011.649616

Craig, S. L., McInroy, L. B., McCready, L. T., Di Cesare, D. M., & Pettaway, L. D. (2015). Connecting without fear: Clinical implications of the consumption of information and communication technologies by sexual minority youth and young adults. *Clinical Social Work Journal, 43*(2), 159–168. doi:10.1007/s10615-014-0505-2

D'Augelli, A. R., Grossman, A. H., & Starks, M. T. (2006). Childhood gender atypicality, victimization, and PTSD among lesbian, gay, and bisexual youth. *Journal of Interpersonal Violence, 21*, 1462–1482.

Denizet-Lewis, B. (2009, September 23). Coming out in middle school. *The New York Times.* Retrieved from http://www.nytimes.com/2009/09/27/magazine/27out-t.html

Diagnostic and Statistical Manual of Mental Disorders: DSM-5. (2013). Washington, DC: American Psychiatric Association.

Diamond, L. M. (2005). A new view of lesbian subtypes: Stable versus fluid identity trajectories over an 8-year period. *Psychology of Women Quarterly, 29*, 119–128. doi:10.1111/j.1471-6402.2005. 00174.x

Diamond, L. M. (2006). *Rethinking positive adolescent female sexual development.* San Francisco, CA: Jossey-Bass.

Diamond, L. M. (2012). The desire disorder in research on sexual orientation in women: Contributions of dynamical systems theory. *Archives of Sexual Behavior, 41*(1), 73–83. doi:10.1007/s10508-012-9909-7

Drasin, H., Beals, K. P., Elliott, M. N., Lever, J., Klein, D. J., & Schuster, M. A. (2008). Age cohort differences in the developmental milestones of gay men. *Journal of Homosexuality, 54*(4), 381–399. doi:10.1080/00918360801991372

Drescher, J. (2015). Out of DSM: Depathologizing homosexuality. *Behavioral Sciences, 5*(4), 565–575. http://doi.org/10.3390/bs5040565

Dunlap, A. (2016). Changes in coming out milestones across five age cohorts. *Journal of Gay & Lesbian Social Services: The Quarterly Journal of Community & Clinical Practice, 28*(1), 20–38. doi:10.1080/10538720.2016.1124351

Ehrensaft, D. (2011). *Gender born, gender made.* New York, NY: The Experiment.

Eldahan, A. I., Pachankis, J. E., Rendina, H. J., Ventuneac, A., Grov, C., & Parsons, J. T. (2016). Daily minority stress and affect among gay and bisexual men: A 30-day diary study. *Journal of Affective Disorders, 190*, 828–835. doi:10.1016/j.jad.2015.10.066

Equality Federation. (2016). Facts on nondiscrimination laws. Retrieved from http://equalityfederation.org/fairnessproject/facts/

Everett, B. (2015). Sexual orientation identity change and depressive symptoms: A longitudinal analysis. *Journal of Health and Social Behavior, 56*(1), 37–58. doi:10.1177/0022146514568349

Farr, R. H., Diamond, L. M., & Boker, S. M. (2014). Female same-sex sexuality from a dynamical systems perspective: Sexual desire, motivation, and behavior. *Archives of Sexual Behavior*, 43(8), 1477–1490. doi:10.1007/s10508-014-0378-z

Farr, R. H., Forssell, S. L., & Patterson, C. J. (2010a). Gay, lesbian, and heterosexual adoptive parents: Couple and relationship issues. *Journal of GLBT Family Studies*, 6(2), 199–213. doi:10.1080/15504281003705436

Farr, R. H., Forssell, S. L., & Patterson, C. J. (2010b). Parenting and child development in adoptive families: Does parental sexual orientation matter? *Applied Developmental Science*, 14(3), 164–178. doi:10.1080/10888691.2010.500958

Fassinger, R. E., & Arseneau, J. R. (2007). "I'd rather get wet than be under that umbrella": Differentiating the experiences and identities of lesbian, gay, bisexual, and transgender people. In K. J. Bieschke, R. M. Perez, K. A. DeBord, K. J. Bieschke, R. M. Perez, & K. A. DeBord (Eds.), *Handbook of counseling and psychotherapy with lesbian, gay, bisexual, and transgender clients* (2nd ed., pp. 19–49). Washington, DC: American Psychological Association.

Federal Interagency Working Group on Improving Measurement of Sexual Orientation and Gender Identity in Federal Surveys. (2016). Current measures of sexual orientation and gender identity in federal surveys. https://s3.amazonaws.com/sitesusa/wp-content/uploads/sites/242/2014/04/WorkingGroupPaper1_CurrentMeasures_08-16.pdf

Fernández, M., Guerra, P., Díaz, M., Garcia-Vega, E., & Álvarez-Diz, J. A. (2015). Nuevas perspectivas en el tratamiento hormonal de la disforia de género en la adolescencia [New perspectives in the hormonal treatment of gender dysphoria in adolescence]. *Actas Españolas de Psiquiatría*, 43(1), 24–31.

Fite, P. J., Williford, A., Cooley, J. L., DePaolis, K., Rubens, S. L., & Vernberg, E. M. (2013). Patterns of victimization locations in elementary school children: Effects of grade level and gender. *Child & Youth Care Forum*, 42(6), 585–597. doi:10.1007/s10566-013-9219-9

Forssell, S. L., Gamache, P., & Dwan, R. (2017). *Approaches to interventions with LGBT populations*. Manuscript in preparation, Department of Psychology, The George Washington University, Washington, DC, 65.

Fox, J., & Ralston, R. (2016). Queer identity online: Informal learning and teaching experiences of LGBTQ individuals on social media. *Computers in Human Behavior*, 65, 635–642. doi:10.1016/j.chb.2016.06.009

Fredriksen-Goldsen, K. I., Kim, H., Shiu, C., Goldsen, J., & Emlet, C. A. (2015). Successful aging among LGBT older adults: Physical and mental health-related quality of life by age group. *The Gerontologist*, 55(1), 154–168. doi:10.1093/geront/gnu081

Friedman, M. S., Koeske, G. F., Silvestre, A. J., Korr, W. S., & Sites, E. W. (2006). The impact of gender-role nonconforming behavior, bullying, and social support on suicidality among gay male youth. *Journal of Adolescent Health*, 38, 621–623.

Galton, F. (1883). Nurture and nature. In *Inquiries into human faculty and its development* (pp. 177–182). New York, NY: MacMillan Co. doi:10.1037/14178-020

Galupo, M. P., Mitchell, R. C., & Davis, K. S. (2015). Sexual minority self-identification: Multiple identities and complexity. *Psychology of Sexual Orientation and Gender Diversity*, 2(4), 355–364. doi:10.1037/sgd0000131

Golombok, S., Spencer, A., & Rutter, M. (1983). Children in lesbian and single-parent households: Psychosexual and psychiatric appraisal. *Journal of Child Psychology and Psychiatry, 24,* 551–572.

Gottman, J. M., Levenson, R. W., Swanson, C., Swanson, K., Tyson, R., & Yoshimoto, D. (2003). Observing gay, lesbian, and heterosexual couples' relationships: Mathematical modeling of conflict interaction. *Journal of Homosexuality, 45,* 65–91.

Gottman, J. S. (1990). Children of gay and lesbian parents. In F. W. Bozett & M. B. Sussman (Eds.), *Homosexuality and family relations* (pp. 177–196). New York, NY: Harrington Park Press.

Grant, J. E., Odlaug, B. L., Derbyshire, K., Schreiber, L. R., Lust, K., & Christenson, G. (2014). Mental health and clinical correlates in lesbian, gay, bisexual, and queer young adults. *Journal of American College Health, 62,* 75–78.

Grau, G., & Shoppmann, C. (Eds.). (2013). *The hidden Holocaust? Gay and lesbian persecution in Germany 1933–45.* New York, NY: Routledge.

Green, R. (1985). Gender identity in childhood and later sexual orientation: Follow-up of 78 males. *American Journal of Psychiatry, 142*(3), 339–341.

Greytak, E. A., Kosciw, J. G., & Boesen, M. J. (2013). Putting the "T" in "resource": The benefits of LGBT-related school resources for transgender youth. *Journal of LGBT Youth, 10*(1–2), 45–63. doi:10.1080/19361653.2012.718522

Grossman, A. H. (2006). Physical and mental health of older lesbian, gay, and bisexual adults. In D. Kimmel, T. Rose, & S. David (Eds.), *Lesbian, gay, bisexual and transgender aging: Research and clinical perspectives* (pp. 53–69). New York, NY: Columbia University Press.

Grossman, A. H., & D'Augelli, A. R. (2007). Transgender youth and life-threatening behaviors. *Suicide and Life-Threatening Behavior, 37*(5), 527–537. doi:10.1521/suli.2007.37.5.527

Grov, C., Bimbi, D. S., Nanín, J. E., & Parsons, J. T. (2006). Race, ethnicity, gender, and generational factors associated with the coming-out process among gay, lesbian, and bisexual individuals. *Journal of Sex Research, 43*(2), 115–121. doi:10.1080/00224490609552306

GSA Network. (2017). https://gsanetwork.org/

Haldeman, D. C. (2012). Sexual orientation conversion therapy: Fact, fiction, and fraud. In S. H. Dworkin, M. Pope, S. H. Dworkin, & M. Pope (Eds.), *Casebook for counseling lesbian, gay, bisexual, and transgendered persons and their families* (pp. 297–306). Alexandria, VA: American Counseling Association.

Hamer, D. H., Hu, S., Magnuson, V. L., Hu, N., & Pattatucci, A. L. (1993). A linkage between DNA markers on the X chromosome and male sexual orientation. *Science, 261*(5119), 321–327. doi:10.1126/science.8332896

Harawa, N. T., Williams, J. K., Ramamurthi, H. C., Manago, C., Avina, S., & Jones, M. (2008). Sexual behavior, sexual identity, and substance abuse among low-income bisexual and non-gay-identifying African American men who have sex with men. *Archives of Sexual Behavior, 37*(5), 748–762. doi:10.1007/s10508-008-9361-x

Hatzenbuehler, M. L. (2014). Structural stigma and the health of lesbian, gay, and bisexual populations. *Current Directions in Psychological Science, 23*(2), 127–132. doi:10.1177/0963721414523775

Hatzenbuehler, M. L., McLaughlin, K. A., Keyes, K. M., & Hasin, D. S. (2010). The impact of institutional discrimination on psychiatric disorders in lesbian, gay, and bisexual populations: A prospective study. *American Journal of Public Health*, *100*(3), 452–459. doi:10.2105/AJPH.2009.168815

Hatzenbuehler, M. L., O'Cleirigh, C., Grasso, C., Mayer, K., Safren, S., & Bradford, J. (2012). Effect of same-sex marriage laws on health care use and expenditures in sexual minority men: A quasi-natural experiment. *American Journal of Public Health*, *102*(2), 285–291. doi:10.2105/AJPH.2011.300382

Hein, L. C., & Matthews, A. K. (2010). Reparative therapy: The adolescent, the psych nurse, and the issues. *Journal of Child and Adolescent Psychiatric Nursing*, *23*(1), 29–35. doi:10.1111/j.1744-6171.2009.00214.x

Herek, G. M., & Garnets, L. D. (2007). Sexual orientation and mental health. *Annual Review of Clinical Psychology*, *3*, 353–375.

HHS: Assistant Secretary for Health. (2012). *LGBT health and well-being: U.S. Department of Health and Human Services recommended actions to improve the health and well-being of lesbian, gay, bisexual, and transgender communities*. Washington, DC: U.S. Department of Health and Human Services.

High, K. P., Brennan-Ing, M., Clifford, D. B., Cohen, M. H., Currier, J., Deeks, S. G., ... Volberding, P. (2012). HIV and aging: State of knowledge and areas of critical need for research: A report to the NIH Office of AIDS Research by the HIV and Aging Working Group. *Journal of Acquired Immune Deficiency Syndromes*, *60* (Supplement 1), S1–S18.

Hill, D. B., & Menvielle, E. (2009). "You have to give them a place where they feel protected and safe and loved": The views of parents who have gender-variant children and adolescents. *Journal of LGBT Youth*, *6*, 243–271.

Hill, D. B., Menvielle, E., Sica, K. M., & Johnson, A. (2010). An affirmative intervention for families with gender variant children: Parental ratings of child mental health and gender. *Journal of Sex & Marital Therapy*, *36*, 6–23.

Hooker, E. (1957). The adjustment of the male overt homosexual. *Journal of Projective Techniques*, *21*, 18–31.

Huebner, D. M., Thoma, B. C., & Neilands, T. B. (2015). School victimization and substance use among lesbian, gay, bisexual, and transgender adolescents. *Prevention Science*, *16*(5), 734–743. doi:10.1007/s11121-014-0507-x

Hurd, Z. (2015). American Geriatrics Society care of lesbian, gay, bisexual, and transgender older adults position statement. *Journal of the American Geriatrics Society*, *63*(3), 423–426. doi:10.1111/jgs.13297

IOM (Institute of Medicine). (2011). *The health of lesbian, gay, bisexual, and transgender people: Building a foundation for better understanding*. Washington, DC: The National Academies Press.

James, S. E., Herman, J. L., Rankin, S., Keisling, M., Mottet, L., & Anafi, M. (2016). *The report of the 2015 U.S. Transgender Survey*. Washington, DC: National Center for Transgender Equality.

Katz-Wise, S. L. (2014). Sexual fluidity in young adult women and men: Associations with sexual orientation and sexual identity development. *Psychology and Sexuality*, *6*, 189–208. doi:10.1080/19419899.2013.876445

Katz-Wise, S. L., & Hyde, J. S. (2015). Sexual fluidity and related attitudes and beliefs among young adults with a same-gender orientation. *Archives of Sexual Behavior*, *44*(5), 1459–1470. doi:10.1007/s10508-014-0420-1

Katz-Wise, S. L., Reisner, S. L., Hughto, J. W., & Keo-Meier, C. L. (2016). Differences in sexual orientation diversity and sexual fluidity in attractions among gender minority adults in Massachusetts. *Journal of Sex Research*, 53(1), 74–84. doi:10.1080/00224499.2014.1003028

Kenneady, D. A., & Oswalt, S. B. (2014). Is Cass's model of homosexual identity formation relevant to today's society? *American Journal of Sexuality Education*, 9(2), 229–246. doi:10.1080/15546128.2014.900465

Keuroghlian, A. S., Shtasel, D., & Bassuk, E. L. (2014). Out on the street: A public health and policy agenda for lesbian, gay, bisexual, and transgender youth who are homeless. *American Journal of Orthopsychiatry*, 84(1), 66–72. doi:10.1037/h0098852

Kinsey, A. C., Pomeroy, W. B., & Martin, C. E. (1998/1948). *Sexual behavior in the human male*. Bloomington, IN: Indiana University Press.

Kinsey, A. C., Pomeroy, W. B., Martin, C. E., & Gebhard, P. H. (1998/1953). Bloomington, IN: Indiana University Press.

Kosciw, J. G., Greytak, E. A., Palmer, N. A., & Boesen, M. J. (2014). *The 2013 National School Climate Survey: The experiences of lesbian, gay, bisexual and transgender youth in our nation's schools*. New York, NY: GLSEN.

Kurdek, L. A. (1998). Relationship outcomes and their predictors: Longitudinal evidence from heterosexual married, gay cohabiting, and lesbian cohabiting couples. *Journal of Marriage and the Family*, 60, 553–568.

Kurdek, L. A. (2001). Differences between heterosexual-nonparent couples and gay, lesbian, and heterosexual-parent couples. *Journal of Family Issues*, 22, 727–754.

Kurdek, L. A. (2004). Are gay and lesbian cohabiting couples really different from heterosexual married couples? *Journal of Marriage and Family*, 66, 880–900.

Kurdek, L. A. (2005). What do we know about gay and lesbian couples? *Current Directions in Psychological Science*, 14(5), 251–254. doi:10.1111/j.0963-7214.2005.00375.x

Kuyper, L., & Bos, H. (2016). Mostly heterosexual and lesbian/gay young adults: Differences in mental health and substance use and the role of minority stress. *Journal of Sex Research*, 53(7), 731–741. doi:10.1080/00224499.2015.1071310

Lambda Legal. (2010). *When health care isn't caring*. New York, NY: Lambda Legal.

Lambda Legal. (2016). Your rights. Retrieved December 2, 2016, from http://www.lambdalegal.org/your-rights

Lament, C. (2015). Transgender children: Conundrums and controversies—An introduction to the section. *The Psychoanalytic Study of the Child*, 68, 13–27.

Lawrence, A. A. (2010). Proposed revisions to gender identity disorder diagnoses in the DSM-5. *Archives of Sexual Behavior*, 39, 1253–1260.

LeVay, S. (1996). *Queer science: The use and abuse of research into homosexuality*. Cambridge, MA: The MIT Press.

LeVay, S. (2011). *Gay, straight, and the reason why: The science of sexual orientation*. New York, NY: Oxford University Press.

Li, Q. (2006). Cyberbullying in schools: A research of gender differences. *School Psychology International*, 27, 1–14. doi:10.1177/0143034306064547

Makadon, H. J., Mayer, K. H., Potter, J., & Goldhammer, H. (Eds.). (2015). *The Fenway guide to lesbian, gay, bisexual, and transgender health* (2nd ed.). Philadelphia, PA: American College of Physicians Press.

Malley, E., Posner, M., & Potter, L. (2008). *Suicide risk and prevention for lesbian, gay, bisexual, and transgender youth.* Newton, MA: Education Development Center. Retrieved from http://www.samaritanbehavioralhealth.com/files/SPRC_LGBT_Youth.pdf

Mallon, G. P. (1994). Counseling strategies with gay and lesbian youth. In T. DeCrescenzo (Ed.), *Helping gay and lesbian youth: New policies, new programs, new practice* (pp. 75–91). New York, NY: Harrington Park Press/Haworth Press.

Marshal, M. P., Sucato, G., Stepp, S. D., Hipwell, A., Smith, H. A., Friedman, M. S., ... Markovic, N. (2012). Substance use and mental health disparities among sexual minority girls: Results from the Pittsburgh girls study. *Journal of Pediatric and Adolescent Gynecology, 25,* 15–18.

Mavandadi, S., Zanjani, F., Ten Have, T. R., & Oslin, D. W. (2009). Psychological well-being among individuals aging with HIV: The value of social relationships. *Journal of Acquired Immune Deficiency Syndromes, 51*(1), 91–98. doi:10.1097/QAI.0b0 13e318199069b

McConnell, E. A., Birkett, M. A., & Mustanski, B. (2015). Typologies of social support and associations with mental health outcomes among LGBT youth. *Journal of LGBT Health, 2*(1), 55–61.

Menvielle, E., & Hill, D. B. (2010). An affirmative intervention for families with gender-variant children: A process evaluation. *Journal of Gay & Lesbian Mental Health, 15*(1), 94–123. doi:10.1080/19359705.2011.530576

MetLife. (2006). *Out and aging: The MetLife study of lesbian and gay baby boomers.* Westport, CT: MetLife Mature Market Institute.

Meyer, I. H. (2003). Prejudice, social stress, and mental health in lesbian, gay, and bisexual populations: Conceptual issues and research evidence. *Psychological Bulletin, 129,* 674–697.

Meyer, I. H. (2015). Resilience in the study of minority stress and health of sexual and gender minorities. *Psychology of Sexual Orientation and Gender Diversity, 2*(3), 209–213. doi:10.1037/sgd0000132

Meyer-Bahlburg, H. L. (2005). Introduction: Gender dysphoria and gender change in persons with intersexuality. *Archives of Sexual Behavior, 34*(4), 371–373. doi:10.1007/s10508-005-4335-8

Miller, M. (2016, November 18). No rest at rest home: Fighting bias against gays and lesbians. *The New York Times.* Retrieved from http://www.nytimes.com/2016/11/19/your-money/lgbt-senior-housing-case-fight-bias.html?_r=0

Mustanski, B., & Liu, R. T. (2013). A longitudinal study of predictors of suicide attempts among lesbian, gay, bisexual, and transgender youth. *Archives of Sexual Behavior, 42,* 437–448.

National LGBT Health Education Center. (2015). *Collecting sexual orientation and gender identity data in electronic health records: Taking the next steps.* Boston, MA: Fenway Institute.

Okami, P., Olmstead, R., & Abramson, P. R. (1997). Sexual experiences in early childhood: 18-year longitudinal data from the UCLA Family Lifestyles Project. *Journal of Sex Research, 34*(4), 339–347. doi:10.1080/00224499709551902

Orel, N. A., & Fruhauf, C. A. (2015). The intersection of culture, family, and individual aspects: A guiding model for LGBT older adults. In N. A. Orel, C. A. Fruhauf, N. A. Orel, & C. A. Fruhauf (Eds.), *The lives of LGBT older adults: Understanding challenges and resilience* (pp. 3–24). Washington, DC: American Psychological Association. doi:10.1037/14436-001

Page, M. L., Lindahl, K. M., & Malik, N. M. (2013). The role of religion and stress in sexual identity and mental health among lesbian, gay, and bisexual youth. *Journal of Research on Adolescence, 23*(4), 665–677. doi:10.1111/jora.12025

Patterson, C. J., & Farr, R. H. (2011). Coparenting among lesbian and gay couples. In J. P. McHale, K. M. Lindahl, J. P. McHale, & K. M. Lindahl (Eds.), *Coparenting: A conceptual and clinical examination of family systems* (pp. 127–146). Washington, DC: American Psychological Association. doi:10.1037/12328-006

Payne, E. (2013, July 8). Group apologizes to gay community, shuts down "cure" ministry, *CNN*. Retrieved from http://www.cnn.com/2013/06/20/us/exodus-international-shutdown/

Perrin, E. C., & Siegel, B. S. (2013). Promoting the well-being of children whose parents are gay or lesbian. *Pediatrics, 131*(4), e1374–e1383. doi:10.1542/peds.2013-0377

Pew Research Poll. (2013). http://www.pewsocialtrends.org/2013/06/13/a-survey-of-lgbt-americans/

Pilkington, N. W., & D'Augelli, A. R. (1995). Victimization of lesbian, gay, and bisexual youth in community settings. *Journal of Community Psychology, 23*(1), 34–56. doi:10.1002/1520-6629(199501)23:1<34::AID-JCOP2290230105>3.0.CO;2-N

Poteat, V. P., Sinclair, K. O., DiGiovanni, C. D., Koenig, B. W., & Russell, S. T. (2013). Gay–straight alliances are associated with student health: A multischool comparison of LGBTQ and heterosexual youth. *Journal of Research on Adolescence, 23*, 319–330.

Reisner, S., Vetters, R, Leclerc, M., Zaslow, S., Wolfrum, S., Shumer, D., & Mimiaga, M. (2015). Mental health of transgender youth in care at an adolescent urban community health center: A matched retrospective cohort study. *Journal of Adolescent Health, 56*, 274–279.

Richards, C., Bouman, W. P., Seal, L., Barker, M. J., Nieder, T. O., & T'Sjoen, G. (2016). Non-binary or genderqueer genders. *International Review of Psychiatry, 28*(1), 95–102. doi:10.3109/09540261.2015.1106446

Rieger, G., Linsenmeier, J. W., Gygax, L., & Bailey, J. M. (2008). Sexual orientation and childhood gender nonconformity: Evidence from home videos. *Developmental Psychology, 44*(1), 46–58. doi:10.1037/0012-1649.44.1.46

Riggle, E. B., Wickham, R. E., Rostosky, S. S., Rothblum, E. D., & Balsam, K. F. (2016). Impact of civil marriage recognition for long-term same-sex couples. *Sexuality Research & Social Policy: A Journal of the NSRC, 14*, 223–232. doi:10.1007/s13178-016-0243-z

Roe, S. L. (2015). Examining the role of peer relationships in the lives of gay and bisexual adolescents. *Children & Schools, 37*, 117–124.

Rosario, M., Schrimshaw, E. W., & Hunter, J. (2012). Risk factors for homelessness among lesbian, gay, and bisexual youths: A developmental milestone approach. *Children and Youth Services Review, 34*(1), 186–193. doi:10.1016/j.childyouth.2011.09.016

Rosenfeld, M. J. (2014). Couple longevity in the era of same-sex marriage in the United States. *Journal of Marriage and Family, 76*(5), 905–918. doi:10.1111/jomf.12141

Rushton, J. P. (1990). Sir Francis Galton, epigenetic rules, genetic similarity theory, and human life-history analysis. *Journal of Personality, 58*, 117–140.

Savin-Williams, R. C. (2016). *Becoming who I am: Young men on being gay*. Cambridge, MA: Harvard University Press.

Savin-Williams, R. C., & Ream, G. L. (2003). Sex variations in the disclosure to parents of same-sex attractions. *Journal of Family Psychology, 17*(3), 429–438. doi:10.1037/0893-3200.17.3.429

Sears, B., & Mallory, C. (2011). *Documented evidence of employment discrimination & its effects on LGBT people*. https://williamsinstitute.law.ucla.edu/wp-content/uploads/Sears-Mallory-Discrimination-July-20111.pdf

Shidlo, A., & Schroeder, M. (2002). Changing sexual orientation: A consumers' report. *Professional Psychology: Research and Practice, 33*(3), 249–259. doi:10.1037/0735-7028.33.3.249

Shifrin, F., & Solis, M. (1992). Chemical dependency in gay and lesbian youth. *Journal of Chemical Dependency Treatment, 5*(1), 67–76. doi:10.1300/J034v05n01_06

Shilo, G., & Savaya, R. (2012). Mental health of lesbian, gay, and bisexual youth and young adults: Differential effects of age, gender, religiosity, and sexual orientation. *Journal of Research on Adolescence, 22*(2), 310–325.

Shippy, R., Cantor, M. H., & Brennan, M. (2004). Social networks of aging gay men. *The Journal of Men's Studies, 13*(1), 107–120.

Toomey, R. B., Card, N. A., & Casper, D. M. (2014). Peers' perceptions of gender nonconformity: Associations with overt and relational peer victimization and aggression in early adolescence. *The Journal of Early Adolescence, 34*(4), 463–485. doi:10.1177/0272431613495446

Tremble, B. (1993). Prostitution and survival: Interviews with gay street youth. *Canadian Journal of Human Sexuality, 2*(1), 39–45.

Troiden, R. R. (1988). Homosexual identity development. *Journal of Adolescent Health Care, 9*, 5–13.

Valanis, B. G., Bowen, D. J., Bassford, T., Whitlock, E., Charney, P., & Carter, R. A. (2000). Sexual orientation and health: Comparisons in the women's health initiative sample. *Archives of Family Medicine, 9*(9), 843–853.

Varjas, K., Meyers, J., Kiperman, S., & Howard, A. (2013). Technology hurts? Lesbian, gay, and bisexual youth perspectives of technology and cyberbullying. *Journal of School Violence, 12*, 27–44. doi:10.1080/15388220.2012.731665

von Krafft-Ebing, R. (2013/1886). *Psychopathia sexualis: A medico-forensic study*. London, UK: Butterworth-Heinemann.

Wallien, M. S. C., & Cohen-Kettenis, P. T. (2008). Psychosexual outcome of gender-dysphoric children. *Journal of the American Academy of Child & Adolescent Psychiatry, 47*, 1413–1423.

Watson, R. J., Wheldon, C. W., & Russell, S. T. (2015). How does sexual identity disclosure impact school experiences? *Journal of LGBT Youth, 12*(4), 385–396. doi:10.1080/19361653.2015.1077764

Weinberg, M. S., & Bell, A. P. (1972). *Homosexuality: An annotated bibliography*. New York, NY: Harper and Row.

Whitton, S. W., Kuryluk, A. D., & Khaddouma, A. M. (2015). Legal and social ceremonies to formalize same-sex relationships: Associations with commitment, social support, and relationship outcomes. *Couple and Family Psychology: Research and Practice, 4*(3), 161–176. doi:10.1037/cfp0000045

Wilson, B. M., & Kastanis, A. A. (2015). Sexual and gender minority disproportionality and disparities in child welfare: A population-based study. *Children and Youth Services Review, 58*, 11–17. doi:10.1016/j.childyouth.2015.08.016

World Professional Association for Transgender Health—(WPATH). (2011). *Standards of care for the health of transsexual, transgender, and gender nonconforming people*, 7ª version.

Zucker, K. J. (2008). Children with gender identity disorder: Is there a best practice? *Neuropsychiatrie de l'Enfance et de l'Adolescence, 56*(6), 358–364.

3

Making Psychology Trans-Inclusive and Trans-Affirmative: Recommendations for Research and Practice

Riddhi Sandil and Shane Henise*

> It is revolutionary for any trans person to choose to be seen and visible in a world that tells us we should not exist.
> —Laverne Cox, transgender actress and advocate

In the past 30 years, psychology has focused on understanding the identity of an individual from a holistic and systemic perspective (Sue, 2001). Research suggests it is important to study an individual while concurrently understanding their context and environment, a shift from the individualistic perspective that was dominant during the inception stages of the field (Marcus & Hamedani, 2010; Sue & Sue, 2008). In today's digital and social world, media exerts substantial influence on the culture and psyche of an individual and thus is a critical component in understanding not only an individual's narrative but also the perception of people and communities (Bryant & Oliver, 2009; Henry, 1999; Mahtani, 2001; Wong & Halgin, 2006). Similar to what happens with other minority identities, media has played a large role in shaping the transgender narrative and ultimately public opinion on transgender people and issues.

Transgender identity first entered media culture in the 1950s with Christine Jorgenson, a World War II veteran who decided to transition after leaving the military. The headlines remained mostly positive, reading "Ex-GI Becomes Blonde Beauty: Operations Transform Bronx Youth" (*New York Daily News*, 1952).

After Jorgenson, the depictions became more and more negative, following into tropes of either victims or villains. In her seminal novel *Whipping Girl*, Julia Serano outlined two distinct portrayals of transgender individuals, which she labeled the "deceptive" to "pathetic" transsexuals (Serano, 2007). These tropes were largely the only representation of transgender people for most of U.S. history until relatively recently.

The shift in media representation was first prompted in 2014 by Laverne Cox's honest portrayal of transgender experience as Sophia Burset in the Netflix

---

*Authorship shared equally

series *Orange Is the New Black*. As she gained media attention for being one of the first transgender actresses to appear in a transgender role, she used her platform to advocate for the transgender community and help shape opinions. The "transgender tipping point" (as proclaimed on the cover of *Time* magazine) occurred after Cox appeared on Katie Couric's show and refused to answer any questions about her medical transition and genitals. She explained, "I do feel there is a preoccupation with that. The preoccupation with transition and surgery objectifies trans people. And then we don't get to really deal with the real lived experiences" (Steinmetz, 2014).

Facing widespread bigotry and hatred, transgender people experience double the rate of unemployment in the general population, with rates for transgender people of color up to four times the national employment rate. A recent major survey, *Injustice at Every Turn* (Grant et al., 2011), uncovered that:

- Forty-three percent of employers would prefer to hire a less qualified cisgender candidate than a more qualified transgender candidate.
  - Even when people secured jobs within the workforce, 90 percent of transgender individuals reported experiencing harassment, mistreatment, or discrimination in the workplace.
- In an attempt to avoid discrimination, transgender people have hidden their gender or gender transition at work (71%) or have entered an underground economy (such as sex work) for work (16%).
- Those who have lost their jobs due to bias also experience vast consequences, such as *four times the rate of homelessness.*
- Despite all these barriers, the vast majority of transgender people felt more comfortable at work and said that their job performance approved once they were able to live truthfully (71%).
- The transgender population experiences suicide at astronomical rates, higher than almost any other population, with 41 percent of transgender individuals having attempted suicide in their lifetimes.
- In a recent year, there were 22 known murders of transgender people in the United States alone, and 19 of those murdered were transgender people of color. Twenty of those murdered were on the transfeminine spectrum (Dalton, 2015).
- Even when attempting to receive help for medical issues, 19 percent of transgender people report being refused medical care, and 50 percent of individuals said they had to teach their medical providers about adequate transgender care.
- There is growing research that also suggests that gender-nonconforming transgender individuals and individuals who belong to multiple disadvantaged groups may experience higher rates of discrimination than gender-conforming/racially privileged trans people (Miller & Grollman, 2015).

Because of widespread discrimination, harassment, and violence, health outcomes for transgender people reveal alarming levels of social and economic marginalization. Transgender individuals have much higher rates of HIV prevalence; smoking, drug and alcohol use; and suicide attempts.

These statistics are perhaps exacerbated by the continued discrimination and bigotry the transgender population experiences. According to the Transgender Law Center, it is still legal in 31 states in the United States to be fired or evicted for being a transgender person, as these states have no legal protections based on gender identity. Transgender individuals also have limited access to bathrooms they feel safe to use, and some states are even currently trying to pass legislation to prevent individuals from using the bathroom that corresponds with their gender identity. Nonbinary-identified trans individuals are often left out of the conversation entirely and are forced into unsafe or unfavorable situations when gender-neutral bathrooms are not an option (Levitt & Ippolito, 2014). Despite no reported instances of transgender individuals attacking others in restrooms, there are many documented cases of transgender people experiencing violence when attempting to use the restroom.

Thus, given the violence and trauma experienced by transgender populations, it is important that psychology continue to examine service delivery for this vulnerable population. While psychology has made strides in expanding its understanding of the experience of transgender populations, there continue to exist gaps in research and practice. This chapter aims to provide a comprehensive overview of how psychology has worked with the trans population in research and practice. First, this chapter will provide an overview of the key terms and definitions associated with this population. Second, the history of transgender research in psychology will be discussed, with particular attention paid to ensuring that research practices in psychology are socially just and affirming for transgender populations. Last, recommendations for culturally sensitive clinical practices will be provided, as existing research indicates that transgender populations often report therapy to be another avenue where their gender identities are overlooked or oppressed (Lev, 2004). It should also be noted that transgender populations will be referred to as trans people, trans populations, and trans interchangeably throughout this chapter.

KEY TERMS AND CONCEPTS

With growing definitions and fluidity of both gender identity and sexual orientation, the two concepts are often conflated. Put most simply, gender identity refers to how you conceptualize your gender; sexual orientation refers to what gender you see yourself being with. However, both are important and central to discussions of the LGBT experience.

While people of diverse sexual orientations and genders have existed throughout history, prevalence rates are hard to quantify. Because census and other measures of population do not always adequately capture transgender identities or experiences, it is nearly impossible to determine how many people are transgender. Generally the choice options for gender do not reflect the transgender experience and only inquire about a person's biological sex. In addition, with the increasing rates of violence against the trans community, many people do not feel safe to live as their authentic selves and thus might not self-report their transgender identities.

As there are many concepts related to the transgender experience, it is important to understand some key concepts and terms that are associated with the transgender experience. According to the National Center for Transgender Equality (2014) some main definitions are the following:

Gender Identity: One's internal sense of gender. This can include not only identifying with our binary conceptions of man and woman but also identifying as a combination of both genders or neither.

Gender Presentation: The way that one expresses their gender to the outside world. We express our gender through many cues, including hairstyles, clothing choices, and mannerisms. However, it is important to note that, due to multiple factors, gender presentation and gender identity do not always match.

Transsexual: A term that has been traditionally used to describe the transgender experience but is somewhat limited. Transsexual people are a subset of transgender individuals who identify with the gender considered opposite their sex assigned at birth and have taken medical and social steps to transition. Some individuals within the transgender community do not choose the label transsexual because of its connection to a history of medical categorization, or because they do not feel they need to take medical steps to align their gender identities and presentations.

Transgender: "Transgender" is an umbrella term used to describe anyone whose gender identity does not align with the sex they were assigned at birth (American Psychological Association [APA], 2015). Transgender individuals have many diverse expressions of not only gender identity but also sexual orientation.

Transphobia: Negative feelings of disgust or fear toward people who identify as transgender or people who are perceived to be gender nonconforming. This can manifest as either *external transphobia* (prejudicial attitudes from friends, coworkers, or within social or healthcare systems) or *internalized transphobia*, in which trans individuals internalize negative messages that they have heard about their own identities or experiences (Nadal, Skolnik, & Wong, 2012).

Cisgender: A term used to describe people whose gender identity matches the gender they were assigned at birth. Most simplistically, this refers to people who are "not transgender." However, using the term "cisgender" offers a description that explains this, instead of suggesting normality or abnormality.

Nonbinary Identified: In the same way that "transgender" is used as an umbrella term to encompass many trans identities, "nonbinary" is also an umbrella term used to express many experiences. The term generally refers to people who feel their gender does not fit into binary conceptualizations of men and women. Nonbinary identities include:

Genderqueer: "Genderqueer" people can identify as both a man and a woman, or oscillating between the two, or hold their own definition and identify as including multiple genders.

Agender: People who identify as agender feel their gender falls outside of the male/female binary. This can include identifying with a third or alternate gender or feeling they do not have a gender.

Two-Spirit: A recognized third gender in indigenous cultures. Two-spirit people are individuals who identify with both female and male gender roles. Said to have "two spirits," one male and one female, two-spirit people have traditionally been regarded as spiritual elders within Native American communities.

TRANSGENDER REPRESENTATION IN RESEARCH

Timeline and History of Transgender Research

With growing visibility and attention toward the transgender community, transgender research has experienced a boom in the past decade (Levitt & Ippolito, 2014). However, historically transgender perspectives have been housed within the context of the larger LGBT community in research. Because many researchers have failed to distinguish accurately between the terms "sexuality" and "gender," it has been hard to capture which population is actually being studied (Moradi, Mohr, Worthington, & Fassinger, 2009).

In addition to a problematic conflation of gender and sexuality in previous research, there has been an assumption that these terms are linked and cannot be separated. Individuals who chose to transition were thought to have done so in order to better be suited to obtain heterosexual relationships with members of the now opposite sex. This inaccurate assumption not only erased the experiences of lesbian and gay transgender individuals but also informed early diagnostic criteria for obtaining access to hormone replacement therapies (Benson, 2013).

In addition to confusion in defining transgender populations, it was also hard to obtain accurate data based on the history of grouping LGBT participants together within research populations (Fassinger & Arseneau, 2007). While transgender individuals do share similar experiences of oppression, transgender individuals are often more stigmatized than their cisgender lesbian, gay, and bisexual counterparts (Bauerband & Galupo, 2014). Frequently overshadowed by the L, G, and B communities, transgender people are stigmatized within multiple spaces, which only leads to further isolation. Previous works (Birkett, Newcomb, & Mustanski, 2014) examining LGBT identity have shown that transgender individuals experience heightened levels of psychological distress and victimization, but, without examining the transgender experience separately, it is hard to distinguish between identities within the transgender umbrella.

This theme, referred to as "assumption of universal transgender experience" in the transgender microaggression research first outlined by Nadal, Skolnik, and Wong (2012), has been common in both research and clinical work with transgender clients. The assumption that all transgender people have the same experience can involve people assuming what medical interventions trans people wish to pursue, what their sexual orientations are, and even that being transgender automatically means people are uncomfortable with their bodies or experiences in the first place.

Galupo, Henise, and Davis (2014) went on to expand the research by looking at experiences across different transgender identities while examining experiences of microaggressions within the context of friendship. They found that, while microaggression frequency differed depending on the identity of the friend, transgender individuals experienced microaggressions in all contexts of friendships, including in cisgender LGB and transgender friendships. This research highlights how pervasive transphobia can be across multiple contexts, even in relationships one would consider the most supportive.

Other researchers (Smith, Shin, & Officer, 2012) have argued that counselors thinking and enforcing sex and gender in binary terms can enact microaggressions. The authors also discuss examining the use of hierarchical-position language ("I [as a cisgender person] affirm your [transgender] identity") and ways the lack of gender-neutral language within the counseling dyad can constitute microaggressions as well.

Studies of Psychological Well-Being in Transgender Individuals

Due to a myriad of internal and external factors negatively impacting people who identify as transgender, it is easy to see how negative mental health outcomes are highly prevalent in this population. Previous literature has outlined higher rates of psychological distress (e.g., depression, anxiety, suicide, and self-injurious behavior) in the transgender community compared to the cisgender population (Meier & Labuski, 2013). The rates differ greatly based on the samples and what identities are being represented within literature that has examined this issue.

Often researchers make attempts to describe prevalence of difficulties in trans populations without considering in context all the complexities and factors that could be contributing to the high prevalence rates. Research that has looked at mental health functioning of transgender populations has found trans people are often not only normal in their functioning but above average in intelligence (Gómez-Gil, Vidal-Hagemeijer, & Salamero, 2008). However, because of persistent and exceedingly harmful discrimination and harassment transgender individuals experience in school settings, many do not feel safe to continue their educations or do not feel supported in their educational endeavors. Indeed, a study of trans persons' economic attainment, *Understanding Issues Facing Transgender Americans*, by the Movement Advancement Project (2016), has shown that the large majority of transgender people make less than $10,000 a year.

Transgender Resilience

Moving forward, psychology should begin to shift the narrative to more positive outlooks on the transgender experience. While it is important to remain mindful of discrimination, prejudice, and negative outcomes that have occurred due to systemic and interpersonal barriers for transgender people, there is a pressing need for a lens of positive psychology and resilience within the transgender community.

Transgender people utilize many aspects of resilience despite negative factors that may impede their journey. Singh and McKleroy (2010) described some of these methods of resilience, particularly for transgender people of color, such as pride in their gender or ethnic or racial identities, recognizing and navigating gender and racial/ethnic oppression, and cultivating spirituality and hope for the future.

The first major tool of resilience used was pride in their ethnic or racial identity. While participants in the study by Singh and McKleroy (2010) described this as a process, they explained that, once developed, pride served as a helpful tool in trans persons' efforts to bounce back after experiencing prejudice.

Another major resilient act employed by participants in the Singh and McKleroy (2010) study was recognizing and navigating gender and racial/ethnic oppression. Being able to recognize oppressive systems and attitudes helped participants better advocate for themselves. Lastly, individuals in this study cultivated spirituality and hope for the future as a method for coping with traumatic life events.

Perhaps one of the biggest studies to date on positive aspects of the transgender experience was done by Riggle, Rotosky, McCants, and Pascale-Hague (2011). They described many ways their participants viewed identifying as transgender through a positive lens. These were outlined as congruency (between their inner feelings and outer appearance), personal growth and resiliency, empathy, strength of interpersonal relationships, feeling participants had gained unique perspectives/insights, living beyond the binary, and engaging in activism. Maintaining a commitment to positive views of transgender identity in both research and practice will hopefully inform future narratives and attitudes toward transgender individuals.

A recent study looking at trans resilience (Breslow et al., 2015) uncovered buffers transgender individuals use to combat minority stress (e.g., internalized transphobia and stigma awareness). While this research found that resilience was strongly associated with lower levels of psychological distress, it was not as strong a moderator between minority stress and psychological distress as predicted by the original research hypothesis. These findings speak to the fact that, while resilience can act as an important buffer against psychological distress for transgender individuals, it is important that members of this community also have access to external resources and supports, such as family, friendships, and adequate health care.

Guidelines for Best Practices in Conducting Research on the Transgender Population

It is imperative that any person wishing to study the transgender population begin by being well informed about the painful history of stigmatization of the transgender community. Researchers must remain mindful of the current state of transgender issues within the larger culture and become aware of how vast the implications of their research can be for members of the community. Before beginning the research, researchers should become aware of their own biases in terms of gender identity and the transgender experience. The assumption that gender is binary, termed "genderist," could lead to the erasure of many transgender individuals' experience (Martin & Meezan, 2003).

One of the best ways to ensure that research is representative of the sample it wishes to describe is to include members of those communities in the conceptualization, implementation, and analysis phases of the research project. Research teams that want to study transgender populations should include transgender research team members. Similarly, if participants need to interface with a member of the research team, it is helpful for them to see someone they feel can understand their experience. If the research team does not include a transgender member, Martin and Meezan (2003) suggest that the researchers immerse themselves in the culture of their participants to become adequately knowledgeable about the challenges and issues facing the community.

In becoming familiar with issues facing the transgender community, researchers should pay special attention to the history of exploitation of transgender individuals in research studies. In addition, data should be collected on participants' gender identities and sexual orientations and should not be assumed. There are so many diverse experiences within the transgender umbrella that any research where the only selection is "transgender" remains somewhat limited.

Green and dickey (2007) have proposed the following guidelines for research on transgender populations:

1. There are many diverse experiences under trans identity, and researchers should be inclusive of all identities.
2. Language is very important when studying the trans community, and participants should be given spaces to self-identify their gender when possible.
3. Mutual respect (i.e., taking a stance of non-pathology) is essential when researching the transgender population for both the researcher and the participants.
4. Researchers must become aware of their own cultural biases in regard to gender and take all appropriate measures to ensure that they avoid bias in their manuscripts.
5. Because being transgender is experienced so differently based on social location, research must take an intersectional lens and approach wherein multiple cultural identities are brought into research discussions.
6. Studies that include trans in the design (e.g., LGBT) must be include all LGBT groupings in the data and interpretation or the T must be left out of the title.
7. Every step of the research process must be inclusive of trans people and trans communities (including consultation, collaboration, and presence on research teams).
8. Pay special attention to research presumptions in design and questioning within the study, particularly in regard to gender assumptions.

9. Ensure that all data reported are accurate to the transgender community. Use individuals' self-designations of gender and sexual orientation to discuss results, and avoid assuming information gathered applies to all members of the trans community.

MOVING TOWARD A TRANS-INCLUSIVE APPROACH IN CLINICAL PRACTICE

While the concerns of transgender individuals have only been highlighted in the last couple decades in psychology (Levitt & Ippolito, 2014; Zimmerman, 2015), research on clinical issues with transgender populations can be traced back to the early 1900s. In *The Transvestites: An Investigation of the Erotic Drive to Disguise*, the author, Magnus Hirschfeld, suggested that it is necessary to examine *psychic stress* experienced by transgender individuals (Hirschfeld, 2003). Along with outlining psychological distress that often emerges from not adhering to the binary structure of gender in Western society, Hirschfeld also stressed that sexuality and gender should be thought of as separate constructs that could not be used synonymously.

Along with Hirschfeld, the study of transgenderism and transexualism continued into the mid-1900s with seminal works by David Cauldwell (also responsible for the introduction of the term "transsexual"), Alfred Kinsey, and Harry Benjamin. Harry Benjamin later went on to study transgender individuals across the country, subsequently suggesting that gender-confirming surgery was the only path to psychological well-being and "cure" for transsexualism, refuting the viability of psychotherapy for symptom and distress relief for this population (Benjamin, 1964).

Harry Benjamin, perhaps, was one of the most impactful individuals when we examine standards for clinical care for transgender populations. Along with focusing on the physical representation of one's gender, Benjamin suggested that transgender individuals were "trapped" in a body that did not match their internal sense of gender (Benjamin, 1966). In 1979, the Harry Benjamin International Gender Dysphoria Association (HBIGDA) published the first set of guidelines for treating transexualism. These guidelines included specific mandates for eligibility for gender-confirming procedures. For example, transgender individuals who wished to pursue hormone replacement treatment (HRT) or sex reassignment surgery (SRS) had to live as "the opposite gender" for one year, and medical professionals were responsible to serve as gatekeepers for individuals seeking SRS and HRT (Benson, 2013). This gatekeeping took the form of needing approval from mental health providers (e.g., letters of recommendation and counseling) before an individual could move toward gender-affirming procedures (HBIDGA, 2001). HBIGDA is now known as the World Professional Association for Transgender Health (WPATH). While the latest WPATH standards allow flexible timeframes for considering SRS and HRT, there still remain issues of healthcare providers determining if an individual is ready for these procedures and essentially controlling a transgender individual's ability to affirm their gender (Benson, 2013; Lev, 2004).

Interestingly, a year after the introduction of the HBIGDA standards of care and the year that homosexuality was removed as a psychiatric disorder, the *Diagnostic and Statistical Manual (DSM-III)* introduced transexualism and gender identity disorder (GID) as two new psychiatric diagnoses (American Psychiatric Association [APA], 1980). Both disorders included dissatisfaction and discomfort with one's *biological sex* (APA, 1980). Further, a desire to alter one's physical body was also used as a diagnostic criterion for both these disorders. While transexualism carried with it a timeframe (an interest for at least two years in altering one's body), GID was hallmarked by persistent and pervasive psychological distress connected with a discrepant internal sense of gender and assigned sex at birth (APA, 1980).

DSM-IV removed transexualism as a disorder but retained GID, and this was classified under Sexual Disorders (APA, 1994). Subsequently, the *DSM-5* removed GID, replacing it with gender dysphoria, a change meant to reduce the stigmatization of transgender individuals (Lev, 2007). Further, APA commented that, by highlighting dysphoria (discomfort experienced by some transgender individuals), the focus of treatment could be on reducing distress, as opposed to focusing on the *disordered* individual (APA, 2013).

While the psychiatric community is moving toward focusing on discomfort and distress experienced by transgender populations, there continues to be oppression of this population, especially from the lens of gender identity pathology (Lev, 2007). As many researchers have highlighted, using GID or gender dysphoria as a diagnosis is not necessarily affirming for transgender individuals (Benson, 2013; Lev, 2004; Walworth, 1997).

APA now acknowledges that disorders exist within cultural norms and that naming a condition a disorder, while important for receiving care and insurance reimbursement, can be a stigmatizing and dehumanizing experience for the individual (APA, 2013). The need for a diagnosis to receive care and the assertion that there are prescribed and universal normal expressions of gender have been deemed problematic and restricting for transgender individuals (Bockting, 2009; Lev, 2004, 2007). In fact, one might argue that it is not the transgender individual who has deficits, but rather the deficiencies lie in the inability of society to affirm and support all gender experiences and identities (Bartlett, Vasey, & Bukowski, 2000).

Given the problematic history of *treating* GID and the continued pathologizing of transgender people, it is not surprising that transgender clients report being mistrustful of mental health practitioners. This mistrust is exacerbated by the heightened imbalance of power between a mental health provider and a transgender client given the need for approval and permission from the care provider to receive gender-affirming medical procedures, such as SRS and HRT (Lev, 2004). This dynamic often leads to transgender clients withholding information or providing misinformation in therapy, particularly if they do not experience the care provided trans-affirmative, as they do not want their HRT or SRS treatment delayed due to misperceptions by uninformed therapists (Prosser, 1998; Walworth, 1997).

Given this mistrust, it is essential that mental healthcare providers move toward a transpositive approach to therapy and psychological practice. Introduced in 2002, the transpositive approach asserts that psychologists and other care providers disrupt the process of pathologizing of transgender individuals by recognizing their clients' lived experience of gender identity and dysphoria. Furthermore, transpositive providers demonstrate awareness and knowledge of their own biases and judgments with regard to gender and gender identity; use guidelines and recommendations within reason when working with transgender individuals (thereby demonstrating a commitment to flexibility and creativity in care); and let clients lead the discussion of gender, thus allowing clients to set the tone and regulate their gender-actualization journey (Raj, 2002). Given that psychology has historically focused on pathologizing transgender clients and not examining the pervasive destructiveness of transphobia in society, it is essential that care providers not only adopt a transpositive approach in their clinical work but also actively demonstrate their commitment to and advocacy for removing transphobia at a broader level (Carroll & Gilroy, 2002).

Mental healthcare providers can actively promote a transpositive approach to psychotherapy by adhering to recommendations for socially just practices with transgender clients. These include awareness of gender and gender biases; training and advanced coursework in working with transgender clients; creating a clinical environment inclusive and supportive of transgender clients; recognizing systemic transphobia; and being aware of guidelines for practice published by the American Counseling Association (ACA) and other professional organizations. Further recommendations for practice are presented in the next section.

RECOMMENDATIONS FOR PRACTICE

Given that transgender individuals have had mistrust toward the counseling professions and often report therapy to be an unhelpful experience, it is important that practitioners engage in the following suggestions in order to provide a transpositive treatment environment.

Awareness of One's Own Gender and Gender Biases

It is estimated that a mental healthcare provider will provide services to at least one transgender or gender-nonconforming client in their lifetime whether they are aware of their client's gender or not (Goethals & Schwiebert, 2005; Korell & Lorah, 2007). Thus, it is essential that mental healthcare providers be able and equipped to provide competent care to this population. Sue and Sue (2008) state that awareness of one's own assumptions and biases is a critical component of multicultural competence, especially when working with clients who are culturally different. Furthermore, ethical guidelines dictate that counselors must examine their own biases and assumptions about various cultural groups and honor a client's self-determination and culture (APA, 2010). Thus, it is imperative that mental healthcare providers are active in exploring their own gender identity and how their own journey has shaped their worldview (Singh & Burnes, 2010).

The importance of self-awareness is critical given that most individuals are socialized into a rigid, binary organization of gender, which often does not allow for gender variance and nonconformity. This socialization can lead to holding oppressive attitudes and, often, an unaccepting stance toward transgender clients (Reicherzer, Steves, & Patton, 2007). It is important to note that an oppressive attitude might not necessarily translate into overt transphobia but can be manifested in more subtle and covert ways. For example, a mental healthcare provider might be uncomfortable about their client's gender and thus refrain from asking questions related to gender identity; a counselor might be unaware that their client does not subscribe to binary pronouns and thus mispronoun their client; psychologists might make assumptions about their clients' gender identity based on their presentation. Therefore, it is critical that a practitioner continually engage in self-examination to avoid/reduce transphobia in treatment.

Training and Graduate Coursework

Along with exploring and building awareness of gender and gender identity, it is important for clinicians to increase their knowledge regarding transgender health and well-being. Studies have found that transgender clients report lack of therapist education on transgender issues as the most frequent factor that leads to therapist-induced harm in treatment (Rachlin, 2002; Sanchez, Sanchez, & Danoff, 2009). Studies have further suggested that clinicians often report lower efficacy in working with LGBT populations, as therapists have not been exposed to targeted training and coursework in their graduate institutions (Rutherford, McIntyre, Daley, & Ross, 2012; Rutter, Estrada, Ferguson, & Diggs, 2008). It is also important to note that these studies tend to clump gender and sexual minorities into one entity even though there exist significant differences in the experiences of these unique populations (Zimmerman, 2015).

In 2005, APA's Task Force on Gender Identity and Gender Variance was created to examine the needs of transgender populations seeking clinical care. This task force found that, even though 33 percent of psychology graduate students and practicing psychologists had provided services to a transgender client, only 25 percent of psychology graduate students and psychologists endorsed feeling proficient in working with transgender populations. Thus, APA strongly recommended that training competency be established for providing culturally competent treatment to transgender populations (APA, 2009).

This necessary attention to transgender clients in psychology led to the development of several competencies and clinical guidelines for practitioners working with transgender clients (ACA, 2010; Carroll, Gilroy, & Ryan, 2002; Singh, Boyd, & Whitman, 2010). The APA formally adopted guidelines for practice with transgender and gender nonconforming persons in 2015 (APA, 2015). These guidelines draw from existing models, such as standards for working with multicultural clients (Sue, Arredondo, & McDavis, 1992) and feminist multicultural frameworks that affirm and validate the experience of culturally different clients (Burnes et al., 2010; Goodman et al., 2004).

Even though guidelines for trans-affirmative practice have been endorsed by professional organizations, such as APA and ACA, it is still unclear whether they are being implemented in graduate psychology training programs (Singh & Burnes, 2010; Zimmerman, 2015). Given that being responsible for culturally consistent treatment is a critical component of being a multiculturally sensitive and ethical practitioner (Sue et al., 1992), it is imperative that clinicians educate themselves on the history of transgender identities, relevant clinical issues that face the community, and systemic oppression experienced by transgender individuals, and familiarize themselves with guidelines for best practice when working with the transgender community (Carroll & Gilroy, 2002).

Perceived Therapist Variables

As stated earlier, the relationship between transgender clients and mental healthcare providers has been tenuous, given the heightened power imbalance that exists when a therapist acts as both a gatekeeper and confidant (Lev, 2004). This, coupled with therapist ignorance and transphobic attitudes, has made counseling too often an unsafe environment where transgender clients end up feeling invalidated and hurt as opposed to affirmed and supported (Association for Lesbian, Gay, Bisexual, and Transgender Issues in Counseling, 2009; Bockting, Robinson, Benner, & Scheltema, 2004). Thus, transgender clients often report being dissatisfied with therapy, which further impacts their desire to seek and continue with psychological care (Lev, 2004).

Benson (2013) interviewed transgender clients to understand their experiences in mental health counseling. Participants shared their reasons for seeking counseling, financial concerns regarding treatment, and experiences with "problems with practice" (Benson, 2013, p. 29). These ranged from participants having to educate their counselors on matters related to gender diversity and counselors being unsure of the difference between gender and sexual orientation. Participants were also unsure whether their therapists understood their concerns or could adequately help them. Other therapist variables that emerged in this study were the importance of "therapist reputation" and "transgender affirmative therapy" (Benson, 2013, pp. 31, 32). Transgender clients reported seeking out therapists who were either recommended by community members or were visible in the community as activists and allies. Additionally, therapists who advertised their expertise and willingness to work with the community were considered more helpful and sought after by transgender clients. Lastly, therapists who validated their clients' gender identity and who did not need education regarding gender and transgender experiences were considered to be the most helpful by transgender clients (Benson, 2013). Thus, therapist reputation, expertise, and community perception were critical factors in determining client satisfaction.

Bauer et al. (2009) outline ways in which healthcare providers engage in *institutional and informational erasure of transgender individuals*. One enactment of this is by not having transgender-affirming language in information and intake forms. Transgender identity is overlooked when information regarding gender identity is restricted to a binary structure (e.g., "are you male or female?"). Along with having oppressive language in healthcare–related paperwork, healthcare providers might engage in discrimination against transgender patients if patients' genders or preferred names do not match with what is listed on their healthcare records or insurance information. In order to promote a transpositive environment, it is critical that healthcare providers ensure that language on their paperwork and in their practice is not restricted to the binary and includes affirmation of all gender identities (Bauer et al., 2009; Benson, 2013; Transgender Law and Policy Institute, 2005). Additionally, Bockting et al. (2004) suggest that a therapist can demonstrate their transpositive approach by ensuring that there are transgender identity–related reading materials and informational print resources in waiting rooms and therapist offices.

Recognizing Transphobia and the Impact of Oppression on Transgender Clients

As outlined earlier, transgender individuals face a myriad of concerns linked to continued oppression in a society that only values a traditional understanding of gender. Statistics show that transgender populations are at substantially higher risk for self-harm, suicide, substance abuse, contracting HIV and other sexually transmitted infections, and being more vulnerable to psychiatric illnesses, such as depression and anxiety (Kenagy, 2005; Liu & Mustanski, 2012; Mustanski, Garofalo, & Emerson, 2010; Nemoto, Bödeker, & Iwamoto, 2011; Nemoto, Operario, Keatley, Han, & Soma, 2004).

Historically, psychologists and other mental healthcare providers have attributed the aforementioned risks to the transgender client's gender (Korell & Lorah, 2007). This attribution not only further pathologizes and alienates transgender clients but also might inaccurately reflect some lived realities of transgender populations. Research has suggested that clinicians be prudent when considering the concerns of transgender clients and not assume that a transgender client seeks therapy because of distress surrounding their gender identity (Sennott & Smith, 2011). Thus, therapists are encouraged to shift their clinical lens to the framework that societal transphobia makes transgender clients more susceptible to psychological distress and for this reason seek psychological care (Bauer et al., 2009; Lev, 2004).

Along with the risk factors outlined earlier, transphobia also impacts access to affirming, high-quality healthcare for transgender clients (Ansara, 2010; Bauer et al., 2009; Sennott & Smith, 2011). As suggested earlier, transgender clients frequently receive oppressive care because healthcare professionals do not have adequate training with regard to this population and often enact their transphobic attitudes toward transgender clients (Bauer et al., 2009; Benson, 2013; Lev, 2004).

Further, societal transphobia also manifests itself in workplace discrimination for transgender clients, which then leads to unemployment and sustained economic inequities. Thus, transgender clients often are uninsured and might not seek out healthcare given both lack of financial resources and a distrust of healthcare professionals (Bockting, Huang, Ding, Robinson, & Rosser, 2005; Lev, 2004).

Transgender individuals are the targets of pervasive transphobic microaggressions and have often survived severely traumatic incidents (Namaste, 2000; Reicherzer, Patton, & Glowiak, 2011). While other minority individuals are able to seek social support from their families, friends, and other extended networks, transgender individuals often report feeling isolated from their communities of support, as these very same individuals are responsible for imposing transphobic attitudes on transgender individuals (Namaste, 2000). Thus, it is important for mental healthcare providers to be active agents of change in reducing transphobia and thereby improving the well-being of transgender clients.

CONCLUDING COMMENTS

Given their unique positionality in society, transgender individuals have continually experienced systemic oppression, which has led to psychological distress and lower life satisfaction for this population. Unfortunately, psychology has contributed to transphobia and transphobic attitudes through ignorance and overlooking the needs of this population. Systemic injustice continues to be the experience of many transgender individuals. For example, during the course of the preparation of this manuscript, North Carolina passed the Public Facilities Privacy & Security Act, a law that mandates that individuals use restrooms that are applicable for their *biological sex* and not their *gender identity*. Citing issues of privacy and safety, this law suggests that transgender individuals are a threat to the general public and thus must be restricted to bathrooms that correspond to their genitalia as opposed to their gender (Kopan & Scott, 2016).

Thus, it is critical that advocacy for and protection of transgender clients be on the forefront for psychology. This can be achieved by examining our own gender identities and transphobia; engaging in research practices that are non-exploitive and reflective of the needs of the community; providing safe therapeutic environments; and, lastly, adopting a resilience-focused approach to the conceptualization and care of transgender populations in research and practice.

Given the ongoing perpetuation of transphobia in all aspects of the U.S. society, it is essential that psychology further continue its work to meet the needs of this vulnerable yet resilient population. By continuing to expand its understanding of gender and gender identity, psychology can ultimately serve the needs of all individuals, including those who perhaps have been on the margins of marginalization.

REFERENCES

American Counseling Association. (2010). Competencies for counseling with transgender clients. *Journal of LGBT Issues in Counseling, 4,* 135–159. doi:10.1080/ 15538605.2010.524839

American Psychiatric Association. (1980). *DSM-III: Diagnostic and statistical manual of mental disorders.* Washington, DC: Author.

American Psychiatric Association. (1994). *DSM-IV: Diagnostic and statistical manual of mental disorders.* Washington, DC: Author.

American Psychiatric Association. (2013). Gender dysphoria. Retrieved from http:// www.dsm5.org/documents/gender%20dysphoria%20fact%20sheet.pdf

American Psychological Association, Task Force on Gender Identity and Gender Variance. (2009). *Report of the Task Force on Gender Identity and Gender Variance.* Washington, DC: Author.

American Psychological Association. (2010). Ethical principles of psychologists and code of conduct (2002, Amended 2016). Retrieved from http://www.apa.org/ethics/code/

American Psychological Association. (2015). Guidelines for psychological practice with transgender and gender nonconforming people. *American Psychologist, 70,* 832–864. doi:10.1037/a0039906

Ansara, Y. G. (2010). Beyond cisgenderism: Counselling people with non-assigned gender identities. In L. Moon (Ed.), *Counselling ideologies: Queer challenges to heteronormativity.* Surrey, England: Ashgate, Aldershot.

Association for Lesbian, Gay, Bisexual, and Transgender Issues in Counseling. (2009). *Competencies for counseling with transgender clients.* Alexandria, VA: Author.

Bartlett, N. H., Vasey, P. L., & Bukowski, W. M. (2000). Is gender identity disorder in children a mental disorder? *Sex Roles, 43,* 753–785. doi:10.1023/A:1011004431889

Bauer, G. R., Hammond, R., Travers, R., Kaay, M., Hohenadel, K. M., & Boyce, M. (2009). "I don't think this is theoretical; this is our lives": How erasure impacts health care for transgender people. *Journal of the Association of Nurses in AIDS Care*, 20, 348–361. doi:http://dx.doi.org/10.1016/j.jana.2009.07.004

Bauerband, A. L., & Galupo, M. P. (2014). The gender identity reflection and rumination scale: Development and psychometric evaluation. *Journal of Counseling & Development*, 92, 219–231. doi:10.1002/j.1556-6676.2014.00151.x

Benjamin, H. (1964). Nature and management of transsexualism with report on 31 operated cases. *Western Journal of Surgical Obstetrics Gynecology*, 72, 105–111.

Benjamin, H. (1966). *The transsexual phenomenon*. New York, NY: Julian Press.

Benson, K. E. (2013). Seeking support: Transgender client experiences with mental health services. *Journal of Feminist Family Therapy*, 25, 17–40. doi:10.1080/08952833.2013.755081

Birkett, M., Newcomb, M. E., & Mustanski, B. (2014). Does it get better? A longitudinal analysis of psychological distress and victimization in lesbian, gay, bisexual, transgender, and questioning youth. *Journal of Adolescent Health*, 56, 280–285. doi:10.1016/j.jadohealth.2014.10.275

Bockting, W., Robinson, B., Benner, A., & Scheltema, K. (2004). Patient satisfaction with transgender health services. *Journal of Sex & Marital Therapy*, 30, 277–294. doi:10.1080/00926230490422467

Bockting, W. O. (2009). Transforming the paradigm of transgender health: A field in transition. *Sexual & Relationship Therapy*, 24, 103–107. doi:10.1080/14681990903037660

Bockting, W. O., Huang, C. Y., Ding, H., Robinson, B., & Rosser, B. R. (2005). Are transgender persons at higher risk for HIV than other sexual minorities? A comparison of HIV prevalence and risks. *International Journal of Transgenderism*, 8, 123–131. doi:10.1300/J485v08n02_11

Breslow, A. S., Brewster, M. E., Velez, B. L., Wong, S., Geiger, E., & Soderstrom, B. (2015). Resilience and collective action: Exploring buffers against minority stress for transgender individuals. *Psychology of Sexual Orientation and Gender Diversity*, 2, 253–265. doi:10.1037/sgd0000117

Bryant, J., & Oliver, M. B. (Eds.). (2009). *Media effects: Advances in theory and research* (3rd ed.). New York, NY: Routledge.

Burnes, T. R., Singh, A. A., Harper, A. J., Harper, B., Maxon-Kann, W., Pickering, D. L., & Hosea, J. U. (2010). American Counseling Association: Competencies for counseling with transgender clients. *Journal of LGBT Issues in Counseling*, 4, 135–159. doi:10.1080/15538605.2010.524839

Carroll, L., & Gilroy, P. J. (2002). Transgender issues in counselor preparation. *Counselor Education & Supervision*, 41, 233–242. doi:10.1002/j.1556-6978.2002.tb01286.x

Carroll, L., Gilroy, P. J., & Ryan, J. (2002). Counseling transgendered, transsexual, and gender-variant clients. *Journal of Counseling and Development*, 80, 131–139.

Dalton, D. (2015). The 22 trans women murdered in 2015. *The Daily Dot*. Retrieved from http://www.dailydot.com/politics/trans-women-of-color-murdered/

Fassinger, R. E., & Arseneau, J. R. (2007). "I'd rather get wet than be under that umbrella": Differentiating the experiences and identities of lesbian, gay, bisexual, and transgender people. In R. P. Pere, K. A. DeBoard, & K. J. Bieschke (Eds.), *Handbook of counseling and psychotherapy with lesbian, gay, bisexual, and transgender clients* (2nd ed., pp. 19–49). Washington, DC: American Psychological Association.

Galupo, M. P., Henise, S. B., & Davis, K. S. (2014). Transgender microaggressions in the context of friendship: Patterns of experience across friend's sexual orientation and gender identity. *Psychology of Sexual Orientation and Gender Diversity, 1,* 461–470.

Goethals, S. C., & Schwiebert, V. L. (2005). Counseling as a critique of gender: On the ethics of counseling transgendered clients. *International Journal for the Advancement of Counselling, 27,* 457–469. doi:10.1007/s10447-005-8206-8

Gómez-Gil, E., Vidal-Hagemeijer, A., & Salamero, M. (2008). MMPI-2 characteristics of transsexuals requesting sex reassignment: Comparison of patients in prehormonal and presurgical phases. *Journal of Personality Assessment, 90,* 368–374.

Goodman, L. A., Liang, B., Helms, J. E., Latta, R. E., Sparks, E., & Weintraub, S. R. (2004). Training counseling psychologists as social justice agents: Feminist and multi-cultural principles in action. *The Counseling Psychologist, 32,* 793–836. doi: 10.1177/0011000004268802

Grant, J. M., Mottet, L. A., Tanis, J., Harrison, J., Herman, J. L., & Keisling, M. (2011). *Injustice at every turn: A report of the National Transgender Discrimination Survey.* Washington, DC: National Center for Transgender Equality and National Gay and Lesbian Task Force.

Green, E., & dickey, l. m. (2007, March). *Considerations for research with trans subjects and communities.* Paper presented at FORGE Forward, Milwaukee, WI. Retrieved April 1, 2016, from http://trans-academics.org/considerations_research_t

Henry, F. (1999). *The racialization of crime in Toronto's print media: A research project.* Toronto, Ontario: School of Journalism, Ryerson Polytechnic University.

Hirschfeld, M. (2003). *Transvestites: The erotic drive to cross-dress* (M. A. Lomnardi-Nash, Trans.). New York, NY: Prometheus Books. (Original work published 1910).

Kenagy, G. P. (2005). Transgender health: Findings from two needs assessment studies in Philadelphia. *Health & Social Work, 30,* 19–26. doi:10.1093/hsw/30.1.19

Kopan, T., & Scott, E. (2016). North Carolina governor signs controversial transgender bill. Retrieved from http://www.cnn.com/2016/03/23/politics/north-carolina-gender-bathrooms-bill/

Korell, S. C., & Lorah, P. (2007). An overview of affirmative psychotherapy and counsel-ing with transgender clients. In K. J. Bieschke, R. M. Perez, & K. A. DeBord (Eds.), *Handbook of counseling and psychotherapy with lesbian, gay, bisexual, and transgender clients* (pp. 271–288). Washington, DC: American Psychological Association.

Lev, A. I. (2004). *Transgender emergence.* New York, NY: Harworth Clinical Practice Press.

Lev, A. I. (2007). Transgender communities: Developing identity through connection. In K. J. Bieschke, R. M. Perez, & K. A. DeBord (Eds.), *Handbook of counseling and psychotherapy with lesbian, gay, bisexual, and transgender clients* (2nd ed., pp. 147–176). Washington, DC: American Psychological Association.

Levitt, H. M., & Ippolito, M. R. (2014). Being transgender: The experience of transgen-der identity development. *Journal of Homosexuality, 61,* 1727. doi:10.1080/00918369.2014.951262

Liu, R. T., & Mustanski, B. (2012). Suicidal ideation and self-harm in lesbian, gay, bisex-ual, and transgender youth. *American Journal of Preventive Medicine, 42,* 221–228. doi: http://dx.doi.org/10.1016/j.amepre.2011.10.023

Mahtani, M. (2001). Representing minorities: Canadian media and minority identities. *Canadian Ethnic Studies, 33,* 99–133.

Marcus, H. R., & Hamedani, M. G. (2010). Sociocultural psychology: The dynamic inter-dependence among self systems and social systems. In S. Kitayama & D. Cohen (Eds.), *Handbook of cultural psychology* (pp. 3–39). New York, NY: Guilford.

Martin, J. I., & Meezan, W. (2003). Applying ethical standards to research and evalua-tions involving lesbian, gay, bisexual, and transgender populations. *Journal of Gay & Lesbian Social Services, 15*, 181–201. doi:10.1300/J041v15n01_12

Meier, S. C., & Labuski, C. M. (2013). The demographics of the transgender population. In A. K. Baumle (Ed.), *International handbook on the demography of sexuality* (pp. 289–327). Dordrecht, Netherlands: Springer Netherlands.

Miller, L. R., & Grollman, E. A. (2015). The social costs of gender nonconformity for transgender adults: Implications for discrimination and health. *Sociological Forum, 30*, 809–831. doi:10.1111/socf.12193

Moradi, B., Mohr, J., Worthington, R., & Fassinger, R. (2009). Counseling psychology research on sexual (orientation) minority issues: Conceptual and methodological challenges and opportunities. *Journal of Counseling Psychology, 56*, 5–22. doi:10.1037/a0014572

Movement Advancement Project. (2018). *Understanding issues facing transgender Americans*. Retrieved June 25, 2017, from www.lgbtmap.org/file/understanding-issues-facing-transgender-americans.pdf

Mustanski, B. S., Garofalo, R., & Emerson, E. M. (2010). Mental health disorders, psychological distress, and suicidality in a diverse sample of lesbian, gay, bisexual, and transgender youths. *American Journal of Public Health, 100*, 2426–2432. doi:10.2105/AJPH.2009.178319

Nadal, K. L., Skolnik, A., & Wong, Y. (2012). Interpersonal and systemic microaggressions toward transgender people: Implications for counseling. *LBGT Issues in Counseling, 6*, 55–82. doi:10.1080/15538605.2012.648583

Namaste, V. (2000). *Invisible lives: The erasure of transsexual and transgendered people*. New York, NY: University of Chicago Press.

National Center for Transgender Equality. (2014). Transgender terminology. Retrieved from http://www.transequality.org/issues/resources/transgender-terminology

Nemoto, T., Bödeker, B., & Iwamoto, M. (2011). Social support, exposure to violence and transphobia, and correlates of depression among male-to-female transgender women with a history of sex work. *American Journal of Public Health, 101*, 1980–1988. doi:10.2105/AJPH.2010.197285

Nemoto, T., Operario, D., Keatley, J., Han, L., & Soma, T. (2004). HIV risk behaviors among male-to-female transgender persons of color in San Francisco. *American Journal of Public Health, 94*, 1193–1199. doi:10.2105/AJPH.94.7.1193

New York Daily News. (1952, December 1). Ex-Gi becomes blonde bombshell. *New York Daily News*. Retrieved from http://www.christinejorgensen.org/MainPages/Home.html

Prosser, J. (1998). *Second skins: The body narratives of transsexuality*. New York, NY: Columbia University Press.

Rachlin, K. (2002). Transgender individuals' experiences of psychotherapy. *The International Journal of Transgenderism, 6*, 97–1003.

Raj, R. (2002). Towards a transpositive therapeutic model: Developing clinical sensitivity and cultural competence in the effective support of transsexual and transgendered clients. *The International Journal of Transgenderism, 6*, 97–1003.

Reicherzer, S., Patton, J., & Glowiak, M. (2011). Counseling transgender trauma survivors. Retrieved from http://www.counseling.org/Resources/Library/VISTAS/2011-V-Online/Article_97.pdf

Reicherzer, S., Steves, M., & Patton, J. (2007). Transgenders, Vestidas, Hijra, Kathoey: Responding to cultural expressions of gender identity. Retrieved from http://citeseerx.ist.psu.edu/viewdoc/download?doi=10.1.1.455.1136&rep=rep1&type=pdf

Riggle, E. D., Rotosky, S. S., McCants, L. E., & Pascale-Hague, D. (2011). The positive aspects of transgender self-identification. *Psychology & Sexuality*, 2, 147–158. doi:10.1080/19419899.2010.534490

Rutherford, K., McIntyre, J., Daley, A., & Ross, L. E. (2012). Development of expertise in mental health service provision for lesbian, gay, bisexual and transgender communities. *Medical Education*, 46, 903–913. doi:10.1111/j.1365-2923.2012.04272.x

Rutter, P. A., Estrada, D., Ferguson, L. K., & Diggs, G. A. (2008). Sexual orientation and counselor competency: The impact of training on enhancing awareness, knowledge and skills. *Journal of LGBT Issues in Counseling*, 2, 109–125. doi:10.1080/15538600802125472

Sanchez, N. F., Sanchez, J. P., & Danoff, A. (2009). Health care utilization, barriers to care, and hormone usage among male-to-female transgender persons in New York City. *American Journal of Public Health*, 99, 713–719. doi:10.2105/AJPH.2007.132035

Sennott, S., & Smith, T. (2011). Translating the sex and gender continuums in mental health: A transfeminist approach to client and clinician fears. *Journal of Gay & Lesbian Mental Health*, 15, 218–234. doi:10.1080/19359705.2011.553779

Serano, J. (2007). *Whipping girl: A transsexual woman on sexism and the scapegoating of femininity*. New York, NY: Seal Press.

Singh, A. A., Boyd, C. J., & Whitman, J. S. (2010). Counseling competency with transgender and intersex persons. In J. Cornish, B. A. Schreier, L. I. Nadkarni, L. Metzger, & E. R. Rodolfa (Eds.), *Handbook of multicultural counseling competencies* (pp. 415–441). Hoboken, NJ: Wiley.

Singh, A. A., & Burnes, T. R. (2010). Shifting the counselor role from gatekeeping to advocacy: Ten strategies for using the competencies for counseling with transgender clients for individual and social change. *Journal of LGBT Issues in Counseling*, 4, 241–255. doi:10.1080/15538605.2010.525455

Singh, A. A., & McKleroy, V. S. (2010). "Just getting out of bed is a revolutionary act": The resilience of transgender people of color who have survived traumatic life events. *Traumatology*, 17, 34–44. doi:10.1177/1534765610369261

Smith, L. C., Shin, R. Q., & Officer, L. M. (2012). Moving counseling forward on LGB and transgender issues: Speaking queerly on discourses and microaggressions. *The Counseling Psychologist*, 40, 385–408. doi:10.1177/0011000011403165

Steinmetz, K. (2014). Laverne Cox talks to Time about the transgender movement. *Time.com*. Retrieved September 13, 2014, from http://time.com/132769/transgender-orange-is-thenew-black-laverne-cox-interview

Sue, D. W. (2001). Multidimensional facets of cultural competence. *The Counseling Psychologist*, 29, 790–821. doi:10.1177/0011000001296002

Sue, D. W., Arredondo, P., & McDavis, R. J. (1992). Multicultural counseling competencies and standards: A call to the profession. *Journal of Counseling & Development*, 70, 477–486. doi:10.1002/j.1556-6676.1992.tb01642.x

Sue, D. W., & Sue, D. (2008). *Counseling the culturally different: Theory and practice* (5th ed.). New York, NY: Wiley.

Transgender Law and Policy Institute. (2005). Ways that colleges and universities meet the needs of transgender students. Retrieved March 21, 2016, from http://www.transgenderlaw.org/college/index.htm

Walworth, J. (1997). Sex reassignment surgery in male-to-female transsexuals: Client satisfaction in relation to selection criteria. In B. Bullough, V. L. Bullough & J. Elias (Eds.), *Gender blending* (pp. 325–373). Amherst, NY: Prometheus Books.

Wong, F., & Halgin, R. (2006). The "model minority": Bane or blessing for Asian Americans? *Journal of Multicultural Counseling and Development, 34,* 38–49.

Zimmerman, V. (2015). Clinical psychology students' perceived training in working with transgender clients: An exploratory study. *Doctoral Papers and Masters Projects.* Paper 25.

4

How Contemporary Psychoanalysis Contributes to LGBT Psychology: Examining and Addressing Gender Fluidity and Diversity as We Slide toward 21st-Century Transformations

Shara Sand

Psychoanalysis has an uneven history and reputation, when it comes to LGBT issues. Sigmund Freud was a fierce defender of LGBT civil rights and social inclusion and stood up for LGBT freedom at no small cost to his career prospects and income (Gay, 1998); collaborated closely with Magnus Hirschfeld, the founder of the first LGBT advocacy and research organization in Europe (Hirschfeld, 2000); and believed gayness (at least in men; women confused him) was not something that could or needed to be "fixed" (Freud, 1950). Some of his followers, especially in the United States, used—most psychoanalysts today would say, grievously and enragingly misused—some now debunked psychoanalytic ideas to condemn gayness as pathological (Bieber, 1965; Ovesey, 1955; Socarides, 1968).

But that has long since not been the prevalent view in psychoanalysis. Psychoanalytic organizations and institutes train and welcome LGBT members, Generations of gay, lesbian, bisexual, trans, and ally psychoanalytic clinicians have made important contributions to understanding LGBT experience, through the opportunities psychoanalytic theories and methods perhaps uniquely allow for understanding the rich fabric of LGBT lives (among the most recent and influential: Corbett, 2001, 2008, 2009a, 2009b, 2011, 2016; D'Ercole & Drescher, 2013; Domenici & Lesser, 2016; Downey & Friedman, 1998; Drescher, 1997, 2008, 2014; Drescher, D'Ercole, & Schoenberg, 2014; Ehrensaft, 2009, 2011, 2015; Gherovici, 2011; Glassgold & Iasenza, 2000; Grossman, 2001; Hoffman et al., 2001; Iasenza, 2002; Isay, 1997, 2010; Layton, 2000; Lesser & Schoenberg, 2013; Lewes, 2009; Magee & Miller, 2013; Rottnek, 1999; Roughton, 2001, 2002, 2003; Schwartz, 2013; Zaretsky, 1997).

In this chapter, I hope to give an example and a flavor for how psychoanalytically informed clinical work can enrich contemporary LGBT possibilities. A warning, you will find that my style of thinking, writing, and working is fairly personal, like the styles of many contemporary psychoanalysts. I hope you will find mine a useful, contributing voice in this volume's chorus.

INTRODUCTION

I have found my practice increasingly filled with young, and sometimes not so young, people who identify as transgender, gender nonconforming, gender non-binary, or gender diverse. I am an out lesbian and have recently acknowledged that I have always been gender nonconforming—in 20th-century terminology, a tomboy who never grew out of it. This is not something I generally share with patients, but perhaps they read me as such anyway—pants, tailored style, very short hair, and no dresses, stockings, heels, or makeup, ever.

My experience with gender diversity in others and myself has at times challenged certain psychoanalytic tenets that are part of how I was trained to practice and think. I was taught the gender binary and heterosexuality are normal and that any variation is pathological. I do not believe that, but the impact of that legacy can linger.

There is little written that explores clinical work with those who are gender diverse; Ehrensaft (2009, 2011, 2015), Gherovici (2011), and Suchet (2011) are exceptions. I think the following questions form a basis that helps formulate a non-pathologizing, psychoanalytically informed clinical approach: How does one conceptualize a person who does not feel comfortable in their gender, and how is that understanding framed? How does someone conceptualize the person whose sexual orientation changes as the result of their gender change, but what a psychoanalyst would call their object choice—the kind of person they desire and seek out for sexual intimacy—does not? What about the person whose object choice and sexual orientation change? How does one understand shifts in sexual attachments, or the lack thereof?

I hope to begin to answer some of these questions.

Until recently, psychoanalysis primarily pathologized those for whom congruence between their birth-assigned physical selves and their self-determined psychic selves is not possible, painting them as suffering from psychotic or delusional processes. There continues to be a tendency of many clinicians to view gender-diverse patients as having unstable object choices, problematic attachments, immature relational capacities, and borderline features (Socarides, 1978). The gender-binary world is much easier to parse and understand, which is why psychoanalysis may struggle with its ability, emerging but conflictually so in our times, to engage in conceptualizing non-dichotomous gender and sexual constructs.

However, it is the lack of inherent or necessary dichotomy that forms the basis of the narratives of gender-diverse patients. There is no word for a third gender, an in-between-male-and-female. Thus, gender-diverse people can often initially struggle with how they want to be seen by others and how they can express themselves in a manner that reflects their unique identity. Unfortunately, if this issue cannot be successfully resolved, the incongruence of gender and psyche can be extraordinarily painful—so much so that suicide attempts among gender-diverse populations are three times that of the general population (Peterson, Copps-Smith, & Conard, 2016). This chapter will look at the gender nonbinary via clinical vignettes and rock 'n' roll lyrics dating back more than 40 years. Emerging through the discussion that follows, I hope the reader will find ways in which a psychoanalytically informed therapeutic approach, which focuses on the dynamics of the patient's inner, subjective experience, can make their utility felt.

GENDER NONBINARY: THE CHALLENGE OF "THEY"

It can be a particular challenge to those who have not felt such extreme discomfort with their gendered selves to develop the empathy to effectively help those who fall on the gender-diverse spectrum. It is for this reason that I have chosen to present brief snapshots of my work with a few patients as a way of illuminating how to work, psychoanalytically, with those for whom gender is not a given but rather comes to entail a complex construction of a differently gendered self.

Z. walked into my office for the first time and presented as intelligent and confident, but somewhat uncomfortable in herself. She discussed in a well-articulated way her distress regarding the sexism and misgendering that were occurring in the piano studio at the elite, urban conservatory where she was studying. Z. presented as female-bodied, slightly overweight, with shoulder-length, dark hair and a very voluptuous appearance.

In discussing the upsetting situation that brought her to therapy, Z. indicated she identified as gender nonbinary and saw herself in a middle space, neither male nor female. I recorded the usual background history; Z. had also had a few bewildering therapy experiences as a child, in which she surmised "they must have been psychoanalysts; they never said anything and just stared at me."

I asked Z. why she had contacted me from among the available counselors at the school. Her reply was anticipated: "Because you deal with gender and sexuality." She said it as if it were a dare; her body language was guarded and suspicious. I inquired how the session had felt so far, and she told me, "You didn't cringe at the word 'misgendered,' and you didn't ask me what it meant, either; so we'll see." I had passed the first test (McLemore, 2016), and with the clear sense of being judged, I noticed I had unconsciously started nodding; consciously, I wanted to be accepted, and so did Z.

I then asked Z. what gender pronoun was preferred and was surprised by her reaction. She look stunned, shrunk into herself, and then, in the smallest of voices, said, "They"; a moment later, they were in tears. I let their tears flow and gently asked what they were feeling. They responded, "No one has ever asked me that before." Their disbelief and gratefulness settled over the room; they could begin to trust me.

Z. went on to describe a sexual assault at 18 by a known assailant. They reported a disappointing therapy experience in which the therapist repeatedly related their gender issues to this assault. They reported their awareness of their gender identity was in place before the assault and that they left that treatment feeling misheard and misunderstood.

Z. said they felt that they thought they might be agender and possibly attracted to women but felt they were primarily asexual. Perhaps issues regarding their sexuality may have turned out to be related to the assault, but we were unable to explore this secondary to time constraints in the treatment relationship that was available to us.

I introduce Z. because I think it is important to note that transgender and gender-diverse persons are not always visibly identifiable but are, increasingly in our society, articulating their identities in a variety of ways (Hansbury, 2011). The numbers are still small but are growing as more young people realize the core of their dissatisfaction is their gendered position in the world. What is new are the numbers of people acknowledging they identify as gender diverse and do not feel the pressure to identity as cisgender, thus normative. The language of gender diversity and the language typically used by millennials are very different from the language of the Baby Boomers; the associations and vocabulary used to define gender and sexuality from the late 20th century are often obsolete and increasingly are replaced with terms offering more subtle descriptors. As I listen to my gender-diverse patients, I cannot help but feel middle aged, with a reckless youthfulness that has long passed and wistfulness for what I feel I am missing.

An important change is the linguistic appropriation of the word "they," which is now being used as a pronoun, in the singular, in place of she or he. For those who do not identify as male or female, "they" presents as a genderless term, an indication of a gender-diverse identity that cannot be presumed to be either male or female. "They" is a pronoun of the carving out of a new space to exist distinctly from either male or female. This is not a de-identification with the gender binary but rather the result of never identifying with the expected gendered behavior. For many it creates a freer sense of self, one that no longer cringes when hearing a gendered description of self with which there is a negative identification. In psychoanalytic psychotherapy with people who disidentify with the cisgender normative, the form and texture of these new, emerging identifications, captured by the use of "they" as a pronoun, become uniquely capable of being appreciated.

WHAT CAN BE LEARNED FROM POPULAR MUSIC: GENDER AND SEXUAL FLUIDITY VIA THE VOICE OF ROCK 'N' ROLL

Those who are gender diverse often present with gender dysphoria, depression, anxiety, and complex issues regarding romantic relationships. Since there is very little psychoanalytic literature exploring transgender life, there is little in the way of treatment approach recommendations other than the utilization of empathy and understanding (Saketopoulou, 2011, 2014; Suchet, 2011).

Because there is so little theoretical or clinical literature, I turn to popular music to give a broader view of the transgender, the gender diverse, and the diversity in sexual experience. Popular music has always been ahead of the game and pushed the boundaries, long before psychoanalysis. This is consistent with one line of development of psychoanalytic theory and methods, which have long drawn on experiences powerfully captured in art, literature, and music to understand clinical and intrapsychic realities (Blum, 2013). I start in the '70s and trace the gender-diverse and sexually diverse trajectory of lyrics through almost 50 years of music. My patients' stories should be heard with an ear to these lyrics, which ring so true to the experiences of many.

I thought of the soundtrack of my youth and the way I was drawn to songs that explicitly mention gender and sexual fluidity. My musical memories landed on the Kinks's "Walk on the Wild Side" (1970) and "Lola" (1972), songs inspired by the sexual adventures of both Ray Davies and the late Lou Reed.

The Kinks's lyrics are very clear and in many ways shocking for the times. Sexual freedom and sex before marriage were new cultural behaviors when these songs debuted, and the change in societal norms had not even begun to absorb LGBTQ people (and then, of course, only lesbians and gay men, at first). When interviewed almost 50 years after writing these songs, Ray Davies is said to have stated that, unless closely listened to, the meaning of these lyrics was not obviously apparent (Baxter-Moore, 2006). The songs raised no eyebrows, as might have been the case if the songs were titled "I Dated a Drag Queen." I believe these songs are important because, in an unknowing way, the Kinks may have set the stage for the normalizing of gender fluidity and diversity. These examples from popular music illustrate the concepts of sexual and gender fluidity that have always existed in society, long before psychoanalysis began to entertain the non-pathological nature of these constructs. I include some samples next.

From "Walk on the Wild Side":

Shaved her legs and then he was a she

From "Lola":

Why she walk like a woman and talk like a man

The late, great David Bowie, the first man I saw wearing makeup and a unitard, wrote "Rebel, Rebel" (1974):

She's not sure if you're a boy or a girl

The thread continues with Ani DiFranco singing "In and Out" in 1992:

Some days the line I walk turns out to be straight, other days the line tends to deviate

Moving to the 21st century, the examples of gender fluidity present rather differently.
J. D. Samson sings, in "Who Am I to Be So Free":

We found options that were better than a man

And lastly, Christine and the Queens (2015):

She's a man now

These lyrics capture something LGBT-affirming psychoanalysts have learned clinically and begun to theorize through our work with patients diverse in gender and sexual identity and expression. This captures a social and cultural shift; psychoanalytic psychotherapy and LGBT psychoanalytic theories are now beginning to conceptualize the impact of these shifts on the emotional lives and behaviors of LGBT people diverse in their personal gender and sexual realities.

KEEPING PACE WITH THE TIMES

Unlike the Kinks, there are no apologies or hidden identities heard from the contemporary artists cited previously who cross sexual and gender borders. Artists have always pushed boundaries, in part because they frequently live on the edge of societal acceptance and are less concerned with social approval. Thus we can take a page from their book as contemporary psychoanalytic clinicians engaged in work with LGBT populations move psychoanalysis forward to the perspective that sexual and gender fluidity is not pathological but rather a more genuine way of expressing aspects of the self that are present.

How can we translate our theories and these lyrics into therapies helpful to the lived experience of our LGBTQ patients? We need to begin eschewing the relevance of "why" someone is trans, gender diverse, or nonconforming. Just as "why someone is LGB" is a question that has mattered less and less in treatment as the focus has become how to live a life of queer contentment, the same is true for diverse, fluid gender and sexual expressions and identities. The currency of the language used to define contemporary gender and sexual desires has changed, and the generational divide means that, when we work with those who traverse the gender and sexuality continuum, we need to listen even more carefully.

There is an acceptance of aspects of life in this century that did not exist for those who came of age in the 20th century. It is on the backs of the giants of those early days (Iasenza, 1995; Isay, 2010/1989) who have given me the privilege that I can write this chapter today. As I thought more and more about this chapter, the same question kept coming to mind: What is new in the LGBTQ arena of psychoanalytic thinking?

Queer psychoanalysts do not have century-old cases to fall back on and to re-analyze; Freud's Dora anyone (Freud, 1997)? Therefore, what are we writing about, or not writing about, and what should be explored and addressed? The path psychoanalysis finally came to walk in the very late 20th century was almost in sync with the culture in its thinking about gender and sexuality. It is necessary for our thinking to continue to evolve if we are to be able to stay current with the generations that follow us and even more if psychoanalysis is to make the contribution it is able to make to the advancement of LGBT communities it now actively serves.

I thought of the major queer psychoanalytic writers, and a few straight allies of the present who have come to prominence since the turn of the century, and the list is neither long nor overly prolific, though the writing is of impeccable quality. Melanie Suchet (2011), Avgi Saketopoulou (2014), Ken Corbett (2001, 2008, 2009a, 2009b, 2011, 2013, 2016), Diane Ehrensaft (2009, 2011, 2015), Muriel Dimen (2014), and Adrienne Harris (2011) are among the most productive authors. There are many additional queer authors and a few straight ones who are also currently writing and considering 21st-century sexuality and gender identity along with their language and behavior. These authors have all addressed important issues regarding gender and sexuality in the LGBTQ community, including gender transitions among adults (Suchet, 2011) and the meaning of words and labels (Harris, 2011; Saketopoulou, 2014; Suchet, 2011). Many write of working with transgender children and adults (Corbett, 2008, 2009b, 2011, 2016; Ehrensaft, 2015; Hansbury, 2011; Saketopoulou, 2014), while some write from a more experience distant, theoretical position (Dimen, 2014; Harris, 2011).

As I followed the labyrinth of gender and sexual theorizing, I thought of those who identify as transgender and the sometimes humiliating, always awkward question that is heard: "What are you?" This question is posed to those who are trans, especially those who are gender nonconforming or appear androgynous. However, in our times, it is not just those who are trans rewriting gender scripts but also those who are genderqueer or gender nonconforming or ascribe to a new androgyny, embodying a middle ground that may be free from conventional notions of gender constancy and the gender binary. Many wish there were a third word to describe this gender that is neither male nor female. Some wish the obsession about gender by others would disappear. Perhaps psychoanalysis, when it can truly listen to our patients' experiences of gender without the assumption of the pathological, can be a useful voice in this contemporary search for a way through to a better, more free understanding of gender. Only then we will be able to help those who live on the gender continuum find a way to be comfortable in their bodies without the need for explanation.

LANGUAGE AND FLUID IDENTITIES

There is a small but significant population, primarily consisting of teenagers and young adults (millennials) as far as I can tell, who decry the lack of appropriate descriptors for their gender and sexual identities. The truth is, maybe we need more and better descriptors. The binary dualities, when used as exclusive categories, do not fit the generation or the times.

Thus, it is important to continue to consider language when examining gender as perceived by those in early adulthood. Psychoanalysis values words and has created its own language to represent the unconscious and human behavior. This language is used to interpret, express empathy, ask for clarification, and attend to nuance and tone as well as to content. The 21st-century language brought to us by the millennial generation has redefined gender and sexual identities. It is not that millennials have made up new identities, but rather that they are articulating them, and that collective articulation has illuminated the limitations of formerly hegemonic categories and words. Twentieth-century terms have been found narrow and constricting; thus, a myriad of descriptions for gender and sexuality are emerging. The changing language surrounding gender signals that the times indeed have changed. Psychoanalysts have just begun to produce writings on transgender realities and perspectives, as well as gender-nonconforming people, whose insights and impact help clinicians think about gender and sexuality in more nuanced ways. The language will begin to change in a positive, more freeing, and more inclusive direction (Ehrensaft, 2011; Saketopoulou, 2014).

When I discuss language, I am referring especially to a new set of pronouns. These pronouns are now increasingly included in e-mail signatures to help ensure an accurate understanding of identity. We are all familiar with he/him/his and she/her/hers. How about ze/hir/hirs? And they/them? These are pronouns now widely used by those on the gender spectrum as well as by their cisgender allies—including the American Psychological Association, whose guidelines for work with trans and gender-nonconforming persons now ask all psychologists proactively to specify their preferred pronouns (American Psychological Association, 2015).

It remains to be seen what other new pronouns may be created to identify the gendered self. Many are familiar with the term "transgender," but not as many are familiar with "cisgender," meaning gender that is concordant with one's birth-assigned gender. And what about "gender nonconforming," referring to those who do not identify as transgender but do not identify as cisgender, either? For those who find gender nonconforming offensive, seeing nonconforming as a pejorative label, there is the use of "gender diverse."

As a sign of shifting times, when my cisgender, heterosexual teenage son was leaving on a trip, I asked him for a hug. He replied, "You mean, a bro slap." I did not really know what this was but got a huge slap on my back and responded by giving him the same. When my partner asked for a hug, she said, "I want a cozy mommy hug." He responded by rolling his eyes and said, "That is so gender normative." Being who she is in the world, my partner just said, "I want a cozy hug, not a slap that sends me flying across the room."

We were both surprised that, in my son's male teenage world, he was scolding us about the confines of gender normativity. He also buys girls' socks and stretches them over his size 11 feet because they are pretty. The 21st-century seems to offer a differently gendered space, and more and more millennials, straight and gay, are eschewing rigid gender norms.

When speaking of labels, one is speaking of identity. How language helps or hinders that construction is important, especially if identity is considered as a social and generational construction as well as a highly personalized and individual psychological reality. The generational and social changes in the first decades of this century have been remarkable. Ending much, if not all, anti-LGBT legal and social discrimination and providing equal marriage status to LGBTQ people have occurred at a rapid pace. Psychoanalysis has not kept pace in addressing these changes in the consulting room but is making notable efforts. Articles about the children of same-sex parents navigating unchartered waters are found among research journals but mostly not, yet, psychoanalytic journals.

Parenting issues and how conception occurs can unleash a barrage of awkward questions fired in rapid succession: Did you use a donor? Your brother? A friend? Such questions are rarely addressed in the literature. Psychoanalysis is not—yet, at least—writing about the teen with two moms or two dads who is closeted about their family. Psychoanalysis is also not yet writing about extended family members and their responses to becoming grandparents, aunts, and uncles to a child to whom they may or may not be related genetically. We have not yet described in print how we are working with those whose partners/husbands/wives are transitioning from one gender to the next. What about the children seeing their parents undergo shifts in gender?

We have not yet come to clear understandings about how we will work with this generation of trans children and teens and their sometimes reluctant or confused parents. Psychoanalysis can certainly have a voice in issues regarding medically and psychologically appropriate ages for childhood transition. But we have not yet figured out how we will work with trans adults who grew up as trans children. These phenomena that the field has rarely seen before now come to psychoanalytic clinicians in greater numbers. Perhaps much of what psychoanalysis can offer, at the present historical and cultural juncture, is our openness to bringing our tools and understandings to the previously uncharted terrains of LGBT mental health. We must use what we know about the roles of inner, subjective experience, the unconscious and inner conflicts, and the ways they can find expression and healing in psychoanalytically informed psychotherapies, as important tools in LGBT-affirmative clinical work.

Z. AND THE GUARDED SELF

Going back to Z.: Our work ended when they graduated and returned home. When we talked about terminating, their sadness permeated the room. They had never felt heard before, always feeling invisible, except when performing. They feared being overwhelmed by the sexual trauma they had experienced earlier in life and having no one with whom to talk at the time or before our work together began. They mostly felt there would be a sadness and loss without our twice-weekly sessions, which they feared would result in an alienated internal retreat. Z. also did not want to need or miss me; that was felt to entail the risk of making me real, thus resulting in Z. feeling vulnerable, a feeling they decried each time it arose.

Approximately one month before termination, Z. announced with a placid expression I had never seen, that they had found the off switch and had chosen to put the painful thoughts away for a while instead of waiting until they were unconsciously dissociated. My inquiry prompted the response I anticipated; such a strategy seemed a good way to handle the end of school, finals, their recital, and a conscious attempt to not to be distracted by psychic pain. We also discussed Z.'s anxiety about becoming too emotionally close or dependent on me in the face of losing me.

Z. chose to continue working with me until the school year ended. We discussed material that was less traumatic—beginning a career, living at home with their brother, mother, and stepfather after many years away, and locating a new clinician who could support them in their identity and help to manage the trauma and its antecedents and consequences.

In my brief treatment with Z., I believe what was most important was my acute attunement to and awareness of their need to be recognized in a very specific way. Contemporary gender terms are complex and comprise a language that needs to be known, as this becomes the lexicon used to describe experiences of gender and sexuality. Z. did not have to come in and explain their identity; they felt able to trust that I would respect their choices. When telling me "they" is their pronoun of choice, they said, "I hope you're not one of those grammar police types." The truth is I am, but, with difficulty, I leave it out of my clinical work, as I know that being the grammar police is alienating and will not help the person sitting before me.

WHO SHOULD I DATE?

I would now like to present briefly two more cases where issues of gender and sexuality fell along the spectrum of possibility. I recently began work with a Chinese trans man. Originally born in China to parents who were low-level scientists and would be considered lower middle class, he came to the United States for advanced educational opportunities. He has a PhD in physics and worked in the Midwest for several years before coming to New York to pursue a PhD in finance.

X. came in with a very specific issue. He asked me, "Whom should I date?"

X. has been transgender for many years and always dated somewhat traditional Chinese women in the United States. He had begun to detect a pattern. "After a few months, I am dropped for a regular straight guy . . . . Sometimes, I am even more handsome than them," he would rail. "I can even make more money. Why does this happen?"

I asked X. about his transition, and he told me he always dressed like a boy and always thought he was a boy. He started therapy when he was in college, in China, and it helped him understand who he was. He identified as lesbian at that time because he liked women but still felt something was not quite right. When he came to the United States, he began to identify as trans. His parents are not very accepting because they fear he will cut his body and have his breasts removed, which is widely considered taboo in Chinese culture. X. is in touch with his parents on an occasional basis but does not plan on returning to China. He feels the United States is a country much more receptive to how he needs to express himself.

X. reported transitioning while in Chicago. It did not feel difficult. He explained, "I'd put on men's clothes and shoes, get a short haircut and just be a man. No one really questioned it." X. is of medium height with a slight build and very small breasts. When I asked if he was on testosterone, he answered no. He felt his voice was low enough; his breasts were not visible, and, he explained, Americans have a "terrible time determining the gender of Chinese people anyway." I asked if his name was particularly masculine or feminine; he asked why I wanted to know, stating, "Americans don't understand Chinese names and their gender." I agreed with him but wanted to know about the perception of other Chinese people. He told me his name can be for either a man or a woman.

We returned to his dilemma, whom to date. The lack of a sustained relationship of more than a year with a heterosexual Chinese woman had made him feel disheartened. He dreamed of a wife and children. He believed lesbians were not attracted to him because of his masculine appearance, though a subset of lesbians is attracted to very masculine-identified women. He was correct that some lesbians might not want their identity to change if they were to be perceived as heterosexual for partnering with someone so masculine.

As we talked, the solution became apparent to X.: bisexual women may be attracted to him without a disturbance due to their more fluid sexual identity. He had previously dated only Chinese women because they were the ones to whom he was attracted. He longed for cultural similarity, to remind him of and connect him with the country he left behind. However, after his explorations in therapy, X. decided to consider being more culturally fluid if it would increase his romantic prospects. He would be more flexible and consider dating women who were not Chinese.

X. was the first trans person with whom I have worked who said his transition was "not a problem." Perhaps it had to do with the freedom of not living in a country with the more rigid rules of the Chinese regime. Perhaps it had to do with living and dressing as a boy from early childhood, which may have allowed for an unusually smooth adaptation. X. felt that, because he had excelled in school, he was allowed his "eccentricities."

X. was very concrete in his pursuit of a relationship and eventually began a low dose of testosterone to deepen his voice from its already-solid alto to a high tenor. He began to sport a tie on a regular basis. He reported feeling more masculine and confident in his pursuit of a wife. Every time he dates a new woman, I hear from him. He wants to assess the possibilities that she may be right for him and figure out what he can do to win her over. He is never interested in insight, just a wife. I realize this and hope he finds one soon.

This is not a typical analytic case. X. is perfectly willing to identify in the category that will bring him love, connection, and family. X.'s awareness that he will not be returning to China motivates his deep desire to get married and have a family, things he feels he cannot access in his homeland. Unlike Z., who clings to language because their sense of self is elusive, language has little meaning for X.: "Transman, lesbian, I don't care; I just want a pretty girl to marry." There is no interest in exploring his indifference to a gender identifier; his confidence in what he can offer someone has made his need for labels feel like a redundancy. His desire for a relationship supersedes his need to be seen as male or female; his gender is a matter of convenience (Goldner, 2011; Suchet, 2011). A psychoanalytic approach to his therapy is relevant primarily because it helps identify the dynamics of his subjective experience.

WHAT SHOULD I WEAR?

I worked with an upper-middle-class young Caucasian man, Y., a junior in college, for a handful of sessions. Y. came with a desire that had left him feeling ashamed, excited, and confused. He wanted to dress in women's clothes but not in the high fashion of drag queens or anything as fetishistic as cheerleading outfits or uniforms. He wanted to dress in the soft and flowing material of sundresses and women's tank tops; he wanted to see himself in soft pastels and pretty sandals. He was very clear that he was straight, after having tried a few sexual encounters with boys when he first felt the desire to dress as a female in high school. He reported he did not care for these experiences and had had girlfriends ever since.

I did not have much time with Y., maybe five or six sessions before he would return home for the summer, so I could inquire only so much. His dressing was connected to the tactile feel of women's clothing and a desire to express femininity more complex to do in his male body. He was aware that he was less masculine in appearance and behavior than his father and brother and that this might have contributed to his desire. However, he still wanted to have the experience of dressing as a woman. One day he said, "I don't know what this is even called and I have no idea how to buy women's clothes."

I let Y. know he had transvestite desires that seemed to come from a place of wanting to express femininity that was constricted by societal mores and his relationships to his father and brother. He replied that he could never compete with them and that dressing in women's clothes felt like a way to express how he felt about femininity and himself (Corbett, 2009).

I assured Y. that I would help him find a way to express himself. We talked about the clothes he liked and where he could possibly shop in his somewhat liberal suburban community. I found this amusing, awkward, and intimidating. I do not know much about stereotypical female clothing and am a bit color-blind, so I felt somewhat unprepared for the task. Nonetheless, we moved forward and talked about bras, breast size, and the fact that dresses are not sold by neck size. He was a small, slender guy but sized himself as a small man, not a medium-sized woman, and together we tried to find his female clothing size, leaving accommodations for tight-fitting or loose-fitting clothes. We talked about hiding his genitals and resources that might be equipped with more specifics that I could provide. He had no idea one could buy clothing and return it, as I suggested he do if he wanted to try things on at home.

Y. was grateful at the end of our brief work and skipped out of my office and into the summer sun. I had a fantasy of him returning to treatment showing me a nice wardrobe of pastel sundress and sandals he had purchased. I imagined him satisfying a fantasy that he never dreamed possible, truly feeling female.

Y. did not return after summer break. Nonetheless, I like to think I provided a space and a way for him to think about his gender that gave him the freedom to experience his multi-gendered self.

CONCLUSION

In writing this chapter, my own youthful nostalgia resulted in fond memories, of a tattoo and associations to gender and sexuality from the last quarter of 20th century. I realized that today's hot and bothered LGBTQ youth use different language to define themselves, their genders, and their sexual desires. Heterosexual youth seem to define themselves as they always have, though the language of their sexuality seems to have shifted. They are more aware and accepting of gender and sexual fluidity. There is not the same need for conformity among all, and many seem comfortable with sexual and gender identities that differ from their own. There are new words to learn, and there are words being used in alternative ways that are not merely fads. If these words are foreign and unknown, they should be learned. They are the language used by those born from approximately 1980 forward. As psychoanalysts, we often work with a wealthier and older population. If working with a younger population is not part of your repertoire, then it is even more important to become comfortable moving beyond the gender binary and embracing those who do not experience themselves as either male or female. These younger people will eventually be older, and we can find them in our offices.

This chapter, in the form of its writing as well as in its content, exemplifies the free-association method that is at the core of psychoanalysis. I have tried to trace for you ways in which my clinical work and my evolving ideas about the subjective experience of sexual and gender fluidity have begun to take shape, and continue to evolve, informed by my open and affirmative encounters with my patients' subjective sexuality and gender experience, and have invited you, in the reading, to travel along with me. If, in the process, you have come to appreciate that contemporary psychoanalysis is markedly different from classical psychoanalysis, or, perhaps more accurately, common perceptions of what psychoanalysis is, both within the broader psychology community and in the broader society, then I have made my point. We are part of LGBT psychology and will continue to be.

Will Rogers said, "Get with the times or get left behind." This is an approach to psychology of a group that ponders, that rewrites ideas, and that at times seems rooted in the past and fixated on constructs that are outdated and do not apply to current societal contexts. But psychoanalysis is also a generative wellspring of new ideas. There is a need to move beyond the gender binary, and there is a need to embrace those who do not experience themselves as either male or female. That is what I, and the substantial number of LGBT-affirmative psychoanalytic clinicians, believe and advance.

REFERENCES

American Psychological Association. (2015). Guidelines for psychological practice with transgender and gender nonconforming people. *American Psychologist, 70,* 721–754.

Bieber, I. (1965). Homosexuality—A psychoanalytic study of male homosexuality. *The British Journal of Psychiatry, 111,* 195–196.

Blum, H. (2013). *Psychoanalysis and the arts.* London, UK: Karnac.

Baxter-Moore, N. (2006). "This Is where I belong"—Identity, social class, and the nostalgic Englishness of Ray Davies and the Kinks. *Popular Music and Society*, 2, 145–165.

Corbett, K. (2001). Faggot = loser. *Studies in Gender and Sexuality*, 2, 3–28.

Corbett, K. (2008). Gender now. *Psychoanalytic Dialogues*, 18, 838–856.

Corbett, K. (2009a). *Boyhoods: Rethinking masculinities.* New Haven, CT: Yale University Press.

Corbett, K. (2009b). Boyhood femininity, gender identity disorder, masculine presuppositions, and the anxiety of regulation. *Psychoanalytic Dialogues*, 19, 353–370.

Corbett, K. (2011). Gender regulation. *The Psychoanalytic Quarterly*, 80, 441–459.

Corbett, K. (2013). Shifting sexual cultures, the potential space of online relations, and the promise of psychoanalytic listening. *Journal of the American Psychoanalytic Association*, 61, 25–44.

Corbett, K. (2016). *A murder over a girl: Justice, gender, junior high.* New York, NY: Henry Holt.

D'Ercole, A., & Drescher, J. (2013). *Uncoupling convention: Psychoanalytic approaches to same-sex couples and families.* New York, NY: Routledge.

Dimen, M. (2014). Both given and made: Commentary on Saketopoulou. *Journal of the American Psychoanalytic Associations*, 62, 807–813.

Domenici, T., & Lesser, R. C. (Eds.). (2016). *Disorienting sexuality: Psychoanalytic reappraisals of sexual identities.* New York, NY: Routledge.

Downey, J. I., & Friedman, R. C. (1998). Female homosexuality: Classical psychoanalytic theory reconsidered. *Journal of the American Psychoanalytic Association*, 46, 471–506.

Drescher, J. (1997). From preoedipal to postmodern: Changing psychoanalytic attitudes toward homosexuality. *Gender & Psychoanalysis*, 2, 203–216.

Drescher, J. (2008). A history of homosexuality and organized psychoanalysis. *Journal of the American Academy of Psychoanalysis and Dynamic Psychiatry*, 36, 443–460.

Drescher, J. (2014). *Psychoanalytic therapy and the gay man.* New York, NY: Routledge.

Drescher, J., D'Ercole, A., & Schoenberg, E. (2014). *Psychotherapy with gay men and lesbians: Contemporary dynamic approaches.* New York, NY: Routledge.

Ehrensaft, D. (2009). One pill makes you boy, one pill makes you girl. *International Journal of Applied Psychoanalytic Studies*, 6, 12–24.

Ehrensaft, D. (2011). *Gender born, gender made.* New York, NY: The Experiment.

Ehrensaft, D. (2015). Listening and learning from gender-nonconforming children. *The Psychoanalytic Study of the Child*, 68(1), 28–56.

Freud, S. (1950). A letter from Freud. *American Journal of Psychiatry*, 107, 786–787.

Freud, S. (1997). *Dora: An analysis of a case of hysteria.* New York, NY: Simon and Schuster.

Gay, P. (1998). *Freud: A life for our time.* New York, NY: W.W. Norton & Company.

Gherovici, P. (2011). *Please select your gender: From the invention of hysteria to the democratizing of transgenderism.* New York, NY: Routledge.

Glassgold, J. M., & Iasenza, S. (2000). *Lesbians and psychoanalysis: Revolutions in theory and practice.* New York, NY: Simon and Schuster.

Goldner, V. (2011). Trans: Gender in free fall. *Psychoanalytic Dialogues*, 21, 159–171.

Grossman, G. (2001). Contemporary views of bisexuality in clinical work. *Journal of the American Psychoanalytic Association*, 49(4), 1361–1377.

Hansbury, G. (2011). King-Kong & Goldilocks: Imagining transmasculinities through the trans-trans dyad. *Psychoanalytic Dialogues*, 21, 210–220.

Harris, A. (2011). Gender as strange attractor. *Psychoanalytic Dialogues*, *21*, 230–238.

Hirschfeld, M. (2000). *The homosexuality of men and women*. Amherst, NY: Prometheus Books.

Hoffman, L. G., Hevesi, A. G., Lynch, P. E., Gomes, P. J., Chodorow, N. J., Roughton, R. E., . . . Vaughan, S. (2001). Homophobia: Analysis of a "permissible" prejudice: A public forum of the American Psychoanalytic Association and the American Psychoanalytic Foundation. *Journal of Gay & Lesbian Psychotherapy*, *4*, 5–53.

Iasenza, S. (1995). Platonic pleasures and dangerous desires: Psychoanalytic theory, sex research, and lesbian sexuality. In J. M. Glassgold & S. Iasenza (Eds.), *Lesbians and psychoanalysis: Revolutions in theory and practice* (pp. 345–373). New York, NY: Simon and Schuster.

Iasenza, S. (2002). Beyond "lesbian bed death": The passion and play in lesbian relationships. *Journal of Lesbian Studies*, *6*, 111–120.

Isay, R. A. (1997). *Becoming gay: The journey to self-acceptance*. New York, NY: Macmillan.

Isay, R. A. (2010/1989). *Being homosexual: Gay men and their development*. New York, NY: Vintage.

Layton, L. B. (2000). The psychopolitics of bisexuality. *Studies in Gender and Sexuality*, *1*, 41–60.

Lesser, R., & Schoenberg, E. (2013). *That obscure subject of desire: Freud's female homosexual revisited*. New York, NY: Routledge.

Lewes, K. (2009). *Psychoanalysis and male homosexuality*. Northvale, NJ: Jason Aronson.

Magee, M., & Miller, D. C. (2013). *Lesbian lives: Psychoanalytic narratives old and new*. New York, NY: Routledge.

McLemore, K. (2016, November 10). A minority stress perspective on the trans individuals' experiences with misgendering. *Stigma and Health*. Retrieved 6/25/10'7 from http://psycnet.apa.org/psycinfo/2016-54169-001/

Ovesey, L. (1955). The pseudohomosexual anxiety. *Psychiatry*, *18*, 17–25.

Peterson, M. A., Copps-Smith, E., & Conard, L. A. (2016, August 19). Suicidality, self-harm, and body dissatisfaction in transgender adolescents and emerging adults with gender dysphoria. *Suicide and Life-Threatening Behavior*. Retrieved June 24, 2014. from http://onlinelibrary.wiley.com/doi/10.1111/sltb.12289/full

Rottnek, M. (Ed.). (1999). *Sissies and tomboys: Gender nonconformity and homosexual childhood*. New York, NY: NYU Press.

Roughton, R. E. (2001). Four men in treatment: An evolving perspective on homosexuality and bisexuality, 1965 to 2000. *Journal of the American Psychoanalytic Association*, *49*, 1187–1217. doi:10.1111/sltb.12289

Roughton, R. E. (2002). Rethinking homosexuality: What it teaches us about psychoanalysis. *Journal of the American Psychoanalytic Association*, *50*, 733–763.

Roughton, R. E. (2003). The International Psychoanalytical Association and homosexuality. *Journal of Gay & Lesbian Psychotherapy*, *7*, 189–196.

Saketopoulou, A. (2011). Minding the gap: Intersections between gender, race, class in work with gender variant children. *Psychoanalytic Dialogues*, *21*(2), 192–209.

Saketopoulou, A. (2014). Developmental considerations in treating transsexual patients analytically. *Journal of American Psychoanalytic Association*, *62*(5), 773–806.

Schwartz, A. E. (2013). *Sexual subjects: Lesbians, gender and psychoanalysis*. New York, NY: Routledge.

Socarides, C. W. (1968). A provisional theory of aetiology in male homosexuality: A case of preoedipal origin. *The International Journal of Psycho-Analysis, 49,* 27.

Socarides, C. W. (1978). Transsexualism and psychosis. *International Journal of Psychoanalytic Psychotherapy, 7,* 373–384.

Suchet, M. (2011). Crossing over. *Psychoanalytic Dialogues, 21*(2), 172–191.

Zaretsky, E. (1997). Bisexuality, capitalism and the ambivalent legacy of psychoanalysis. *New Left Review, 223,* 67–89.

5

LGBT Psychology and Ethnic Minority Perspectives: Intersectionality

Barbara C. Wallace and Erik Santacruz

Numerous scholars, researchers, and clinicians have embraced the *intersectionality framework* for conceptualizing ethnic minority issues for LGBT populations. These conceptualizations have encompassed the challenge of negotiating multiple and intersecting stigmatized identities and systems of oppression, given racial, ethnic, gender, socioeconomic, and cultural influences upon diverse LGBT populations (Blosnich, Hanmer, Yu, Matthews, & Kavalieratos, 2016; Cochran & Mays, 2016; Greene & Spivey, 2017; Stall et al., 2016). The necessity of using an intersectionality framework was inferred by the Institute of Medicine (IOM, 2011) when they acknowledged how there are not only discrete populations to consider (i.e., lesbians, gay men, bisexual women, bisexual men, transgender men, transgender women) but also racial, ethnic, and other cultural influences shaping each population's experiences and health. Advancing intersectionality is viewed as consistent with the American Public Health Association's mission of working to improve the public health and achieve equity in health status for all (Bowleg, 2012). Intersectionality is the "critical, unifying, and long overdue theoretical framework for which public health has been waiting" (Bowleg, 2012, p. 1272). The intersectionality framework has also been endorsed by the American Psychological Association (APA, 2012) in their Guidelines for Psychological Practice with Lesbian, Gay, and Bisexual Clients, specifically, with regard to the impact of the social and cultural environment upon identity for diverse LGBT clients.

This chapter will follow the rationale of the APA (2012) in using the intersectionality framework for considering issues of diversity among LGB individuals "who are members of racial, ethnic, and cultural minority groups" who must "negotiate the norms, values, and beliefs regarding homosexuality and bisexuality of both mainstream and minority cultures" (p. 20). Such factors may constitute "a significant source of psychological stress" impacting "health and mental health" (p. 20). Specifically, this chapter will (1) provide an overview of the roots and impact of the concept of intersectionality; (2) discuss how intersectionality operates for those who have multiple stigmatized identities and experience multiple oppressions; (3) review heterosexism, heteronormativity, microaggressions, and violence as key sources of stress for those who are both sexual and racial/ethnic minorities; (4) highlight how intersectionality provides a new paradigm for theory, research, and practice; (5) cover advances in research and resultant recommendations for clinical practice that have followed from the adoption of the intersectionality paradigm; (6) offer cases illustrating the possibilities for those who are both sexual and racial/ethnic minorities displaying psychological vulnerability and psychological resilience—depending on the factors operating in their lives; and, (7) conclude by highlighting the need for an essential focus on training in cultural competence and related topics while offering a guiding definition for the minimum essential competence of cultural humility—while also offering final recommendations for future directions in research.

PART I: OVERVIEW OF THE ROOTS AND IMPACT OF THE CONCEPT OF INTERSECTIONALITY

One may locate the roots of the concept of intersectionality in the work of Black feminists in the Combahee River Collective (Cole, 2009). The Combahee River Collective (1974–1980) was formed in Boston by a group of young African American women and lesbians upon their return from the inaugural public meeting of the National Black Feminist Organization (NBFO) in 1973 in New York City; the group's name has roots in how Harriet Tubman freed 750 slaves in 1864 near the Combahee River in South Carolina (Ford, 2010). In the Combahee River Collective Statement, a key tenet of their manifesto constituted the root of the concept of intersectionality; specifically, the difficulty in separating "race from class from sex oppression," given the lived experience of these oppressions as occurring simultaneously (Cole, 2009, p. 170). According to Smith (2000), one of the cofounders of the Combahee River Collective, their "concept of the simultaneity of oppression" is "one of the most significant ideological contributions of Black feminist thought"; the concept of the simultaneity of oppression acknowledges the combined experience of "race, class, sex, and homophobia" (p. xxxiv). Similarly, others have hailed the concept of intersectionality as a highly significant contribution arising from feminist studies (Cole, 2009, p. 171; McCall, 2005; Risman, 2004). More specifically, the Combahee River Collective's (1977) Statement included the following:

> The most general statement of our politics at the present time would be that we are actively committed to struggling against racial, sexual, heterosexual, and class oppression, and see as our particular task the development of integrated analysis and practice based upon the fact that the major systems of oppression are

interlocking. The synthesis of these oppressions creates the conditions of our lives. As Black women we see Black feminism as the logical political movement to combat the manifold and simultaneous oppressions that all women of color face. (p. 1)

According to Smith (2000), their Black feminist analysis followed from recognition of how "racism and sexism had formed a blueprint" for mistreatment, as "psychic violence and material abuse" and multiple oppression (p. xxxvi). The emergent ideology encourages "political action that will change the very system that has put us down" (p. xxxvii).

Thus, a group of young African American women and lesbians that included Smith boldly pioneered the ideology (Smith, 2000) underpinning what Crenshaw (1995) eventually called *intersectionality*. While advancing critical race theory, Crenshaw (1995) deployed the concept of intersectionality in order to disrupt the tendency to view race and gender as exclusive or separate categories, while urging concurrent considerations of class, sexual orientation, age, and color, and to also locate women of color within overlapping systems of subordination that create their "unique vulnerability" to "converging systems of domination" (p. 367).

PART II: INTERSECTIONALITY FOR MULTIPLE STIGMATIZED IDENTITIES AND MULTIPLE OPPRESSIONS

Intersectionality is "grounded in the lived experience and critique of those at the convergence of multiple stigmatized identities" (Cole, 2009, p. 179). Intersectionality is a concept and framework with the capacity for encompassing the lived experience of those individuals facing multiple oppressions, such as racial/ethnic minorities who are also sexual minorities—whether African American, Latino/a, or other LGBT people of color (Cole, 2009).

The intersectionality framework when used in research permits investigating multiple and intersecting stigmatized identities and systems of oppression (e.g., Gamson & Moon, 2004). Greene and Spivey (2017) acknowledged the *double and triple marginalization* faced by African American sexual minorities—given the complex interaction between multiple identities arising from their race, gender, and sexual orientation. Further, some experience the effects of a *multiple minority or marginalized status*, as social identities in complex dynamic interaction across the life span; for example, there are identities linked to gender, ethno-racial identity, social class, sexual orientation, physical ability, and culture. Living at the "nexus of those identities, and the structural inequities associated with those identities" can leave these individuals "predisposed to psychological vulnerability as well as psychological resilience, depending on other factors in their lives" (p. 186).

Indeed, on the basis of race alone, African Americans have long suffered oppression, as systematic unjust treatment from slavery to the present; this includes structural racism that confers widespread disadvantages, which negatively impact physical and mental health (Kelly & Hudson, 2017). The disadvantages that continue up to the present day include African American same-sex couples and their children experiencing the lowest socioeconomic status (SES) and highest levels of poverty compared to their white counterparts (Badgett, Durso, & Schneebaum, 2013). Further, there are disadvantages that accrue from the stress of anti-Black bias, racial profiling, discriminatory law enforcement practices by police, and microaggressions (Kelly & Hudson, 2017). These microaggressions include daily discrimination in the form of intentional or unintentional racial slights and insults, as described by Pierce (1995) and Sue et al. (2007). The negative consequences that follow for African Americans from exposure to such stressors include internalizing negative stereotypes of themselves and their race (Kelly & Hudson, 2017).

While there is tremendous diversity among Latino/as, a consideration involves how they, too, face minority stress. This follows from Meyer's (2010) expanded considerations within the minority stress theory that encompass LGB people of color and their experiences of social stress. For Latino/as, migration and acculturation experiences are a source of stress, including pressure to adopt their host culture and bicultural stress "relating to the push and pull" between their culture of origin and dominant U.S. culture; and other sources of stress include the oppression and barriers commonly encountered within institutions (Marano & Roman, 2017). Velez, Moradi, and DeBlaere (2015) acknowledged how, for Latino/as with a racial/ethnic *and* sexual minority status, there is a potential unique and interactive relationship between racist and heterosexist external and internalized oppressions and mental health status.

PART III: THE STRESS OF HETEROSEXISM, HETERONORMATIVITY, MICROAGGRESSIONS, AND VIOLENCE

Consistent with Meyer's (2010) expanded conceptualization of the minority stress theory to encompass those who are both sexual and racial/ethnic minorities, it is vital to consider the sources of stress impacting them. As with all sexual minorities, there is *heterosexism* or discrimination against homosexuals—being akin to the homophobia that is a dislike and prejudice against homosexuals and the transphobia that is a dislike and prejudice against transgender people; all of these have roots in a toxic heteronormativity—"the belief that heterosexuality and traditional male and female roles are the only sexual orientation and gender norms" (Greene & Spivey, 2017, p. 182). The social context in the United States dictates a compulsory heteronormativity. Some will deny being a sexual minority, given the potency of the associated stigma, potentially reflecting *internalized homophobia*. As an essential feature of our society, heteronormativity "creates a hostile social environment" for negotiation by all sexual minorities, including everyday discrimination and hostility that range from microaggressions to life-threatening violence (p. 183).

Research has shown that the microaggressions experienced by those who are *both* sexual minorities and racial/ethnic minorities were linked to depression and perceived stress (Balsam, Molina, Beadnell, Simoni, & Walters, 2011). Balsam et al. (2011) concluded that "heterosexism in racial/ethnic minority communities may be particularly harmful to the mental health" of LGBT people of color (p. 15). Their work supported that of others (e.g., Greene, 1994) who suggested there were "higher levels of heterosexism in racial/ethnic minority communities than in society at large" (p. 15).

The reality is that we all live in a heteronormative society in the United States, with the majority of Americans "inevitably" internalizing some homophobia (Meyer, 2015, p. 41). Moreover, the socialization process that inculcates idealization of heterosexuality begins in childhood via countless messages that privilege heterosexuality. This justifies a "focus on changing the social conditions that give rise to homophobia" (p. 41). With regard to the example of the social condition of anti-queer violence, it is important to avoid viewing it "as the product of homophobia," as this serves to reduce the problem to the individual level of a prejudiced individual, thus minimizing the problem. As, as a social condition, anti-queer violence must be viewed as the broader issue regarding how society has encouraged all societal members to think of heterosexuality as superior to homosexuality (p. 41).

There are dangerous and negative consequences that follow from using a narrow, individual-level framework that focuses exclusively on homophobia—specifically, the marginalization of sexual minorities who experience violence based on their race *and* gender identity (Meyer, 2015). Meyer (2015) emphasized how lesbian and transgender women are victims of sexual assault at disproportionately high rates—especially transgender women of color. Transgender women were found to account for the vast majority of all anti-LGBT homicide victims, suggesting especially pernicious antitransgender hate and prejudice. Further, a body of evidence indicates that Black LGBT people, in general, are exposed to police-based violence at higher rates than their white peers. Such evidence has served to reveal how contemporary anti-queer violence has multiple roots, going beyond homophobia and discrimination based on sexual orientation to include inequalities based on race, class, and gender.

For Meyer (2015), a primary focus on homophobia in research "has inadvertently reinforced the interests of LGBT people who are oppressed predominantly based on their sexuality" (p. 43)—meaning, those who are most likely white and middle-class gay men find their interests advanced via a narrow focus on individual-level homophobia. Research must go beyond advancing the interests of the dominant group of white gay men who enjoy race and class privileges. Research, scholarship, and advocacy work must also move beyond homophobia and take "seriously the experiences of LGBT people who are oppressed in multiple ways" on the broader societal level (p. 43).

PART IV: INTERSECTIONALITY AS PROVIDING A NEW PARADIGM FOR THEORY, RESEARCH, AND PRACTICE

The implications following from the concept of intersectionality are far more expansive than merely considering "the lived experience" of those with "multiple stigmatized identities" (Cole, 2009, p. 179). What has emerged is an entire new paradigm for theory and research that provides "new ways of understanding the complex causality that characterizes social phenomena" (p. 179). Intersectionality has justified a multidisciplinary approach and guided research within disciplines as varied as women's studies, Black feminist studies, social epidemiology, sociology, critical race theory, legal studies, and psychology (Bowleg, 2008).

For example, intersectionality was embraced by sociologists in order for research to more concretely specify how sexuality is intertwined with the "cultural creation of other categories of inequality" such as race, class, and gender (Gamson & Moon, 2004, p. 49). Queer theory has argued that sexuality is inevitably intertwined with, and "even sometimes constitutive of, power relations" (p. 49). There are also power differentials to be considered across the categories of "gender, race, ethnicity, sexuality, dis/ability, nationality, citizenship, creed, class, geographical location, age, landedness, employment, health, caste, and so on" (das Nair & Butler, 2012, p. 3).

Psychologists have paralleled the work of sociologists in seeking to increasingly study the "effects of race/ethnicity, gender, social class, and sexuality" in relation to a range of outcomes; these outcomes include health, well-being, personal identity, social identity, and political identity and action (Cole, 2009). This advance has been deemed vital, given psychology's neglect in investigating simply race and gender in tandem—let alone other potential categories of identity, such as class or sexuality (Cole, 2009). Obstacles for psychology focusing simply on race and gender in tandem have included (Cole, 2009) the following: the tendency to simplify models and omit variables or statistically control for membership in other categories outside the variable of interest; the lack of guidelines for empirical work using the intersectionality framework; and, the perception that research within the intersectionality framework would necessitate large samples—deemed prohibitive—while necessitating use of an interdisciplinary team to "triangulate the problem" (Cole, 2009, p. 170). Psychologists should consider and investigate the social categories of gender, race, class, and sexuality *simultaneously*—even as such research involves more complexity (p. 179). Indeed, such research is a necessity in a "stratified society" (p. 179).

Similarly, the field of public health has witnessed calls for research that can encompass greater complexity. Arising from a focus on health disparities, experts have cautioned against the "silver bullet trap"—meaning, the expectation that "a single intervention" is sufficient, while multifaceted approaches are required to address health disparities (IOM, 2012, p. 74). Yet, there is a hesitancy to conduct research on multifaceted interventions on the part of funding institutions and policy makers; this follows from research that involves "going at a problem from multiple directions and on multiple levels" being "necessarily messy and complex" (p. 74). The "silver bullet" approach also constitutes reductionism in research; no one factor is at the root cause of health disparities, as multiple factors are operating (IOM, 2012, p. 77).

Intersectionality is viewed as ideal for investigating complex multidimensional issues, such as the "entrenched health disparities and social inequality among people from multiple historically oppressed and marginalized populations"; this necessitates the application of "novel and complex multidimensional approaches" (Bowleg, 2012, p. 1272). A focus on such complex and multidimensional issues effectively mirrors the experiences of the vulnerable populations disproportionately experiencing adverse health outcomes. Despite a large body of research in pubic health that is focused on such multiply oppressed populations, what is rare is the actual deployment of the intersectionality paradigm. The intersectionality paradigm is absent in theoretical frameworks, methodological designs, statistical analyses, and the interpretations of findings. A fundamental problem rests in public health experts persisting in viewing categories such as women and minorities as mutually exclusive, whereas these categories "intersect" in the "lives of racial/ethnic minority women" (p. 1267). Intersectionality forces attention to socially constructed social identities—while no one "social category or form of social inequality" is considered more salient than another (p. 1271). What is essential is acknowledgment of social identities as "multiple and interlocking" or "intersecting"—as foundation knowledge for "understanding the complexities of health disparities for populations from multiple historically oppressed groups" (p. 1267). There is no need for public health scholars to wait for a methodological revolution wherein the methodological challenges of intersectionality are resolved before proceeding to incorporate intersectionality into theory, research questions, research measures, analyses, and interpretations of data (p. 1269). What is sufficient is an "intersectionality-informed stance" that considers how multiple categories of identity intersect (p. 1269). At a minimum, researchers need to ensure the collection of data on race, ethnicity, age, SES, gender/transgender categories, sexual identity, sexual behavior, and disability status (Bowleg, 2012). However, "simply asking questions about demographic difference or comparing different social groups does not constitute intersectionality research" (Bowleg, 2008, p. 323). The interpretation of findings must occur with use of an interdisciplinary approach that locates the sample historically and socioeconomically (Bowleg, 2012).

Indeed, numerous researchers have called for use of an intersectionality framework in health research with sexual minorities (Cochran & Mays, 2016). This follows from how intersectionality has been deemed ideal for addressing marginalized, vulnerable, and socially disadvantaged populations (Carbado, Crenshaw, Mays, & Tomlinson, 2013) and for use in racial/ethnic health disparities research—toward the elimination of health disparities (Cochran & Mays, 2016; Kilbourne, Switzer, Hyman, Crowley-Matoka, & Fine, 2006; Thomas, Quinn, Butler, Fryer, & Garza, 2011). Yet, use of the intersectionality framework in health disparities research for sexual minorities has just begun (Cochran & Mays, 2016).

As another major strength for research, intersectionality directs attention to the *macrosocial-structural level—or to social determinants of health, social inequality, ecological or ecosocial influences*—where multiple social inequalities, such as racism, heterosexism, sexism, and classism, intersect as systems of privilege and oppression (Bowleg, 2012). Intersectionality privileges "a focus on structural-level factors rather than an exclusive focus on the individual"—which is "likely to facilitate the development of structural-level" interventions (p. 1271). This is consistent with the global movement to focus on social determinants of health (e.g., Marmot, 2005; Marmot & Bell, 2009; Marmot et al., 2008). Even when the intersectionality paradigm focuses on the individual level, the intersection of multiple interlocking identities "at the micro level" is conceptualized as reflecting "multiple and interlocking structural-level inequality at the macro levels of society" (Bowleg, 2012, p. 1267). The result is the provision of a critical unifying public health framework, as a vital "interpretive and analytical framework for reframing how public health scholars conceptualize, investigate, analyze and address disparities and social inequality in health" (p. 1267). This unifying public health framework holds the potential for ending the tendency for public health to examine the systems of privilege and oppression (i.e., racism, sexism, heterosexism) separately and independently (p. 1267). Instead, intersectionality forces attention to a diverse array of intersections among the categories of "race, ethnicity, gender, sexual orientation, SES, disability, and immigration and acculturation status" as well as primary language (p. 1269). The result is a "unifying language and theoretical framework for public health" (p. 1271).

Also, intersectionality examines the health of multiply historically oppressed and marginalized populations "in their own context and from their vantage point[s], rather than their deviation from the norms" established via research with white middle-class subjects (Bowleg, 2012, p. 1269). For example, public health prevention adopted use of the term "MSM" (men who have sex with men) for Blacks and Latinos versus use of the terms "gay" or "bisexual," which did not resonate with them—indicating consideration of the vantage point of these men. As another example, there was a recommended avoidance of references to women negotiating condom use, as this was deemed unrealistic and inapplicable to poor women. There is also the intersectionality paradox where assumptions about what it means to have a high-status identity, paradoxically, do not apply to Black middle-class men and women; for example, this is illustrated via the "disproportionate rates of infant mortality among highly educated Black women and homicide rates among Black middle-class men" (p. 1269).

Thus, intersectionality as a paradigm and framework has served to forge *culturally appropriate* research, practice, and policy. This involves research, practice, and policy arising from the *cultural vantage point* of diverse LGBT clients versus merely extending what has been done with whites or white LGBT clients to people of color or LGBT populations of color.

PART V: ADVANCES IN RESEARCH AND PRACTICE WITHIN THE INTERSECTIONALITY PARADIGM

The use of an intersectionality paradigm has also permitted advances in research, with a growing body of studies conducted with sexual minorities who are also people of color (Sarno, Mohr, Jackson, & Fassinger, 2015). Sarno et al. (2015) recognized as vital the advance in research involving the provision of guidelines for how to integrate intersectionality into research (e.g., Bowleg, 2012; Bowleg, Burkholder, Teti, & Craig, 2009; Cole, 2009).

Advances via Mixed Methods/Qualitative Identity Research with Black Sexual Minorities

As an example of an advance in research, Bowleg et al. (2009) deployed mixed methods within an intersectionality paradigm. They examined the relationship between having a *lesbian or bisexual identity* and having a *racial identity* for Black lesbian and bisexual women (LBW)—with regard to being "out" about one's sexual orientation. Results showed that Black LBW who were "more strongly identified with being lesbian versus Black LBW were more likely than those who were less strongly identified as lesbian or bisexual and/or more strongly identified as Black to be out and talking about their sexual orientation" (p. 162). Bowleg et al. (2009) cautioned that their measures forced women to consider their race versus their sexual orientation identifications as independent, separate, and unidimensional; however, intersectionality theory posits that these identities are interdependent and mutually constitutive. Further, for many Blacks these "social identities intersect inextricably" (p. 163). Also, coming out did not emerge as reflecting the "pinnacle of psychological well-being," given no relationship between coming out, active coping, and self-esteem (p. 163). The Black LBW emerged as quite different from white middle-class LBW— where coming out was associated with lower psychological distress, lower suicidal ideation, greater social support, higher self-esteem and positive affect, and lessened anxiety. Also, the Black LBW emerged as being motivated to "maintain relationships with their families and communities, despite heterosexism, because these relationships provide a buffer against racial oppression"— findings aligning with those of others (p. 163). Also, the negotiation of the complexities of maintaining family and community ties involved covert acknowledgment without overt discussion of their sexual minority status (Bowleg et al., 2009).

By way of another example of advances in qualitative research from an intersectionality framework, Bowleg's (2013) data about Black gay and bisexual men revealed the following: they felt their racial identities were primary while also describing intersectionality for their race, gender, and sexual identities; the men experienced as a particular challenge their encounters with negative stereotypes and with racial microaggressions within both the larger society and white LGBT communities; the men coped with heterosexism in Black communities along with pressure to conform to a masculine gender role; and, they felt their being out conferred upon them personal benefits such as psychological growth, feelings of liberation from traditional gender and heteronormative roles, and the option to explore new experiences (Bowleg, 2013). This resilience for the Black MSM in the Bowleg (2013) research was characterized as a potentially untold story deserving further study via qualitative, mixed methods and quantitative research—especially population-level research, given the power of narratives to illuminate intersectionality-facilitated resilience. Findings echoed the assertion by Greene (1995) that intersectionality may result in highlighting evidence of a greater resilience among Black sexual minority populations and among transgender youth of color (Singh, 2013).

Advances via Quantitative Identity Research with Latino/as

Permitting advances in research with an intersectionality framework, Velez et al. (2015) considered how the multiple oppressions of racism and heterosexism combined to impact mental health, permitting a focus on the interactions of oppressions related to subjects' different identities. Velez et al. (2015) found some support for the combination of external and internalized oppressions being related to greater psychological distress, and only internalized oppressions were "related uniquely to lower psychological well-being" (pp. 25–26). Implications for counseling, therapy, and prevention with sexual minority Latino/a clients covered how it is vital to attend to the client's internalization of racism or heterosexism and links to psychological well-being, and it is also important to attend to their experiences of external racist and heterosexist discrimination with links to psychological distress. Also, sexual minority Latino/a individuals with low internalized oppression experience protection against negative mental health outcomes associated with high external oppression, and, in contrast, those with low internalized racism "may experience a self-esteem cost when external racism is high" (p. 29). This may follow from how high levels of racism are a personal threat and "tax their sense of mastery in resisting that same form of oppression" (p. 29). Clinicians may need to support clients in harnessing their "full repertoire of oppression resisting strategies, including the transfer of coping strategies across identities," as suggested by prior qualitative studies (p. 29).

In this regard, Greene and Spivey (2017) emphasized how, where a client has healthy coping strategies rooted in having one marginalized identity, they can use what they have learned to cope with another marginalized identity—for example, being able to mentally challenge the negative assertions of others about them while maintaining a healthy identity. Further, the cross-oppression transfer of strategies may encompass "confronting prejudice, creating safe spaces or support networks, actively cultivating self-acceptance, and accessing spiritual or religious support"—as per the prior work of others (Velez et al., 2015, p. 28). For example, African American MSM are likely to share greater affinity with church members—in terms of their attitudes, beliefs, and norms—than with white members of the LGBT community (Meyer, 2001).

Advances in Quantitative Research with Diverse MSM

Fields et al. (2013) found that, within a sample of HIV-positive African American men, about half had experienced any interpersonal trauma (e.g., sexual assault, child sexual assault, other physical assault). Of note, about half of those with such a trauma history had experienced at least one nondiscrimination-related traumatic experience in their lifetimes—whether related to their being gay, African American, or HIV-positive. The experience of any discrimination-related interpersonal trauma was significantly associated with engagement in unprotected anal intercourse (UAI) with any male partner and with an HIV-positive male partner—thereby being engaged in greater risk-taking. On the other hand, the experience of interpersonal trauma that was *not* associated with discrimination was not significantly associated with engagement in UAI. The findings underscored how future researchers need to separate out discrimination-related trauma from nondiscrimination-related trauma. The results were viewed as being consistent with the minority stress model; "sexual minority individuals who experienced discrimination-related stressors showed greater adverse" mental health outcomes, ranging from symptoms of depression to suicidal ideation, in comparison to sexual minorities without the experience of discrimination-related stressors (p. 878). Fields et al. (2013) viewed their findings as being aligned with those of others who suggested engagement in increased sexual risk behavior was likely a maladaptive coping strategy, or an avoidance or escape strategy, in response to the stressors of discrimination. Providers were urged to consider the potential negative impact of discrimination-related trauma on health (Fields et al., 2013).

Other research conducted with a sample of predominantly racial/ethnic minority young MSM (YMSM) aged 18–19 (94.7% Hispanic and Black non-Hispanics) underscored the importance of paying attention to the disadvantages associated with class that exacerbate risks associated with racial/ethnic minority status (Halkitis & Figueroa, 2013). Research findings identified how low SES and being foreign born/having an immigrant status were associated with greater engagement in unprotected risky sexual behavior and, therefore, with the risk of HIV transmission among YMSM. SES and foreign-born status were deemed to be likely parts of a causal path associated with higher levels of psychosocial burdens, as per the perspective of syndemics theory. Halkitis and Figueroa (2013) concluded that comprehensive and holistic approaches to HIV prevention need to focus upon the "interactive effects of race, culture, sexual orientation, SES and foreign-born status" that increase HIV risk (p. 188). Such factors must be considered simultaneously when developing YMSM prevention programming and policies for the protection of YMSM (Halkitis & Figueroa, 2013).

Advances in Mental Health Research with Racial/Ethnic Sexual Minorities

Regarding mental health approaches to racial/ethnic sexual minorities, it must be acknowledged how "LGB people of color can have positive racial/ethnic and LGB identities and form strong affiliations to both communities" (Meyer, 2010, p. 443). The focus on those who are both racial/ethnic and sexual minorities has raised essential questions regarding "risk versus resilience," including whether a double minority status has translated into facing greater risk, as the double jeopardy hypothesis, encompassing exposure to both homophobia and racism (p. 443) suggests, and whether a double minority status has led to higher levels of resilience, as the resilience hypothesis suggests. These are core questions about social stress as a potential cause of mental disorders (p. 443). The resilience hypothesis posits that "in part because of their experiences with racism prior to coming out, Black LGB individuals are inoculated against the effects of stress related to homophobia and may actually fare better than LGB Whites" (p. 447). As a result, Black LGB individuals may have a greater capacity to cope with minority stress in comparison to LGB whites.

Regarding the resilience hypothesis, some data have been supportive, while more research is needed (Meyer, 2010; Moradi, DeBlaere, & Huang, 2010). Other data do not support the minority stress hypothesis and are contrary to the double jeopardy hypothesis when examining Black and Latino/a LGB persons. The minority stress hypothesis is supported by a body of research, including that from a meta-analysis of large-scale studies showing that "as predicted, LGB individuals had more mood, anxiety, and substance-use disorder than heterosexuals" (Meyer, 2010, p. 448). Contrary to this well-established finding, LGB people of color *do not* evidence more mental disorders in comparison to LGB whites. This same pattern holds for Blacks in the U.S population in general, with Blacks *not* showing a higher prevalence of psychiatric disorders when compared to whites in the general population (Meyer, 2010).

An emergent question for which there is as yet no answer follows from such data: "If, as we know, Blacks are exposed to greater stress, and if, as we believe, stress causes mental health problems," then the logical question to ask next is this, as per Meyer (2010): Why do Blacks in the United States, both LGB and heterosexual, not have a "resultant excess in mental disorders in comparison to White?" (p. 449). A possible answer is that resilience among Black populations reduces their risk, while future research is needed that involves "greater specification of how resilience may be implicated in the causal relationship of stress and mental health" (p. 449). Complicating future research is how resilience "cannot be directly observed" (p. 449). Meanwhile, a core resilience argument is that, because Blacks have good coping skills, including "not only personal but also community-wide coping resources," then their "coping overcomes the potential negative effects of stress" (p. 450). Future research that explores and resolves these questions and issues has the potential to address fundamental "inconsistencies in social stress theory" that arise from the findings of Black resilience (p. 450). Future research needs to also consider the role of group-level resources such as *affirmative social support* and *access to role models* that may serve to counter societal stressors of prejudice and discrimination.

Evidence of resilience for Black sexual minorities as well as differences from White sexual minorities has arisen from qualitative data (Meyer, 2010). Whereas White have been shown to view racial/ethnic identity as less important than sexual identity, Meyer (2010) found no evidence that "LGB identity collides with Black identity and with an affiliation with the Black community and culture" (p. 446). More specifically, Meyer (2010) found the following:

> ... Our interviewers asked probing questions to get to the purported identity clash, but time and again they were rebuffed by the respondents. More often than not, men and women, bisexual- and gay/lesbian-identified, and younger and older respondents rejected the idea of identity conflict. They did not deny the stress of homophobia, especially homophobia in the Black church, but they clearly differentiated between the external sources of stress and internal identity cohesiveness. Our Black respondents perceived rejection and homophobia in their social environments: family, friends, religious figures, and the community at large. But that rejection did not lead them to doubt their own identities. Sometimes they chose to deal with homophobia by swallowing frustration or anger to protect relationships with family and churches; at other times they chose to move to more accepting churches. Some chose to stand up and demand acceptance in their families and communities, and others contemplated doing so. (p. 446)

Meyer (2010) offered a compelling conclusion that is suggestive of great resilience among those who have both a racial/ethnic and sexual minority identities:

"LGB people of color are at the intersection of identities related to race/ethnicity and sexual orientation, and this intersection creates a new unified identity that cannot be split" (p. 451). This reflects tremendous progress away from the now antiquated question, "Are you Black first or are you queer?" (p. 451).

Thus, the use of an intersectionality framework has served to advance research in several ways. First, it has permitted advances in the area of substantiating the *resilience* characterizing Blacks who are sexual minorities as well as potentially other sexual minority people of color. Second, it has permitted the advance of documenting the positive attribute of a *unified identity* rooted in both a sexual minority and racial/ethnic identity. Third, it permits appreciation of the *good coping skills* used by Blacks who are sexual minorities as well as potentially other sexual minority people of color. In this manner, the chapter has come full circle by initially asserting how the intersectionality framework was needed to encompass the simultaneity of multiple oppressions suffered by sexual minority people of color and then reviewing the associated experience of multiple structural inequities or multiple oppressions for sexual minority people of color, and then, subsequently, in moving toward closing, the chapter has highlighted the multiple positive attributes that may emerge for sexual minority people of color —including *resilience, a unified identity, and good coping skills.* The latter development, as outlined in this chapter, underscores the value in what Greene and Spivey (2017) were noted as asserting early in the chapter—that is, experiences of living at the nexus of multiple identities and multiple systems of oppression, as captured by the concept of intersectionality, can leave sexual minority individuals with "psychological vulnerability as well as psychological resilience, depending on other factors in their lives" (p. 186).

PART VI: ILLUSTRATIVE CASES HIGHLIGHTING KEY CONCEPTS

Several cases will be presented in this section in order to illustrate both the possibilities of psychological vulnerability and psychological resilience (i.e., Greene & Spivey, 2017) and the kind of factors operating in the lives of sexual minorities of color—as brought to light through this chapter's discussion of intersectionality. Key concepts covered in this chapter are *italicized* in the cases next, serving to illustrate central aspects of intersectionality and the varied factors that may be operating in the lives of clients who are both sexual minorities and racial/ethnic minorities.

John and David are in a long-term relationship. African American professional men ages 36 and 38, respectively, they were "legally married two years ago." They entered couple's counseling following David's disclosure of an extramarital affair. The couple felt as though they had "little to no social support" for their marriage and perceived feelings of envy on the part of some friends. David's infidelity emerged as an act of sabotaging their marriage while acting out his "often feeling un-deserving of his luck" in having John as a life partner. David's *psychological vulnerability* and behavior of sabotaging his marriage emerged as rooted in a *lack of affirmative social support* for their marriage; a *lack of access to role models* to counter feeling undeserving of his life partner—factors linked to *both racist and heterosexist external and internalized oppressions*, and, the historical delegitimizing within society of any kind of long-term loving sexual relationships among Black men. This followed from a widespread *toxic heteronormativity* in society, which David and John regularly encountered—reflecting the role of *factors operating on the macrosocial-structural level as social determinants*. Also common were experiences of *microaggressions* from both homophobic and heterosexist Black family/community/church members and racist Whites in the LGBT community. The focus in counseling was on finding new sources of *affirmative social support* for their marriage while fostering a legitimizing of their love as "valid and real"—as their heartfelt desire. This included exposure to new *role models* for stable gay marriage upon their joining a "gay-affirming" church. Positive outcomes included both partners evidencing over time a greater *psychological resilience* and the deployment of more *adaptive coping skills* for dealing with the ongoing stress of *heteronormativity* and *microaggressions*. Couple's counseling also successfully focused on rebuilding trust within their relationship, given David's infidelity.

Rosa, as a 22-year-old Afro-Latina Dominican lesbian, is dating a 21-year-old Puerto Rican lesbian named **Anna**. Both attend a local college where they are active in the Gay-Straight Alliance that was established on campus in the aftermath of daily *microaggressions* and incidents of *anti-LGBT hate and discrimination* on campus. Recent vandalism on campus included hate messages, such as "*God hates gays; Kill Faggots; The only good Faggot is a dead one; Die Dykes*; and, *Get a Dick Dyke*." Rosa sought out counseling at the college health center, given her increasing feelings of depression. Regarding her *perceived stress and depression*, Rosa discussed in counseling the impact of her being a lesbian and also having dark brown skin color. Rosa was facing the *triple jeopardy* and *stress of multiple oppressions* as a woman, lesbian, and Afro-Latina. She reported "unfair grading" practices and classroom humiliation by a white male professor as indicative of *racism*. Also, after Rosa took her girlfriend, Anna, home to meet her family, essentially coming out, Rosa faced rejection; this was reflective of the *high levels of heterosexism* in her Afro-Latino family and church community. Rosa's counseling sessions focused on her acquisition of *coping skills* in response to *multiple oppressions*—that is, *the stress of heterosexism* in her family and church community; *racism* in the classroom; and *anti-LGBT hate and discrimination* on campus. Thus, *macrosocial-structural factors, or multiple social determinants* played a role in Rosa's *psychological vulnerability to depression*.

Jo, born Jocelyn, is a 38-year-old African American transgender man in a committed long-term relationship with **Sheila**. Jo self-identifies as "a trans man." He has elected to not take any testosterone steroids, "not pack a penis," and not pursue surgery. Jo works in construction and has been routinely harassed by coworkers due to their *transphobia*. He has felt the need to repeatedly leave construction sites in search of those with more welcoming supervisors and coworkers—"I just walked away." As a result, Jo has also coped with financial strain—suggesting his *triple* *jeopardy from being a sexual minority, racial minority, and having a low SES.* Due to a pervasive *heteronormativity*, Jo has experienced tremendous *prejudice and discrimination* in all societal contexts—being called "bulldagger, cross dresser, and a man" with hate and disdain. As an adolescent, Jo experienced *anti-queer, violence* on a regular basis as well as *police violence* that reflected a combination of *racial profiling, discriminatory law enforcement practices by police,* as well as *transphobia and hate.* The reality that Black LGBT people, in general, are victims of *police-based violence* at higher rates than their White counterparts was the Jo's lived experience across most of his life span. Once during *police violence,* Jo suffered a severe beating that injured his face and one of his eyes. Thereafter, Jo began coping with near-daily experiences of *microaggressions, transphobia, and hate* by telling himself to "remain calm and walk away." Jo also accomplished full self-acceptance of his uniqueness within *a unified identity as a sexual and racial minority*—as evidence of an impressive *resilience.* By age 30, Jo was able to enter into a stable loving relationship with a femme lesbian, Sheila (one year younger than Jo), who provided tremendous *social support.* Sheila and Jo were referred for couple's counseling by the physician Sheila sought out, given plans for Sheila to become pregnant. The physician sought to further enhance their *social support,* given likely stress from widespread societal *heteronormativity* and their decision to pursue a pregnancy.

Hector is a 19-year-old Mexican American gay man, entered therapy at an urban adolescent clinic, given a recent diagnosis of HIV. The year before his HIV diagnosis, Hector had moved into an urban, gay-friendly environment, leaving his family in a Southern border state. Hector had entered the United States at age eight, as one of four children born to migrant farm workers. His history of a *lower SES, foreign-born/immigrant status, higher levels of psychosocial burdens,* and entrance into the unfamiliar urban bar scene combined in conferring upon Hector *the risk of greater engagement in unprotected sex—as per syndemics theory.* These factors created a general *psychological vulnerability,* including the emergence of a serious depression upon receipt of his HIV diagnosis. Thus, Hector was referred to the YMSM group in the clinic. Hector felt "different" within the group while struggling with the *push and pull between his culture of origin and the dominant U.S. culture.* Where most of the White YMSM in the group reported they "gave up family and church" to come out, Hector felt a deep enduring "connection" to both his family and church. He felt the group was "not a safe space" for him to talk about these enduring connections or related concerns. Though he never discussed his sexual orientation with his family, Hector felt his family "knew"—while they had an unspoken "understanding to never talk about it openly." There was also an incident where a White male from the group approached him outside of the clinic, saying, "I want some meat fresh off the boat," as a derogatory reference to his immigrant status while coming on to him sexually. Hector felt deeply offended by this painful *microaggression.* When Hector shared this experience with the YMSM group leader, the leader responded with laughter and a comment about Hector being oversensitive. This was experienced as yet another *microaggression.* When Hector told his primary care physician at the clinic that the YMSM group was "not working out for," him the physician said Hector was being lazy and needed to engage in more activities like the group. The physician's *negative stereotyping* of Hector as lazy was experienced as yet another *microaggression.* Hector began to feel even more *depressed* *from the stress* of attending the clinic. He left the clinic due to the *stress of oppression and barriers to full participation*, including the experience of multiple *microaggressions* and the *clash of cultural/family/church values* within the YMSM group. He went online and found a Latino/a psychologist with whom he was able to open up about his *"traumatic experiences of discrimination* at that clinic." Meanwhile, Hector's discrimination-related traumatic experiences had actually served to exacerbate his depression and contributed to a relapse to UAI with other YMSM participating in the bar scene. This engagement in risky sex appeared to be a *maladaptive coping strategy, or an avoidance or escape strategy, in response to the stressors of discrimination.*

The goal in presenting these cases was to provide practitioners with concrete examples of the potential range of diverse LGBT clients whose experiences are best understood utilizing the intersectionality framework. The intent has been to thereby empower practitioners to draw upon the new base of knowledge advanced in this chapter in their actual clinical practice. This base of knowledge, as shown via the cases, includes recognition of dual processes worthy of emphasis, as follows: (1) there were intersections among clients' multiple interlocking identities at the micro level, and (2) the clients' experiences reflected multiple and interlocking structural-level inequalities or multiple oppressions that negatively impacted them, which were operating at the macro levels of society, as social determinants of their physical and mental health (i.e., as per Bowleg, 2012).

PART VII: CONCLUSION

This chapter has covered key issues for LGBT ethnic minorities using a focus on intersectionality—including the roots of the concept, the impact of the broader intersectionality framework, the influence of intersectionality in advancing research, and the applicability of intersectionality to clinical practice with sexual and racial/ethnic minorities. However, there are serious limitations to this chapter that follow from the omission of training guidelines for varied professionals with regard to the acquisition of cultural competence, multicultural competence, and cultural humility. A focus on increasing cultural competence (Butler et al., 2016) and cultural humility (Hub & Staff, 2016) is essential for work with sexual and racial/ethnic minorities. Indeed, in another context (Wallace, 2016), numerous topics were identified as vital for the training of varied professionals as well as for their clients, as follows: how to acquire essential racial-cultural skills or practical coping skills for coping in encounters with those presenting diversity or difference; how to execute coping responses to the stress of perceiving racism and oppression; how to recognize, overcome, and emerge free from any personal engagement in racism, oppression, or White privilege while pursuing positive identity development; and, how to recognize, respond to, and cope with microaggressions in order to avoid a negative impact on health and psychological well-being (Wallace, 2016). Such training is beyond the scope of this chapter, while deemed absolutely vital for scholars, researchers, practitioners, and advocates working with or on behalf of those presenting both a sexual orientation and racial/ethnic minority status.

However, this chapter made an important relevant assertion earlier in the discussion: the intersectionality framework has actually served to forge *culturally appropriate* research, practice, and policy. This has followed from how—within the intersectionality framework—research, practice, and policy arise directly from considerations of the *cultural vantage point* of diverse LGBT clients. This is consistent with the essence of *cultural humility*, as expressed by others (i.e., Tervalon & Murray-Garcia, 1998), while constituting a minimum essential competence for professionals codified within an original definition introduced in this chapter, below.

In this chapter, *cultural humility* may be defined as a characteristic of those professionals (i.e., researchers, clinicians, advocates) who are able to thoroughly inquire into and ascertain the cultural vantage point of those who are "diverse and different" within our society. Such professionals ascertain this cultural vantage point, given how they respectively pose questions and then genuinely listen to clients as they offer their responses to questions. Professionals are able to learn the nature of a client's experiences and what makes them unique as a human being, as a consequence of genuine listening. The professional is not arrogant, does not act superior to the client, and does not convey an attitude that they "know everything." Instead, the provider exudes a genuine humility while being comfortable in admitting that they need to learn about the client's culture and cultural experiences *from* the individual client; assumptions and judgments about the client's culture and cultural experiences are not made by the professional. Instead, the professional's cultural humility allows them to be respectful, accepting, and open to learning about an individual client's experience of their culture. This includes being open to learning about how the client's cultural experiences combine with other experiences (e.g., gender, SES, disability, immigration and acculturation status, primary language) to make them a unique human being. Thus, the professional with cultural humility does not enter into an interpersonal encounter with a set of assumptions about the client, does not engage in cultural stereotyping, and does not make any negative judgments about the individual client or their culture. When a client is interacting with a professional who has cultural humility, the client feels free to express or not express information about themselves and their culture. However, the client consistently perceives the professional as open, accepting, and not making any judgments about them, regardless of what they choose to share (or not share) about their culture and cultural experiences.

In closing, recommendations for future directions in research with ethnic minority LGBT populations, including from the intersectionality framework, should be considered. While it has been asserted that racial/ethnic minorities have been largely invisible in the psychological research literature, and we need to learn more about sexual minorities of color, what must be rectified is the deficit in knowledge with regard to those groups that are other than Black or Latino (Meyer, 2010). For example, Chou, Asnaani, and Hoffman (2011) documented the experience of perceiving racial discrimination for the three major ethnic groups in the United States, including Asian Americans along with Hispanics and African Americans. Chou et al. (2011) documented significant associations between perceived racial discrimination for all three ethnic groups with varied psychopathology—that is, major depressive disorder, panic disorder, agoraphobia, substance use disorders, and posttraumatic stress disorder—as racism can be traumatic. Thus, future research with sexual minorities needs to follow suit in expanding beyond a primary focus on Blacks and Latino/as—while this chapter reflects the limitation of such a primary focus.

REFERENCES

American Psychological Association (APA). (2012). Guidelines for psychological practice with lesbian, gay, and bisexual clients. *American Psychologist, 67*(1), 10–42.

Badgett, M. V., Durso, L. E., & Schneebaum, A. (2013). *New patterns of poverty in the lesbian, gay, and bisexual community.* Los Angeles, CA: eScholarship. University of California, The Williams Institute, UCLA School of Law. Retrieved from http://williamsinstitute.law.ucla.edu/wp-content/uploads/LGB-Poverty-Update-Jun-2013.pdf

Balsam, K. F., Molina, Y., Beadnell, B., Simoni, J., & Walters, K. (2011). Measuring multiple minority stress: The LGBT people of color microaggressions scale. *Cultural Diversity and Ethnic Minority Psychology, 17*(2), 163.

Blosnich, J. R., Hanmer, J., Yu, L., Matthews, D. D., & Kavalieratos, D. (2016). Health care use, health behaviors, and medical conditions among individuals in same-sex and opposite-sex partnerships: A cross-sectional observational analysis of the Medical Expenditures Panel Survey (MEPS), 2003–2011. *Medical Care, 54*(6), 547–554.

Blosnich, J. R., Marsiglio, M. C., Gao, S., Gordon, A. J., Shipherd, J. C., Kauth, M., Brown, G.R., & Fine, M. J. (2016). Mental health of transgender veterans in US states with and without discrimination and hate crime legal protection. *American journal of public health, 106*(3), 534–540.

Bowleg, L. (2008). When Black+ lesbian+ woman≠ Black lesbian woman: The methodological challenges of qualitative and quantitative intersectionality research. *Sex Roles, 59*(5–6), 312–325.

Bowleg, L. (2012). The problem with the phrase "women and minorities": Intersectionality, an important theoretical framework for public health. *American Journal of Public Health, 102*(7), 1267–1273.

Bowleg, L. (2013). "Once you've blended the cake, you can't take the parts back to the main ingredients": Exploring how Black gay and bisexual men describe and experience intersectionality. *Sex Roles, 68*(11), 754–767.

Bowleg, L., Burkholder, G., Teti, M., & Craig, M. L. (2009). The complexities of outness: Psychosocial predictors of coming out to others among Black lesbian and bisexual women. *Journal of LGBT Health Research, 4*(4), 153–166.

Butler, M., McCreedy, E., Schwer, N., Burgess, D., Call, K., Przedworski, J., . . . Kane, R. L. (2016). *Improving cultural competence to reduce health disparities.* Comparative Effectiveness Review No. 170. (Prepared by the Minnesota Evidence-based Practice Center under Contract No. 290-2012-00016-I.) AHRQ Publication No. 16- EHC006-EF. Rockville, MD: Agency for Healthcare Research and Quality.

Carbado, D. W., Crenshaw, K. W., Mays, V. M., & Tomlinson, B. (2013). Intersectionality. *Du Bois Review: Social Science Research on Race, 10*(2), 303–312.

Chou, T., Asnaani, A., & Hoffman, S. G. (2011). Perception of racial discrimination and psychopathology across three U.S. ethnic groups. *Cultural Diversity and Ethnic Minority Psychology, 18*(1), 74–81.

Cochran, S. D., & Mays, V. M. (2016). A strategic approach to eliminating sexual orientation-related health disparities. *American Journal of Public Health, 106*(9), e4.

Cole, E. R. (2009). Intersectionality and research in psychology. *American Psychologist, 64*(3), 170–180.

Combahee River Collective. (1977). The Combahee River Collective Statement. *Black feminist organizing in the seventies and eighties.* Retrieved from http://americanstudies. yale.edu/sites/default/files/files/Keyword%20Coalition_Readings.pdf

Crenshaw, K. W. (1995). Mapping the margins: Intersectionality, identity politics, and violence against women of color. In K. W. Crenshaw, N. Gotanda, G. Peller, & K. Thomas (Eds.), *Critical race theory: The key writing that formed the movement* (pp. 357–383). New York, NY: The New Press.

das Nair, R., & Butler, C. (2012). Introduction. In R. das Nair & C. Butler (Eds.), *Intersectionality, sexuality and psychological therapies: Working with lesbian, gay and bisexual diversity* (pp. 1–8). Hoboken, NJ: John Wiley & Sons.

Fields, E. L., Bogart, L. M., Galvan, F. H., Wagner, G. J., Klein, D. J., & Schuster, M. A. (2013). Association of discrimination-related trauma with sexual risk among HIV-positive African American men who have sex with men. *American Journal of Public Health, 103*(5), 875–880.

Ford, L. E. (2010). *Encyclopedia of women and American politics.* New York, NY: Infobase Publishing.

Gamson, J., & Moon, D. (2004). The sociology of sexualities: Queer and beyond. *Annual Review of Sociology, 30,* 47–64.

Greene, B. (1994). Lesbian and gay sexual orientations: Implications for clinical training, practice, and research. In B. Greene & G. Herek (Eds.), *Psychological perspectives on lesbian and gay issues: Vol. 1. Lesbian and gay psychology: Theory, research, and clinical applications* (pp. 1–24). Thousand Oaks, CA: Sage.

Greene, B. E. (1995). Addressing racism, sexism, and heterosexism in psychoanalytic psychotherapy. In J. M. Glassgold & S. Iasenza (Eds.), *Lesbians and psychoanalysis: Revolutions in theory and practice* (pp. 145–159). New York, NY: The Free Press.

Greene, B., & Spivey, P. (2017). Sexual minority couples and families: Clinical considerations. In S. Kelly (Ed.), *Diversity in couple and family therapy: Ethnicities, sexualities, and socioeconomics* (pp. 181–201). Santa Barbara, CA: Praeger/ABC-CLIO, LLC.

Halkitis, P. N., & Figueroa, R. P. (2013). Sociodemographic characteristics explain differences in unprotected sexual behavior among young HIV-negative gay, bisexual, and other YMSM in New York City. *AIDS Patient Care and STDs, 27*(3), 181–190.

Hub, R. R., & Staff, M. (2016). Cultural humility with lesbian, gay, bisexual, and transgender populations: A novel curriculum in LGBT health for clinical medical students. *MedPortal Publications*, 9. Retrieved from http://doi.org/10.15766/mep_2374-8265.9542

Institute of Medicine (IOM). (2011). *The health of lesbian, gay, bisexual, and transgender people: Building a foundation for better understanding.* Washington, DC: The National Academies Press.

Institute of Medicine (IOM). (2012). *How far have we come in reducing health disparities? Progress since 2000—Workshop summary.* Institute of Medicine of the National Academies. Washington, DC: The National Academies Press.

Kelly, S., & Hudson, B. N. (2017). African American couples and families and the context of structural oppression. In S. Kelly (Ed.), *Diversity in couple and family therapy: Ethnicities, sexualities, and socioeconomics* (pp. 3–32). Santa Barbara, CA: Praeger/ABC-CLIO, LLC.

Kilbourne, A. M., Switzer, G., Hyman, K., Crowley-Matoka, M., & Fine, M. J. (2006). Advancing health disparities research within the health care system: A conceptual frame-work. *American Journal of Public Health, 96*(12), 2113–2121.

Marano, M. R., & Roman, E. (2017). Latino couples and families. In S. Kelly (Ed.), *Diversity in couple and family therapy: Ethnicities, sexualities, and socioeconomics* (pp. 63–90). Santa Barbara, CA: Praeger/ABC-CLIO, LLC.

Marmot, M. (2005). Social determinants of health inequalities. *The Lancet, 365*(9464), 1099–1104.

Marmot, M. G., & Bell, R. (2009). Action on health disparities in the United States: Commission on social determinants of health. *Journal of the American Medical Association, 301*(11), 1169–1171.

Marmot, M., Friel, S., Bell, R., Houweling, T. A., Taylor, S., & Commission on Social Determinants of Health. (2008). Closing the gap in a generation: Health equity through action on the social determinants of health. *The Lancet, 372*(9650), 1661–1669.

McCall, L. (2005). The complexity of intersectionality. *Signs, 30*(3), 1771–1800.

Meyer, D. (2015). *Violence against queer people: Race, class, gender, and the persistence of anti-LGBT discrimination.* New Brunswick, NJ: Rutgers University Press.

Meyer, I. H. (2001). Why lesbian, gay, bisexual, and transgender public health? *American Journal of Public Health, 91*, 856–859.

Meyer, I. H. (2003). Prejudice, social stress, and mental health in lesbian, gay, and bisexual populations: Conceptual issues and research evidence. *Psychological Bulletin, 129*(5), 674–697.

Meyer, I. H. (2010). Identity, stress, and resilience in lesbians, gay men, and bisexuals of color. *The Counseling Psychologist, 38*(3), 442–454.

Meyer, I. H. (2013). Prejudice, social stress, and mental health in lesbian, gay, and bisexual populations: Conceptual issues and research evidence. *Psychology of Sexual Orientation and Gender Diversity, 1*(S), 3–26.

Moradi, B., DeBlaere, C., & Huang, Y. P. (2010). Centralizing the experiences of LGB people of color in counseling psychology 1Ψ7. *The Counseling Psychologist, 38*(3), 322–330.

Pierce, C. (1995). Stress analogs of racism and sexism: Terrorism, torture, and disaster. In C. V. Willie, P. P. Reiker, B. M. Kramer, & B. S. Brown (Eds.), *Mental health, racism, and sexism* (pp. 277–293). New York, NY: Routledge.

Risman, B. J. (2004). Gender as a social structure: Theory wrestling with activism. *Gender & Society, 18*(4), 429–450.

Sarno, E. L., Mohr, J. J., Jackson, S. D., & Fassinger, R. E. (2015). When identities collide: Conflicts in allegiances among LGB people of color. *Cultural Diversity and Ethnic Minority Psychology, 21*(4), 550–559.

Singh, A. A. (2013). Transgender youth of color and resilience: Negotiating oppression and finding support. *Sex Roles, 68*(11–12), 690–702.

Smith, B. (2000). Introduction. In B. Smith (Ed.), *Home girls: A black feminist anthology* (pp. xxi–lix). New Brunswick, NJ: Rutgers University Press.

Stall, R., Matthews, D. D., Friedman, M. R., Kinsky, S., Egan, J. E., Coulter, R. W., . . . Markovic, N. (2016). The continuing development of health disparities research on lesbian, gay, bisexual, and transgender individuals. *American Journal of Public Health, 106*(5), 787–789.

Sue, D. W., Capodilupo, C. M., Torino, G. C., Bucceri, J. M., Holder, A., Nadal, K. L., & Esquilin, M. (2007). Racial microaggressions in everyday life: Implications for clinical practice. *American Psychologist, 62*(4), 271–286.

Tervalon, M., & Murray-Garcia, J. (1998). Cultural humility versus cultural competence: A critical distinction in defining physician training outcomes in multicultural education. *Journal of Health Care for the Poor and Underserved, 9*(2), 117–125.

Thomas, S. B., Quinn, S. C., Butler, J., Fryer, C. S., & Garza, M. A. (2011). Toward a fourth generation of disparities research to achieve health equity. *Annual Review of Public Health, 32*, 399–416.

Velez, B. L., Moradi, B., & DeBlaere, C. (2015). Multiple oppressions and the mental health of sexual minority Latina/o individuals. *The Counseling Psychologist, 43*(1), 7–38.

Wallace, B. C. (2017). Ethnic minority perspectives on heath and psychological well-being. In T. Copper & M. Skewes (Eds.), *Social issues in living color: Challenges and solutions from the perspective of ethnic minority psychology* (Vol. 3, pp. 1–30). Santa Barbara, CA: Praeger.

6

Intersectional Feminism and LGBTIQQA+ Psychology: Understanding Our Present by Exploring Our Past

Deanna N. Cor and Christian D. Chan

For the past several decades, research and larger societal conversations have focused on the experiences and needs of individuals holding minority sexual and gender identities (Meyer, 2010, 2014, 2016). The United States has seen significant paradigm shifts in recent years that suggest increased equality for the entire lesbian, gay, bisexual, transgender, intersex, queer, questioning, agender, and asexual (LGBTIQQA+) community as a whole. However, there exist a large number of people within this population who have not reaped the benefits of these changes. Among this group, discrimination has come from both within and outside of the community. Often, White, gay, cisgender males have the loudest and most readily listened to voices as evidenced by the push for marriage equality at the expense of rights for trans folks. This reality relegates cisgender LGB women and gender-nonbinary individuals to a silent and frequently invisible existence—oppressed within their own community.

It is likely that there is another force within this population impacting the nuances of this movement toward equality for the entire community. The purpose of this chapter is to present the audience with an expansion beyond unidimensional perspectives while developing a working knowledge of the historical traditions of the LGBTIQQA+ political movement, feminism, and intersectionality. Feminism has played a crucial and inclusive role in the LGBTIQQA+ movement. As a result, this chapter seeks to provide relevant information regarding the ways the three waves of feminism, and more recently intersectional feminism, have impacted the individual and collective mental health of the LGBTIQQA+ community. The chapter will begin with an overview of feminist history, theory, and clinical application in the mental health professions. From there, the authors will explore intersectionality theory and its connection to feminism as a means to understanding the multitude of identities and experiences of LGBTIQQA+ individuals. It is also vital to explore discrimination within this community and its relevance to feminist theory, including the subtle and overt manners through which discrimination and exclusion take place at the micro, meso, and macro levels (Cao, Roger Mills-Koonce, Wood, & Fine, 2016; Few-Demo, Humble, Curran, & Lloyd, 2016; Higa et al., 2014; Hong & Garbarino, 2012; Kosciw, Palmer, & Kull, 2015). The LGBTIQQA+ population as a whole has been subject to a range of discriminatory action, and the authors will provide an overview of the impact of discrimination on mental health. Finally, intersectional feminism will provide the foundation for understanding resilience and strength within the LGBTIQQA+ community.

POSITIONALITY

We would be remiss if we did not also acknowledge aspects of our own identities and their potential, and, likely, their impact on the writing of this chapter. Dr. Cor identifies as a White, queer, able-bodied counselor educator in the Pacific Northwest. She has immersed herself in the work of growing and developing culturally competent mental health counselors through honest dialogue and increased self-awareness.

Dr. Chan identifies as a queer, multiethnic, second-generation Asian American, Catholic, cisgender male. His ethnic identities stem from Filipino, Chinese, and Malaysian heritages. Growing up as the child of two immigrants in Southern California, his upbringing took place in a middle-class family. He also identifies as able-bodied.

Though we are members of the broader LGBTIQQA+ community, we could not possibly speak for or represent the experiences of the entire population. Rather, our goal is to contribute to the literature by highlighting the integral part intersectional feminism has played in advancing this cause.

OVERVIEW OF FEMINISM AND INTERSECTIONAL FEMINISM

What Is Feminism?

It is impossible, we believe, to discuss the LGBTIQQA+ movement for equity without exploring the ways (intersectional) feminism and feminist theory have enhanced and been an integral part of society's transformation. We are sure you noticed that the word "intersectional" was in parentheses in the previous sentence, and we feel it necessary to expand on why this is the case. Simply put, in the history of the feminist movement, including women's suffrage, many women were not invited to a seat at the table. Women of color, trans women, and nonbinary folks were silenced and excluded from this imperative conversation. It would not be until the 1990s, when Dr. Kimberlé Crenshaw (1988, 1989, 1991) coined the term *intersectionality*, that mainstream feminism became aware of the ways in which their movement worked to recapitulate systems of oppression. More time will be devoted to intersectionality throughout this chapter.

It is of utmost importance to utilize a common definition to understand the foundation of feminism. It can be useful to begin by acknowledging what feminism is *not*. Feminism is not hatred toward men. Feminism is not a belief that women are superior. Feminism is certainly not a confirmation of the gender binary. In fact, feminism seeks to disrupt rigid ideas about femaleness, maleness, and how individuals are treated based on those arbitrary and socially constructed categories. According to bell hooks, a powerful and significant voice of feminist thought, "Feminism is a movement to end sexism, sexist exploitation, and oppression" (hooks, 2000).

Laura Brown describes feminism as radically reconstructing "social systems so as to deprivilege hierarchies of power based on gender" (Brown, 2011). Brown draws a direct correlation between feminism and the gay civil rights movement in the 1960s, 1970s, and 1980s. She eloquently writes, "Butch dykes and radical faeries—the brave, unassimilated, and unassimilatable faces of the movement—were decoupling biological sex from gender. We were thinking about how to be women and men in the world in new and exciting ways, embodying the projects of feminism" (p. 672). Feminism, Brown notes, encourages us to shatter dominant ideology and thinking.

LGBTIQQA+ folks have lived countless lives on the outside of the dominant paradigm. As we draw closer to equality, feminism allows us to remember and embrace what makes us different from mainstream culture. Feminism reminds us that we have come far, but our work is far from over.

We may also benefit from seeking to explore what feminism *is*. Feminism is equality. Feminism is the disruption of hegemony and systemic oppression. Feminism is acknowledging and working to dismantle the patriarchy. If this is true, feminism is inherently antiracist, antihomophobic, anticissexist, antitransphobic, and anticlassist.

However, feminism has also been dominated by the voices and experiences of White women who have called for their own equality and their own rights without acknowledging their personal role in perpetuating systems of oppression. Feminism has intersected with various aspects of identity since its conception, and many authors have called specifically for the acknowledgment and disruption of racism in the feminist movement (Bailey & Miller, 2015; hooks, 1995, 2010). hooks writes:

> Women, all women, are accountable for racism continuing to divide us. Our willingness to assume responsibility for the elimination of racism need not be engendered by feelings of guilt, moral responsibility, victimization, or rage. It can spring from a heartfelt desire for sisterhood and the personal, intellectual realization that racism among women undermines the potential radicalism of feminism. It can spring from our knowledge that racism is an obstacle in our path that must be removed. More obstacles are created if we simply engage in endless debate as to who put it there (2010, p. 31).

Self-proclaimed feminists who are White and cisgender must recognize that they, too, have been situated in a system that values dominance, imperialism, and suppression and that they, too, are responsible for creating and ending racism.

The same, of course, should be said for discrimination within the feminist movement. What about women who were assigned male at birth but do not ascribe to the concept of binary genders? Even the most feminist institutions have too often excluded trans women and gender-nonconforming people from their halls. Historically, women's colleges, for example, have experienced their own upheaval and paradigm shift as they begin to explore what it means to be a "woman" (Weber, 2016).

INTERSECTIONALITY THEORY

The development of intersectionality theory continues to create a multidisciplinary presence in the negotiation of identity politics, multiculturalism, social justice, scholarship, and practice. With its expanse for creative perspectives, intersectionality has formed largely as a result of the theoretical and philosophical underpinnings of multiple disciplines, demonstrating a wide applicability.

In line with this creative and multidimensional perspective, the tenets of intersectionality theory draw from the evolution and contributions of multiple disciplines to redefine the meaning of cultural and social identity. Significantly connecting many of these constructs together from several disciplines, intersectionality demonstrates these interconnected relationships in intersectionality's applicability to identifying a social justice agenda that speaks to eradicating social inequities. Within this social justice framework, intersectionality aims at disrupting the norms often representing privileged groups in power.

The saturation of intersectionality literature (Carbado, Crenshaw, Mays, & Tomlinson, 2013; Cole, 2008, 2009; Collins, 2004; Crenshaw, 1989, 1991; McCall, 2005; Warner, 2008) often occurs heavily in specific disciplines (e.g., law, sociology, psychology) while creating a foundation for other applied disciplines (e.g., management, higher education, economics, business, counseling). Mapping its history, scholars often pinpoint intersectionality principles as a model for praxis, yet sometimes the theory remains nebulous due to its multiple applications. As a result, scholars and practitioners adopting an intersectionality framework engage an imperative to constantly investigate its historical trajectory, including a comprehension of the foundational movements influencing the tenets of intersectionality. Tying in personal experiences of oppression to reflect injustice and inequality of social structures, intersectionality continues to remain well supported and widely discussed through an evidence base, offering a wealth of operational definitions to move a theoretical approach into practice (Bilge, 2013; Bowleg, 2008, 2012; Cho, 2013; Carbado et al., 2013; Clarke & McCall, 2013; Collins & Bilge, 2016; Corlett & Mavin, 2014; McCall, 2005;

Nash, 2008; Parent, DeBlaere, & Moradi, 2013; Warner, 2008; Warner, Settles, & Shields, 2016; Warner & Shields, 2013). More importantly, intersectionality offers the context to illuminate social justice philosophies and practices with LGBTIQQA+ communities through integrating its roots in feminist movements originally focused exclusively on women's issues.

OVERVIEW OF INTERSECTIONALITY

Early Historical Sources

Despite the recently growing presence of intersectionality in conceptual and empirical literatures, a discussion of intersectionality cannot be explained without an overarching understanding of the major philosophical and political movements guiding its notions. Intersectionality emerged largely during the early work of Dr. Kimberlé Crenshaw (1989, 1991), who postulated that women of color were not reflected in political movements for women's rights as demonstrated specifically within the legal system. Thus, there were significantly more difficult challenges and consequences for women of color who were not reflected in the overall changes to social structures—namely, legislation and protections (Crenshaw, 1991). The problematic context surrounding these issues was the subsequent invisibility and victimization of women of color, considering the lack of protections against violence against women. Crenshaw (1989, 1991) critiqued that feminist movements and women's rights movements disproportionately reflected individuals still operating with privilege, primarily White women. Consequently, the omission of Black women as a multiply marginalized group operated with the veil that feminist movements and women's issues successfully identified problematic practices. In contrast, these movements reflected the voices of a select few who were marginalized in one identity and privileged in another identity. According to Crenshaw (1990, 1991), it was an inaccurate grounding understanding for a progressive feminist movement targeting women's rights and eradicating women's issues in social structures.

In order to expose the discrepancies within women's rights movements, Crenshaw coined the term "intersectionality" (1989, 1991) to critically examine the missing components within feminist movements, although many other scholars had commented extensively on the assumptions and misrepresentation placed on multiply marginalized groups (Anzaldúa, 1987; hooks, 1981, 1984, 1989; Lorde, 1984; Moraga & Anzaldúa, 1983). In order to further her critique, she offered that antidiscrimination law could not remain predicated on a "single axis of analysis" (Crenshaw, 1989, p. 193).

Collins (1986) similarly ignited the intersectional movement through observing the "interlocking nature of oppression" often responsible for disconnecting women of color from intellectual and academic spaces in addition to other social contexts. Specifically, Crenshaw (1989, 1991) and Collins (1990) asserted that the voices of women of color remained lost in the portrayal of movements targeted at eradicating racism and sexism. In an attempt to counteract these sources of oppression, women of color were often ignored in light of men of color taking an active stance in movements against racism, while White women gained additional power within women's rights movements.

Despite intentions to develop social justice movements to challenge oppression and social inequality, the experiences of women of color were excluded and lost, leading to multiple forms of discrimination and marginalization for a group at the ends of multiple minority statuses (Yuval-Davis, 2006). A more problematic notion in the personal experiences occurring at the micro level was the hegemonic structure of power relations at the macro level of social structures, which only relayed access to resources and power for groups commonly retaining privilege and power.

Philosophical Shifts in Research

The formation of intersectionality has operated in multiple directions to address social inequalities in a variety of disciplines. In particular, the evolution of intersectionality has resulted in multifaceted patterns, which warranted an extended description of the seminal source material. Although scholarship in intersectionality has exponentially grown and diversified, scholars often attend to the manner in which intersectionality has resulted in secondhand interpretations of the source material (Bowleg, 2008; Yuval-Davis, 2006). These scholars identify the challenge of explicating the complex interpretation of intersectionality but remain largely critical of the nuances between additive and intersectional approaches (Corlett & Mavin, 2014).

This critique extends to the development of intersectionality and intercategorical approaches to focus on mutually shaping categories of identity and existence. Scholars actively debating the grounds of intersectionality have argued that interpretations of intersectionality are far more saturated with evidence on additive and multiplicative approaches, which often reduce oppression to discrete categories (e.g., racism, sexism, heterosexism, classism) in efforts to demonstrate the effects of multiple forms of discrimination and oppression or multiple minority stress.

Although these approaches have presented a worthwhile argument in considering overlapping inequalities, scholars point to the consequent danger in limiting intersectionality to focus on the addition and multiplication of categories of oppression in attempts to represent the experiences of marginalized groups. Separating marginalized identity categories as exclusively discrete categories acts counterintuitively to the underlying philosophy of intersectionality, which reflects the significant influence each identity category carries within an individual's unique lived experience.

Nonetheless, it is important to highlight the methods by which evidence in mental health has covered intersectionality as a framework. For example, there are numerous studies identifying the purpose and methodological design of additive and multiplicative approaches. Primarily, many of these studies' methodological designs explore minority stress in the framework of multiple minority stress and health disparities based on multiple forms of oppression.

At the confluence of racial/ethnic minority and sexual minority statuses in LGBT people of color, numerous researchers have identified the presence of increased suicide rates, poorer mental health outcomes, and decreased measures of wellness (Bostwick et al., 2014; Calabrese, Meyer, Overstreet, Haile, & Hansen, 2015; Frost, Lehavot, & Meyer, 2015; Meyer, 2010, 2014). With a focus on quantitative measures, many of these studies demonstrate the immense impact of oppression and discrimination on mental health, especially in the context of LGBT mental health.

Scholars (Bowleg, 2008; Corlett & Mavin, 2014; Yuval-Davis, 2006) denote the limiting structure often presented through additive and multiplicative designs when used in an attempt to represent social inequities and the experiences of groups falling in the societal margins. The major challenge in identifying these experiences often refers to the complex and varied experience of groups carrying multiple minority statuses scholars encounter when aiming to shed light on the multidimensional experience of identity.

As other scholars negotiate the direction of intersectionality research (Parent et al., 2013; Shields, 2008; Warner, 2008; Warner & Shields, 2013), there is a significant movement to involve interactionist and intersectional designs (Corlett & Mavin, 2014), largely evidenced by the resurgence of qualitative research focused on intersectionality. Rather than simplifying experiences of marginalization as mathematically confined data, research on intersectionality has emerged with additional qualitative studies using interactionist or intersectional designs to elicit the voices of individuals identifying with marginalized groups. These complex experiences are the result of lived experience derived from mutually shaping identities that weave together. Interactionist and intersectional approaches make strong arguments that lived experiences are reflections of the personal, political, and temporal nature of identity politics and social structures, which detail the complex power relations connected to social structures and personal experiences (McCall, 2005; Shields, 2008). Additionally, the development of intersectional and interactionist approaches formulates a resistance to the earlier traditions of additive and multiplicative approaches, given that many researchers attempting to investigate intersectional experiences were not directly experiencing the same intersections of social identities as those of the participants they studied.

Conceptualizations of LGBT mental health can also benefit from the framework of intersectionality by analyzing the description and meaning attached to categories of social identity. Multiple scholars (McCall, 2005; Walby, Armstrong, & Strid, 2012) innately emphasize the variety of approaches that become utilized in establishing and approaching social categories.

Specifically, McCall (2005) explained three approaches to explicate the complex notion of intersectionality as a framework for the study of social categories: the "anticategorical," "intercategorical," and "intracategorical" (p. 1773). Anticategorical approaches promote a movement away from describing social identity as limited to the naming conventions of a single category with the purpose of expanding on the experience existing beyond the confines of the social category (McCall, 2005). In contrast, the intercategorial approach utilizes commonly described social categories as strategic tools to identify social inequalities, power relations, social location, and problems situated within oppression (McCall, 2005). The intracategorical approach operates as the midpoint between the two other approaches, with the intention to describe ever-growing, complex, lived experience utilizing pre-existing social categories (McCall, 2005).

At the Intersection of Feminism and Mental Health

There exists a storied history between feminism and psychology. To understand the shared connection between feminism and mental health, Rutherford and Pettit suggest we understand the history of feminism "and/in/as" psychology (2015, p. 223). Feminism *and* psychology denotes the tension between a political movement and a scientific discipline and the efforts of participants in each to "problematize" the other (p. 223). Feminism *in* psychology speaks to when feminists sought to alter the content, methodologies, and populations of psychology. Finally, feminism *as* psychology outlines the shared space between these two ideas.

Brief Description on Principles

Intersectionality theory makes its significant contribution to LGBTIQQA+ mental health, feminism, and social justice through relying on its foundational principles, its paradigm for praxis, and its expansion of social justice to sexuality and gender identity. Intersectionality originated from the convergence of the feminist (specifically Black feminist) and critical race theory paradigms (Carbado et al., 2013), eliciting a social justice praxis to disrupt the norms and, most notably, the visible perspectives on social inequality, oppression, and marginalization.

Historically, intersectionality pushes the boundaries as a constantly developing and evolving paradigm and construct, which explains its increasing adaptation and application to numerous disciplines. While Carbado et al. (2013) extensively describe this movement, they offer significant arguments for its global application as intersectionality analysis.

Intersectionality has provided a framework for critical thinking and critical consciousness to move beyond the reduced approaches of singular categories on the basis that lived experience and social identity operate on multiple identities (e.g., race, ethnicity, sexuality, affectional orientation, gender identity, ability status, spirituality, social class, regional identity). In its essence dedicated to social justice, intersectionality expands on the experience of culture through identifying overlapping visible and invisible identifications with experiences of oppression and discrimination.

The processes of identity development for each social category are mutually shaping and constitute interconnected and interlocking processes (Bowleg, 2008, 2012). Compartmentalizing these categories as singular processes would invalidate the experience of lived identity (Cole, 2008, 2009; Parent et al., 2013; Shields, 2008; Singh, 2013; Velez, Moradi, & DeBlaere, 2015). A significant juxtaposition of each of the categories critically examines the manner in which privilege and oppression persist as complex, intersecting constructs tied to personal and social identity. Collins and Bilge (2016) focus primarily on six themes that identify an intersectional analysis to organize and highlight particular foci: (a) power; (b) relationality; (c) social context; (d) complexity; (e) social justice; and (f) social inequality.

Intersectional Feminism, LGBTIQQA+ Populations, and Advocacy

Although the advent of intersectionality occurred at the birth of effort to counteract both racism and sexism, it has demonstrated potential for demarginalizing the experience of sexuality and gender identity as well, through exploring heterosexism and genderism. Its critical analysis not only expands to identify the invisibility often faced at the crossroads of sexual identity, affectional orientation, and gender identity, but it also exposes hegemonic power relations and patriarchal expressions of masculinity and power in social structures (Cho, 2013; Cronin & King, 2010; Monro, 2010; Strolovitch, 2012; Veenstra, 2013).

In relation to hegemony and patriarchy, intersectionality demarcates the reality that sexual and gender expression is not limited and relegated to heterosexist norms often reflecting individuals in the majority (e.g., male, heterosexual, cis, White). This phenomenon points to the values attending to queer theory and intersectional feminism as a disruption of heteronormative representations of sexuality and gender identity as the privileged notion of power (Strolovitch, 2012).

Even more informative is the ability intersectionality fosters to build coalitions on the basis that interlocking relations of oppression exist at the level of sexual identity and gender identity (Cho, 2013), thus giving an avenue for identifying social injustices for sexual and gender minorities. In addition, these coalitions formulate a basis for ally development, considering that groups that are "othered" could operate as advocates for those impacted by heterosexism and genderism.

Intersectionality and feminism coalesce in a collaborative fashion to inform the centrality of experiences operating within the diversity of sexual identity, affectional identity, and gender identity. Primarily, intersectionality and feminism influence principles frequently associated with queer theory (Cannon, Lauve-Moon, & Buttell, 2015; Chevrette, 2013; Gedro & Mizzi, 2014; McCann, 2016; Misgav, 2016; Showden, 2012)—a theoretical framework intended to demarginalize and disrupt heteronormativity, homophobia, heterosexism, and genderism while fostering a focus on sexual, affectional, and gender diversity (Goodrich, Luke, & Smith, 2016; Valocchi, 2005).

Queer theory takes these principles into account by engaging an antiassimilationist perspective—members of the LGBTIQQA+ community are far better represented by their intersections and do not necessarily wish to assimilate to heteronormative restrictions. As queer theory utilizes a political agenda, it politicizes identities by using narratives to counter privilege, power, and dichotomous thinking in institutions. This sociopolitical agenda takes on an oppositional and defiant voice intended to disrupt systems of power.

POWER, PRIVILEGE, AND OPPRESSION

The LGBTIQQA+ community is a beautiful representation of intersectionality. Each member of this community holds a sexual orientation and a gender identity. This, of course, includes identities such as agender and asexual. The LGBTIQQA+ umbrella cuts across race/ethnicity, socioeconomic status, ability status, and religious/spiritual orientation. This "salad bowl" of diverse identity offers a rich depiction of the range of experiences of LGBTIQQA+ folks (Ruth & Davis, 2014).

Our work is incomplete if we do not consider the intersection of identity while also exploring the intersections of power, privilege, and oppression. One study found that folks identifying as lesbians and gay men, bisexuals, and heterosexuals who had experienced any same-sex sexual partners in their lifetime to be at higher risk of the onset of posttraumatic stress disorder (Roberts, Austin, Corliss, Vandermorris, & Koenen, 2010).

Understanding the experiences of lesbian, gay, bisexual, transgender, and queer folks is to understand their experiences with domination, subjugation, and, ultimately, subversion and rebellion. Members of this community are at greater risk of experiencing violence and trauma.

Covert and Overt Forms of Bias and Discrimination

While changes have begun to occur in the ways mental health professionals conceptualize sexuality and gender variance, individuals identifying within the LGBTIQQA+ community still experience both overt and covert forms of discrimination. *Overt discrimination* describes instances of prejudice that occur individually or systemically and that are explicitly based on a person's gender identity. *Covert discrimination* refers to subtle forms of bias that are often hidden and difficult to discern except by people of minoritized status. These are also referred to as microaggressions.

Derald Wing Sue and colleagues have studied the effects of racial microaggressions and explored implications for clinical practice (2007). Recently, research is being conducted to explore microaggressions in the LGBTIQQA+ community. Sue et al., (2007) defined microaggressions as "brief and commonplace daily verbal, behavioral, or environmental indignities, whether intentional or unintentional, that communicate hostile, derogatory, or negative slights and insults toward individuals from a marginalized population." Further, Sue and colleagues have stated that "perpetrators of microaggressions are often unaware that they engage in such communications while interacting with culturally different people" (Sue et al., 2007).

Homophobia, Heterosexism, Sexism, and Genderism

From an intersectional feminist perspective, these four concepts are inextricably tied in U.S. society. The Association for Lesbian, Gay, Bisexual, and Transgender Issues in Counseling (ALGBTIC) provides the following definitions (ALGBTIC, 2009; ALGBTIC LGBQQIA Competencies Taskforce et al., 2013; Harper et al., 2012): Homophobia refers to an aversion, fear, hatred, or intolerance of individuals who are lesbian, gay, bisexual, queer, or questioning or of things associated with our culture or way of being. Homophobia is often used to target the way that gender norms are being challenged by LGBTIQQA+ individuals. Folks in the LGBTIQQA+ community can experience internalized homophobia, which is the belief that they are indeed deserving of ill treatment due to their identities. Heterosexism connects to the ideas of systemic and institutionalized oppression. It represents an ideological system that denies, denigrates, ignores, marginalizes, and stigmatizes anyone who identifies as LGBTIQQA+ by seeking to silence or make invisible their lives and experiences. Heteronormativity refers to an ideology that suggests heterosexual relationships and cultural standards are considered "normal" and preferred. The ALGBTIC Competencies Taskforce et al. (2013) defines sexism as oppression, harassment, discrimination, prejudice, and microaggressions targeted toward people because of their biological sex. Sexism is linked to heterosexism because it is based on a set of behaviors that are considered appropriate for women or men, which include expectations about engaging in heterosexual relationships. "Cisexism" is a similar term that highlights the preferential treatment and advantages afforded to cisgender individuals. Finally, "genderism" refers to oppression, harassment, and discrimination based on a person's gender, gender identity, and gender expression. Often, people in the LGBTIQQA+ community experience genderism as a result of departure from expected gender performance that is largely based on one's biological sex (ALGBTIC LGBQQIA Competencies Taskforce, 2013).

U.S. society has instituted these forms of discrimination to ensure dominance over non-LGBTIQQA+ folks. Pharr (2014) asserts that homophobia has been used as a weapon of sexism because it is linked to heterosexism: "Heterosexism and homophobia work together to enforce compulsory heterosexuality and that bastion of patriarchal power, the nuclear family" (p. 166).

Arguments for "family values" often harken back to the days in which men and women ascribed and subscribed to rigid gender roles, including heterosexual sexual activity, bearing and raising 1.5 children, women wearing dresses and engaging in household activities such as cooking and cleaning, and men seen as breadwinners whose only job was to provide financially for the family.

These unyielding assignments seek to reinforce the idea that any departure away from these norms is pathological, sinful, and a threat to "American" values. Pharr highlights the socialization of this oppression beginning in childhood: "Children know what we have taught them, and we have given clear messages that those who deviate from standard expectations are to be made to get back in line" (2014, p. 167).

Homonormativity

Homonormativity is a separate concept but similar to heteronormativity. As outlined previously, heteronormativity not only refers to the institutionalized value that praises and prefers heterosexual culture, but heteronormativity also assumes that one's gender is aligned with one's biological genitalia. This ideology suggests that heterosexuality and cisgender identities are assumed "normal," and any variance in sexuality and gender identity is therefore abnormal.

Duggan (2003) defines homonormativity as an approach that does not seek to disrupt heteronormativity. Rather, this ideology upholds and sustains heteronormative assumptions and institutions and praises the alignment of gay culture with heterosexual values.

Self and Hudson (2015) suggest that race also intersects with homonormativity. They note that homonormative Whiteness refers to regulating norms that constitute the dominant queer body as White and male and center polar ideas of Whiteness and masculinity as normal (Self & Hudson, 2015).

Evidence of homonormativity can be seen in the focus of the marriage equality movement. LGBTIQQA+ culture has often pushed against the institution of marriage (van Eeden-Moorefield, Martell, Williams & Preston, 2011). Lifting up celebrities such as Neil Patrick Harris and Ellen DeGeneres can be examples of ways society praises homonormativity and seeks to further subjugate any queer person who falls outside of this rigid box.

As queer theorists disrupt traditional and privileged constructions of normative experience, they frequently cite the antiassimilationist lens that coincides fluidly with the arguments positioned by intersectional thinking. Interrogating privileged identity categories propels critical thinking to fully understand the diversity within and between categories, which accentuates the linkages among mutually constitutive categories.

Homonormativity acts counterintuitively to lenses positioned by queer and intersectional theoretical frameworks by invalidating diverse representations and expressions within the LGBTIQQA+ community. Instead, homonormativity perpetuates the reproduction of the hegemonic organization of power relations and social stratification within social structures through privileging particular identities and narratives within the community.

Consequently, intersectional feminism involves an oppositional and resistive stance to privileging within the community and, ultimately, against dominant forms of horizontal oppression, where oppression can occur within marginalized communities. Intersectional feminism also politicizes identities, unifying the multiplicity of the LGBTIQQA+ community to bring the community together as a political act to interrupt heteronormative systems of power. Intersectional feminism acts in tandem with this movement to lift up the lived experiences of diversity for members who compose the community, illustrating that members of the community are unique through their intersecting and mutually constitutive identities (e.g., race, ethnicity, sexuality, affection, gender identity, ability status, spirituality, social class, region). This viewpoint interrogates privileged narratives within the community to eradicate perpetuated forms of oppression.

Compounding Effects of Discrimination

Several researchers argue vehemently about mental health issues and utilization of services for people of color within the LGBTQQIA+ community (Balsam, Molina, Beadnell, Simoni, & Walters, 2011; Hein & Scharer, 2013; Meyer, 2010). While people of color within the community face numerous deleterious effects on their mental health and well-being, they are subjugated to navigating multiple converging forms of oppression compounding barriers to proper care for mental health. These issues illustrate the social, cultural, and political claims affecting people of color within the community across social structures that limit access to resources and services (Meyer, 2010). Complicating these issues for people of color are the heterosexism, genderism, and racism influencing an integral factor in well-being, mental health, isolation, and suicidality (Bowleg, 2008, 2012, 2013; Durso & Meyer, 2013; Frost et al., 2015; Meyer, 2010, 2013, 2014; Wilson et al., 2016).

Invisible Identities

It is vital to acknowledge the very real fact that, within the LGBTIQQA+ community, there exist a plethora of kinds of discrimination. Even among a group intimately aware of the pain of oppression and subjugation, hierarchies have been established to lift up the voices of some while silencing the voices and experiences of others. As outlined in the preceding section, homonormativity stems from heteronormativity and encourages LGBTIQQA+ folks to move closer to resembling White, straight, cisgender, able-bodied men. So what about members of the community for whom this conformity feels inappropriate?

Bisexuality, Asexuality, and the Experience of Agender Individuals

The challenges experienced by the LGBTIQQA+ community extend to advocacy that fully represents the illustriously diverse nature of sexual identity, affectional identity, and gender identity. Intersectionality promulgates the diversity that exists within and between categories (Smooth, 2013) by attending to postmodern constructions of identity categories. Given this observation, intersectionality adds to the construction upheld by queer theorists (Duong, 2012) to illuminate diverse experiences. While engaging advocacy and experiences attached to other identities, it is vital to increase the visibility and advocacy for bisexual, asexual, and agender members of the LGBTIQQA+ community to prevent consistent erasure (Barker & Langdridge, 2008; Flanders, 2015; Flanders & Hatfield, 2014; Marcus, 2015; Sergent-Shadbolt, 2015). Accounting for these identities transcends the boundaries and dichotomous thinking generally imposed on sexuality, affection, and gender identity (Lugg, 2003, 2006; Lugg & Murphy, 2014; Misgav, 2016), often a reproduction of hetero- and homonormative pressures.

Lifting up lived experiences in conjunction with the expansion of identities among members of the LGBTIQQA+ community elicits an oppositional defiance of the norms instituted by groups historically in power. Identifying the complexities inherent within these identities and experiences represents a constantly evolving process that engages a relationship with historical, social, cultural, and political claims.

Bisexual, asexual, and agender persons concomitantly operate within multiple layers of identities that fully exhibit the magnitude of gender identity, gender expression, sexuality, and affection. Given the historical movement and expansion of the LGBTIQQA+ community, there are extensions of discrimination, marginality, microaggressions, silence, and invisibility to bisexual, asexual, and agender communities.

Of particular note, some of this complexity has to do with the attributes the complicated nature of "passing" inculcated as a demonstrative experience that exemplifies both marginality and privilege (Baldwin et al., 2015; Marrs &

Staton, 2016; Tasker & Delvoye, 2015). Bisexual, asexual, and agender individuals have the capacity to pass as other identities within the spectrum of sexuality, affection, and gender identity.

Most notably, other individuals within and outside the LGBTQQIA+ community generate numerous assumptions about these specific identities by imposing heterosexual, cisgender, and heteronormative expressions on this set of identities. Examples include indicating bisexuality, asexuality, and agender as phases or assuming the identity is a cover for a dichotomous identification (e.g., gay/heterosexual, cisgender/transgender). These dichotomies exemplify the erasure proliferated within LGBTIQQA+ communities by removing these other less visible identities and their unique viewpoints from efforts to organize as a community and engage in social action. As a result, such erasure disconnects bisexual, asexual, and agender members of the community (Toft, 2014; Tweedy, 2015).

Muñoz-Laboy, Parker, Perry, and Garcia (2013) observed and discussed this issue of conflating both heteronormativity and homonormativity in ways the LGBTIQQA+ community treats the bisexual community, arguing that bisexual individuals experience both forces. This attribution disengages and invalidates other community members' identities within the community, reinforcing dominance and heternormativity, which run counter to the purposes set forth by queer theory and intersectionality theory.

Trans and Gender-Nonconforming Individuals

The 2015 U.S. Transgender Survey (USTS) was the largest and most comprehensive exploration of experiences of trans folks ever conducted in the United States,—gleaning 27,715 responses from participants in all 50 states, all U.S. territories, and military bases overseas (James et al., 2016). The results revealed that 39 percent of respondents experienced psychological distress in the month prior to the survey, as compared to five percent of the general population. Ten percent of respondents indicated a family member was violent toward them after coming out; eight percent were kicked out of their homes. Rates of poverty were significantly higher for respondents, largely attributed to the 15 percent unemployment rate—three times higher than the national average. Children in K–12 settings who identify as trans or gender-nonconforming reported rates of verbal harassment at 54 percent, physical assault at 24 percent, and sexual violence at 13 percent.

In each of these categories, individuals of color faced significantly higher rates of discrimination. While rates of poverty were significantly higher for all respondents surveyed, trans folks of color reported increased rates of poverty, including people who are Latino/a (43%), American Indian (41%), multiracial (40%), and Black (38%).

These experiences of overt discrimination have significant, adverse impacts on a person's well-being. According to the USTS, a staggering 40 percent of respondents reported attempting suicide as compared to 4.6 percent of the general population in the United States (Kochanek, Murphy, Anderson, & Scott, 2004).

As societal opinions begin to shift, it is possible that overt discrimination may begin to decrease as public displays of violence or harassment become less acceptable, though currently rates of violence toward trans individuals are startling. However, equally troubling are experiences of covert discrimination. Nadal, Skolnik, and Wong (2012) conducted a qualitative study with nine participants who identified as transgender female or male. This study found several important themes of microaggressions experienced by these participants when interacting with cisgender individuals. These themes of microaggressions included the use of transphobic and incorrectly gendered terminology, discomfort or disapproval of transgender experience, and the assumption of sexual pathology or abnormality.

Experiences of both covert and overt forms of discrimination occur in mental health settings as well. The USTS found that 22 percent of respondents indicated they were denied equal treatment and verbally or physically harassed in a drug and alcohol treatment facility. Carroll and Gilroy note that one study found clinicians discouraged clients from undergoing sex reassignment surgery because of "somatically inappropriate body types and facial features" (2002, p. 233). These findings, along with the significantly higher than average suicide rates, support the need for competent and ethical clinical practices and improved treatment of individuals identifying as trans in mental health settings.

RESILIENCE

Understanding the historical insights and philosophical underpinnings of the intersectional feminist theoretical framework in an effort to deconstruct and reconstruct the promise for negotiating authenticity and expression among range of members of the LGBTQQIA+ community seems to be a worthy pursuit. The underlying principles of intersectional feminism hold that efforts toward the discovery of diversity in the LGBTIQQA+ community are necessary, and are not yet finished, and work in conjunction with eradicating problematic systems contributing to social injustices.

Attending to personal experiences in juxtaposition with larger systemic issues also captures the explicit and implicit complexities inherent in the core of issues first identified by feminist movements targeted to addressing women's issues and sexism. Intersectionality emerged from the convergence of feminism, specifically Black feminism, and critical race theory; its principles then brought forth tenets associated with another critically informed paradigm, queer theory, which contests the institutionalization of heteronormativity, homophobia, transphobia, and genderism.

This coalescence of critically informed theories highlights a historical context significant in marginalized communities. Considering the histories connected to marginalized communities provides opportunities to map significant changes that hold potential to fortify resilience and instill hope.

Building on the work of Collins (2004), the instrumental concept of the outsider-within lens applies dynamically to the LGBTQQIA+ community, embodying intersections within the community as well as knowledge constructed from awareness of systems of oppression and privilege. Systems predicated on traditional and privileged narratives and viewpoints were invented to otherize, dehumanize, and devalue communities subjugated to this stratification. In contrast, Collins (2004) prominently offered the outsider-within viewpoint to promote the knowledge produced from the vantage points of marginalized communities, especially when marginalized identities intersect with privilege.

Because marginalized communities successfully navigate these systems of power daily, they can also be involved in the process of unraveling the broken pieces of oppressive systems. However, folks with privileged identities must work consciously and intentionally to understand their roles in decentering privilege and demarginalizing oppression. Negotiating the construction of this knowledge problematizes systems of oppression and enriches formative experiences to develop coalitions and advocacy. Consequently, intersectional feminism channels energy into the LGBTQQIA+ community and movement through illustrating diversity within and between; increasing capital stemming from navigating systems of power; and illuminating value and voice in marginalized communities.

REFERENCES

ALGBTIC LGBQQIA Competencies Taskforce, Harper, A., Finnerty, P., Martinez, M., Brace, A., Crethar, H. C., ... Kocet, M. (2013). Association for Lesbian, Gay, Bisexual, and Transgender Issues in Counseling Competencies for counseling with lesbian, gay, bisexual, queer, questioning, intersex, and ally individuals: Approved by the ALGBTIC board on June 22, 2012. *Journal of LGBT Issues in Counseling, 7*, 2–43.

Anzaldúa, G. (1987). *Borderlands/La frontera*. San Francisco, CA: Aunt Lute Books.

Association for Lesbian, Gay, Bisexual, and Transgender Issues in Counseling. (2009). *Competencies for counseling with transgender clients*. Alexandria, VA: Author.

Bailey, M., & Miller, S. J. (2015). When margins become centered: Black queer women in front and outside of the classroom. *Feminist Formations, 27*, 168–188.

Baldwin, A., Dodge, B., Schick, V., Hubach, R. D., Bowling, J., Malebranche, D., ... Fortenberry, J. D. (2015[2014]). Sexual self-identification among behaviorally bisexual men in the midwestern United States. *Archives of Sexual Behavior, 44*, 2015–2026. doi:10.1007/s10508-014-0376-1

Balsam, K. F., Molina, Y., Beadnell, B., Simoni, J., & Walters, K. (2011). Measuring multiple minority stress: The LGBT People of Color Microaggressions Scale. *Cultural Diversity and Ethnic Minority Psychology*, *17*, 163–174. doi:10.1037/a0023244

Barker, M., & Langdridge, D. (2008). II. Bisexuality: Working with a silenced sexuality. *Feminism & Psychology*, *18*, 389–394. doi:10.1177/0959353508092093

Bilge, S. (2013). Intersectionality undone: Saving intersectionality from feminist intersectionality studies. *Du Bois Review*, *10*, 405–424. doi:10.1017/S1742058X13000283

Bostwick, W. B., Meyer, I., Aranda, F., Russell, S., Hughes, T., Birkett, M., & Mustanski, B. (2014). Mental health and suicidality among racially/ethnically diverse sexual minority youths. *American Journal of Public Health*, *104*, 1129–1136. Retrieved from http://proxygw.wrlc.org/login?url=http://search.proquest.com/docview/1538587431?accountid=11243

Bowleg, L. (2008). When black + lesbian + woman ≠ black lesbian woman: The methodological challenges of qualitative and quantitative intersectionality research. *Sex Roles*, *59*, 312–325. doi:10.1007/s11199-008-9400-z

Bowleg, L. (2012). The problem with the phrase *women and minorities:* Intersectionality—An important theoretical framework for public health. *American Journal of Public Health*, *102*, 1267–1273. doi:10.2105/AJPH.2012.300750

Bowleg, L. (2013). "Once you've blended the cake, you can't take the parts back to the main ingredients": Black gay and bisexual men's descriptions and experiences of intersectionality. *Sex Roles*, *68*, 754–767.

Brown, L. S. (2011). A look back at "new voices, new visions": The view from here. *Psychology of Women Quarterly*, *35*, 671–675. doi:10.1177/0361684311426687

Calabrese, S. K., Meyer, I. H., Overstreet, N. M., Haile, R., & Hansen, N. B. (2015). Exploring discrimination and mental health disparities faced by black sexual minority women using a minority stress framework. *Psychology of Women Quarterly*, *39*, 287–304. doi:10.1177/0361684314560730

Cannon, C., Lauve-Moon, K., & Buttell, F. (2015). Re-theorizing intimate partner violence through post-structural feminism, queer theory, and the sociology of gender. *Social Sciences*, *4*, 668–687. doi:10.3390/socsci4030668

Cao, H., Roger Mills-Koonce, W., Wood, C., & Fine, M. A. (2016). Identity transformation during the transition to parenthood among same-sex couples: An ecological, stress-strategy-adaptation perspective. *Journal of Family Theory & Review*, *8*, 30–59. doi:10.1111/jftr.12124

Carbado, D. W., Crenshaw, K. W., Mays, V. M., & Tomlinson, B. (2013). Intersectionality. *Du Bois Review*, *10*, 303–312. doi:10.1017/S1742058X13000349

Carroll, L., & Gilroy, P. J. (2002). Transgender issues in counselor preparation. *Counselor Education & Supervision*, *41*, 233–241. doi:10.1002/j.15566978.2002.tb01286.x

Chevrette, R. (2013). Outing heteronormativity in interpersonal and family communication: Feminist applications of queer theory "Beyond the sexy streets." *Communication Theory*, *23*, 170–190. doi:10.1111/comt.12009

Cho, S. (2013). Post-intersectionality: The curious reception of intersectionality in legal scholarship. *Du Bois Review*, *10*(2), 385–404. doi:10.1017/S1742058X13000362

Clarke, A. Y., & McCall, L. (2013). Intersectionality and social explanation in social science research. *Du Bois Review*, *10*, 349–363. doi:10.1017/S1742058X13000325

Cole, E. R. (2008). Coalitions as a model for intersectionality: From practice to theory. *Sex Roles*, *59*, 443–453. doi:10.1007/s11199-008-9419-1

Cole, E. R. (2009). Intersectionality and research in psychology. *American Psychologist, 64,* 170–180. doi:10.1037/a0014564

Collins, P. H. (1986). Learning from the outsider within: The sociological significance of black feminist thought. *Social Problems, 33,* S14–S32. doi:10.2307/800672

Collins, P. H. (1990). *Black feminist thought: Knowledge, consciousness and the politics of empowerment.* New York, NY: Routledge.

Collins, P. H. (2004). Learning from the outsider within: The sociological significance of black feminist thought. In S. Harding (Ed.), *The feminist standpoint theory reader* (pp. 103–126). New York, NY: Routledge.

Collins, P. H., & Bilge, S. (2016). *Intersectionality.* Malden, MA: Polity Press.

Corlett, S., & Mavin, S. (2014). Intersectionality, identity and identity work. *Gender in Management, 29,* 258–276. doi:10.1108/GM-12-2013-0138

Crenshaw, K. (1988). Race, reform, and retrenchment: Transformation and legitimation in antidiscrimination law. *Harvard Law Review, 101,* 1331–1387. Retrieved from http://www.jstor.org/stable/pdf/1341398.pdf

Crenshaw, K. (1989). Demarginalizing the intersection of race and sex: A black feminist critique of antidiscrimination doctrine, feminist theory and antiracist politics. *University of Chicago Legal Forum, 1989,* 139–167.

Crenshaw, K. (1991). Mapping the margins: Intersectionality, identity politics, and violence against women of color. *Stanford Law Review, 43,* 1241–1299. doi:10.2307/1229039

Cronin, A., & King, A. (2010). Power, inequality and identification: Exploring diversity and intersectionality amongst older LGB adults. *Sociology, 44,* 876–892. doi:10.1177/0038038510375738

Duggan, L. (2003). *The twilight of equality? Neoliberalism, cultural politics, and the attack on democracy.* Boston, MA: Beacon Press.

Duong, K. (2012). What does queer theory teach us about intersectionality? *Politics & Gender, 8,* 370–386. doi:10.1017/S1743923X12000360

Durso, L. E., & Meyer, I. H. (2013). Patterns and predictors of disclosure of sexual orientation to healthcare providers among lesbians, gay men, and bisexuals. *Sexuality Research and Social Policy, 10,* 35–42. doi:10.1007/s13178-012-0105-2

Few-Demo, A. L., Humble, Á. M., Curran, M. A., & Lloyd, S. A. (2016). Queer theory, intersectionality, and LGBT-parent families: Transformative critical pedagogy in family theory. *Journal of Family Theory & Review, 8,* 74–94. doi:10.1111/jftr.12127

Flanders, C. E. (2015). Bisexual health: A daily diary analysis of stress and anxiety. *Basic and Applied Social Psychology, 37,* 319–335. doi:10.1080/01973533.2015.1079202

Flanders, C. E., & Hatfield, E. (2014). Social perception of bisexuality. *Psychology & Sexuality, 5,* 232–246. doi:10.1080/19419899.2012.749505

Frost, D. M., Lehavot, K., & Meyer, I. H. (2015). Minority stress and physical health among sexual minority individuals. *Journal of Behavioral Medicine, 38,* 1–8. doi:10.1007/s10865-013-9523-8

Gedro, J., & Mizzi, R. C. (2014). Feminist theory and queer theory: Implications for HRD research and practice. *Advances in Developing Human Resources, 16,* 445–456. doi:10.1177/1523422314543820

Goodrich, K. M., Luke, M., & Smith, A. J. (2016). Queer humanism: Toward an epistemology of socially just, culturally responsive change. *Journal of Humanistic Psychology, 56,* 612–623. doi:10.1177/0022167816652534

Harper, A., Finnerty, P., Martinez, M., Brace, A., Crethar, H., Loos, B., . . . Lambert, S. (2012). Association for Lesbian, Gay, Bisexual, and Transgender Issues in Counseling (ALGBTIC) competencies for counseling with lesbian, gay, bisexual, queer, questioning, intersex and ally individuals. Retrieved from http://www.counseling.org/docs/ethics/algbtic-2012-07

Hein, L. C., & Scharer, K. M. (2013). Who cares if it is a hate crime? Lesbian, gay, bisexual, and transgender hate crimes—Mental health implications and interventions. *Perspectives in Psychiatric Care, 49*, 84–93. doi:10.1111/j.1744-6163.2012.00354.x

Higa, D., Hoppe, M. J., Lindhorst, T., Mincer, S., Beadnell, B., Morrison, D. M., . . . Mountz, S. (2014[2012]). Negative and positive factors associated with the well-being of lesbian, gay, bisexual, transgender, queer, and questioning (LGBTQ) youth. *Youth & Society, 46*, 663–687. doi:10.1177/0044118X12449630

Hong, J. S., & Garbarino, J. (2012). Risk and protective factors for homophobic bullying in schools: An application of the social-ecological framework. *Educational Psychology Review, 24*, 271–285. doi:10.1007/s10648-012-9194-y

hooks, b. (1981). *Ain't I a woman: Black women and feminism*. Boston, MA: South End Press.

hooks, b. (1984). *Feminist theory: From margin to center*. Cambridge, MA: South End Press.

hooks, b. (1989). *Talking back: Thinking feminist, thinking black*. Boston, MA: South End Press.

hooks, b. (1995). Feminism and militarism: A comment. *Women's Studies Quarterly, 23*, 58–64.

hooks, b. (2000). *Feminism is for everybody: Passionate politics*. Cambridge, MA: South End Press.

hooks, b. (2010). Racism and feminism: The issue of accountability. In S. M. Pitcher (Ed.), *Localizing/Glocalizing oppression: A critical exploration of race, class, gender, and sexuality* (pp. 15–31). San Diego, CA: Cognella.

James, S. E., Herman, J. L., Rankin, S., Keisling, M., Mottet, L., & Ana, M. (2016). *Executive summary of the report of the 2015 U.S. Transgender Survey*. Washington, DC: National Center for Transgender Equality.

Kochanek, K. D., Murphy, S. C., Anderson, R. N., & Scott, C. (2004). Deaths: Final data for 2002. *National Vital Statistics Reports, 53*. Retrieved from http://www.cdc.gov/nchs/data/nvsr/nvsr53/nvsr53_05.pdf

Kosciw, J. G., Palmer, N. A., & Kull, R. M. (2015). Reflecting resiliency: Openness about sexual orientation and/or gender identity and its relationship to well-being and educational outcomes for LGBT students. *American Journal of Community Psychology, 55*, 167–178. doi:10.1007/s10464-014-9642-6

Lorde, A. (1984). *Sister outsider: Essays and speeches*. Trumansburg, NY: Crossing Press.

Lugg, C. (2003). Sissies, faggots, lezzies, and dykes: Gender, sexual orientation and new politics of education? *Educational Administration Quarterly, 39*, 95–134.

Lugg, C. A. (2006). Thinking about sodomy: Public schools, legal panopticons, and queers. *Educational Policy, 20*, 35–58. doi:10.1177/0895904805285374

Lugg, C. A., & Murphy, J. P. (2014). Thinking whimsically: Queering the study of educational policy-making and politics. *International Journal of Qualitative Studies in Education, 27*, 1183–1204. doi:10.1080/09518398.2014.916009

Marcus, N. C. (2015). Bridging bisexual erasure in LGBT-rights discourse and litigation. *Michigan Journal of Gender & Law, 22*, 291–344. Retrieved from http://proxygw.wrlc

.org/login?url=http://search.proquest.com.proxygw.wrlc.org/docview/1853603959?
accountid=11243

Marrs, S. A., & Staton, A. R. (2016). Negotiating difficult decisions: Coming out versus passing in the workplace. *Journal of LGBT Issues in Counseling*, *10*, 40–54. doi:10.1080/15538605.2015.1138097

McCall, L. (2005). The complexity of intersectionality. *Signs*, *30*, 1771–1800. doi:10.1086/426800

McCann, H. (2016). Epistemology of the subject: Queer theory's challenge to feminist sociology. *Women's Studies Quarterly*, *44*, 224–243. doi:10.1353/wsq.2016.0044

Meyer, I. H. (2010). Identity, stress, and resilience in lesbians, gay men, and bisexuals of color. *The Counseling Psychologist*, *38*, 442–454. doi:10.1177/0011000009351601

Meyer, I. H. (2013). Prejudice, social stress, and mental health in lesbian, gay, and bisexual populations: Conceptual issues and research evidence. *Psychology of Sexual Orientation and Gender Diversity*, *1*, 3–26. http://dx.doi.org/10.1037/2329-0382.1.S.3

Meyer, I. H. (2014). Minority stress and positive psychology: Convergences and divergences to understanding LGBT health. *Psychology of Sexual Orientation and Gender Diversity*, *1*, 348–349. doi:10.1037/sgd0000070

Meyer, I. H. (2016). The elusive promise of LGBT equality. *American Journal of Public Health*, *106*, 1356–1358. doi:10.2105/AJPH.2016.303221

Misgav, C. (2016). Some spatial politics of queer-feminist research: Personal reflections from the field. *Journal of Homosexuality*, *63*, 719–721. doi:10.1080/00918369.2015.1112191

Monro, S. (2010). Sexuality, space and intersectionality: The case of lesbian, gay and bisexual equalities initiatives in UK local government. *Sociology*, *44*, 996–1010. doi:10.1177/0038038510375743

Moraga, C., & Anzaldúa, G. (Eds.). (1983). *This bridge called my back: Writings by radical women of color* (2nd ed.). New York, NY: Kitchen Table/Women of Color Press.

Muñoz-Laboy, M., Parker, R., Perry, A., & Garcia, J. (2013). Alternative frameworks for examining Latino male bisexuality in the urban space: A theoretical commentary based on ethnographic research in Rio de Janeiro and New York. *Sexualities*, *16*, 501–522. doi:10.1177/1363460713487367

Nadal, K. L., Skolnik, A., & Wong, Y. (2012). Interpersonal and systemic microaggressions toward transgender people: Implications for counseling. *Journal of LGBT Issues in Counseling*, *6*, 55–82. doi:10.1080/15538605.2012.648583

Nash, J. C. (2008). Re-thinking intersectionality. *Feminist Review*, *89*, 1–15. doi:10.1057/fr.2008.4

Parent, M. C., DeBlaere, C., & Moradi, B. (2013). Approaches to research on intersectionality: Perspectives on gender, LGBT, and racial/ethnic identities. *Sex Roles*, *68*, 639–645. doi:10.1007/s11199-013-0283-2

Pharr, S. (2014). Homophobia as a weapon of sexism. In P. S. Rothenberg & K. S. Mayhew (Eds.), *Race, class, and gender in the United States* (9th ed., pp. 163–172). New York, NY: Worth.

Roberts, A. L., Austin, S. B., Corliss, H. L., Vandermorris, A. K., & Koenen, K. C. (2010). Pervasive trauma exposure among US sexual orientation minority adults and risk of posttraumatic stress disorder. *American Journal of Public Health*, *100*, 2433–2441.

Ruth, R., & Davis, D. (2014). European Americans. In L. H. Cousins (Ed.), *Encyclopedia of human services and diversity* (pp. 498–499). Thousand Oaks, CA: Sage Publications. doi:10.4135/9781483346663.n213

Rutherford, A., & Pettit, M. (2015). Introduction: Feminism and/in/as psychology: The public sciences of sex and gender. *History of Psychology*, *18*, 223–237. doi:10.1037/a0039533

Self, J. M., & Hudson, K. M. (2015). Dangerous waters and brave space: A critical feminist inquiry of campus LGBTQ centers. *Journal of Gay & Lesbian Social Services*, *27*, 216–245. doi:10.1080/10538720.2015.1021985

Sergent-Shadbolt, J. (2015). Revolving doors and new identities: A report into new bisexuality research in Aotearoa/New Zealand. *Women's Studies Journal*, *29*, 42–49. Retrieved from http://proxygw.wrlc.org/login?url=http://search.proquest.com.proxygw.wrlc.org/docview/1757275999?accountid=11243

Shields, S. A. (2008). Gender: An intersectionality perspective. *Sex Roles*, *59*, 301–311. doi:10.1007/s11199-008-9501-8

Showden, C. R. (2012). Theorising maybe: A feminist/queer theory convergence. *Feminist Theory*, *13*, 3–25. doi:10.1177/1464700111429898

Singh, A. A. (2013). Transgender youth of color and resilience: Negotiating oppression and finding support. *Sex Roles*, *68*, 690–702. doi:10.1007/s11199-012-0149-z

Smooth, W. G. (2013). Intersectionality from theoretical framework to policy intervention. In A. R. Wilson (Ed.), *Situating intersectionality: Politics, policy, and power*. New York, NY: Palgrave Macmillan.

Strolovitch, D. Z. (2012). Intersectionality in time: Sexuality and the shifting boundaries of intersectional marginalization. *Politics & Gender*, *8*, 386–396. doi:10.1017/S1743923X12000372

Sue, D. W., Capodilupo, C. M., Torino, G. C., Bucceri, J. M., Holder, A. M. B., Nadal, K. L., & Esquilin, M. (2007). Racial microaggressions in everyday life: Implications for clinical practice. *American Psychologist*, *62*, 271–286. doi:10.1037/0003-066X.62.4.271

Tasker, F., & Delvoye, M. (2015). Moving out of the shadows: Accomplishing bisexual motherhood. *Sex Roles*, *73*, 125–140. doi:10.1007/s11199-015-0503-z

Toft, A. (2014). Re-imagining bisexuality and Christianity: The negotiation of Christianity in the lives of bisexual women and men. *Sexualities*, *17*, 546–564. doi:10.1177/1363460714526128

Tweedy, A. E. (2015). A bisexual perspective on law school hiring. *Columbia Journal of Gender and Law*, *31*, 82–86.

Valocchi, S. (2005). Not yet queer enough: The lessons of queer theory for the sociology of gender and sexuality. *Gender & Society*, *19*, 750–770. doi:10.1177/0891243205280294

van Eeden-Moorefield, B., Martell, C. R., Williams, M., & Preston, M. (2011). Same sex relationships and dissolution: The connection between heteronormativity and homonormativity. *Family Relations*, *60*, 562–571.

Veenstra, G. (2013). The gendered nature of discriminatory experiences by race, class, and sexuality: A comparison of intersectionality theory and the subordinate male target hypothesis. *Sex Roles*, *68*, 646–659. doi:10.1007/s11199-012-0243-2

Velez, B. L., Moradi, B., & DeBlaere, C. (2015). Multiple oppressions and the mental health of sexual minority Latina/o individuals. *The Counseling Psychologist*, *43*, 7–38. doi:10.1177/0011000014542836

Walby, S., Armstrong, J., & Strid, S. (2012). Intersectionality: Multiple inequities in social theory. *Sociology*, *46*, 224–240. doi:10.1177/0038038511416164

Warner, L. R. (2008). A best practices guide to intersectional approaches in psychological research. *Sex Roles, 59,* 454–463. doi:10.1007/s11199-008-9504-5

Warner, L. R., Settles, I., & Shields, S. (2016). Invited reflection: Intersectionality as an epistemological challenge to psychology. *Psychology of Women Quarterly, 40,* 171–176. doi:10.1177/0361684316641384

Warner, L. R., & Shields, S. A. (2013). The intersections of sexuality, gender, and race: Identity research at the crossroads. *Sex Roles, 68,* 803–810. doi:10.1007/s11199-013-0281-4

Weber, S. (2016). "Womanhood does not reside in documentation": Queer and feminist student activism for transgender women's inclusion at women's colleges. *Journal of Lesbian Studies, 20,* 29–45. doi:10.1080/10894160.2015.1076238

Wilson, P. A., Meyer, I. H., Antebi-Gruszka, N., Boone, M. R., Cook, S. H., & Cherenack, E. M. (2016). Profiles of resilience and psychosocial outcomes among young black gay and bisexual men. *American Journal of Community Psychology, 57,* 144–157. doi:10.1002/ajcp.12018

Yuval-Davis, N. (2006). Intersectionality and feminist politics. *European Journal of Women's Studies, 13,* 193–209. doi:10.1177/1350506806065752

7

Caught at the Intersections: Microaggressions toward Lesbian, Gay, Bisexual, Transgender, and Queer People of Color

Kevin L. Nadal, Tanya Erazo, Julia Schulman,
Heather Han, and Tamara Deutsch

Since 2007, the study of microaggressions, subtle forms of discrimination that target various historically marginalized groups, has increased exponentially in psychology, counseling, social work, and education (Nadal, 2013; Nadal, Whitman, Davis, Erazo, & Davidoff, 2016; Wong, Derthick, David, Saw, & Okazaki, 2014). Studies have demonstrated that microaggressions are prevalent in the lives of many communities, including people of color, women, members of religious minority groups, people with disabilities, people with mental illness, and lesbian, gay, bisexual, transgender, and queer (LGBTQ) people (Nadal et al., 2016).

Despite this, most studies to date have focused on how individuals experience microaggressions as a result of their singular identities (e.g., race, gender, ability, ethnicity), not taking into account how microaggressions can be influenced by intersectional identities (e.g., being a woman of color, being a queer person with a disability). For instance, when examining racial microaggressions, earlier studies have used qualitative methods to ask people of color about their experiences with subtle racial discrimination (e.g., Rivera, Forquer, & Rangel, 2010; Sue et al., 2008; Sue, Bucceri, Lin, Nadal, & Torino, 2010), without inquiring directly about how participants' genders, sexual orientations, ages, social classes, sizes, and other aspects of identity may influence their experiences. While it is likely that a primary identity (e.g., race) may be the focus of a microaggression (e.g., when someone makes a subtle racist remark, it is clearly race-related), it is likely that other identities influence how the microaggression manifests and the impact the interaction has on an individual. The purpose of this chapter is to explore the concept of intersectional microaggressions, or "subtle forms of discrimination based on an individual's multiple social identities," (Nadal, 2013, p. 36) and the impacts of these incidents on the mental health of LGBTQ people of color.

MICROAGGRESSIONS: A REVIEW OF THE LITERATURE

Microaggressions are brief, commonplace, daily, verbal, behavioral, and environmental slights and indignities that send denigrating and harmful messages to various people, particularly those who belong to historically marginalized groups (Nadal, 2013; Sue, 2010). Microaggressions are said to take three forms (Sue, 2010): microinvalidations (statements, usually unconscious, that dismiss the lived experiences of marginalized groups), microassaults (statements and behaviors, often deliberate, that convey bias), and microinsults (statements and behaviors that communicate subtle negative attitudes toward marginalized groups). While people of diverse races, ethnicities, sexual orientations, genders, and other identities face microaggressions frequently, microaggressions are usually unacknowledged unless confronted or pointed out by the people targeted by microaggressions. Sue (2010) describes a "Catch-22" for individuals targeted by microaggressions—if they respond, there are potential consequences for their safety, jobs, psychological well-being, and more; however, if they do not respond, they frequently feel regret, resentment, anger, and other emotions, often leading to rumination about the inaction. Sue et al. (2007) argue that subtle yet pervasive discrimination can affect self-esteem, anger, and frustration levels even more than traditional, overtly discriminatory behaviors.

Sue et al. (2007) created a microaggressions taxonomy that highlighted themes of racial microaggressions that affect people of color. The first theme, *alien in one's own land*, perpetuates the idea that people of color do not belong in the United States; this occurs primarily for Latino/as and Asian Americans, who are typically assumed to be foreigners, even though many have lived in the United States their whole lives or come from families that have been living in the United States for generations. The second theme, *ascription of intelligence*, refers to the notion that intelligence levels are narrated through the lens of racial stereotypes (e.g., when Black Americans are complimented for being "articulate" or Asian Americans are assumed to be good at math and sciences). The third theme, *color blindness*, occurs when White people refuse to acknowledge race and convey that racism does not exist and that people of color should assimilate into the dominant White culture. The fourth theme, *criminality/assumption of criminality*, refers to the false belief that people of color are criminals solely based on their race/appearance. The fifth theme, *denial of individual racism*, occurs when a person refuses to acknowledge their individual racial biases (e.g., saying "I'm not racist; I have a Black friend"). The sixth theme, *myth of meritocracy*, transpires when White people deny that race influences success and supports the notion that everyone moves forward based on talent and hard work (e.g., saying that, if people of color worked harder, they could be better represented in high social positions). The seventh theme, *pathologizing cultural values and communication styles*, occurs when White culture and a White style of communication are assumed to be the best or only acceptable values or ways of communicating. Finally, the eighth theme, *second-class citizen*, describes how White people are given better customer service or treated better than people of color, implying that White people are more deserving of good treatment and that people of color should expect and accept substandard treatment.

Drawing from this taxonomy, qualitative studies have affirmed that people of color indeed experience these microaggressions; people of color identify these experiences as race-related or as microaggressions; and people of color report negative impacts of such experiences on their mental health and well-being. For example, studies with Latino/as (Rivera et al., 2010), Black Americans (Sue et al., 2008), and Asian Americans (Sue et al., 2010) have confirmed how the themes presented in the taxonomy affect different racial groups in nuanced ways. Quantitative research has found that racial microaggressions give rise to multiple negative effects on people of color, including depressive symptoms and negative affect (Nadal, Griffin, Wong, Hamit, & Rasmus, 2014); higher levels of anxiety and underage binge drinking (Blume, Lovato, Thyken, & Denny, 2012); suicide and suicidal ideation (O'Keefe, Wingate, Cole, Hollingsworth, & Tucker, 2015); lower self-esteem (Nadal, Wong, Griffin, Davidoff, & Sriken, 2014); lower levels of psychological well-being (Nadal, Wong, Sriken, Griffin, & Fujii-Doe, 2015); and emotional intensity (Wang, Leu, & Shoda, 2011). It is clear that racial microaggressions negatively affect people of color; however, it is unclear how other identities may influence some of these factors.

Previous studies have also examined microaggressions based on sexual orientations, gender identities, and combinations of these factors. Similar to participants in studies on racial microaggressions, LGBQ participants (Nadal, Issa, et al., 2011) and transgender participants (Nadal, Skolnik, & Wong, 2012) identify a spectrum of microaggressions they face. The first theme, *heterosexist and transphobic terminology*, refers to the many words that denigrate LGBTQ people— phrases such as "that's so gay" communicate that being gay is weird or different. The second theme, *endorsement of heteronormative or gender-binary culture and behaviors*, involves statements that describe heteronormative relationships or cisgender identities as the norm. The third theme, *assumption of universal LGBTQ experience*, involves instances in which heterosexual people assume all LGBTQ people are the same (e.g., being surprised to learn of a woman's lesbian identity because she is not seen as "butch"). The fourth theme, *exoticization*, involves instances in which LGBTQ people are treated as tokens, objects, or animals (e.g., asking invasive questions about sex or treating gay people as comic relief). The fifth theme, *discomfort or disapproval of the LGBTQ experience*, transpires when people behave negatively toward LGBT people (e.g., displaying obvious disgust in response to same-sex couples showing affection). The sixth theme, *denial of societal heterosexism*, occurs when heterosexual people invalidate the existence of homophobia, heterosexism, and transphobia. The seventh theme, *assumption of sexual pathology/abnormality*, describes incidents in which LGBTQ people are oversexualized and assumed to be sexually deviant. The eighth theme, *denial of individual heterosexism/transphobia*, occurs when a person denies they could have been heterosexist or transphobic, such as by insisting they cannot be homophobic because they have a gay friend.

Subsequent qualitative studies[1] on microaggressions have confirmed these themes and added others. Platt and Lenzen (2013) described the theme of *under-sexualization*, describing the notion that heterosexual people were tolerant of LGBTQ people if LGBTQ people did not widely discuss their relationships or romantic and sex lives. In a study of transgender people, participants identified a common theme of *denial of bodily privacy*, demonstrated when cisgender people ask transgender individuals invasive questions about their anatomy or sexual practices (Nadal et al., 2012). In a study with bisexual women, participants identified microaggression themes including *pressure to change* (i.e., assumptions the bisexual person should "choose" the sexual orientation that matches their relationship), *LGBTQ legitimacy* (i.e., statements that convey that bisexuals are not legitimate members of an inclusive LGBTQ community), and *dating exclusion* (i.e., comments or behaviors that pressure bisexual people about who they can or cannot date; Bostwick & Hequembourg, 2014).

Participants in qualitative studies reported that experiencing microaggressions made them feel distressed, affected their ability to be comfortable identifying as LGBTQ, and contributed to chronic, negative mental health outcomes, such as anxiety, depression, and posttraumatic stress disorder (PTSD; Nadal, Issa, et al., 2011; Nadal, Yong, et al., 2011). Quantitative studies have found that heterosexist microaggressions were predictors of psychological distress (Woodford, Kulick, Sinco, & Hong, 2014); lower self-esteem and negative feelings about sexual orientation identity (Wright & Wegner, 2012); and anxiety and distress (Woodford, Paceley, Kulick, & Hong, 2015). It is therefore evident that LGBTQ people experience and can identify microaggressions in their lives and that microaggressions have a negative impact on their mental health. However, these studies leave unclear how *multiple* identities (e.g., race, gender, sexual orientation) may affect LGBTQ people's experiences of microaggressions.

Following the tenets of intersectionality theory, which holds that a person's multiple identities influence the ways they experience and navigate the world (see Crenshaw, 1989), studies have explored how multiple identities impact the types of microaggressions a person encounters and how those experiences influence mental health. One study developed an LGBT People of Color Microaggressions Scale (LGBT-PCMS) to examine racial microaggressions, heterosexist microaggressions, and intersectional microaggressions that LGBTQ people face.

---

[1]Qualitative research explores reasoning, themes, and opinions that provide insight into a certain topic or problem.

Salient findings included that "LGBTQ Asian American participants reported significantly more microaggressive experiences and resultant distress than LGBTQ African Americans and Latina/os while LGBTQ men of color reported significantly more microaggressive experiences/distress than LGBTQ women of color" (Balsam, Molina, Beadnell, Simoni, & Walters, 2011). Another study introduced the Gendered Racial Microaggressions Scale for Black Women. This scale examined Black women's experience of intersectional microaggressions and found evidence of four kinds of microaggressive experiences the study population faced, including assumptions of beauty and sexual objectification; being silenced and marginalized; the "strong Black woman" stereotype; and the "angry Black woman" stereotype (Lewis & Neville, 2015).

In qualitative studies, Bowleg (2013) found that Black American gay and bisexual men reported experiencing racial microaggressions from the general LGBTQ community while also experiencing heterosexism and pressure to conform to gender roles from the Black community. Follins (2014) reported similar findings in qualitative interviews with gay Black and Latino men, who cited microaggressions related to being sexually objectified, treated as aliens in their own land, and being negatively stereotyped with other attributes of Black and Latino people. Finally, a qualitative secondary analysis study used raw data from 19 focus groups from previously published microaggression studies with 80 participants (Nadal et al., 2015). The authors identified eight themes of intersectional microaggressions: "exoticization of women of color; gender stereotypes for lesbians and gay men; disapproval of LGBTQ identity within racial/ethnic and/or religious communities; assumption of inferior status for women of color; invisibility and desexualization of Asian men; assumptions of inferiority and/or criminality for men of color; gender stereotypes for Muslim individuals; and women of color as spokespersons" (Nadal et al., 2015).

While all of the findings discussed have merit, there have been no known studies that have used racially mixed samples of gender-diverse participants who identify as LGBQ people of color to explore the manifestation of intersectional microaggressions.

METHODOLOGY

The present study used consensual qualitative research (CQR; Hill et al., 2005) to examine microaggressions LGBQ-identifying individuals who also identified as people of color experience. Recognizing that transgender people may also identify as LGBQ, transgender and gender-nonconforming people were not recruited for this study, as gender identity should not be conflated with sexual orientation and would benefit more from separate examination. The study met the standards of and was approved by the researchers' Institutional Review Board.

Participants

The research team recruited both college and community participants from a large, metropolitan, urban region in the northeastern United States. A total of 16 individuals participated across four focus groups and identified in multiple ways. Eight participants identified as men, seven identified as women, and one did not list a gender. Participants were largely born in the United States (N = 14); two were born outside the United States (one in Brazil, and another in Iran). Participants self-identified their race/ethnicities as Black or African American (N = 10), Asian (N = 3), Native American (N = 1), Black/Latino (N = 1), and Latino/Middle Eastern (N = 1). Participants identified their sexual orientations as gay (N = 7), lesbian (N = 3), bisexual (N = 2), queer (N = 1), queer/pansexual (N = 1), homosexual/same gender loving (N = 1), and asexual (N = 1). Participants' average age was 27.5 and ranged from 23 to 57. Most participants reported having no religion (N = 7) or being atheist or agnostic (N = 2); some identified as Catholic (N = 3) or Christian (N = 2); one person identified as "nondenominational" and another as "Israelite." Educational level was diverse, ranging from "high school" to "PhD." For further demographic details, see Table 7.1.

Researchers

Our research team consisted of one male professor, one female doctoral student, two female master's students, one male master's student, and two female undergraduate students. The racial/ethnic identities of data analysts included mixed-race, White, Hispanic, Latino/a, Black, and Asian American; sexual orientation identities included heterosexual, pansexual, and bisexual. The principal investigator in this study is a professor with extensive CQR training and over 16 years' experience in qualitative research. All data analysts received in-depth CQR training and, prior to starting data collection, convened to discuss study expectations and potential biases. The aim of this dialogue was to minimize impacts of researcher bias throughout the coding process (Hill, Thompson, & Williams, 1997).

Procedures

As opposed to individual interviews, focus groups encourage an open dialogue about experience (Krueger & Casey, 2009). Hence, focus groups were conducted, proceedings were transcribed, and then transcript content was categorized into themes. Focus groups lasted 60–90 minutes and followed a semi-structured interview format, with open-ended questions and related follow-ups. The interview questions aimed to elicit narratives concerning experiences with microaggressions, particularly those related to race/ethnicity,

Table 7.1
Demographic Information of Participants

Gender	Age	Race	Ethnicity	Sexual Orientation	Religion	Occupation	Education	Place of Birth
Female	27	African American	African American	Lesbian	Catholic	Student	PhD candidate	Bronx, NY
Female	27	African American	African American	Lesbian	Catholic	Student	Bachelor's degree	Bronx, NY
Female	26	Black	Not specified	Gay	None	None	High school	New York, NY
Female	31	American Indian	American Indian	Lesbian	None	Archivist	Graduate school	Baltimore, MD
Female	27	East Indian	East Indian	Asexual	Atheist	Freelance artist	Bachelor's degree	Iran
Female	23	Asian	Chinese	Queer/Pansexual	Agnostic	Student, tutor	High school	New York, NY
Female	57	Black	Not specified	Bi	Not specified	Substitute teacher	BS in education	Virginia
Male	32	Black	African American	Gay	N/A	Student	Some college	Atlanta, GA
Male	30	Black	African American	Gay	None	Production	BA	Miami, FL
Male	28	Asian	Chinese	Queer	–	Support worker	Bachelor's degree	Los Angeles, CA
Male	27	African American	Black/African	Gay	Christian/Pentecostal	Data administrator	Some college	Brooklyn, NY
Male	33	Black	African American	Homosexual/Same gender loving	Christian	HIV test counselor	BA	Bronx, NY
Male	32	African American	Not specified	Gay	None	CNA at senior care building	Certified Nursing Assistant	United States
Male	26	African American/Hispanic	Black	Bisexual	Catholic	Stock/Sales associate	Third-year college student	Far Rockaway, NY
Male	46	Latino/Middle-Eastern	Jew	Gay	Israelite	Teacher/Educator	PhD (Anthropology)	Brazil
Not specified	54	Black	African American	Gay	Nondenominational	Educator	Not specified	United States

sexual orientation, and the intersection of both. All focus group facilitators identified as female, while facilitators and observers represented diverse racial backgrounds and sexual orientations. This was done to make participants feel they were in a safe environment among peers.

At the end of the interview, participants were asked to provide any additional thoughts they wished to offer. Facilitators and observers met after the conclusion of each group to discuss their observations and process their own reactions and experiences. Audio records of the focus group discussions were transcribed verbatim by the research team, maintaining the linguistic fillers and other nuances of colloquial speech.

Analysis

The four focus group transcripts were analyzed using CQR procedures (Hill et al., 1997). Coding teams held various meetings to discuss and categorize the data. In between these meetings, individual coding team members augmented data analysis by individually identifying and categorizing quotations and then meeting again with coders to discuss their findings. These meetings ensured that all the data had been attended to and that consensus was reached on all quotations and domains. The resultant list of domains and quotations was collectively agreed upon as accurately reflecting and categorizing the data reported by participants.

RESULTS

Participant responses were initially organized in four, overarching domains: microaggressions based on identity groups, microaggression themes, reactions to microaggressions, and enactors of microaggressions (see Table 7.2). Domains serve as broad categorizations of participants' responses and are sometimes further broken down into specific themes. The first domain referred to how participants experienced some microaggressions based on themes of race/ethnicity, others based on sexual orientation, and some related to the intersection of racial/ethnic identity and sexual orientation. The second domain involved the thematic content of microaggressions and the messages that they communicated. This domain was comprised of three themes: feeling unwelcomed, assumptions of criminality, and assumptions of abnormality. The third domain encompassed four themes: behavioral reactions, emotional reactions, cognitive reactions, and mental health impacts. Lastly, the fourth domain, enactors of microaggressions, listed the perpetrators of said microaggressions. These could be family members, service providers, strangers, employers, coworkers, and friends. A visual representation of the domains and themes is found next:

Table 7.2
Types and Domains of Microaggressions

DOMAIN 1: Microaggressions Based on Identity Groups	DOMAIN 2: Microaggression Themes	DOMAIN 3: Reactions to Microaggressions	DOMAIN 4: Enactors of Microaggressions
Theme 1: Race/ethnicity	Theme 1: Assumption of criminality	Theme 1: Behavioral reactions	(e.g., family members, employers, coworkers, strangers, and service providers)
Theme 2: Sexual orientation	Theme 2: Feeling unwelcomed	Theme 2: Emotional reactions	
Theme 3: Intersectional microaggressions	Theme 3: Assumptions of abnormality	Theme 3: Cognitive reactions	
		Theme 4: Mental health impacts	

After intently reviewing all of the audio recordings and transcripts of the focus groups the participants took part in, the research team chose domains and themes that repeatedly emerged in participants' responses. In order for a piece of narrative to be classified as reflective of a domain, it had to meet one of two criteria: the participant explicitly described an event as meeting a domain (i.e., stating that an incident was related to their race/ethnicity and/ or sexual orientation; describing their reactions as cognitive, affective, or behavioral; or reporting a mental health impact), or the research team collectively believed the participant's response yielded sufficient evidence to codify the quotation into a particular domain. Quotations from participants were then placed under the chosen domains. This section will offer myriad quotations from research participants that best exemplify the spirit of the domains and themes.

Domain 1: Microaggressions Based on Identity Groups
Theme 1: Race/Ethnicity

Many responses reflected microaggressions related to race or ethnicity; these were further divided into subcategories reflecting the manifestation of the microaggression: verbal and behavioral. Verbal microaggressions occurred when participants were attended to differently because of their race/ethnicity or asked particular things based on assumptions about their racial or ethnic group. One male participant described a common occurrence he experienced in social settings:

> When I'm in a bar, you know, drinking, like White people would come up to me, asking me questions . . . . After you talk to them and they'll come out of line with these questions, you know? Uh, just because I'm Black, I'm supposed to be raised in the 'hood . . . . I'm like, you know, I wasn't raised in the 'hood, so why are you coming up to me asking me these crazy questions? You know what I mean? So I kind of . . . I . . . I'm always offended.

Similarly, a Black culinary student shared how he was often assigned to cook certain types of dishes and attributed it to his race:

> [My supervisor will tell me,] "You got the collard greens, and macaroni and cheese, and the fried chicken." And you're assigned to cook it, and you're like. "I'm a culinary student so . . . . Are you actually saying that that's all I'm able to do because I'm Black? Are you going for the stereotypical thing or whatever?"

Experiences like these match the themes of assumptions of stereotypes and exoticization of Sue et al. (2007), in which people of color are often stereotyped or tokenized in various ways.

Participants also recalled being treated differently on the basis of their race or ethnicity. One woman shared an incident when she was asked to show her receipt upon exiting a retail shop, when others did not have to do so:

> So, the White couple, the guy threw out his bag and the security guy saw that. The security guy saw that he had a mug or whatever and he was walking through the door. He didn't stop him. "Have a nice night, sir" . . . And it's the same thing with the woman. She did the same thing, he didn't stop her . . . . Now, I'm Black. I have like five more M&Ms in my bag, eating. And I guess I look like shit, but whatever it is, he decides to stop me. "Did you pay for that?" I'm like, "Why are you asking me? You didn't ask them, why are you asking me? Yes, I paid for it". "Can I see your receipt?" "No." So it became a whole thing because you have to give me a plausible reason why I have to show my receipt when the other two people didn't?

Another participant described how she recognized that police officers treated her differently from her White peers:

> This was when I was in high school. So I was being searched by police, and it was weird because first of all this police officer was White and had a history of stopping only the Black or minority people. I don't know that much of what happened. He just searched my bag and that was it; I forgot what he told me . . . but I did feel a little bit upset that he did search me and he let the like a lot of White people go without being searched.

With both of these examples, participants recognized that their race played a part in how people treated them, particularly in comparison to White people.

Theme 2: Sexual Orientation

Participants revealed a number of microaggressions based on their sexual orientation identities, with both verbal and behavioral manifestations. Verbal microaggressions in this category ranged from stereotypical comments to direct personal attacks. One participant was told by his grandmother, "Y'all homosexuals gonna catch that homosexual disease which is HIV." Another participant, after offering a homeless man money, was told, "I don't ask money from faggots."

One speaker discussed microaggressions that occur within the LGBTQ community: "Even in the gay community I have seen a lot of friends of my gay male friends who are like 'Oh, she's a lesbian, blah, blah.'" She perceived comments like these as indicative of the stigma of lesbian women perpetrated by gay men.

Participants experienced different treatment on the basis of sexual orientation as well. One man described disclosing his orientation to his business partner: "From that time forward my business partner started treating me in a very, very different way. He didn't call me anymore. He wanted me to be his partner because he knows I can make money for him, but the relationship is over." This type of microaggression matches what Nadal, Yong, et al. (2011) refer to as discomfort or disapproval of the LGBQ experience. When LGBQ people's friends or family members are not comfortable with their sexual orientation, it is common for them to lose friendships or close relationships.

Theme 3: Intersectional Microaggressions

Participants revealed microaggressions associated with the intersection of their racial/ethnic and sexual orientation identities. One participant described an instance with a crime victim service, which he viewed as related to both his racial and gay identities:

> He said to me, after all these questions treating me like absolutely . . . like I was less than, he said, "So where do you work?" I said, "I'm an educational researcher for Harvard University." He said, "Oh I'm sorry, you know, I asked you those questions like that because, you know, sometimes, we have to make sure folks are telling the truth and sometimes they lie and sometimes they aren't being honest." And I thought to myself, "No, you thought I was just some ignorant Black person on 125th Street at that hour of night; you had no idea who you were dealing with and now you realize that you're dealing with me . . . that I can write and I know what to do and who I work for." All of it was rooted in two things: my being Black and my being a gay man.

Another participant believed that his identity as both a gay male and Latino was what prompted his students to ask him if he needed a green card: "But they are always asking the director of the school if I'm straight or if I'm a gay guy. And I'm also offered like green cards. I'm an American citizen, but the White students always are offering a green card."

One male participant described how he perceived that a male healthcare professional treated him differently because of race and sexual orientation, treating him as a second-class citizen and a sexual deviant. When he sought medical attention for a problem in his anal region, he noticed that the medical practitioner "tip-toed" and "didn't want to touch [him]." He continued, "This was a professional. So the way he was acting, I am like, I'm almost certain that it was because who I loved and how I loved and other things, that came into play in terms as to how he handled the situation."

One woman described the street harassment she experiences as a result of stereotypes about the intersection of her race and gender:

All the street harassment that I [experience], it is racially motivated even if they do not [say it]. "Oh there is like an East Asian woman, and East Asian women are submissive . . . . She won't talk back or you know respond in any way . . . if I catcall her or touch her or anything."

Another woman described an interaction with a school counselor that she attributed to the intersection of her race and gender:

I was going to med school and my counselor um said to me, "Why are you going to med school? Why don't you try to be a physician's assistant or a nurse?" And like, "Why? Why can't I be a doctor? I mean I have the grades. My grades show that I have the grades. Um is it 'cause I'm Black? Or is it because I'm a woman? Or what is it, you know?"

The experiences of these queer women of color matched what was found in a previous study of intersectional microaggressions by Nadal et al. (2015), in which women of color were often viewed in racialized and sexualized ways and as doubly inferior because of race, gender, or both.

Domain 2: Microaggression Themes
Theme 1: Assumption of Criminality

Most participants described microaggressions in which they were assumed to be criminal or dangerous, matching the original microaggression taxonomy of Sue et al. (2007). A few participants discussed "being followed in stores" or being perceived as "sketchy." One male speaker shared a recurrent experience of being viewed as villainous in his neighborhood:

> I live in like a gentrified area of Brooklyn, and I could be walking in the street with a hoodie on and walking behind a Caucasian female and she will grab her purse or her wallet and will make me feel some kind of way. You know, walking right behind her, just she and I on the same block walking down the street . . . . That she thinks that I'm gonna take her wallet or want to rob her.

Theme 2: Feeling Unwelcomed

Several participants reported being made to feel unwelcome in their careers, their educational pursuits, or their own cultures and families. One participant recalled being advised that she should pursue a vocation teaching in a "multicultural setting" instead of pursuing a doctoral degree. She stated, " 'Go to the 'hood and go lift those kids up and don't bother in higher [education] because you're not wanted there!' [That's] kinda what I got from it, but she thought she was steering me in the right direction, helping me."

Similarly, one woman described her experience interviewing for a job for a creative technology corporation. Someone thought she was applying for a lower-level position. She shared, "They thought I was going for the office clerk/secretary job . . . . They thought I was a Spanish girl from the ghetto . . . . They thought that I was like not there for that particular position." While there is nothing wrong with secretarial work, the assumption that people of color could not hold executive or higher-paying positions is a microaggression.

Theme 3: Assumptions of Abnormality

Some participants experienced microaggressions that communicated that they were deviant or perverse. One participant described the negative perception of sexual orientation in his culture, particularly in relation to social class:

> It's hate. It is not intolerance. It's pure hate. It's hate because homosexuality in Brazil is related with incompetence. It's related with poverty. It's related with a subculture . . . . If I'm from the bourgeoisie, if I'm homosexual, I am just a guy with a weird habit. If I'm a poor guy and gay, I'm a freak, a faggot, and I cannot even have my own life.

Participants described how culture influenced how others perceived them and treated them. This parallels previous literature (e.g., Nadal, 2013) that being a queer person of color comes with experiences of racism, homophobia, or both.

Domain 3: Reactions to Microaggressions

Identification of discriminatory experiences led participants to describe various ways in which they respond to these situations. Reactions were categorized as behavioral, emotional, or cognitive reactions or as having mental health implications.

Theme 1: Behavioral Reactions

Behavioral reactions were the most common responses participants reported. Speakers notably identified situations in which they had had to modify their behavior and hide their sexuality to avoid being subject to discrimination. This desire to "pass" was often accompanied by a heightened sense of vigilance and a fear of detection. One participant described how he has adapted to modify his behavior so as not to draw attention from others and to avoid becoming victimized: "When I'm on the train at the end of the Bronx, okay I gotta—obviously I would 'straighten up.'"

Many participants described how their behaviors were related to the intersections of race/ethnicity and sexual orientation. One participant described a constant pressure from society to hide aspects of herself:

> [I think of my identity]. . . all the time. Um. I think being a Black masculine lesbian is like . . . I mean, it's not a bad thing, but it's like one of the worse things you can be in society. So I feel pressured all the time to dress different, speak different, to talk different, talk about different things. I feel pressured all the time, really all the time, to be different and unlike myself.

Another participant described how his cultural background shapes how he behaves during family gatherings to avoid potential victimization due to his sexuality:

> My parents are Sudanese, so being around them, you know, they're accepting of me, but when we're around the family, you know, I'm forced to act as, you know, like a straight guy; something that I'm not, you know what I mean?

All of the participants described thinking about their multiple identities frequently and how doing so changes how they act and navigate the world.

Theme 2: Emotional Reactions

When participants described their experiences of microaggressions, the research team noticed prominent affective reactions—emotions ranging from feelings of embarrassment, feeling terrible, feeling offended, and to feeling distress. One participant explained how she feels when society constantly pressures her to hide her identity: "Well it makes you feel terrible. You know. It sucks that, uh, just being myself is not good enough."

Embarrassment was another frequently reported emotional reaction. One participant described his experience after an unpleasant interaction with a coworker due to his double minority status: "I felt uncomfortable, a little bit embarrassed [because] I'm Black and I'm gay."

Theme 3: Cognitive Reactions

While participants described different types of cognitive reactions, rationalization was the most frequently used. Participants used this reaction to ameliorate the denigrating messages microaggressions communicate. One participant described how they cope with other people's reactions to their various identities:

> It used to bother me but I've reached a point where it's like, if you don't like how I dress or how I look then just kick rocks because this is me. This is my life. You don't pay my bills or control me or anything, so it's your problem.

For others, experiences of discrimination reinforced empowerment or a positive sense of self. One participant described feeling empowered by microaggressions because they have taught him to appreciate certain qualities in himself: "I've learned to view it in a very positive way. I discovered that we do have this powerful body language that straight people, they don't have it. But we developed it." Being empowered and confident in oneself and using positive framing allow participants to cope with various forms of discrimination and appear to protect them from negative mental health consequences.

Theme 4: Mental Health Impacts

Participants delineated some of the ways that microaggressions affected their mental health. Negative metal health outcomes cited included general mental distress, depression, and hypervigilance in social relationships. One participant described how cumulative microaggressions caused an unwelcome alertness in social relationships and how discrimination took a mental toll:

> It makes you, you know, think twice about people, letting people into your life, and letting people take your energy, letting people throw negative things. How much you're going to take, how much you're going to tolerate. It has its toll on you. It makes it kind of hard.

Another participant recalled being disheartened and experiencing depression: "It was awful. I went into deep depression because I felt how ... how ... how wicked, how awful you people could be that you could go to this extent."

Not all participants described their experiences of microaggressions as all negative, however. Many participants described being able to adapt and utilize negative incidents as fuel for self-betterment and motivation. One participant shared how she was able to draw on repeated instances of microaggressions for motivation in her career: "You'll face it again, so try to make a positive spin again because it did motivate me to become like a Web designer or a mobile app designer." So, while microaggressions can be extremely painful, some can use such experiences to better themselves.

Domain 4: Enactors of Microaggressions

Participants described a variety of kinds of instances when they had felt offended, as a result of experiences with family, employers, coworkers, strangers, and service providers. One participant described how he felt when he experienced a verbal microaggression from a stranger in a public setting: "So I kind of … I'm always offended. You know, I never … I don't know, I mean, sometimes I'll entertain it, you know, because of the fact that I'm in a bar … but it's always offensive when they do that. You know what I mean?"

Participants described feeling especially hurt or sad when the perpetrators of microaggressions have intimate relationships with them:

> But coming from the family it hurts more. I mean, even when I'm close to my mother, in the back of my mind that statement that she always told me … that you know she wished all gay people die and go to hell …. Even though she has that, she plays a role that she's over it, but deep down inside my mother still …. I can still see it …. And it's hard, but I mean I love her to death but ….Every time I see her, that statement always sits.

As this quotation conveys, for many participants, negative emotions that result from microaggressions are not easy to heal from. When these negative feelings are internalized, they may lead to internalized homophobia or internalized heterosexism, harmful for mental health.

DISCUSSION

This study's findings clearly establish that LGBQ people of color experience an array of microaggressions in their daily lives. When study participants were asked about their experiences with subtle discrimination, they were able to identify microaggressions based on their race, gender, and sexual orientation. This replicates findings from a burgeoning line of quantitative and qualitative research and supports an impression that—while social changes might have some ways of lessening the historical burdens of racial oppression, misogyny, homophobia, and transphobia—racist, sexist, and homophobic microaggressions continue to oppress members of racial/ethnic minority groups, women, and LGBQ people.

While participants in this study reported some microaggressions that were explicitly intersectional in nature, lending some credence to the researchers' guiding sense that this understudied phenomenon deserves further research attention and is a problem that needs to be addressed in community and clinical interventions, participants had a more difficult time identifying microaggressions that targeted more than one of their identities. One possible explanation is that the participants had not experienced as many intersectional microaggressions as we hypothesized. However, an alternate explanation might be that they do encounter intersectional microaggressions but do not have the language to process or express these experiences fully. This may occur because the intended target and message of the microaggression are clear to the perpetrator; the victim must assume which or how many identities were attacked.

In the study participants' credible experience, microaggressions are abundant and perpetrated by family members, colleagues and employers, service providers, and strangers. The sheer volume and diversity of enactors of the reported racial microaggressions, sexual orientation microaggressions, and intersectional microaggressions were staggering. Microaggressions were credibly reported to occur with regularity in presumably safe and intimate private and social spaces as well as in the outside world.

Findings from this study indicate that microaggressions are a pervasive factor in the lives of LGBQ people of color and that—while they can sometimes trigger the development of positive self-regard and resilience—their effect is often deeply painful and disempowering and can lead to negative mental health impacts.

This study leaves unanswered the pathways through which these positive and, more often, negative effects develop. Future studies regarding enactors of microaggressions, and the varying effects microaggressions perpetrated by different enactors (e.g., family members versus health providers) may have on LGBQ people of color, would be helpful in quantifying the mental health impacts on this population. Similarly, how microaggressions do their damage—process issues—can be a fruitful target of future study.

Participants were quickly able to report myriad offenses committed as a result of their racial identities, sexual orientation identities, or both, leading to an array of emotional reactions and mental health consequences, both immediately after experiencing microaggressions and in terms of their cumulative impact. In spite of this, many participants retrospectively attributed positive mental health outcomes to enduring microaggressions and did not endorse negative mental health impacts. In hindsight, at least, many participants expressed gratitude for the resilience and fortitude negative experiences of microaggressions have given them. By overcoming adversity—whether based on racism, sexism, homophobia, or a combination—several participants described themselves as feeling stronger or propelling themselves forward despite others' ignorant viewpoints. The mechanisms through which this resilience-building capacity develops, and what kinds of interventions might foster its further development, would be an important focus of further study.

The sample studied in this research endeavor was small and metropolitan. It is hoped that future studies can explore whether, as current findings suggest, the adverse mental health impacts LGBQ people of color experience in response to microaggressions are generalizable. Researchers are also encouraged to examine the experiences of transgender people of color and other groups with multiple oppressed identities (e.g., LGBTQ people with disabilities, people of color with disabilities) in response to the diverse kinds of microaggressions, to further understand intersectionality theory and its implications for the understanding of microaggression theory. In undertaking further explorations in this important line of inquiry, there will be opportunities to understand how multiple identities impact the types of discrimination people experience, the ways people cope or are resilient, and the ways systems and institutions can change in order to foster safer spaces for marginalized people. In this sense, advances in LGBTQ psychology can have positive impact on populations far beyond queer communities.

REFERENCES

Balsam, K. F., Molina, Y., Beadnell, B., Simoni, J., & Walters, K. (2011). Measuring multiple minority stress: The LGBT People of Color Microaggressions Scale. *Cultural Diversity and Ethnic Minority Psychology, 17*, 163.

Blume, A. W., Lovato, L. V., Thyken, B. N., & Denny, N. (2012). The relationship of microaggressions with alcohol use and anxiety among ethnic minority college students in a historically white institution. *Cultural Diversity and Ethnic Minority Psychology, 18*, 45–54.

Bostwick, W., & Hequembourg, A. (2014). "Just a little hint": Bisexual-specific microaggressions and their connection to epistemic injustices. *Culture, Health & Sexuality, 16*, 488–503.

Bowleg, L. (2013). "Once you've blended the cake, you can't take the parts back to the main ingredients": Black gay and bisexual men's descriptions and experiences of intersectionality. *Sex Roles, 68*, 754–767.

Crenshaw, K. (1989). Demarginalizing the intersection of race and sex: A black feminist critique of antidiscrimination doctrine, feminist theory and antiracist politics. *University of Chicago Legal Forum, 1989*, 139–167.

Follins, L. D. (2014). Young Black and Latino gay men's experiences with racial microaggressions. In S. C. Howard (Ed.), *Critical articulations of race, gender, and sexual orientation* (pp. 47–63). Lanham, MD: Lexington Books.

Hill, C. E., Knox, S., Thompson, B. J., Williams, E. N., Hess, S. A., & Ladany, N. (2005). Consensual qualitative research: An update. *Journal of Counseling Psychology, 52*, 196–205.

Hill, C. E., Thompson, B., & Williams, E. (1997). A guide to conducting consensual qualitative research. *The Counseling Psychologist, 25*, 517–572.

Krueger, R. A., & Casey, M. A. (2009). *Focus groups: A practical guide for applied research* (4th ed.).Thousand Oaks, CA: Sage Publications.

Lewis, J A., & Neville, H. A. (2015). Construction and initial validation of the Gendered Racial Microaggressions Scale for Black Women. *Journal of Counseling Psychology, 62*, 289–302.

Nadal, K. L. (2013). *That's so gay! Microaggressions toward the lesbian, gay, bisexual, and transgender community*. Washington, DC: American Psychological Association.

Nadal, K. L., Davidoff, K. C., Davis, L. S., Wong, Y., Marshall, D., & McKenzie V. (2015). A qualitative approach to intersectional microaggressions: Understanding influences of race, ethnicity, gender, sexuality, and religion. *Qualitative Psychology, 2*, 147–163.

Nadal, K. L., Griffin, K. E., Wong, Y., Hamit, S., & Rasmus, M. (2014). The impact of racial microaggressions on mental health: Counseling implications for clients of color. *Journal of Counseling & Development, 92*, 57–66.

Nadal, K. L., Issa, M., Leon, J., Meterko, V., Wideman, M., & Yinglee, W. (2011). Sexual orientation microaggressions: "Death by a thousand cuts" for lesbian, gay, and bisexual youth. *Journal of LGBT Youth, 8*, 234–259.

Nadal, K. L., Skolnik, A., & Wong, Y. (2012). Interpersonal and systemic microaggressions toward transgender people: Implications for counseling. *Journal of LGBT Issues in Counseling, 6*, 55–82.

Nadal, K. L., Whitman, C. N., Davis, L. S., Erazo, T., & Davidoff, K. C. (2016). Microaggressions toward lesbian, gay, bisexual, transgender, queer and genderqueer people: A review of the literature. *Annual Review of Sex Research*. Advanced online publication. doi:10.1080/00224499.2016.1142495

Nadal, K. L., Wong, Y., Griffin, K. E., Davidoff, K., & Sriken, J. (2014). The adverse impact of racial microaggressions on college students' self-esteem. *Journal of College Student Development, 55*, 462–474.

Nadal, K. L., Wong, Y., Issa, M., Meterko, V., Leon, J., & Wideman, M. (2011). Sexual orientation microaggressions: Processes and coping mechanisms for lesbian, gay, and bisexual individuals. *Journal of LGBT Issues in Counseling, 5*, 21–46.

Nadal, K. L., Wong, Y., Sriken, J., Griffin, K., & Fujii-Doe, W. (2015). Racial microaggressions and Asian Americans: An exploratory study on within-group differences and mental health. *Asian American Journal of Psychology, 6*, 136–144. doi:10.1037/a0038058

O'Keefe, V. M., Wingate, L. R., Cole, A. B., Hollingsworth, D. W., & Tucker, R. P. (2015). Seemingly harmless racial communications are not so harmless: Racial microaggressions lead to suicidal ideation by way of depression symptoms. *Suicide and Life-Threatening Behavior, 45*, 567–576.

Platt, L. F., & Lenzen, A. L. (2013). Sexual orientation microaggressions and the experience of sexual minorities. *Journal of Homosexuality, 60*, 1011–1034.

Rivera, D., Forquer, E. E., & Rangel, R. (2010). Microaggressions and the life experience of Latina/o Americans. In D. W. Sue (Ed.), *Microaggressions and marginality: Manifestation, dynamics, and impact* (pp. 59–84). New York: Wiley & Sons.

Sue, D. W. (2010). *Microaggressions and marginality: Manifestation, dynamics, and impact*. New York, NY: Wiley.

Sue, D. W., Bucceri, J. M., Lin, A. I., Nadal, K. L., & Torino, G. C. (2010). Racial micro-aggressions and the Asian American experience. *Asian American Journal of Psychology*, *13*, 88–101.

Sue, D. W., Capodilupo, C. M., Torino, G. C., Bucceri, J. M., Holder, A. B., Nadal, K. L., & Esquilin, M. (2007). Racial microaggressions in everyday life: Implications for clinical practice. *American Psychologist*, *62*, 271–286.

Sue, D. W., Nadal, K. L., Capodilupo, C. M., Lin, A. I., Rivera, D. P., & Torino, G. C. (2008). Racial microaggressions against Black Americans: Implications for counsel-ing. *Journal of Counseling and Development*, *86*, 330–338.

Wang, J., Leu, J., & Shoda, Y. (2011). When the seemingly innocuous "stings": Racial microaggressions and their emotional consequences. *Personality and Social Psychology Bulletin*, *37*, 1666–1678. doi:10.1177/0146167211416130

Wong, G., Derthick, A. O., David, E. J. R., Saw, A., & Okazaki, S. (2014). The *what*, the *why*, and the *how*: A review of racial microaggressions research in psychology. *Race and Social Problems*, *6*, 181–200.

Woodford, M. R., Kulick, A., Sinco, B. R., & Hong, J. S. (2014). Contemporary heterosexism on campus and psychological distress among LGBQ students: The mediating role of self-acceptance. *American Journal of Orthopsychiatry*, *84*, 519–529.

Woodford, M. R., Paceley, M. S., Kulick, A., & Hong, J. S. (2015). The LGBQ social climate matters: Policies, protests, and placards and psychological well-being among LGBQ emerging adults. *Journal of Gay & Lesbian Social Services*, *27*, 116–141.

Wright, A. J., & Wegner, R. T. (2012). Homonegative microaggressions and their impact on LGB individuals: A measure validity study. *Journal of LGBT Issues in Counseling*, *6*, 34–54.

8

Addictions and Substance Abuse in the LGBT Community: New Approaches

Barbara C. Wallace and Erik Santacruz

As we focus on addictions and substance abuse in the LGBT community, it is vital to heed advice to avoid the stigmatization, stereotyping, or pathologizing of the LGBT community (Abdulrahim, Whiteley, Moncrieff, & Bowden-Jones, 2016). Data from the largest nationally representative sample of sexual minorities, to date, make clear that most *had not* engaged in substance use and most *did not* meet criteria for problematic substance use (McCabe, Hughes, Bostwick, West, & Boyd, 2009). Both in the United States and globally, the majority of the members of the LGBT community do not use substances, and, among those who do use substances, the majority are able to do so without any associated harm (Abdulrahim et al., 2016).

Yet, this chapter will present a body of evidence documenting the manner in which sexual minority adults present a particularly high prevalence and heightened risk for substance involvement (e.g., alcohol, drugs) in comparison to heterosexuals, including across the life span. More specifically, this chapter will cover the following topics: (1) the diagnosis of substance use disorder and prevalence patterns among sexual minority groups; (2) club drug, poly-drug, alcohol, cigarette, prescription drug, and opioid use patterns; and (3) meeting the needs of diverse clients—such as those presented in a series of illustrative cases—via new approaches and advances in treatment, including future directions in research.

THE DIAGNOSIS OF SUBSTANCE USE DISORDERS AND PREVALENCE PATTERNS

The fifth edition of the *Diagnostic and Statistical Manual of Mental Disorders (DSM-5)* of the American Psychiatric Association (APA, 2013) provides the contemporary standard for diagnosing *substance use disorders*. In *DSM-5*, a diagnosis of a substance use disorder requires evidence of meeting two or more of

the following criteria within a 12-month period: evidence of engaging in hazardous use; experiencing social/interpersonal problems related to use; neglecting
major role obligations in order to use; experiencing withdrawal; demonstrating
tolerance, meaning using larger amounts/over longer periods of time; reporting
repeated attempts to quit/control use; reporting a great deal of time engaged in
using; manifesting physical/psychological problems related to use; reporting
activities that were given up in order to use; and reporting craving—as a major
change from DSM-IV to permit use of biological treatments (Hasin et al.,
2013). Possibilities include also using the *DSM-5* to diagnosis co-morbidity
where clients present additional disorders—that is, depression, anxiety, posttraumatic stress disorder, and bipolar disorder (Wallace, 2005).

Prevalence Patterns for Sexual Minority Youth

Compared to heterosexual youth, a meta-analysis found that LGB youth
reported significantly higher rates of substance use; and, there were large effect
sizes found in a meta-analysis for the relationship between sexual orientation
and lifetime cigarette use, injection drug use, and a composite drug use variable
(Marshal et al., 2008). The odds of substance use for LGB youth were 190 percent
higher, on average, than for heterosexuals, 340 percent higher for bisexual
youth, and 400 percent higher for female sexual minority youth. Links between
sexual orientation and substance use were strongest for LGB youth with victimization histories (Marshal et al., 2008).

LGB youth engage in both more alcohol use and heavy drinking in comparison to heterosexual youth (Talley, Hughes, Aranda, Birkett, & Marshal, 2014).
Data for those aged 13–18 were more likely to report lifetime and past-month
alcohol use; an earlier age initiation of drinking alcohol; and past-month heavy
episodic drinking—including at a higher frequency of drinking days. Sexual
minority girls reported higher rates of lifetime alcohol use (81.3%) in comparison to heterosexual girls (66.9%), heterosexual boys (65.6%), and sexual minority boys (68.9%) and higher rates of past-month heavy episodic drinking (30%)
in comparison to heterosexual girls (16.4%), heterosexual boys (19.3%), and
sexual minority boys (25.4%; Talley et al., 2014).

Research on substance use among transgender youth has been nearly nonexis-
tent (Institute of Medicine [IOM], 2011). Others indicated there is an elevated
risk for transgender youth relative to heterosexuals (Heck et al., 2014; Hotton,
Garofalo, Kuhns, & Johnson, 2013).

Prevalence Patterns for Older Sexual Minority Adults

With increasing age, substance use disorders decline in prevalence. However,
adult LGBT individuals start with higher rates of substance use disorders in

comparison to age-matched heterosexuals (McCabe et al., 2009; Yarns, Abrams, Meeks, & Sewell, 2016).

Also, data indicated that, for all sexual minority groups, alcohol use decreases with age; however, these changes occur at later ages and tend to be smaller in comparison to rates for heterosexuals (Hughes, Wilsnack, & Kantor, 2016). For example, sexual minority women's (SMW) rates of alcohol consumption were found to defy a significant decline by age when comparing younger and middle-aged groups to older age groups; this was unlike the decline observed for women in the general population. SMW aged 50 and older were significantly more likely to engage in excessive drinking when compared to age-matched heterosexual women; the same pattern prevailed for gay and bisexual men aged 50 and older when compared to age-matched heterosexual men. Older gay men aged 41–60 had higher rates of alcohol problems (19%) in comparison to heterosexual men (7%) in that age group; and for lesbian women aged 41–60, findings showed they were three times more likely to report alcohol problems (15%) in comparison to heterosexual women (4.5%) in that age group (Hughes et al., 2016).

Other findings have indicated that, for older men who have sex with men (MSM), the use of alcohol and other drugs is associated with an increased likelihood of engaging in high-risk sexual behavior; and data have shown that drinking among older MSM when engaging in sex was associated with engaging in more high-risk sex in comparison to younger MSM (Heath, Lanoye, & Maisto, 2012). Older age has also been shown to predict increased use of opioids for nonmedical use (Yarns et al., 2016).

Prevalence Patterns for SMW

Evidence indicated greater risk for SMW—that is, lesbian and bisexual women—engaging in heavy alcohol use and having a greater prevalence of alcohol use disorders across the life span compared to heterosexual women (Wilson, Gilmore, Rhew, Hodge, & Kaysen, 2016). A large national sample found lesbians were 3.6 times more likely and bisexual women 2.9 times more likely to meet criteria for past-year alcohol dependence (McCabe et al., 2009; Yarns et al., 2016). Others found SMW to be at higher risk for alcohol abuse or hazardous drinking when compared to heterosexual women (Drabble, Trocki, Hughes, Korcha, & Lown, 2013; Hughes et al., 2016; Wilsnack et al., 2008). Higher rates of drinking were found for SMW compared to heterosexual women (Coulter, Marzell, Saltz, Stall, & Mair, 2016).

Some studies found lesbians were more likely to report being in recovery from alcohol with a history of being in treatment and in recovery (Drabble, Midanik, & Trocki, 2005). Consistent research showed that, compared to heterosexual women, lesbians were approximately 7 times more likely and bisexual women about 6.5 times more likely to meet the criteria for alcohol dependence, by

*DSM-IV*criteria. Further, seeking help for alcohol problems was eight times greater for lesbians and four times greater for bisexual women. Regarding experiencing being drunk at least two or more times in the past, SMW were 2.5 times more likely to report this in comparison to heterosexual women. Also, in comparison to heterosexual women, the odds for having experienced two or more negative consequences from drinking alcohol (i.e., fights, arguments, angry partner because of drinking, physician recommendation to cut down, lost time at work, legal problems) were approximately 11 times greater for lesbians and 8 times greater for bisexual women (Drabble et al., 2005). SMW had a higher prevalence of alcohol use disorder and alcohol-related problems (Green & Feinstein, 2012), such as sexual assault and suicidality (Coulter et al., 2016).

For drug use, data showed lesbians were 11–12 times more likely to meet criteria for past-year drug dependence in comparison to age-matched heterosexual women, while there were no statistically significant differences for bisexual women when compared to age-matched heterosexual women (McCabe et al., 2009; Yarns et al., 2016). Yet, research has found bisexual women to have greater use of cannabis in comparison to heterosexual women. Past-year illegal cannabis use was five times greater for bisexual women than for women in general; and greater use of cannabis was associated with higher depression (Robinson, Sanches, & MacLeod, 2016).

Prevalence Patterns for Sexual Minority Men

Regarding sexual minority men—including gay, bisexual, and other MSM—there is also evidence of elevated alcohol use. Data showed gay men were 2.9 times more likely and bisexual men were 4.2 times more likely to meet criteria for past-year alcohol use in comparison to age-matched heterosexual men (McCabe et al., 2009). Regarding being drunk at least two or more times in the past, gay men were nearly three times as likely to report this in comparison to heterosexual men (Drabble et al., 2005). MSM had high rates of heavy alcohol use, alcohol problems, and alcohol-related disorders, while links between HIV acquisition and heavy drinking underscore the urgent public health problem for MSM (Wray et al., 2016). Research showed high rates of alcohol use among urban MSM, including heavy frequent alcohol use and three or more alcohol-related problems (Stall et al., 2001).

Research also indicated that gay men were 4.2 times more likely and bisexual men were 6.3 times more likely to meet criteria for past-year drug dependence in comparison to age-matched heterosexual men (McCabe et al., 2009; Yarns et al., 2016). Data for urban MSM also showed frequent engagement in multiple drug use (Stall et al., 2001). There was a greater risk for MSM being involved in illicit drug use and having related problems (Green & Feinstein, 2012). Drug use before or during sex was associated with increased risk for acquiring HIV (Coffin et al., 2014).

MSM have been shown to use methamphetamine and other amphetamine-type stimulants at rates 10 times higher than those found in the general population (Colfax & Shoptaw, 2005). Methamphetamine has been injected, smoked, snorted, and ingested orally and anally—amphetamine compounds including substances known as speed, ice, tina, crystal, or crank. Ingestion increases energy and sexual desire; and methamphetamine use has been reported to "always" or "often" occur with engagement in sex (p. 195). Methamphetamine use is "a driving force in the transmission of HIV," being associated with increased engagement in sexual risk behavior (e.g., unprotected anal sex with unknown or opposite serostatus partners, syphilis, high numbers of sexual partners, condom breakage, higher viral loads, and compromised adherence and decreased effectiveness of antiretroviral therapy (ART; p. 195).

Prevalence Patterns for Transgender Adults

Researchers have asserted that, relative to other sexual minorities, less is known about transgender persons with regard to substance use disorders, while the available data have suggested elevated risk for this group, also (Flentje, Bacca, & Cochran, 2015; Heck et al., 2014; IOM, 2011; Yarns et al., 2016). Prior research has indicated elevated lifetime alcohol use, marijuana use, and cocaine use for this population (Hoffman, 2014).

Research with a large trans masculine sample (i.e., female-to-male or transgender men) revealed a high burden of discrimination across a variety of settings, including healthcare settings, and substance use to cope with mistreatment (Reisner et al., 2015). Some 1 in 10 reported having been refused healthcare by a provider due to being transgender or gender nonconforming, and 27.6 percent used substances to cope. Data confirmed prior research on associations between substance use and adverse health outcomes, including poor mental health, chronic disease, and infectious disease (Reisner et al., 2015).

Researchers have emphasized how transgender women also engage in high rates of sex work, with as many as 50 percent acknowledging intoxication with drugs and alcohol during sex work (Hoffman, 2014). The HIV prevalence rate of transgender women (27.7%) has been characterized as exceeding that of MSM. Concerns regarding elevated drug/alcohol use include multiple links to the risk of acquiring HIV, as follows: injection drug use (i.e., for intoxication and to achieve feminization with hormones or silicone) is linked with sharing needles and a risk for HIV transmission; lowered inhibitions from drugs/alcohol use are linked with an increased risk of engagement in high-risk sexual behavior, including having multiple partners and condom-less sex; and intoxication with drugs/alcohol is linked to higher engagement in more receptive anal sex and unprotected anal sex, including with commercial sex partners (Hoffman, 2014).

For a diverse sample of transwomen (i.e., male-to-female transgender), two-thirds reported lifetime injection drug use or nonmedically prescribed hormone misuse (Reback & Fletcher, 2014). Lifetime injection drug use or nonmedically prescribed hormone misuse was associated with a 21–125 percent increase in the odds of transwomen being HIV positive (Reback & Fletcher, 2014). Older transgender adults have suffered negative health outcomes from long-term hormone use (IOM, 2011). For intoxicant poly-drug use, alcohol was the most frequently reported, followed by marijuana, methamphetamine use, cocaine, and crack use (Reback & Fletcher, 2014). Recent methamphetamine and crack use were each associated with more than doubling in the estimated odds of transwomen being HIV positive, when controlling for demographics, other substance use, and sexual risk behaviors (Reback & Fletcher, 2014).

Other research with a convenience sample of mostly African American diverse transgender adults (male-to-female, 67.1%; female-to-male, 32.9%) indicated 25.6 percent reported lifetime engagement in nonmedical use of prescription drugs; this included prescription analgesics/painkillers, anxiolytics/anti-anxiety medication, stimulants, and sedatives (Benotsch et al., 2013). Transgender adults also engaged in the lifetime nonmedical use of hormones (30.3%); and those who reported the nonmedical use of prescription drugs (N = 41) were significantly more likely to report use of other substances (alcohol, marijuana, ecstasy, poppers, cocaine, methamphetamine, heroin, and other recreational drugs), suggesting engagement in poly-drug use, compared to those not reporting (N = 114) nonmedical use of prescription drugs. Associated risks from the combined use of alcohol with nonmedical use of prescription drugs place individuals at risk for respiratory failure, seizures, coma, and death. Also, those who reported the nonmedical use of prescription drugs scored significantly higher on measures of depression anxiety, somatic distress, global psychiatric distress, self-esteem, and gender identity discrimination. Perceptions of discrimination due to gender identity were also associated with the nonmedical use of prescription drugs (Benotsch et al., 2013, p. 393).

CLUB DRUG/POLY-DRUG, ALCOHOL, CIGARETTE, PRESCRIPTION DRUG, AND OPIOID USE

Also warranted is a focus on club drug, poly-drug, alcohol, cigarette, prescription drug, and opioid use, including heroin. Common use patterns will be identified.

Club Drug, Poly-Drug, Alcohol, and Viagra Use Patterns

Investigations of club drug use among sexual minorities have noted higher rates for using numerous drugs compared to heterosexuals. These club drugs include cannabis, cocaine, ecstasy (i.e., MDA/Molly), methamphetamine (amphetamines), amyl nitrite (poppers), ketamine, hallucinogens (LSD, PCP, DMT, ayahuasca, mescaline, peyote, psilocybin, salvia), and tranquilizers; poly-drug use also predominates, involving combinations of these drugs (Abdulrahim et al., 2016, p. 1). Additional substances have also been included in the category of club drugs gamma-hydroxybutyric acid (GHB), Rohypnol, heroin, prescription drugs and cold medicines, synthetic cannabinoids (K2/spice), synthetic cathinones (bath salts), steroids (anabolic), as well as tobacco/nicotine (National Institute on Drug Abuse [NIDA], 2012a). Club drugs have been used heavily by MSM; elevated use has also been found in lesbian and bisexual women and transgender women (Abdulrahim et al., 2016; Reisner, Gamarel, Nemoto, & Operario, 2014; Yarns et al., 2016). Female gender has not served as a protective factor for drug use for SMW, while it has tended to be protective for heterosexual women (Green & Feinstein, 2012). Of great concern is how more severe substance use was associated with higher odds for HIV risk (Coffin et al., 2014).

Typically combined with heavy alcohol use, the club drugs methamphetamine, amyl nitrate (poppers), and cocaine have been found to be associated with not only increased sexual libido but also engagement in high-risk sexual behavior (Coffin et al., 2014). This risk has included unprotected anal intercourse, sexually transmitted infections (STIs), condom failure (slippage, breakage), and HIV transmission (Coffin et al., 2014). Further, to cope with erectile dysfunction as a consequence of using club drugs, Viagra has been used, increasing risky sexual behavior (RSB; Yarns et al., 2016).

Methamphetamine, Cocaine/Crack, and Poly-Drug Use

Methamphetamine, cocaine, and crack cocaine dominate the substances that may result in a stimulant use disorder or may be a part of binge or episodic drug use patterns (Washton & Zweben, 2009). Sexual minority youth are also engaged in higher rates of cocaine use compared to heterosexual youth (Sadhir, Stockburger, & Omar, 2016). Research has shown the use of crack cocaine to be among the factors associated with HIV infection in young MSM (Millett, Peterson, Wolitski, & Stall, 2006). Methamphetamine has been identified as the drug with the highest prevalence of use among MSM, and is linked to engagement in high-risk sexual behavior (i.e., unprotected insertive and receptive anal sex, casual partners, condom-less sex) and increased risk of HIV and STI transmission (Mausbach, Semple, Strathdee, Zians, & Patterson, 2007).

Research has also highlighted methamphetamine as the single drug most strongly associated with transwomen being HIV positive (Santos et al., 2014). Data showed a high prevalence of alcohol and substance use with a sample of transwomen (N = 314); 58 percent used alcohol, and 43 percent used other substances; specifically, marijuana (29%), methamphetamine (20.1%), crack cocaine (13.4%), and club drug use (13.1%) were reported. The use of metham-phetamine (i.e., before or during anal intercourse) by transwomen was associated with significantly greater odds of transwomen testing HIV positive, compared to transwomen who did not use methamphetamine within the context of anal intercourse. Also, at least weekly methamphetamine users had greater odds of testing positive for HIV when compared to transwomen who did not use meth-amphetamine. However, crack cocaine use carries great stigma and may have been underreported in the sample; and transwomen using crack and living with HIV likely have higher mortality rates. This may have contributed to selection bias in the sample, which may have led to nonsignificant findings (Santos et al., 2014).

Crack cocaine is the only illicit drug that Black MSM report using at higher rates than other MSM; however, what is not known is the potential role of higher rates of crack cocaine use in contributing to Black MSM being at greatest risk for HIV (Millett et al., 2006). Also, Black MSM were more likely to use crack or cocaine during sex (Millett et al., 2006).

Marijuana within Poly-Drug Use

Marijuana use has also been found in association with sex. Black MSM have been found to engage in particularly high rates of marijuana use, including for general use (60.4%) and as a sex-drug (20.8%; Morgan et al., 2016). When investigating Black MSM and their social network members, findings for those aged 30 and above showed their most commonly used sex-drugs were marijuana (24%), cocaine/crack (25%), and poppers (9.4%; Morgan et al., 2016). For Black MSM aged 30 and below, their most commonly used sex-drugs were marijuana (17.6%), psychedelics (11.1%), and poppers (8.3%). When adjusting for the use of all general-use drugs, sex-drug use of marijuana was significantly associated with engagement in condom-less sex and group sex. Rates of marijuana use are rising among Black men and women (Morgan et al., 2016).

The research findings on marijuana augment evidence that club drugs are linked to a range of negative consequences. These consequences include increased engagement in RSBs, while substance use serves to impair immune function, reduce antiretroviral therapy medication adherence, and thereby increase the risk of HIV transmission (Yarns et al., 2016).

Tobacco/Cigarette Use Patterns

Cigarette smoking commonly occurs in association with alcohol and drug use (Ryan, Wortley, Easton, Pederson, & Greenwood, 2001). As a major public health priority, the burden of tobacco-related morbidity and mortality includes disparities among sexual minorities (Blosnich, Lee, & Horn, 2013). Smoking rates among adult (11%–50%) and adolescent (38%–59%) sexual minorities

(LGB) were found to be higher than national rates for adults (28%) and adolescents (28%–35%) across comparable time periods (Ryan et al., 2001). The transgender population has been included in data showing significant higher LGBT community cigarette smoking rates (32.8%) than those found in the general U.S. adult population (19.5%) and in comparison to heterosexuals (19.5%; Matthews, McConnell, Li, Vargas, & King, 2014). National survey data showed that LGB persons were found to have higher rates of tobacco use (38.5%) in comparison to heterosexuals (25.3%), even as rates of use declined with increasing age for the LGB group (Yarns et al., 2016). National and state surveys also showed higher percentages of sexual minority youth reporting current tobacco/cigarette use (Sadhir et al., 2016).

Examining the population of MSM, their disproportionate burden of ill health includes health burden associated with higher rates of cigarette smoking in comparison to heterosexual men, including higher rates of smoking for young MSM (Abdulrahim et al., 2016; D'Avanzo, Halkitis, Yu, & Kapadia, 2016; Stall, Greenwood, Acree, Paul, & Croates, 1999). Among young MSM, research found the odds of being either a current or former smoker were higher for current users of alcohol or marijuana and higher for those with internalized antihomosexual prejudice (D'Avanzo et al., 2016). A meta-analysis found young MSM aged 13–21 had a cigarette prevalence rate of 41.5–59 percent compared to the national average for 13–21-year-olds of 28–35 percent (Storholm, Halkitis, Siconolfi, & Moeller, 2011). Cigarette smoking has been identified as part of a syndemic among young MSM (i.e., ages 13–29), with a prevalence higher than among heterosexuals and also associated with the use of illicit drugs, alcohol, and pharmaceuticals obtained without a prescription (Storholm et al., 2011).

Among the risk factors for smoking, research has identified internalized homophobia and the stress related to coming out; meanwhile, a body of research has documented higher rates for sexual minorities of stress, depression, alcohol use, and victimization experiences (Blosnich et al., 2013). Daily stress from homophobia, discrimination, victimization, socialization in bars/discrimination in other settings, targeting by the tobacco industry, the stress of coming out, lack of social support (i.e., parents, family, peers), isolation and loneliness, and, alcohol and drug use are all potential factors in high rates of cigarette smoking (Ryan et al., 2001).

Prescription Drug Use, Opioid Analgesics, and Heroin Use

The United States is currently experiencing an epidemic of overdose deaths from opioids, primarily prescription pain relievers and heroin. Indeed, the rate of overdoses has tripled since year 2000 (Davis & Carr, 2016; Rudd, Aleshire, Zibbell, & Gladden, 2016). Older age has been shown to predict increased use of opioids for nonmedical use, while older LGBT adults have evidenced higher rates of certain physical illnesses in comparison to the general population of older adults (Yarns et al., 2016). While more than 30 percent of all adults suffer from acute or chronic pain, among older adults there is a 40 percent prevalence of chronic pain (Volkow & McLellan, 2016). Older adults are more susceptible to chronic pain, which is the most prevalent and debilitating medical condition among Americans; chronic pain is also the most controversial and complex condition to manage, typically involving the use of opioid analgesics. Over-reliance on opioid medications is associated with overdose and addiction (Volkow & McLellan, 2016).

Research has highlighted how many transgender adults engage in the non-medical use of prescription drugs, including opioid analgesics/painkillers, anxiolytics, and sedatives (Benotsch et al., 2013). Rates of alcohol use were shown to be high among transgender adults (72.5%), and the combined use of alcohol with nonmedical use of prescription drugs places individuals at great risk (i.e., respiratory failure, seizures, coma), including the risk of death (Benotsch et al., 2013). Also, prior research showed rates of heroin to be of concern among transgender adults. Data showed 10.3 percent reported the use of heroin (Benotsch et al., 2013). Also, those who abuse alcohol, illicit drugs, and nicotine or have mental disorders (e.g., depression or attention deficit/hyperactivity disorder) are more vulnerable for developing an opioid addiction, upon exposure to opioid analgesics (Volkow & McLellan, 2016). Opioid analgesic misuse has been identified as the strongest predictor of transitioning to heroin; and, heroin is less expensive and often more available than prescription painkillers (Davis & Carr, 2016).

NEW APPROACHES AND ADVANCES IN TREATMENT FOR DIVERSE CLIENTS

Treatment must address the tremendous diversity to be found within the community of sexual minorities, as reflected in the following cases:

Maria is a Puerto Rican lesbian, college educated, insurance broker who, at age 58, was rushed to the emergency room for a near-fatal overdose. Maria combined the painkiller Oxycodone, which she used for lower back pain, with alcohol and marijuana. A long-standing major depressive disorder was exacerbated after a divorce from her wife, including loss of access to their child, contributing to her addiction. The emergency room referred Maria to an outpatient clinic for integrated treatment of her addiction and depression as well as to a specialty pain clinic.

Tommy is a single, gay, HIV-positive, white, male Irish Catholic with a GED who relapsed to compulsive crack cocaine smoking at age 48, after 12 years of stable abstinence. After starting a new job, he felt pressure to drink alcohol with his boss. He eventually relapsed to compulsive crack cocaine smoking, nonadherence to his HIV medication, high-risk sex, and he exchanged sex for drugs/money. Tommy was arrested and mandated to drug treatment, where he was diagnosed with neurological complications from AIDS and depression.

Dang *is a 30-year-old bisexual Asian male with a college degree who reported a recent alcohol blackout and rape involving condom-less anal intercourse. He sought HIV/STI testing from a public health clinic, where he admitted to heavy binge alcohol use and compulsive sexual behavior nearly every weekend with multiple partners, but for "always with condoms." Dang was referred to an outpatient clinic for integrated treatment for his alcohol use, rape trauma, compulsive sexual behavior, and anxiety over disclosing details of his life to his girlfriend.*

Gerri *is a 41-year-old trans masculine Jamaican immigrant whose job as a machine operator was in jeopardy, after he came to work with alcohol on his breath, following all-night drinking and gambling. A supervisor directed Gerri to enter their Employee Assistance Program (EAP), where urine testing revealed marijuana use; he admitted to smoking pot with his girlfriend. The EAP directed him to an inpatient rehabilitation center for his alcohol, marijuana, and gambling issues. Gerri emerged an enthusiast of Gambler's Anonymous and Alcoholics Anonymous. He broke up with his girlfriend, since she was not ready to give up marijuana smoking.*

Kathy, *a 25-year-old White, bisexual Jewish woman, worked as an administrative assistant while pursuing a master's degree. She smoked marijuana daily before and after work and almost continuously on weekends. Her girlfriend sold marijuana, always having a large supply. After a sudden breakup, Kathy was unable to access the large amount of marijuana she had used for over a decade to cope with insomnia and anxiety. She opened up about her issues with her medical doctor and received a referral to a psychiatrist specializing in addiction treatment.*

Stacey *is a 50-year-old biracial transgender woman who reported a long history of poly-drug use, including hormone injections. She suffered severe neck pain from a violent sexual assault, which led to disability and dependence on prescription painkillers. Following mistreatment due to her being transgender, Stacey refused to return to the physician who prescribed the painkillers, eventually shifting to snorting and then injecting heroin. After a friend died from a heroin overdose, Stacey entered inpatient detoxification, followed by entrance into a methadone maintenance treatment program (MMTP). A year later, Stacey pursued gradual detoxification from methadone in a specialized long-term residential therapeutic community (TC).*

Kwame, *a young Black MSM, was 19 and in college, HIV negative, and had a boyfriend who just admitted to being HIV positive. After months of their dating, Kwame sought help for anxiety from the college counseling center. He was referred for PrEP, given inconsistent condom use. PrEP counseling uncovered how condom-less sex was associated with binge use of club drugs (i.e., ketamine, poppers), poly-drug use (i.e., crack, marijuana), and alcohol. He accepted a referral for drug treatment at an outpatient clinic.*

Frankie *is a 68-year-old White gay man with an MBA who was pressured into treatment by his business partner and husband, who was ready for divorce and wanted to sell their business. Frankie reported heavy alcohol use; escalating use of club drugs (i.e., ketamine, poppers, methamphetamine, Viagra); relapsing to compulsive sexual behavior, a pattern from his 30s to 40s; and a relapse to cigarette smoking. Secondhand smoke was exacerbating his husband's asthma. Once in an inpatient rehabilitation center, Frankie was diagnosed with bipolar disorder.*

Bernadette, a 41-year-old African American lesbian with an AS degree working in retail sales, had been married for two years. She was recently placed on probation at work, after a serious lapse in judgment. As a survivor of childhood sexual abuse, Bernadette presented posttraumatic stress disorder as well as severe dependence on alcohol, marijuana, and cocaine. Bernadette's late-night drinking in bars and driving home under the influence compelled her wife to leave their home, triggering Bernadette's recent depression with suicidal ideation. Bernadette entered an outpatient clinic for integrated treatment of her addiction, psychological issues, and trauma.

Louis, a recent immigrant from Peru, South America, is a 16-year-old Latino openly gay male. After being caught smoking marijuana in a high school bathroom, a referral to his guidance counselor allowed Louis to reveal depression and suicidal ideation from severe bullying in school. Louis was referred to an adolescent specialty clinic for marijuana use and depression. At the clinic, Louis admitted to engaging in sex for money with older men, having trouble negotiating condom use, and use of club drugs (e.g., ketamine, poppers, methamphetamine) with heavy binge drinking when he was with these older men.

The cases affirm the IOM's (IOM, 2011) emphasis on the tremendous diversity of the LGBT population, including diversity that follows from age, race/ethnicity, educational level, socioeconomic status, religion, and other characteristics. Fortunately, there are new approaches and advances in treatment for addressing the diversity embodied in the cases of Maria, Tommy, Dang, Gerri, Kathy, Stacey, Kwame, Frankie, Bernadette, and Louis.

Existing Evidence-Based Interventions and Two Core Issues

The discussion of new approaches and advances in treatment necessitates attention to two core issues. The first issue involves the "extent to which interventions widely tested in majority populations can be readily adapted for patients with different ethnic or sociocultural backgrounds" (Anderson, 2006, p. 279), such as being readily adapted with ethnic/racial minority groups or sexual minorities. The second issue involves the "extent to which social factors and cultural differences necessitate different forms of treatment" (p. 279), such as a treatment model created to be culturally relevant and specific for a cultural group. Regarding the first core issue, relevant background includes that, there has been an "inadequate representation of members of ethnic/racial minority groups" in investigations of evidence-based treatments (Whaley & Davis, 2007, p. 563). As a result, there have been related questions as to whether or not these treatments are, therefore, valid for ethnic/racial minorities (Whaley & Davis, 2007).

For example, consider whether it is necessary to conduct research that seeks to replicate findings of what works for heterosexual women with SMW (Green & Feinstein, 2012). Of note, "advocates of cultural competence and empirically supported treatment agree that treatments that have been shown to work with predominantly European American populations should be tried with ethnic/racial minority individuals" (Whaley & Davis, 2007, p. 572). This follows from how ethnic/racial minorities in the United States are viewed as sharing some cultural characteristics with the mainstream society, so it is also reasonable to assume that "culturally specific interventions developed for ethnic/racial minority groups are effective with other cultural groups, including European Americans" (p. 572).

Thus, evidence-based approaches (i.e., "what works") are deemed to be generalizable from one group to another. This includes their use with any of the subgroups of sexual minorities.

Two Types of Treatment Approaches with Sexual Minorities

Following the analysis of Talley (2013), the available evidence base with regard to substance abuse treatment studies that *do* focus exclusively on sexual minorities can be described as falling into two broad types. The first type, *traditional evidence-based treatment*, has involved the administration of empirically supported treatment for substance abuse, which is generalized from heterosexual studies and provided to sexual minorities; for example, this involves generalizing to sexual minority groups use of the evidence-based substance abuse treatment interventions of 12-step facilitation, cognitive behavioral therapy (CBT), contingency management (CM), and motivational interviewing (MI), while materials and messages are merely adapted to the characteristics of the target population. This first type of *traditional evidence-based treatment* involves *minimally altering* evidence-based intervention materials and messages for the target population of sexual minorities, as interventions are adapted to the observable characteristics of the target population (Talley, 2013).

Regarding the previously mentioned core issue covering the extent to which social factors and cultural differences necessitate different forms of treatment (Anderson, 2006), here, most relevant is Talley's (2013) second type of treatment studies conducted with sexual minorities. This second type of treatment study, *culturally tailored treatment for cultural relevance*, has involved implementation of alterations to treatments in an effort to address cultural, social, psychological, environmental, and historical factors conceptualized as contributing to substance abuse in the target population (Talley, 2013). For example, treatments address gay culture and identify acceptance, disclosure of sexual identity, experiences of childhood and/or adulthood victimization, minority stress, potential family rejection, and specific coping strategies for use with peers engaged in substance use. This second type involves *extensively adapting* materials and programs so they are culturally relevant for sexual minorities. There is no "consistent evidence to suggest approaches that extensively adapt materials and programs to be culturally relevant for treatment-seeking LGB individuals are any more successful at reducing or eliminating substance abuse compared with approaches that are minimally altered" (p. 539). Yet, transgender-specific substance abuse treatment and support systems are needed (Hoffman, 2014).

Making the Case That Cultural Adaptations to Evidence-Based Treatments Are Sufficient

On the other hand, there are those who provide compelling support for the value in the first type of *traditional evidence-based treatment* being *minimally altered* for the target population or undergoing a small degree of altering to the observable characteristics of the target population, following Talley (2013). It has been asserted that it is sufficient to engage in *cultural adaptations to evidence-based treatments*, thereby providing more culturally competent services (Whaley & Davis, 2007). Whaley and Davis (2007) define *cultural adaptation* as engaging in any adjustment "to an evidence-based treatment that involves changes in the approach to service delivery, in the nature of the therapeutic relationship, or in components of the treatment itself to accommodate the cultural beliefs, attitudes, and behaviors of the target population" (p. 571). They identify a body of literature in support of their conclusion that "standard empirically supported treatments are efficacious" with ethnic/racial minorities, and "modifications to service delivery may be sufficient cultural adaptations in many cases" (p. 572).

By extension, it follows that to meet the needs of the diverse group of sexual minorities in the illustrative cases means engaging in *cultural adaptations to evidence-based substance abuse treatments* in response to a unique cultural background, religion, sexual orientation, and gender identity. This follows whether for a Puerto Rican lesbian, White, Irish Catholic, bisexual Asian, trans masculine Jamaican immigrant, white Jewish lesbian, biracial transgender woman, young Black MSM, African American lesbian, or adolescent gay male Peruvian immigrant.

Making the Case for Individually Tailored Treatment

There is a history of clinician-delivered therapies being were considered most efficacious because they were individualized and dependent upon interaction with clients (Prochaska, 2008). Thus, what is recommended is to *individualize treatments via the use of tailored interventions* (Prochaska, 2008). Behavior change is viewed as a process that unfolds over time, as individual clients progress at their own pace through stages of change (SOC) that include precontemplation, contemplation, preparation, action, maintenance, and relapse (DiClemente & Velasquez, 2002). In this manner, change is a dynamic individualized process, which requires interventions being tailored to the needs of individual clients, including to their stage of change (Prochaska, 2008).

In contrast to Prochaska's (2008) endorsement of individually tailored treatment, the evidence-based movement sought to standardize therapies by rooting them in the use of treatment manuals. Prochaska (2008) argues that, instead of individual differences being conceptualized as variability to be controlled, individual differences constitute opportunities for tailoring treatment to current needs of the individual. Instead of seeking to control individual differences "as a threat to validity," the use of individually tailored interventions should "be driven by such differences as a foundation for external validity" (p. 72). Well endorsed is Use of individually tailored treatments as the standard of care in substance abuse treatment is well endorsed (e.g., NIDA, 2012b; Wallace, 2005; Washton & Zweben, 2009).

Making the Case for a Multiple-Behavior Paradigm—Addressing Multiple Problems

Despite the reality that many individuals—including those in our illustrative cases—have more than one problem behavior, as per Prochaska's (2008) observation, randomized controlled trials target a single specific problem behavior or condition while evaluating a single specific treatment. However, psychological treatments are not specific to single problem behaviors, despite the tendency to evaluate them as if they are. Prochaska (2008) advocates use of a multiple-behavior paradigm to impact multiple problem behaviors instead of simply treating single problem behaviors. Most noteworthy for population health, the "highest risk and highest cost people are those with multiple behavior problems" (p. 73). Thus, what are needed are "impacts on multiple behaviors" that are treated by tailored communications (p. 75). Clients with a single condition can still receive a single-behavior approach within a multiple-behavior paradigm. Prochaska's (2008) analysis makes the case for new approaches and advances in treatment that seek to impact multiple-behavior outcomes.

Consistent with this, others describe contemporary clients with substance use disorders as "multiproblem," while outlining to address these multiple problems via use of MI and relapse prevention (RP), for example (Wallace, 2005). Multiproblem clients have been described as presenting various combinations of substance use disorders, mental disorders, and behavioral health and physical health issues; this requires tailoring treatment interventions to each individual client's distinct and unique combination of mental, behavioral, and physical problems. This includes recognition of how individual clients may be in different SOC for each of their substance use, mental health, behavioral health, or physical health issues—even though all may be closely interrelated (Wallace, 2005). For example, a multiproblem client may present for treatment as follows: in a *maintenance stage* for adherence to HIV/AIDS medication; in an *action stage* for addressing their severe alcohol use disorder; in a *preparation stage* for addressing their engagement in condom-less anal intercourse; in a *contemplation stage* for addressing their marijuana use; and, in a *precontemplation stage* for addressing their episodic use of methamphetamine and poppers before sex. Or, a multiproblem client may be in an action stage for addressing their alcohol and marijuana substance use disorders but in a contemplation stage for addressing their Oxycodone use for pain and in a precontemplation stage for adherence to prescribed antidepressant medication.

Durvasula and Miller (2014) acknowledge as valuable for addressing more than one problem behavior the use of the evidence-based methadone maintenance treatment program, which provides the legal medication of methadone, as well as counseling and monitoring, while also eliminating the health risks associated with injection heroin use. As an even better example of how psychological treatments may simultaneously impact multiple behaviors, Durvasula and Miller (2014) speak of integrated care systems that can use existing evidence-based treatments, such as CBT and MI, which have proven useful for *both* enhancing adherence to HIV medications and reducing substance use.

Integrated and Comprehensive Care

Hence, new approaches and advances include integrated and comprehensive care models. Such integrated and comprehensive care models permit addressing how clients are caught up in syndemics with impacts from multiple epidemics (e.g., substance abuse, HIV/AIDS, STIs, violence) and multiple health and psychosocial risks (e.g., Halkitis, Wolitski, & Millett, 2013; Singer, 2014). Such clients are conceptualized as multiproblem and in need of integrated and comprehensive care to address impacts from multiple epidemics and health and psychosocial risks (Wallace, 2005). In this same vein, others speak of addressing common triple diagnoses of substance use disorders, HIV/AIDS, and psychiatric comorbidity (Durvasula & Miller, 2014).

Whether the language is of syndemics, multiproblem clients, or clients with triple diagnoses, what must be delivered to clients by practitioners are integrated and comprehensive care models that address all of clients' varied issues, problems, and diagnoses in the same setting (Wallace, 2005). Practitioners are advised to utilize their assessment findings, including those conducted on an ongoing basis across phases of treatment, in order to match clients to treatment interventions (NIDA, 2012b; Wallace, 2005); indeed, a meta-analysis has provided support for the use of such treatment matching (Pearson et al., 2012). For example, treatment matching would need to address the common combination found among HIV-infected MSM of drug and alcohol problems, medication nonadherence, depression, and trauma—necessitating "tailored interventions for MSM" (White, Gordon, & Mimiaga, 2014, p. 321). Substance abuse treatment programs must also be comprehensive in having innovative and state-of-the-art behavioral interventions, such as those that encourage HIV testing, reduction in sexual and drug-related risk behavior, and adherence to medical care (Halkitis et al., 2013).

In this manner, new approaches and advances in treatment include the "adaptation of evidence-based interventions to multiproblem clients in the real world, emphasizing the need to integrate interventions as needed in order to forge a comprehensive treatment approach and tailor treatment for individual clients" (Wallace, 2005, p. 66). Meanwhile, consider parallel developments in empirical research evaluating models that approximate innovative integrated and comprehensive care models by using a psychological treatment to address more than one problem behavior, including the following: a randomized controlled trial with sexually active, HIV-negative MSM with a diagnosis of alcohol use disorder—targeting both drinking and HIV prevention—to examine the comparative efficacy of MI versus a combination of CBT and MI (Morgenstern et al., 2007); a randomized controlled trial with MSM not currently in substance use disorder treatment examining the efficacy of brief MI focused on reducing club drug use and HIV risk behaviors, compared to a four-session education control condition (Morgenstern et al., 2009); and an evaluation of brief personalized feedback (PF) designed to provide individualized feedback on drinking patterns for MSM at risk for engagement in high-risk sex and HIV infection while including elements of MI and RP (Kuerbis, Schaumberg, Davis, Hail, & Morgenstern, 2014).

The Emergent Framework for Delivering New Approaches and Advances in Treatment

The emergent framework for delivering new approaches and advances in the treatment of substance use disorders, or the contemporary standard of care, is the following: an integrative and comprehensive care model that addresses more than one problem behavior through, the use of one or more evidence-based psychological treatments while also being an individualized approach that provides individually tailored care to meet the needs of individual clients (Wallace, 2005; Washton & Zweben, 2009). This follows from principles that guide treatment—that is, that no one method of treatment is deemed superior to all others; adherence to one theoretical model or a particular method of treatment is not required and not recommended; and that it is essential for practitioners to exercise both some degree of fidelity to evidence-based treatment interventions as well as flexibility in responding to individual client needs via individually tailored treatment (NIDA, 2012b; Wallace, 2005; Washton & Zweben, 2009).

The results described by Washton and Zweben (2009) derive from the blending of seemingly disparate and competing substance abuse treatment approaches and treatments, including CBT, MI/motivational enhancement, patient education, 12-step facilitation (TSF), group therapy, supportive psychotherapy, interpersonal therapy, pharmacotherapy, abstinence-based addiction counseling, the SOC model, urine drug testing, a focus on the therapeutic relationship as central to treatment, couples' therapy, and incorporation of the self-medication model where substances are seen as being used to manage affects and address self-regulation deficits (Washton & Zweben, 2009).

In essence, this is the exact same proposal for implementing new approaches and advances in substance abuse treatment with diverse, multiproblem clients, Wallace (2005) recommended that practitioners hold in hand a menu of seven evidence-based and seven state-of-the art integrated treatments and practitioners then select from the menu those to be integrated to create an individually tailored treatment. Wallace's (2005) *menu of evidence-based* options includes a special focus on building a strong therapeutic alliance/social-support network (TASS); MI/motivational enhancement therapy (MI/MET)/brief interventions; CBT/RP/social-skills training (SST); TSF/guidance using Alcoholics or Narcotics Anonymous; individual drug counseling (IDC) or supportive-expressive psychotherapy (SEP); the community reinforcement approach (CRA)/vouchers or CM; and, the Matrix Model—or, a day-treatment approach, or an IEC outpatient model (i.e., I for intensive care four to five days per week, E for extensive care spanning 6–12 months, and C for comprehensive care combining TASS, CBT/RP, IDC, group drug counseling/GDC, drug testing, etc.).

Also reflecting a standard of care, which involves the use of integrated and comprehensive treatments, Wallace (2005) invited practitioners to select interventions from a *menu of state-of-the-art practices* for combining treatments. By way of an example, the integration or combination of MI (i.e., Miller & Rollnick, 2013) and the SOC (DiClemente & Velasquez, 2002) is an item on the menu.

CONCLUSION

What has emerged from this chapter's analysis is how the LGBT community encompasses tremendous diversity. Fortunately, new approaches and advances in treatment permit the forging of an integrated, comprehensive, individually tailored treatment that combines the careful selection of evidence-based and state-of-the-art combinations of approaches. Such integrated, comprehensive, individually tailored treatment may only be categorized as state-of-the art, since it has not as yet been evaluated, given the integration of two or more evidence-based interventions (Wallace, 2005). Also, while some research advances have occurred, practitioners face the reality that where effective strategies evaluated via rigorous clinical trials must still be translated into practice (White, Gordon, & Mimiaga, 2014, p. 321). This is why practitioners are urged to engage in a mixture of fidelity to aspects of evidence-based interventions and flexibility in adapting those interventions in real-world settings with actual clients (Wallace, 2005). There is a need for future ongoing research that examines such comprehensive and integrated care models in order to produce empirically validated recommendations on best practices, which practitioners can implement (Durvasula & Miller, 2014, p. 49). Such research can further build on the progress made thus far in addressing the needs of sexual minorities by investigating the utility of combining psychological treatments in response to syndemics or the realities of the risks faced by multiproblem clients (e.g. Kuerbis et al., 2014; Morgenstern et al., 2007; Morgenstern et al., 2009).

Also, the IOM (2011) has called for all federally funded surveys benefiting from the development and inclusion of standardized measures to ascertain sexual orientation and gender identity. Hence, future research may provide multiple streams of findings that will continue to inform new approaches and advances in the treatment of substance abuse for sexual minorities who are as unique in their presentation as the individuals in the cases—that is, Maria, Tommy, Dang, Gerri, Kathy, Stacey, Kwame, Frankie, Bernadette, and Louis.

REFERENCES

Abdulrahim, D., Whiteley, C., Moncrieff, M., & Bowden-Jones, O. (2016). *Club drug use among lesbian, gay, bisexual and trans (LGBT) people.* London, UK: Novel Psychoactive Treatment UK Network (NEPTUNE).

American Psychiatric Association. (2013). *Diagnostic and statistical manual of mental disorders* (5th ed.). Washington, DC: American Psychiatric Association.

Anderson, N. B. (2006). Evidence-based practice in psychology. *American Psychologist, 61*(4), 271–285.

Benotsch, E. G., Zimmerman, R., Cathers, L., McNulty, S., Pierce, J., Heck, T., . . . Snipes, D. (2013). Non-medical use of prescription drugs, polysubstance use, and mental health in transgender adults. *Drug Alcohol Depend, 132*(1–2), 391–394.

Blosnich, J., Lee, J. G., & Horn, K. (2013). A systematic review of the etiology of tobacco disparities for sexual minorities. *Tobacco Control, 22*(2), 66–73.

Coffin, P. O., Santos, G. M., Colfax, G., Das, M., Matheson, T., DeMicco, E., . . . Herbst, J. H. (2014). Adapted personalized cognitive counseling for episodic substance-using men who have sex with men: A randomized controlled trial. *AIDS and Behavior, 18*(7), 1390–1400.

Colfax, G., & Shoptaw, S. (2005). The methamphetamine epidemic: Implications for HIV prevention and treatment. *Current HIV/AIDS Reports, 2*(4), 194–199.

Coulter, R. W. S., Marzell, M., Saltz, R., Stall, R., & Mair, C. (2016). Sexual-orientation differences in drinking patterns and use of drinking contexts among college students. *Drug and Alcohol Dependence, 160*, 197–204.

D'Avanzo, P. A., Halkitis, P. N., Yu, K., & Kapadia, F. (2016). Demographic, mental health, behavioral and psychosocial factors associated with cigarette smoking status among young men who have sex with men: The P18 cohort study. *LGBT Health, 3*(5), 379–386.

Davis, C. S., & Carr, D. (2016). Physician continuing education to reduce opioid misuse, abuse, and overdose: Many opportunities, few requirements. *Drug and Alcohol Dependence, 163*, 100–107.

DiClemente, C., & Velasquez, M. M. (2002). Motivational interviewing and the stages of change. In W. R. Miller & S. Rollnick (Eds.), *Motivational interviewing: Preparing people for change* (2nd ed., pp. 201–216). New York, NY: Guilford.

Drabble, L., Midanik, L. T., & Trocki, K. (2005). Reports of alcohol consumption and alcohol-related problems among homosexual, bisexual, and heterosexual respondents: Results from the 2000 National Alcohol Survey. *Journal of Studies on Alcohol, 66*, 111–120.

Drabble, L., Trocki, K. F., Hughes, T. L., Korcha, R. A., & Lown, A. E. (2013). Sexual orientation differences in the relationship between victimization and hazardous drinking among women in the National Alcohol Survey. *Psychology of Addictive Behaviors, 27*(3), 639–649.

Durvasula, R., & Miller, T. R. (2014). Substance abuse treatment in persons with HIV/AIDS: Challenges in managing triple diagnosis. *Behavioral Medicine, 40*(2), 43–52.

Flentje, A., Bacca, C. L., & Cochran, B. N. (2015). Missing data in substance abuse research? Researchers' reporting practices of sexual orientation and gender identity. *Drug and Alcohol Dependence, 147*, 280–284.

Green, K. E., & Feinstein, B. A. (2012). Substance use in lesbian, gay, and bisexual populations: An update on empirical research and implications for treatment. *Psychology of Addictive Behaviors, 26*(2), 265–278.

Halkitis, P. N., Wolitski, R. J., & Millett, G. A. (2013). A holistic approach to addressing HIV infection disparities in gay, bisexual, and other men who have sex with men. *American Psychologist, 68*(4), 261–273.

Hasin, D. S., O'Brien, C. P., Auriacombe, M., Borges, G., Bucholz, K., Budney, A., ... Schuckit, M. (2013). DSM-5 criteria for substance use disorders: Recommendations and rationale. *American Journal of Psychiatry, 170*(8), 834–851.

Heath, J., Lanoye, A., & Maisto, S. A. (2012). The role of alcohol and substance use in risky sexual behavior among older men who have sex with men: A review and critique of the current literature. *AIDS and Behavior, 16*(3), 578–589.

Heck, N. C., Livingston, N. A., Flentje, A., Oost, K., Stewart, B. T., & Cochran, B. N. (2014). Reducing risk for illicit drug use and prescription drug misuse: High school gay-straight alliances and lesbian, gay, bisexual, and transgender youth. *Addictive Behaviors, 39*(4), 824–828.

Hoffman, B. R. (2014). The interaction of drug use, sex work, and HIV among transgender women. *Substance Use & Misuse, 49*(8), 1049–1053.

Hotton, A. L., Garofalo, R., Kuhns, L. M., & Johnson, A. K. (2013). Substance use as a mediator of the relationship between life stress and sexual risk among young transgender women. *AIDS Education and Prevention, 25*(1), 62–71.

Hughes, T. L., Wilsnack, S. C., & Kantor, L. W. (2016). The influence of gender and sexual orientation on alcohol use and alcohol-related problems: Toward a global perspective. *Alcohol Research: Current Reviews, 38*(1), 121–132.

Institute of Medicine (IOM). (2011). *The health of lesbian, gay, bisexual, and transgender people: Building a foundation for better understanding.* Washington, DC: The National Academies Press.

Kuerbis, A. N., Schaumberg, K., Davis, C. M., Hail, L., & Morgenstern, J. (2014). Unpacking personalized feedback: An exploratory study of the impact of its components and the reactions it elicits among problem drinking men who have sex with men. *Substance Use & Misuse, 49*(4), 383–394.

Marshal, M. P., Friedman, M. S., Stall, R., King, K. M., Miles, J., Gold, M. A., ... Morse, J. Q. (2008). Sexual orientation and adolescent substance use: A meta-analysis and methodological review. *Addiction, 103*(4), 546–556.

Matthews, A. K., McConnell, E. A., Li, C. C., Vargas, M. C., & King, A. (2014). Design of a comparative effectiveness evaluation of a culturally tailored versus standard community-based smoking cessation treatment program for LGBT smokers. *BMC Psychology*, *2*(1), 1–11.

Mausbach, B. T., Semple, S. J., Strathdee, S. A., Zians, J., & Patterson, T. L. (2007). Efficacy of a behavioral intervention for increasing safer sex behaviors in HIV-positive MSM methamphetamine users: Results from the EDGE study. *Drug and Alcohol Dependence*, *87*(2), 249–257.

McCabe, S. E., Hughes, T. L., Bostwick, W. B., West, B. T., Boyd, C. J. (2009). Sexual orientation, substance use behaviors and substance dependence in the United States. *Addiction*, *104*(8), 1333–1345.

Miller, W. R., & Rollnick, S. (2013). *Motivational interviewing: Helping people changer* (3rd ed.). New York, NY: Guilford Press.

Millett, G. A., Peterson, J. L., Wolitski, R. J., & Stall, R. (2006). Greater risk for HIV infection of black men who have sex with men: A critical literature review. *American Journal of Public Health*, *96*(6), 1007–1019.

Morgan, E., Skaathun, B., Michaels, S., Young, L., Khanna, A., Friedman, S. R., ... UConnect Study Team. (2016). Marijuana use as a sex-drug is associated with HIV risk among Black MSM and their network. *AIDS and Behavior*, *20*(3), 600–607.

Morgenstern, J., Bux, D. A., Jr., Parsons, J., Hagman, B. T., Wainberg, M., & Irwin, T. (2009). Randomized trial to reduce club drug use and HIV risk behaviors among men who have sex with men. *Journal of Consulting and Clinical Psychology*, *77*(4), 645–656.

Morgenstern, J., Irwin, T. W., Wainberg, M. L., Parsons, J. T., Muench, F., Bux, D. A., Jr., ... Schulz-Heik, J. (2007). A randomized controlled trial of goal choice interventions for alcohol use disorders among men who have sex with men. *Journal of Consulting and Clinical Psychology*, *75*(1), 72–84.

National Institute on Drug Abuse (NIDA). (2012a). *Club drugs*. Bethesda, MD: National Institutes of Health. Retrieved from https://www.drugabuse.gov/drugs-abuse/club-drugs

National Institute on Drug Abuse (NIDA). (2012b). *Principles of drug addiction treatment: A research-based guide* (3rd ed.). Bethesda, MD: National Institutes of Health. Retrieved from https://www.drugabuse.gov/sites/default/files/podat_1.pdf

Pearson, F. S., Prendergast, M. L., Podus, D., Vazan, P., Greenwell, L., & Hamilton, Z. (2012). Meta-analyses of seven of the National Institute on Drug Abuse's principles of drug addiction treatment. *Journal of Substance Abuse Treatment*, *43*(1), 1–11.

Prochaska, J. O. (2008). New paradigms for inclusive health care: Toward individual patient and population health. In B. C. Wallace (Ed.), *Toward equity in health: A new global approach to health disparities* (pp. 61–78). New York, NY: Springer Publications.

Reback, C. J., & Fletcher, J. B. (2014). HIV prevalence, substance use, and sexual risk behaviors among transgender women recruited through outreach. *AIDS and Behavior*, *18*(7), 1359–1367.

Reisner, S. L., Gamarel, K. E., Nemoto, T., & Operario, D. (2014). Dyadic effects of gender minority stressors in substance use behaviors among transgender women and their non-transgender male partners. *Psychology of Sexual Orientation and Gender Diversity*, *1*(1), 63–71.

Reisner, S. L., Pardo, S. T., Gamarel, K. E., Hughto, J. M. W., Pardee, D. J., & Keo-Meier, C. L. (2015). Substance use to cope with stigma in healthcare among US female-to-male trans masculine adults. *LGBT Health*, 2(4), 324–332.

Robinson, M., Sanches, M., & MacLeod, M. S. (2016). Prevalence and mental health correlates of illegal cannabis use among bisexual women. *Journal of Bisexuality*, 16(2), 181–202.

Rudd, R. A., Aleshire, N., Zibbell, J. E., & Gladden, R. M. (2016). Increases in drug and opioid overdose deaths-United States, 2000–2014. *MMWR: Mortality Weekly Report*, 64(50–51), 1378–1382. Retrieved from http://www.cdc.gov/mmwr/preview/mmwrhtml/mm6450a3.htm

Ryan, H., Wortley, P. M., Easton, A., Pederson, L., & Greenwood, G. (2001). Smoking among lesbians, gays, and bisexuals: A review of the literature. *American Journal of Preventive Medicine*, 21(2), 142–149.

Sadhir, M., Stockburger, S. J., & Omar, H. A. (2016). Sexual minority (LGBTQ) youth and role of health care provider. *Dynamics of Human Health*, 3(1). Retrieved from http://journalofhealth.co.nz/wp-content/uploads/2016/03/DHH_Hatim_Sexual.pdf

Santos, G. M., Rapues, J., Wilson, E. C., Macias, O., Packer, T., Colfax, G., & Raymond, H. F. (2014). Alcohol and substance use among transgender women in San Francisco: Prevalence and association with human immunodeficiency virus infection. *Drug and Alcohol Review*, 33(3), 287–295.

Singer, M. (2014). The infectious disease syndemics of crack cocaine. *Journal of Equity in Health*, 3(1), 32–44.

Stall, R. D., Greenwood, G. L., Acree, M., Paul, J., & Coates, T. J. (1999). Cigarette smoking among gay and bisexual men. *American Journal of Public Health*, 89(12), 1875–1878.

Stall, R., Paul, J., Greenwood, G., Pollack, L., Bein, E., Crosby, M., ... Catania, J. A. (2001). Alcohol use, drug use and alcohol-related problems among men who have sex with men: The Urban Men's Health Study. *Addiction*, 96(11), 1589–1601.

Storholm, E. D., Halkitis, P. N., Siconolfi, D. E., & Moeller, R. W. (2011). Cigarette smoking as part of a syndemic among young men who have sex with men ages 13–29 in New York City. *Journal of Urban Health*, 88(4), 663–676.

Talley, A. E. (2013). Recommendations for improving substance abuse treatment interventions for sexual minority substance abusers. *Drug and Alcohol Review*, 32(5), 539–540.

Talley, A. E., Hughes, T. L., Aranda, F., Birkett, M., & Marshal, M. P. (2014). Exploring alcohol-use behaviors among heterosexual and sexual minority adolescents: Intersections with sex, age, and race/ethnicity. *American Journal of Public Health*, 104(2), 295–303.

Volkow, N. D., & McLellan, A. T. (2016). Opioid abuse in chronic pain—Misconceptions and mitigation strategies. *New England Journal of Medicine*, 374(13), 1253–1263.

Wallace, B. C. (2005). *Making mandated addiction treatment work*. Lanham, MD: Jason Aaronson/Rowman & Littlefield.

Washton, A. M., & Zweben, J. E. (2009). *Cocaine and methamphetamine addiction: Treatment, recovery, and relapse prevention*. New York, NY: W.W. Norton & Company.

Whaley, A. L., & Davis, K. E. (2007). Cultural competence and evidence-based practice in mental health services: A complementary perspective. *American Psychologist*, 62(6), 563–574

White, J. M., Gordon, J. R., & Mimiaga, M. J. (2014). The role of substance use and mental health problems in medication adherence among HIV-infected MSM. *LGBT Health*, 1(4), 319–322.

Wilsnack, S. C., Hughes, T. L., Johnson, T. P., Bostwick, W. B., Szalacha, L. A., Benson, P., ... Kinnison, K. E. (2008). Drinking and drinking-related problems among heterosexual and sexual minority women. *Journal of Studies on Alcohol and Drugs*, 69(1), 129–139.

Wilson, S. M., Gilmore, A. K., Rhew, I. C., Hodge, K. A., & Kaysen, D. L. (2016). Minority stress is longitudinally associated with alcohol-related problems among sexual minority women. *Addictive Behaviors*, 61, 80–83.

Wray, T. B., Grin, B., Dorfman, L., Glynn, T. R., Kahler, C. W., Marshall, B. L., ... Operario, D. (2016). Systematic review of interventions to reduce problematic alcohol use in men who have sex with men. *Drug and Alcohol Review*, 35(2), 148–157.

Yarns, B. C., Abrams, J. M., Meeks, T. W., & Sewell, D. D. (2016). The mental health of older LGBT adults. *Current Psychiatry Reports*, 18(6), 1–11.

9

Health Disparities and LGBT Populations

Barbara C. Wallace and Erik Santacruz

There is a contemporary public health imperative to address the health disadvantages documented for sexual minorities (Cochran, Björkenstam, & Mays, 2016). This includes the goal of acknowledging and meeting the unique health needs characterizing lesbian, gay, bisexual, and transgender (LGBT) populations (Hollenbach, Eckstrand, & Dreger, 2014).

This chapter will focus on the mental and physical health disparities experienced by LGBT populations in the United States. More specifically, this chapter will accomplish the following: (1) ground the chapter's discussion in definitions of health and health disparities or health inequalities while also covering the concept of health equity, the goal of equity in health for all, the rationale for focusing on vulnerable populations, and the typical outcomes focused upon in a health disparities framework; (2) provide acknowledgment of limitations in research, followed by an overview of the body of research that has documented the mental health disparities and physical health disparities impacting sexual minorities, including by specific sexual minority populations; (3) review the dominant perspectives on LGBT populations that have impacted the delivery of mental and physical healthcare, both historically and in contemporary times, including those with harmful and beneficial impacts; and, (4) offer an overview of solutions for health disparities among LGBT populations burdened by specific disparities. A conclusion will emphasize the importance of society prioritizing a substantial investment in research on LGBT populations' health disparities to ensure progress toward their reduction and elimination.

GUIDING DEFINITIONS, CONCEPTS, AND GOALS

A review of key definitions, concepts, and goals in the field of health disparities provides an important foundation for this chapter. This review serves as vital introduction.

First and foremost, *health* is a state of well-being with physical, emotional, mental, and spiritual dimensions, and is an essential resource to be valued (Wallace, 2008). There are vast differences with regard to the markers and indicators of health across races/ethnicities, diverse groups, special or vulnerable populations, socioeconomic statuses, geographic regions, and countries. The goal of valuing and pursuing equity in health for all has been articulated. Acknowledgment has been given to those historical legacies and forces of oppression, stigmatization, and discrimination that have served to compromise the pursuit of equity in health for all. Emphasis has been placed on paying special attention to those vulnerable groups that have suffered injustice with a negative impact on health. This has necessitated taking action or pursuing social justice in order to address *health disparities* and ensure achievement of *equity in health* or *health equity*, terms often used interchangeably (Wallace, 2008).

Health disparities or *health inequalities* have been defined as those unfair, systematic, and potentially avoidable differences in health, or in major socially determined influences on health, that emerge through comparisons of groups of people with different relative positions in social hierarchies (Braveman, 2006). These unfair differences in health follow from factors such as wealth, power, or prestige. Disadvantages linked to social position adversely impact health or health risks. The resultant goal of pursuing *health equity* necessitates striving to eliminate *health disparities* strongly linked with social disadvantage as well as striving for equal opportunities for all social groups to achieve optimal health. This goal necessitates a focus on improving social conditions for historically disadvantaged groups while removing obstacles to these groups realizing their right to health (Braveman, 2006).

Others have defined *health disparities* as those "observed clinically and statistically significant differences" not explained by the defects of selection bias that are found in empirical research when comparing socially distinct vulnerable and less vulnerable populations, specifically for the following variables: the quality of health care; healthcare use patterns; and health outcomes, including health status across the life span and life expectancy (Kilbourne, Switzer, Hyman, Crowley-Matoka, & Fine, 2006, p. 2114). Noteworthy, these health disparities may reflect gaps or disparities in the quality of care delivered to a vulnerable population better: and can suggest deviations best practices and inferior healthcare outcomes. What is vital in this definition is the requirement that the disparity is occurring in vulnerable populations, meaning those groups that have encountered social discrimination due to "underlying differences in social status, which can lead to potential gaps in health or healthcare" (p. 2115).

Regarding key goals, a focus on health disparities means attending to differences with regard to the incidence of disease, prevalence of disease, and mortality from disease conditions and, specifically, documenting how these differences manifest for various population groups—whether by race, ethnicity, sexual orientation, socioeconomic status, gender, age, education, income, social class, disability, or geographic location (Massetti, Ragan, Thomas, & Ryerson, 2016). Health disparities manifest as a disproportionate burden of disease, disability, injury, and death among vulnerable populations, necessitating action on the federal, state, local agency and private organizational levels in collaboration with communities in order to eliminate health disparities (Frieden, 2013).

OVERVIEW OF MENTAL HEALTH AND PHYSICAL HEALTH DISPARITIES FOR SEXUAL MINORITIES

As introduction to the overview of research on LGBT populations' mental and physical health disparities, consider how Stall et al. (2016) have analyzed the body of available research, noting serious limitations. The body of research has early roots in investigations with small convenience samples of sexual minorities using self-report measures. Research progressed to larger household-based samples obtaining data on morbidity where sexual minorities were omitted or under-represented—a serious limitation; a factor of note is that, historically, most national surveys and registries failed to include questions on sexual identity and sexual behavior. Next, the progression in research was to the contemporary analysis of population-based national survey data that permitted included questions to identify sexual minorities and permitted comparison to heterosexuals; and there is a pioneering highlight in such contemporary research where population-based national survey data not only permit comparison to heterosexuals but also examine the ultimate biological outcome of mortality—that is, the research of Cochran et al. (2016). The contemporary standard being advanced to guide ongoing health disparities research with sexual minorities rests on the use of random samples drawn from the general population, which permit comparison to the general public. Finally, decades of underinvestment in health research with sexual minorities have had a negative impact (Stall et al., 2016).

Overview of Mental Health Disparities for Sexual Minorities

There are numerous studies that have documented serious *mental health disparities* for sexual minorities in comparison to heterosexuals, as follows: estimates from a meta-analysis indicated that up to 80 percent of sexual orientation minorities had experienced some form of harassment across their life span, and stressful social interactions, such as antigay victimization, have been linked to the emergence of serious mental health disparities (Lick, Durso, & Johnson, 2013); negative impacts on mental health have followed from high levels of overall stress, including from personal safety concerns due to lack of social acceptance (U.S. Department of Health and Human Services [USDHHS], 2000); a one-and-a-half to two times greater likelihood of lifetime mood and anxiety disorder in a national study (Bostwick, Boyd, Hughes, West, & McCabe, 2014; Meyer, 2003);

higher rates of suicide attempts, as a particularly robust finding (Cochran & Mays, 2015; Gilman, Cochran, Mays, Ostrow, & Kessler, 2001); a general higher risk for poor mental health (Fredriksen-Goldsen, Kim, Barkan, Muraco, & Hoy-Ellis, 2013) and a higher prevalence of mental disorders (Meyer, 2003); specifically, an elevated risk for anxiety disorders, mood disorders, and substance use disorders; being a sexual orientation minority was a risk indicator for a higher prevalence of mental health disorders and higher use of mental health services (Cochran, Sullivan, & Mays, 2003), and a higher likelihood of a positive history of child maltreatment by parents (Corliss, Cochran, & Mays, 2002), higher risk of lifetime trauma (Roberts, Austin, Corliss, Vandermorris, & Koenen, 2010), and higher exposure to discrimination, victimization, and violence across the life span from childhood to old age (Hollenbach et al., 2014).

Overview of Physical Health Disparities for Sexual Minorities

A body of research has documented significant *physical health disparities* for sexual minorities in comparison to heterosexuals, such as the following: especially robust evidence of health disadvantages linked to higher rates of tobacco use, suicide attempts, and HIV infection among men (Cochran et al., 2016); greater difficulties in accessing health care (Cochran & Mays, 2015); a greater all-cause mortality after adjusting for demographic confounding, in particular, an elevated mortality risk for lesbians, homosexually experienced women, and bisexual men—suggesting a role for sexual orientation–related health disadvantages in creating this vulnerability (Cochran et al., 2016); higher rates of not only cigarette smoking for lesbians and gay men but also of lung cancer, asthma, and cardiovascular disease (Landers, Mimiaga, & Conron, 2011; Stall et al., 2016); a higher prevalence of diagnoses for diabetes and other chronic health conditions, an increased risk for cancer, and higher likelihood of a reported poor general health status (Lick et al., 2013); an elevated risk for varied cancer diagnoses, late cancer detection and treatment, and poorer outcomes that reflected higher rates of risk factors—spanning from higher rates of obesity, alcohol, tobacco use, and nulliparity to nonadherence to screening guidelines (Matthews et al., 2016); and, a greater likelihood of becoming disabled at a younger age (Fredriksen-Goldsen, Kim, & Barkan, 2012).

Also noteworthy, data have revealed that sexual minority nonsmokers remain at greater risk for exposure to secondhand smoke in comparison to heterosexuals, including in both household and workplace settings (Cochran & Mays, 2016; Max, Stark, Sung, & Offen, 2016a). Potential factors operating in the greater rates of cigarette smoking and secondhand smoke exposure for sexual orientation minorities include the bar-focused subculture, the manner in which the tobacco industry had targeted the population, and "stress, and structural stigma and discrimination" (Max, Stark, Sung, & Offen, 2016b). Also of concern were "differential patterns of healthcare access" and tobacco exposure, which may exert "their cumulative effects on mortality in older ages" (Cochran & Mays, 2015, p. 363).

Patterns of Mental and Physical Health Disparities for Specific Sexual Minorities

Research has also revealed patterns of mental health disparities and physical health disparities in specific sexual minority communities. More specifically, there is research on the patterns of mental and physical health disparities for sexual minority men, sexual minority women, bisexuals, transgender populations, adolescent and young adult sexual minorities, and older sexual minorities.

Mental Health Disparities in Sexual Minority Communities

Mental Health Disparities for Sexual Minority Men

Mental health disparities for sexual minority men, usually in research with comparisons to heterosexual men, were found, as follows: four times the odds of a mood disorder (Blosnich, Hanmer, Yu, Matthews, & Kavalieratos, 2016); a higher prevalence of depression, panic attacks, and psychological distress (Cochran et al., 2003); greater likelihood of reported frequent mental distress found in a study using national population data (Cochran et al., 2016); a higher risk for depression, anxiety, suicide attempts, and substance use disorders (Lewis, 2009); a two to four times higher risk for suicidal ideation (King et al., 2008); higher rates of substance abuse, depression, and suicide (USDHHS, 2000); and, higher rates of experiencing parental, emotional, and physical maltreatment during childhood in comparison to heterosexuals (Corliss et al., 2002).

Mental Health Disparities for Sexual Minority Women

Other mental health disparities were found for sexual minority women, in comparison to heterosexual women, including the following: greater likelihood for reporting frequent mental distress (Cochran et al., 2016); a higher prevalence of depression (Koh & Ross, 2006), major depression, and generalized anxiety (Cochran et al., 2003); alcohol use (Butler et al., 2016; Drabble & Trocki, 2005); higher odds of suicide attempts (Cochran & Mays, 2015); higher rates of histories of child and adolescent experiences of emotional, physical, and sexual abuse victimization (Austin et al., 2008); and, specifically, lesbian women were more likely to have experienced both physical and sexual abuse in both childhood and adolescence, in comparison to heterosexual women (Austin et al., 2008). In comparison to lesbians, for bisexual women, specifically, evidence showed a higher risk for mental distress (Fredriksen-Goldsen et al., 2013). Specifically for lesbians, data showed higher rates of alcohol abuse and stress (USDHHS, 2000).

Mental Health Disparities for Transgender Populations

Mental health disparities found for transgender populations included high rates of self-reported mental health problems. This included high rates of mood disorders, tobacco use disorder, posttraumatic stress disorder, and suicide risk (Blosnich, Marsiglio, et al., 2016).

Mental Health Disparities for Adolescent and Young Adult Sexual Minorities

Research has found mental health disparities for adolescent and young adult sexual minorities, as follows: disclosure of sexual orientation by youth was associated with verbal abuse and physical attacks by mothers, physical attacks by fathers, and sibling abuse and abuse from older youth—placing them at risk for social isolation, internal conflict, and engagement in risk behaviors, such as alcohol/drug use (Austin et al., 2008); for female children, displays of gender-nonconforming behavior in childhood created vulnerability for targeting for abuse (Austin et al., 2008); with regard to revictimization after an abuse experience, of those who had any childhood experience of physical abuse, lesbian women were more likely to experience physical abuse revictimization in adolescence, and bisexual and lesbian women were more likely to experience sexual abuse revictimization in adolescence (Austin et al., 2008); gay male adolescents showed a two to three times higher risk of attempting suicide relative to their heterosexual peers (USDHHS, 2000); specifically, higher odds of suicide attempts for sexual minority adolescents in comparison to heterosexual females have been found (Cochran & Mays, 2015); relative to heterosexual youth, sexual minority youth presented an increased risk for substance use disorders, depression, anxiety, and suicide attempts (Lewis, 2009)—including engaging in more serious suicide attempts and making attempts requiring medical attention (Marshal et al., 2011); among rural college students, a higher prevalence of the experience of psychological interpersonal violence (IPV) has been found for LGBT youth, with those with a prior history of IPV in middle/high school showing an increased risk in college—with increased risk also linked to alcohol consumption (Felix, Policastro, Agnich, & Gould, 2016); higher rates of alcohol use for youth and young adults (Butler et al., 2016); and higher rates of engagement in prescription opioid use and tranquilizer use (Kecojevic et al., 2012).

Mental Health Disparities for Older Sexual Minorities

Findings documented for older sexual minorities have included the following: higher rates of poor mental health and excessive drinking, in comparison to heterosexuals, using data from a large population-based study (Fredriksen-Goldsen et al., 2013); specifically, older sexual minority women showed high rates of excessive alcohol drinking and poorer mental health (Emlet, 2016;

Fredriksen-Goldsen et al., 2013); for transgender older adults a higher risk for stress and depression (Emlet, 2016); transgender identity, in comparison to nontransgender identity, was associated with lower socioeconomic status and higher odds of experiencing discrimination, depression, and a history of attempted suicide (Su et al., 2016); specifically for HIV-positive older adults, there were higher odds of having depression, anxiety, suicidal thoughts, or a formal mental health diagnosis, as well as substance abuse issues (Emlet, 2016); the higher the lifetime prevalence of victimization for older sexual minorities, there was evidence of a greater prevalence of depressive symptoms (Emlet, 2016); gay and bisexual men, when compared to heterosexual men, presented a higher ratio of symptoms of psychological distress (Wallace, Cochran, Durazo, & Ford, 2011); and, lesbian and bisexual women were found to present a higher risk for psychological distress in comparison to heterosexual women (Wallace et al., 2011).

Mental Health Disparities for Those with Intersecting Identities

Also worth mention are mental health disparities for those with intersecting identities. Research with a large national probability sample of sexual minorities (LGB) found that sexual orientation discrimination, when combined with other types of discrimination—specifically, racial or ethnic discrimination—was associated with higher odds of having a past-year mental health disorder (Bostwick et al., 2014).

Physical Health Disparities within Sexual Minority Communities
Physical Health Disparities for Sexual Minority Men

There are also numerous physical health disparities specifically for sexual minority men, in comparison to heterosexual men, as follows: higher rates of HIV/AIDS and other sexually transmitted diseases (STDs), as well as difficulties in accessing healthcare (Centers for Disease Control and Prevention [CDC], 2013; Cochran & Mays, 2015; Cochran et al., 2016); an increased risk, specifically for syphilis, gonorrhea, chlamydia, human papillomavirus, and hepatitis A and B (Butler et al., 2016); a higher risk for anal cancer, specifically, in gay men (Darwich et al., 2013); higher likelihood of reported current smoking, daily smoking, and twice the likelihood of experiencing secondhand smoke exposure at home (Max et al., 2016a); bisexual men had the greatest odds of being current smokers and a vulnerability to worse health outcomes from smoking (Max et al., 2016a); a greater likelihood of reported cigarette smoking (Cochran et al., 2016) —and a disturbing interplay with HIV status, given data that smoking may lead to poorer outcomes for those with HIV (Max et al., 2016a); documented poorer outcomes of a higher likelihood of viral load being detectable and greater risk for lung cancer, tuberculosis, chronic obstructive pulmonary disease, pneumonia, cancers associated with human papillomavirus, cardiovascular disease, and bone fractures (Max et al., 2016a); and, specifically for bisexual men, a three times greater likelihood of becoming disabled at a younger age (Fredriksen-Goldsen et al., 2012).

Physical Health Disparities for Sexual Minority Women

Other patterns of physical health disparities for sexual minority women, in comparison to heterosexual women, have been found, as follows: higher rates of cigarette smoking, being current smokers, and secondhand smoke exposure in their homes (Conron, Mimiaga, & Landers, 2010; Max et al., 2016a); negative consequences from lesbians' higher rates of smoking and being overweight (USDHHS, 2000), such as greater odds of heart disease, diabetes, obesity, high cholesterol, and asthma (Blosnich, Hanmer, et al., 2016); greatest odds of being current smokers and a vulnerability to worse health outcomes from smoking (Max et al., 2016a); a one and a half times greater risk of asthma and more than twice the risk of cardiovascular disease (Conron et al., 2010); higher rates of excessive alcohol use (Fredriksen-Goldsen et al., 2013); higher likelihood for lifetime tobacco use, monthly binge drinking, worse overall health, and a lower level of health insurance coverage (Cochran et al., 2016); higher prevalence of cancer risk factors—that is, higher alcohol use, higher rates of obesity, higher rates of never having given birth/nulliparity, and possible higher risk for cardiovascular disease (Butler et al., 2016); and lower likelihood of lifetime or past-year cervical cancer screening via Pap tests despite engagement in higher risk sexual practices (Fallin-Bennett, Henderson, Nguyen, & Hyderi, 2016). Factors found to be related to lack of screening for cervical cancer were fear of discrimination, lower likelihood of disclosing sexual orientation, and low screening knowledge levels (Fallin-Bennett et al., 2016). Specifically, lesbians were found to present twice the risk for becoming physically disabled compared to heterosexual women (Fredriksen-Goldsen et al., 2012). Also, lesbians had the greatest health disadvantages, including the highest rates of obesity, smoking, and recent binge drinking, and lower rates of insurance coverage (Cochran et al., 2016). Specifically for bisexual women, there was also a higher prevalence of limited healthcare access and a higher risk for poor general health (Fredriksen-Goldsen et al., 2013).

Physical Health Disparities for the Transgender Population

For transgender populations, there was evidence of high rates of tobacco use disorder with implications for physical health risks (Blosnich, Marsiglio, et al., 2016). African American transgender male-to-female individuals experienced the most striking higher disparity in HIV/AIDS prevalence (Butler et al., 2016). Compared to cisgender individuals, transgender individuals were more likely to be uninsured, and experiences of discrimination were associated with postponing medical care; and transgender men presented the highest risk for postponing care (Institute of Medicine [IOM], 2011).

Physical Health Disparities for Younger Sexual Minorities

Physical health disparities identified for adolescent and young adult sexual minorities have included higher rates of tobacco use and higher rates of engagement in risky sexual behavior as well as unhealthy weight (Butler et al., 2016); one-third of sexual minority youth indicated engagement in hazardous weight-control behaviors, including vomiting, using laxatives and diet pills, and fasting beyond 24 hours (Hadland, Austin, Goodenow, & Calzo, 2014); and a lack of engagement in recommended levels of physical activity/exercise, or team sports, in comparison to heterosexual youth, which also placed sexual minority youth at risk (Calzo et al., 2014).

Physical Health Disparities for Older Sexual Minorities

Data have documented physical health disparities for older sexual minorities. Fredriksen-Goldsen et al. (2013) reported findings from a large population-based study that found the following for older LGB adults in comparison to heterosexuals: evidence of higher rates of disability; specifically for lesbian and bisexual women, a higher risk of cardiovascular disease and obesity; specifically for gay and bisexual men, a higher risk of poor physical health; and, for gay men, a lower rate of diabetes and higher rate of testing for HIV compared to bisexual men (Fredriksen-Goldsen et al., 2013).

Other research found the following for older sexual minorities, in comparison to heterosexuals: higher rates of poor general health, cigarette smoking, and a reduced level of engagement in activities of daily living; specifically for bisexual women, greater odds of disability and obesity; for transgender older adults, a higher risk for poor physical health, and disability, and an increased risk for living in poverty, experiencing financial barriers and having barriers to access to healthcare; specifically for HIV-positive older adults, higher odds of having hypertension, diabetes mellitus, and arthritis, and a lower level of physical activity; and the higher the lifetime prevalence of victimization for older sexual minorities, then there were findings of poorer general health and greater disability (Emlet, 2016).

Also, older gay and bisexual men, when compared to heterosexual men, presented a higher ratio of hypertension, diabetes, physical disability, and fair/poor health status (Wallace et al., 2011). In comparison to heterosexual women, older lesbian and bisexual women were found to present a higher risk for physical disability (Wallace et al., 2011). Older adults also face special challenges and problems, including that Medicaid and Social Security do not provide spousal benefits for same-sex partners, and some policies fail to extend benefits to same-sex partners, resulting in financial barriers to healthcare (Wallace et al., 2011). There is also the risk that Older adults also present greater health risks due reluctance to seek out healthcare and long-term care, given fear of discrimination and the costly nature of services (Rowan & Giunta, 2016).

DOMINANT PERSPECTIVES ON LGBT POPULATIONS AND IMPACTS ON CARE

A contemporary dominant perspective acknowledges how disparities arise from social systems that perpetuate structural stigma and providers who enact the stigma society has attached to sexual orientation, gender identities, and sexual practices (Eckstrand & Sciolla, 2014). All too often, sexual minorities receive "poor, inadequate, or discriminatory care," as a result of these factors (p. 10). Historically, disparities in healthcare service delivery arose from "egregious discrimination" by the healthcare system—as a structural factor—and, on the social interpersonal level, through the behavior of "individual practitioners" (p. 10).

Practitioners engaged in service delivery, in either the mental health domain or the physical health domain, have been impacted by dominant perspectives, historically and in contemporary times—including harmful and beneficial views. These dominant perspectives are reviewed, as they have impacted the care delivered to LGBT populations.

Perspectives on Factors Relevant to the Mental Health Domain

For the mental health domain—and for mental health professionals—a particularly relevant perspective is embedded in the history of pathologizing homosexual behavior as a mental disorder via the diagnosis of "homosexuality" in the *Diagnostic and Statistical Manual of Mental Disorders (DSM)* published by the American Psychiatric Association and, specifically, in the *DSM-I* and *DSM-II* (Drescher, 2015). It was in 1973 that the diagnosis of homosexuality was removed from the *DSM-II*, permitting a shift in focus to meeting the mental healthcare needs of members of LGBT populations (Drescher, 2015). However, there is a destructive legacy from the history of pathologizing homosexuality that involves reparative therapies and ongoing persistent efforts to "treat" homosexuality with conversion or reorientation therapy (Eckstrand & Sciolla, 2014). Representing a vital shift in dominant perspectives, these interventions are widely deemed potentially harmful by the American Psychiatric Association, American Psychological Association, Society for Adolescent Health and Medicine, and American Academy of Child and Adolescent Psychiatry (Eckstrand & Sciolla, 2014).

There is also a lasting destructive legacy from perspectives pathologizing homosexuality that includes a society-wide stigmatization of sexual minorities (Meyer, 2003). In this regard, there is a compelling minority stress model advanced by Meyer (1995, 2003) that considers the excess social stressors related to stigma and prejudice; the role of distal and proximal causes of distress; and the importance of structural level and individual level interventions. The minority stress model acknowledges the need to focus on oppressors perpetrating sources of stress while abandoning any singular focus on the victims of oppression (Meyer, 2003). The minority stress model also recognizes the large body of social psychology research that highlights the importance of sexual minorities coping with stigma while supporting concepts of individual agency and resilience. Ultimately, sexual minorities may emerge as resilient actors, and not victims, in response to oppressive social conditions (Meyer, 2003)—a pioneering and influential contemporary perspective arising from the minority stress framework.

Further, Meyer's minority stress framework (Meyer, 1995, 2003) permits conceptualizing health disparities among minority groups (Bostwick et al., 2014) while drawing attention to how mental health disparities have roots in social determinants. Individual-level factors (e.g., personality) are not viewed as determinants. Instead, mental health disparities are viewed as socially patterned factors rooted in environmental circumstances, with interplay between individual-level factors and factors in the sociocultural context in which the individual is situated. Moreover, for marginalized minorities, such as LGBT populations in the United States, this context "too often includes institutional and interpersonal discrimination, prejudice and stigma" (p. 35). Further, attention has been focused on the individual's expectation of discrimination experiences, which functions as a stressor that may be additive in nature and result in excess stress that may contribute to higher rates of mental health disorders for sexual minorities (Bostwick et al., 2014).

The minority stress framework's wide influence includes research on institutional discrimination, such as the codification of policies banning gay marriage. There is empirical evidence from a nationally representative sample that has shown that living in states with discriminatory laws serves as a risk factor for the emergence of psychiatric morbidity (e.g., mood disorders, generalized anxiety disorder, alcohol use disorder, psychiatric comorbidity) among LGB populations (Hatzenbuehler, McLaughlin, Keyes, & Hasin, 2010). Others have also recognized the role of social determinants of health, such as social environmental factors, including discriminatory laws (Blosnich, Hanmer, et al., 2016).

Thus, a growing body of empirical research supports the argument that sexual orientation minority disparities in health are linked to the experience of minority stress or the stress of antigay stigma (Lick et al., 2013). This reflects the broad impact of the work of Meyer (1995, 2003) on the dominant perspectives that have been brought to the examination of the experiences of LGBT populations in contemporary times.

Perspectives on Factors Relevant to the Physical Health Domain

Regarding the physical health domain—and for professionals in the medical field—there is also the legacy of harms done by the medical profession. These harms encompass structural level and individual level discrimination and the institutional and interpersonal discrimination, prejudice, and stigma mentioned elsewhere (i.e., Bostwick et al., 2014).

Within the spectrum of sexual minorities, there are also those with differences in sex development (DSD) and with congenital conditions (i.e., atypical development that is chromosomal, gonadal, or anatomic) who have been subject to a medical system that enacted societal stigmatization of DSD (Eckstrand & Sciolla, 2014). The results included the medical profession subjecting children diagnosed with DSD to "highly invasive and sometimes damaging interventions" to "ensure sex and gender normalization" (Eckstrand & Sciolla, 2014, p. 12). Consequences have involved perceived discrimination for those with DSD as well as delayed and avoidant behavior when healthcare was needed. This has also contributed to health disparities, overall, for the spectrum of sexual minorities (Eckstrand & Sciolla, 2014), and has reflected the overall legacy of the harm done by the medical profession from structural level and individual level discrimination that targeted sexual minorities as a stigmatized group.

Extensive research has confirmed perceived discrimination on the part of sexual minorities when they are within the healthcare delivery system—suggesting significant harms being perpetrated (Fallin-Bennett et al., 2016). Also, Lack of insurance may also be a factor in sexual minorities delaying or avoiding seeking healthcare. Yet, it is noteworthy that those who do seek treatment have all too often perceived medical providers to be creating an unwelcoming environment while unknowingly expressing stigma and engaging in discrimination—even when having "the best of intentions" (p. 24). The majority of physicians continue to report lack of formal training in LGBT health issues, including in medical school, during their residencies, and through continuing medical education; and most physicians who received such training evaluated it poorly (Fallin-Bennett et al., 2016).

OVERVIEW OF SOLUTIONS FOR HEALTH DISPARITIES AMONG LGBT POPULATIONS

Regarding solutions for physical and mental health disparities among sexual minorities, there has been an emphasis on the need to achieve health equity (Braveman, 2006; Wallace, 2008). There is consensus on the need for focusing on health equity, in particular, for the most vulnerable populations

(Marmot et al., 2008; Wallace, 2008). In the United States, the CDC has sought to both identify and address those factors associated with the emergence of health disparities among various groups, in an effort to achieve health equity (Frieden, 2013). Further, national priorities have encompassed ensuring access to comprehensive, culturally competent, community-based healthcare (USDHHS, 2000).

Indeed, as a national milestone impacting dominant perspectives, the second overarching goal of *Healthy People 2010* was to eliminate health disparities, including those involving differences occurring due to gender, race, ethnicity, education, income, disability, geographic location, or sexual orientation (USDHHS, 2000). Another influential national milestone, *Healthy People 2020* included among the four overarching goals one of achieving health equity, eliminating health disparities, and improving the health of all groups (USDHHS, 2010) acknowledging the role of social determinants of health (Massetti et al., 2016). Through *Healthy People 2020* initiatives, the USDHHS achieved yet another influential milestone by identifying LGBT people as a national health priority (Emlet, 2016).

Also, *Healthy People 2020* (USDHHS, 2010) acknowledged not only health disparities by sexual orientation but also the value of an ecological approach and the overlapping role of numerous determinants, including the role of social determinants of health, as follows: the physical environment; social environment (i.e., cultural institutions, patterns, beliefs); health services; biology and genetics; individual behavior; and also the key role of policies. Further, all of these factors were seen as collectively impacting health outcomes. In this manner, *Healthy People 2020* intentionally went beyond the work in many health fields of health that had previously focused primarily on individual-level health determinants and interventions (USDHHS, 2010).

As an important milestone impacting dominant perspectives, this advance in *Healthy People 2020* involving a focus on social determinants was consistent with a dominant global shift. Globally, the shift has been toward focusing on social determinants or social factors as the root causes of inequalities in health for the world's most vulnerable populations (Marmot, 2005). Indeed, a major goal was to foster a global movement to promote health equity by focusing on the social determinants of health (Marmot et al., 2008).

As another historic milestone influencing dominant perspectives, specifically within the United States, the National Institutes of Health (NIH) asked the IOM (2011) to convene a consensus committee to answer the following questions: "What is currently known about the health status of LGBT populations? Where do gaps in the research exist? What are the priorities for a research agenda to address these gaps?" (p. 1). This was, in essence, an acknowledgment of the reality of how the health disparities experienced by LGBT individuals had been neglected in research (IOM, 2011). In approaching their work, the

IOM (2011) utilized four conceptual frameworks to evaluate the science on the health status of LGBT populations, as follows: *life-course framework* with attention to how experiences at every stage of life inform subsequent experiences while ensuring an historical perspective (e.g., Cohler & Hammack, 2007); the *minority stress model*, acknowledging chronic stress from stigmatization/prejudice/discrimination (e.g., Meyer, 2003); the *social ecology perspective* that attends to individual- and population-level determinants of health, as in a focus on social environmental factors impacting individuals, while avoiding individual-level victim blaming (e.g., McLeroy, Bibeau, Steckler, & Glanz, 1988); and *intersectionality*, with a focus on multiple and intersecting stigmatized identities and systems of oppression (e.g., Gamson & Moon, 2004). The IOM (2011) reviewed the available evidence that substantiated health disparities across numerous health outcomes for sexual minorities.

Of note, LGBT health disparities were described by the IOM (2011) as unique, while acknowledging the key factor of stigma throughout the historical trajectory of LGBT populations in this nation. Emphasis was placed on the contextual factors that impact the lives of members of the LGBT population. This encompassed not only the effects of stigma but also those laws, policies, demographic factors, and barriers to care that all stem from stigma and are interrelated. This included attention to differential treatment in taxation and insurance that result in less disposable income, financial barriers, and limitations on access to health insurance and healthcare (IOM, 2011). Thus, of note, another milestone in the national effort to reduce health disparities involved the passage of the Affordable Care Act, specifically provisions that require insurer coverage of preventive services without any cost to patients and, increased access to health insurance for the millions across this nation who were previously uninsured (Frieden, 2013).

The IOM (2011) also cited insufficient provider training as contributing to LGBT populations receiving less than optimal care and experiencing discrimination in the healthcare system. These issues were viewed as potentially compounded by an additional stigmatizing identity or status due to race/ethnicity (i.e., intersectionality), being an immigrant, or having low income or limited English proficiency. Challenges regarding the enactment of stigma were viewed as operating on both the personal and structural levels, necessitating attention to the social determinants of health disparities (IOM, 2011). Thus, the IOM (2011) affirmed and followed the essential global shift toward considerations of social determinants as root causes of inequalities for vulnerable populations (i.e., Marmot, 2005; Marmot et al., 2008).

Further, advances have been made at the level of describing those clinical issues considered essential to healthcare delivery with sexual minorities (Ard & Makadon, 2012; ; Eckstrand & Ehrenfeld, 2016; Hollenbach et al., 2014; Makadon, Mayer, Potter, & Goldhammer, 2008). Responses to the LGBT populations' mental and physical health disparities include calls for adequate training to ensure the provision of culturally competent healthcare, which may both streamline healthcare costs and improve the effectiveness of the care provided to sexual minorities (Rowan & Giunta, 2016). Progress has included the provision of practical guidelines for clinicians engaged in primary care (Ard & Makadon, 2012; Eckstrand & Ehrenfeld, 2016; Hollenbach et al., 2014; Makadon et al., 2008).

CONCLUSION

This chapter covered the physical and mental health disparities experienced by LGBT populations in United States. More specifically, the chapter provided (1) key definitions of health, and health disparities, or health inequalities, and reviewed concepts such as health equity, while also discussing the typical outcomes focused upon within the health disparities framework; (2) provided an overview of mental health disparities and physical health disparities for sexual minorities, including by specific sexual minority populations; (3) discussed dominant perspectives on LGBT populations impacting the delivery of mental and physical healthcare; and, (4) delivered an overview of solutions to health disparities for sexual minorities.

As this chapter has established, LGBT populations are, indeed, vulnerable populations characterized by the prevalence of significant and wide-ranging mental and physical health disparities. In light of this chapter's overview, it may be asserted that advances have been made in the dominant perspectives influencing LGBT populations' healthcare. Significant milestones in the field of health disparities mark this progress, even despite harmful history. Hopefully, a much-needed future milestone will be achieved in coming decades—that is, the emergence of an evidence base identifying a range of approaches and interventions that serve to effectively reduce and eliminate health disparities for LGBT populations.

REFERENCES

Ard, K. L., & Makadon, H. J. (2012). *Improving the health care of lesbian, gay, bisexual and transgender (LGBT) people: Understanding and eliminating health disparities*. Boston, MA: The Fenway Institute.

Austin, S. B., Jun, H. J., Jackson, B., Spiegelman, D., Rich-Edwards, J., Corliss, H. L., & Wright, R. J. (2008). Disparities in child abuse victimization in lesbian, bisexual, and heterosexual women in the Nurses' Health Study II. *Journal of Women's Health*, 17(4), 597–606.

Blosnich, J. R., Hanmer, J., Yu, L., Matthews, D. D., & Kavalieratos, D. (2016). Health care use, health behaviors, and medical conditions among individuals in same-sex and opposite-sex partnerships: A cross-sectional observational analysis of the Medical Expenditures Panel Survey (MEPS), 2003–2011. *Medical Care*, 54(6), 547–554.

Blosnich, J. R., Marsiglio, M. C., Gao, S., Gordon, A. J., Shipherd, J. C., Kauth, M., ... Fine, M. J. (2016). Mental health of transgender veterans in US states with and without discrimination and hate crime legal protection. *American Journal of Public Health*, 106(3), 534–540.

Bostwick, W. B., Boyd, C. J., Hughes, T. L., West, B. T., & McCabe, S. E. (2014). Discrimination and mental health among lesbian, gay and bisexual adults in the United States. American *Journal of Orthopsychiatry*, 84(1), 35–45.

Braveman, P. (2006). Health disparities and health equity: Concepts and measurement. *Annual Review of Public Health*, 27, 167–194.

Butler, M., McCreedy, E., Schwer, N., Burgess, D., Call, K., Przedworski, J., ... Kane, R. L. (2016). *Improving cultural competence to reduce health disparities*. Rockville, MD: Agency for Healthcare Research and Quality.

Calzo, J. P., Roberts, A. L., Corliss, H. L., Blood, E. A., Kroshus, E., & Austin, S. B. (2014). Physical activity disparities in heterosexual and sexual minority youth ages 12–22 years old: Roles of childhood gender nonconformity and athletic self-esteem. *Annals of Behavioral Medicine*, 47(1), 17–27.

Centers for Disease Control and Prevention (CDC). (2013, November 22). HIV infection—United States, 2008 and 2010. MMWR. *Morbidity and Mortality Weekly Reports*, Supplement, 62(3), 112–119. Retrieved from https://www.cdc.gov/mmwr/pdf/other/su6203.pdf

Cochran, S. D., Björkenstam, C., & Mays, V. M. (2016). Sexual orientation and all-cause mortality among US adults aged 18 to 59 years, 2001–2011. *American Journal of Public Health*, 106(5), 918–920.

Cochran, S. D., & Mays, V. M. (2015). Mortality risks among persons reporting same-sex sexual partners: Evidence from the 2008 General Social Survey—National death index data set. *American Journal of Public Health*, 105(2), 358–364.

Cochran, S. D., & Mays, V. M. (2016). A strategic approach to eliminating sexual orientation-related health disparities. *American Journal of Public Health*, 106(9), e4.

Cochran, S. D., Sullivan, J. G., & Mays, V. M. (2003). Prevalence of mental disorders, psychological distress, and mental health services use among lesbian, gay, and bisexual adults in the United States. *Journal of Consulting and Clinical Psychology*, 71(1), 52–61.

Cohler, B. J., & Hammack, P. L. (2007). The psychological world of the gay teenager: Social change, narrative, and "normality." *Journal of Youth and Adolescence*, 36(1), 47–59.

Conron, K. J., Mimiaga, M. J., & Landers, S. J. (2010). A population-based study of sexual orientation identity and gender differences in adult health. *American Journal of Public Health*, 100(10), 1953–1960.

Corliss, H. L., Cochran, S. D., & Mays, V. M. (2002). Reports of parental maltreatment during childhood in a United States population-based survey of homosexual, bisexual, and heterosexual adults. *Child Abuse & Neglect*, 26(11), 1165–1178.

Darwich, L., Videla, S., Cañadas, M. P., Piñol, M., García-Cuyàs, F., Vela, S., ... & Can Ruti HIV-HPV Team. (2013). Distribution of human papillomavirus genotypes in anal cytological and histological specimens from HIV-infected men who have sex with men and men who have sex with women. *Diseases of the Colon & Rectum*, 56(9), 1043–1052.

Drabble, L., & Trocki, K. (2005). Alcohol consumption, alcohol-related problems, and other substance use among lesbian and bisexual women. *Journal of Lesbian Studies*, 9(3), 19–30.

Drescher, J. (2015). Out of DSM: Depathologizing homosexuality. *Behavioral Sciences*, 5(4), 565–575.

Eckstrand, K. L., & Ehrenfeld, J. M. (Eds.). (2016). *Lesbian, gay, bisexual, and transgender healthcare: A clinical guide to preventive, primary, and specialist care*. New York, NY: Springer International Publishing.

Eckstrand, K. L., & Sciolla, A. F. (2014). History of health disparities among individuals who are or maybe LGBT, gender nonconforming, and/or born with DSD. In A. D. Hollenbach, K. L. Eckstrand, & A. Dreger (Eds.), *Implementing curricular and institutional climate changes to improve health care for individuals who are LGBT, gender nonconforming, or born with DSD: A resource for medical educators*. Washington, DC: Association of American Medical College. Retrieved from https://members.aamc.org/eweb/upload/Executive%20LGBT%20FINAL.pdf

Emlet, C. A. (2016). Social, economic, and health disparities among LGBT older adults. *Generations*, 40(2), 16–22.

Fallin-Bennett, K., Henderson, S. L., Nguyen, G. T., & Hyderi, A. (2016). Primary care, prevention, and coordination of care. In K. L. Eckstrand & J. M. Ehrenfeld (Eds.), *Lesbian, gay, bisexual, and transgender Healthcare* (pp. 95–114). New York, NY: Springer International Publishing.

Felix, S., Policastro, C., Agnich, L., & Gould, L. A. (2016). Psychological victimization among college students. *Violence and Gender*, 3(1), 42–48.

Fredriksen-Goldsen, K. I., Kim, H. J., & Barkan, S. E. (2012). Disability among lesbian, gay, and bisexual adults: Disparities in prevalence and risk. *American Journal of Public Health*, 102(1), e16–e21.

Fredriksen-Goldsen, K. I., Kim, H., Barkan, S. E., Muraco, A., & Hoy-Ellis, C. P. (2013). Health disparities among lesbian, gay, and bisexual older adults: Results from a population-based study. *American Journal of Public Health*, 103(10), 1802–1809.

Frieden, T. R. (2013). Foreword. In CDC Health Disparities and Inequalities Report-United States, MMWR. *Morbidity and Mortality Weekly Report*, Supplement, 62(3), 1–2. Retrieved from https://www.cdc.gov/mmwr/pdf/other/su6203.pdf

Gamson, J., & Moon, D. (2004). The sociology of sexualities: Queer and beyond. *Annual Review of Sociology*, 30, 47–64.

Gilman, S. E., Cochran, S. D., Mays, V. M., Ostrow, D., & Kessler, R. C. (2001). Risk of psychiatric disorders among individuals reporting same-sex sexual partners in the National Comorbidity Survey. *American Journal of Public Health*, 91(6), 933–939.

Hadland, S. E., Austin, S. B., Goodenow, C. S., & Calzo, J. P. (2014). Weight misperception and unhealthy weight control behaviors among sexual minorities in the general adolescent population. *Journal of Adolescent Health*, 54(3), 296–303.

Hatzenbuehler, M. L., McLaughlin, K. A., Keyes, K. M., & Hasin, D. S. (2010). The impact of institutional discrimination on psychiatric disorders in lesbian, gay, and bisexual populations: A prospective study. *American Journal of Public Health*, 100(3), 452–459.

Hollenbach, A. D., Eckstrand, K. L., & Dreger, A. (Eds.). (2014). *Implementing curricular and institutional climate changes to improve health care for individuals who are LGBT, gender nonconforming, or born with DSD: A resource for medical educators*. Washington, DC: Association of American Medical Colleges. Retrieved from https://members.aamc.org/eweb/upload/Executive%20LGBT%20FINAL.pdf

Institute of Medicine (IOM). (2011). *The health of lesbian, gay, bisexual, and transgender people: Building a foundation for better understanding*. Washington, DC: The National Academies Press.

Kecojevic, A., Wong, C. F., Schrager, S. M., Silva, K., Bloom, J. J., Iverson, E., & Lankenau, S. E. (2012). Initiation into prescription drug misuse: Differences between lesbian, gay, bisexual, transgender (LGBT) and heterosexual high-risk young adults in Los Angeles and New York. *Addictive Behaviors, 37*(11), 1289–1293.

Kilbourne, A. M., Switzer, G., Hyman, K., Crowley-Matoka, M., & Fine, M. J. (2006). Advancing health disparities research within the health care system: A conceptual frame-work. *American Journal of Public Health, 96*(12), 2113–2121.

King, M., Semlyen, J., Tai, S. S., Killaspy, H., Osborn, D., Popelyuk, D., & Nazareth, I. (2008). A systematic review of mental disorder, suicide, and deliberate self harm in lesbian, gay and bisexual people. *BMC Psychiatry, 8*(1), 1–17.

Koh, A. S., & Ross, L. K. (2006). Mental health issues: A comparison of lesbian, bisexual and heterosexual women. *Journal of Homosexuality, 51*(1), 1–26.

Landers, S. J., Mimiaga, M. J., & Conron, K. J. (2011) Sexual orientation differences in asthma correlates in a population-based sample of adults. *American Journal of Public Health, 101*(12), 2238–2241.

Lewis, N. M. (2009). Mental health in sexual minorities: Recent indicators, trends, and their relationships to place in North America and Europe. *Health & Place, 15*(4), 1029–1045.

Lick, D. J., Durso, L. E., & Johnson, K. L. (2013). Minority stress and physical health among sexual minorities. *Perspectives on Psychological Science, 8*(5), 521–548.

Makadon, H. J., Mayer, K., Potter, J., & Goldhammer, H. (2008). *The Fenway guide to lesbian, gay, bisexual, and transgender health*. Philadelphia, PA: ACP Press.

Marmot, M. (2005). Social determinants of health inequalities. *The Lancet, 365*(9464), 1099–1104.

Marmot, M., Friel, S., Bell, R., Houweling, T. A., Taylor, S., & Commission on Social Determinants of Health. (2008). Closing the gap in a generation: Health equity through action on the social determinants of health. *The Lancet, 372*(9650), 1661–1669.

Marshal, M. P., Dietz, L. J., Friedman, M. S., Stall, R., Smith, H. A., McGinley, J., ... Brent, D. A. (2011). Suicidality and depression disparities between sexual minority and heterosexual youth: A meta-analytic review. *Journal of Adolescent Health, 49*(2), 115–123.

Massetti, G. M., Ragan, K. R., Thomas, C. C., & Ryerson, A. B. (2016). Public health opportunities for promoting health equity in cancer prevention and control in LGBT populations. *LGBT Health, 3*(1), 11–14.

Matthews, A. K., Hotton, A., Li, C. C., Miller, K., Johnson, A., Jones, K. W., & Thai, J. (2016). An Internet-based study examining the factors associated with the physical and mental health quality of life of LGBT cancer survivors. *LGBT Health, 3*(1), 65–73.

Max, W. B., Stark, B., Sung, H. Y., & Offen, N. (2016a). Sexual identity disparities in smoking and secondhand smoke exposure in California: 2003–2013. *American Journal of Public Health, 106*(6), 1136–1142.

Max, W. B., Stark, B., Sung, H. Y., & Offen, N. (2016b). Max et al. respond. *American Journal of Public Health, 106*(9), e4–e5.

McLeroy, K. R., Bibeau, D., Steckler, A., & Glanz, K. (1988). An ecological perspective on health promotion programs. *Health Education & Behavior, 15*(4), 351–377.

Meyer, I. H. (1995). Minority stress and mental health in gay men. *Journal of Health and Social Behavior, 36*(1), 38–56.

Meyer, I. H. (2003). Prejudice, social stress, and mental health in lesbian, gay, and bisexual populations: Conceptual issues and research evidence. *Psychological Bulletin, 129*(5), 674–607.

Roberts, A. L., Austin, S. B., Corliss, H. L., Vandermorris, A. K., & Koenen, K. C. (2010). Pervasive trauma exposure among US sexual orientation minority adults and risk of posttraumatic stress disorder. *American Journal of Public Health, 100*(12), 2433–2441.

Rowan, N. L., & Giunta, N. (2016). Lessons on social and health disparities from older lesbians with alcoholism and the role of interventions to promote culturally competent services. *Journal of Human Behavior in the Social Environment, 26*(2), 210–216.

Stall, R., Matthews, D. D., Friedman, M. R., Kinsky, S., Egan, J. E., Coulter, R. W., . . . Markovic, N. (2016). The continuing development of health disparities research on lesbian, gay, bisexual, and transgender individuals. *American Journal of Public Health, 106*(5), 787–789.

Su, D., Irwin, J. A., Fisher, C., Ramos, A., Kelley, M., Mendoza, D. A. R., & Coleman, J. D. (2016). Mental health disparities within the LGBT population: A comparison between transgender and nontransgender individuals. *Transgender Health, 1*(1), 12–20.

U.S. Department of Health and Human Services (USDHHS). (2000). *Healthy people 2010.* Washington, DC: U.S. Department of Health and Human Services, Office of Disease Prevention and Health Promotion. Retrieved from http://www.healthypeople.gov/2010/

U.S. Department of Health and Human Services (USDHHS). (2010). *Healthy people 2020: Framework.* Washington, DC: U.S. Department of Health and Human Services, Office of Disease Prevention and Health Promotion. Retrieved from https://www.healthypeople.gov/sites/default/files/HP2020Framework.pdf

Wallace, B. C. (Ed.). (2008). *Toward equity in health: A new global approach to health disparities.* New York, NY: Springer Publishing Company.

Wallace, S. P., Cochran, S. D., Durazo, E. M., & Ford, C. L. (2011). The health of aging lesbian, gay and bisexual adults in California. *Policy Brief (UCLA Center for Health Policy Research)*, 1–8.

10

Challenges in Moving toward the Resolution, Reduction, and Elimination of Health Disparities for LGBT Populations

Barbara C. Wallace and Erik Santacruz

There is a quandary: The resolution of health disparities among LGBT populations, or making progress from reducing health disparities to their elimination, requires an evidence base on "what works." However, the evidence base at this point is sorely lacking.

Gaps in knowledge hampering progress in resolving, reducing, and eliminating health disparities for sexual minorities involve the science not having established "what works" in numerous areas, as follows: there is a lack of knowledge regarding "what works" in targeting the precise mechanisms operating as factors impacting health, or the drivers of health disparities and health epidemics, or relevant social determinants, including when there are multiple and intersecting stigmatized identities (Blosnich, Marsiglio, et al., 2016; Gamson & Moon, 2004; Hatzenbuehler, Phelan, & Link, 2013; Lick, Durso, & Johnson, 2013; Marmot, 2005; Stall et al., 2016); a lack of knowledge on "what works" with regard to interventions targeting specific health disparities, including the void from a lack of clinical trials on interventions, and a lack of translational research to see what works in implementing and evaluating interventions in routine care settings (Cochran & Mays, 2016; Kilbourne, Switzer, Hyman, Crowley-Matoka, & Fine, 2006; Thomas, Quinn, Butler, Fryer, & Garza, 2011); a knowledge gap about "what works" in terms of delivering LGBT curriculum content and cultural competency training interventions with providers actually translate into provider behavioral change and changes in the patient-provider relationship (Fallin-Bennett, Henderson, Nguyen, & Hyderi, 2016); and a deficiency in not knowing "what works" in transforming the overall clinical system or service delivery system, to produce better patient outcomes (Fallin-Bennett et al., 2016).

Yet, and still, there is an imperative to address the health disparities and unique health needs of sexual minorities (Hollenbach, Eckstrand, & Dreger, 2014). LGBT populations in the United States experience numerous barriers to receipt of quality care, as their experiences include perceived discrimination in the healthcare setting, provider neglect to discuss issues of sexual orientation or gender identity, and lack of provider training on LGBT health issues or inadequate training (Fallin-Bennett et al., 2016). This suggests a vital need for evolution in research and movement toward discovering of "what works."

This chapter will focus upon the progress being made in moving toward the resolution of health disparities, and, specifically, the reduction and elimination of health disparities for sexual minorities through evolutionary steps in research deemed essential to permit establishing an evidence base on "what works." More specifically, this chapter will (1) review weaknesses and advances in health disparities research for LGBT populations and frameworks utilized to propel evolution in health disparities research and (2) present recommended strategies for moving toward solutions and cutting-edge advances to improve healthcare service delivery to LGBT populations, including a focus on cultural competence training for providers as well as other individual-level, provider-level, and system-level approaches in order to reduce and eliminate health disparities. A conclusion will emphasize the importance of society prioritizing a substantial investment in research on LGBT populations' health disparities in order to identify "what works" so as to propel progress toward the resolution, reduction, and elimination of health disparities.

WEAKNESSES AND ADVANCES IN HEALTH DISPARITIES RESEARCH FOR LGBT POPULATIONS

There is a desired standard that has yet to be met through health disparities research with LGBT populations—that is, for clinical practice with LGBT populations to emerges as evidence based (Makadon, Mayer, Potter, & Goldhammer, 2008). It is important to elaborate on the research weaknesses and limitations, and factors barring progress toward clinical practice becoming evidence based. It is also vital to acknowledge advances and to articulate frameworks for propelling evolution in research.

Historically, in the health disparities literature, initially the focus was primarily on comparisons of racial/ethnic minority populations to whites—exposing disparities from data on morbidity and mortality "across a broad spectrum of mostly preventable conditions and diseases," which were viewed as "troubling" gaps necessitating action to eliminate health disparities and foster equity in health (Thomas et al., 2011, p. 3). Indeed, consider how the contemporary study of health disparities is rooted in the 1985 report released by the secretary of the U.S. Department of Health and Human Services (USDHHS), Margaret Heckler—that is, the *Secretary's Task Force Report on Black and Minority Health*; this report specifically documented differences in mortality between whites and minorities using data on excess deaths among minorities from cancer, cardiovascular diseases, diabetes, chemical dependency, homicide, unintentional injuries, and infant mortality (Thomas et al., 2011).

However, when the focus is on research on health disparities for sexual minorities, a long-standing limitation has been observed (Butler et al., 2016). This involves the scant research linking evidence of risk factor disparities (i.e., meaning that sexual minorities experience a higher-risk status for various health conditions and outcomes) to actual intermediate or to longer-term health outcomes. This is the case whether the health condition is cancer or cardiovascular disease or even the final outcome of mortality (Butler et al., 2016).

Pioneering Evolution in Health Disparities Research with LGBT Populations

Fortunately, research is evolving to overcome prior limitations in investigations with sexual minorities. In contemporary pioneering research, as a major advance, Cochran, Björkenstam, and Mays (2016) "capitalized on the recent linkage of National Death Index mortality records through December 31, 2011, to the 2001 to 2010 National Health and Nutrition Examination Survey (NHANES) cohort" data (p. 918). They found an elevated mortality risk for lesbians, homosexually experienced women, and bisexual men, in comparison to their same-sex heterosexual counterparts (Cochran et al., 2016). What emerged was that it was not "sexual orientation, per se, but rather sexual orientation-related health disadvantages" that created this "vulnerability" (p. 920). However, a "statistical adjustment for health differences identified at onset of follow-up eliminated the sexual orientation effect, except for homosexually experienced women" (p. 920). Also, among a subset of sexual minority men, especially bisexual men, HIV infection was found to be an "important morality risk factor" (p. 920).

Despite its limitations, this research is viewed as pioneering, given how the analyses focused on the final outcome of mortality, which has been largely lacking in research with sexual minorities, due to the absence of usable data from population-based national surveys in most studies (Butler et al., 2016). The advance in research embodied in the Cochran et al. (2016) study was made possible because the national population survey data they utilized included vital questions on sexual identity and sexual behavior—major progress.

Need for National Survey and Registry Questions on Sexual Identity and Behavior

On the other hand, there is a long-standing history where questions on sexual orientation and gender identity have been absent from national surveys and national registries (Butler et al., 2016). The result of this limitation in research has been stagnation in the study of sexual minority health disparities, preventing the kind of evolution deemed essential. The consequences are deemed so severe that sexual minority research on health disparities has been described as still being *first-generation* research; meanwhile, research on health disparities for racial and ethnic minority populations has been described as advancing into *fourth-generation* research (Butler et al., 2016).

Conceptualizing Research Weaknesses: Four Generations of Health Disparities Research

More specifically, following the concept of phases of health disparities research advanced by Kilbourne et al. (2006), Thomas et al. (2011) proceeded to identify four phases, or *four generations of health disparities research*, as follows: *first-generation research* with a focus on the detection, identification, and documentation of health disparities while also identifying vulnerable populations; *second-generation research* with a focus on determining causal relationships underlying health disparities, including multiple influential factors and social determinants negatively impacting health status and access to healthcare; *third-generation research* with a focus on identifying solutions to eliminate health disparities while building an evidence base through randomized clinical trials (i.e., do interventions work?) and via transdisciplinary research, community engagement, and translational research; and a proposed *fourth generation* of health disparities research that considers the dynamics of race and racism while addressing structural determinants of health disparities using comprehensive, multilevel interventions as well as via comprehensive evaluation of interventions while also necessitating researcher self-reflection (Thomas et al., 2011).

Of note, Thomas et al. (2011) explained that the dynamics of race and racism and researcher self-reflection emerged as key *fourth-generation* research issues. Regarding race and racism, it is necessary to focus on "the impact of routine exposure to racism on health behaviors and health status" (p. 8). This necessitates researchers also examining their own lived experiences, including the interaction of race, power, and class in their lives, and the need to engage in disciplinary self-critique. Moreover, it was asserted that "only by directly confronting race and racism can we truly eliminate health disparities and achieve health equity" (p. 8). Attention needs to be paid to the underlying societal dynamic power structure, which serves to perpetuate inequities, as structural determinants of health; and to taking action in response to such factors, which may necessitate a role for mixed methods research (i.e., qualitative and quantitative), which can "evaluate comprehensive, multilevel interventions" as components of a guiding paradigm for *fourth-generation* health disparities research (p. 10).

Thus, there are lessons to be learned from the work of Thomas et al. (2011) which largely applies to research on racial/ethnic disparities. Much may be extended to the study of health disparities for LGBT populations. Specifically, there may be implications for focusing on factors such as discrimination, stig-matization, and social marginalization for sexual minorities via research. Also, there is a need for self-reflection with regard to the interpersonal processes of dis-crimination, stigmatization, and social marginalization for not only researchers but also practitioners and diverse providers of physical and mental health services.

An Analysis of LGBT Populations' Health Disparities via the Generation Framework

When the advances in the frameworks guiding racial/ethnic health disparities research are extended to sexual orientation minorities, what emerges is the rela-tive "infancy" of sexual orientation health disparities research (Cochran & Mays, 2016, p. e4). To propel vital evolution, Cochran and Mays (2016) also offered their own interpretation of how there are *four generations for health dispar-ities research for LGBT populations.*

The *first-generation* work of documenting disparities has been proceeding for years (Cochran & Mays, 2016). The assertion that sexual minority research on health disparities is still *first-generation* research has been placed in further con-text by Butler et al. (2016), given their emphasis on how sexual minority research on health disparities is still largely focused on the detection, identifica-tion, and documentation of health disparities (Butler et al., 2016). Of note, such research has advanced from using small convenience samples, to household-based samples, population-based national samples, and random samples drawn from the general population (Stall et al., 2016); however, so much still remains *first-generation research.*

What has just "begun" is *second-generation* research, which "seeks to identify factors that contribute to disparities," using "intersectionality foci and docu-menting the impact of minority stress" (Cochran & Mays, 2016, p. e4). The intersectionality framework has guided research that unpacks examined factors involving the impact of multiple and intersecting stigmatized identities and sys-tems of oppression (e.g., Gamson & Moon, 2004). The intersectionality frame-work calls for research, which unpacks factors impacting health that are linked to a complex reality—that is, "not only are lesbians, gay men, bisexual women, bisexual men, transgender women, and transgender men all discrete populations, but each group is further shaped by racial, ethnic, and other cultural influences" (Institute of Medicine [IOM], 2011, p. 74). A growing body of empirical research supports the argument that sexual orientation minority disparities in health are linked to the experience of minority stress or the stress of antigay stigma (Lick et al., 2013).

Thus, *second-generation* research has been heavily influenced by Meyer's minority stress framework (Meyer, 1995, 2003) as a tremendous strength.

The minority stress model is notable for having synthesized a large body of sociological and psychological literature on stress and coping processes in order to
provide a framework for conceptualizing health disparities among minority
groups (Bostwick, Boyd, Hughes, West, & McCabe, 2014). Yet, it has been
asserted that insufficient research has focused on uncovering social determinants
of sexual orientation minority disparities in health or the causes of the physical
health problems disproportionately impacting this group (Lick et al., 2013).
In addition, others have pointed out the vital need to investigate and expand
the knowledge base regarding the precise mechanisms of how these factors operate to impact health, suggesting a direction in which research needs to evolve
(Blosnich, Marsiglio, et al., 2016; Hatzenbuehler et al., 2013).

Cochran and Mays (2016) envision *third-generation* research focused on
proposing and testing interventions that target specific health disparities.
Third-generation research "lies mostly over the horizon for sexual orientation
research" (p. e4). Cochran and Mays's (2016) vision for *fourth-generation*
research for sexual minorities involves eliminating health disparities by elimination of their root causes, necessitating attention to factors such as "likely social
marginalization and stigmatization" (p. e4)—that is social determinants (i.e., as
per Marmot, 2005). The reality is that the task of advancing evolution in the
field of sexual orientation health disparities research and achieving the goal of
health equity necessitates following the path of science—that is, "building on
findings generated by previous research" (Cochran & Mays, 2016, p. e4).
This implies the maturation of science from first- to second-, to third-, and to
fourth-generation research as outlined by Cochran and Mays (2016).

Three Proposed Phases/Generations of Health Disparities Research for LGBT Populations

Stall et al. (2016) have also sought to propel evolution in research, utilizing
the work of Kilbourne et al. (2006) as a springboard for providing a framework
for the evolution of research. The Stall et al. (2016) framework proceeds across
three phases or generations of health disparities research for LGBT populations, as follows: (1) the research focus starts with *detection of health disparities*;
(2) research proceeds to *understanding health disparities*; and, (3) finally, research
advances to *reduction or elimination of health disparities*—also referred to as *resolution*
(p. 787).

The *first phase/generation, detection of health disparities* has been compromised
by the long-standing under-investment in health research for specific LGBT
populations and especially specific sexual and gender minority populations (Stall
et al., 2016). The first phase of research, involving *detection*, covers the processes
of defining health disparities, defining vulnerable populations (e.g., sexual
minorities, LGBT populations, overlapping sexual minority and racial/ethnic

populations), measuring disparities in these vulnerable populations, considering selection effects (e.g., sample bias, such as greater severity of illness in the sample, obscuring true differences) in research samples and confounding factors (Kilbourne et al., 2006). Much-needed advances in *detection* that have been recommended include addressing the gap in knowledge regarding those distinct health disparities characterizing specific populations within the category of sexual minorities, including by race/ethnicity, and which health disparities are associated with "the greatest burden of disease and mortality among specific sexual and gender minority populations" and among racial/ethnic groups (Stall et al., 2016, p. 788). These findings have implications for the development of interventions that target specific populations' health disparities (Stall et al., 2016). This is consistent with the major recommendation that future research needs to involve the development and evaluation of "targeted health interventions, particularly for lesbians, bisexual men, and homosexually experienced women, who are not commonly the focus for health intervention studies" (Cochran et al., 2016, p. 920).

Hampering progress with regard to the *first phase/generation, detection of health disparities* research, is what remains undetected. Simply, there are surely undetected health disparities for specific LGBT populations, given long-standing limitations in research, including national surveys failing to include questions on sexual identity and behavior (Stall et al., 2016). Advancing to research using interventions to reduce or eliminate health disparities is not possible when health issues remain undetected. It is vital to document "which health disparities are the causes of the greatest burden of disease and mortality" for specific sexual and gender minority populations, given the need to "identify which health disparities should be targeted first in terms of intervention development" (p. 788).

The *second phase/generation for understanding health disparities* may be interpreted as involving several elements, as follows (Stall et al., 2016): utilizing theories to explain the drivers of health disparities in distinct LGBT populations; viewing such drivers or the identification of mechanisms that drive health disparities as providing the rationale for the design of interventions; codifying variables that may be driving mechanisms of health disparities (e.g., biological, behavioral, interpersonal, community, and structural) toward being able to explain "the complex and multilayered causal processes" underlying specific health disparities in distinct LGBT populations, going beyond the identification of the role of minority stress or the chronic stress associated with stigmatization in a heterosexist society (p. 788); and, overall, being able to conceptualize the theoretical relationships among variables and building on empirical advances for purposes of "sound intervention design" (p. 788).

In research undertaking the *second phase/generation task, understanding health disparities*, there may be a focus on identifying determinants of health disparities on the level of the patient/individual, provider, clinical encounter, and health-care system (Kilbourne et al., 2006). This is consistent with the need to pay attention to potential drivers of health disparities (Stall et al., 2016). *Understanding* also requires research investigating the drivers of epidemics or the underlying mechanisms that drive health disparities—identifying factors to be addressed by interventions, including theoretical relationships (Stall et al., 2016).

The *third phase generation task, reducing, resolving, or eliminating health disparities*, necessitates having interventions that meet certain standards and follow specific steps (Stall et al., 2016), including the following: the design of the interventions is directly rooted in second-phase/generation understanding of health disparities using theoretical and empirical advances; there is funding so the emergent interventions "can be subjected to randomized trials to test for efficacy" (p. 788); and the interventions are "finally evaluated for effectiveness part of ongoing public health practice"—as a stage in which ideally emerge are "practical public health tools" available for use to "resolve," reduce, and eliminate health disparities in distinct LGBT populations, as a matter of "social justice" (p. 788).

The *third phase/generation research task, reducing or eliminating health disparities or resolving them*, occurs through the processes of intervention, evaluation of an intervention trial, and then implementation and translation into routine care settings including the development of strategies to promote changes in policy in light of the intervention (Kilbourne et al., 2006). There are gaps in knowledge that can only be filled by empirical advances in research. Filling these gaps in knowledge depends not only on prior advances in identifying the drivers of health disparities, drivers of epidemics, but in identifying through research those underlying mechanisms operating for specific sexual minority populations (Stall et al., 2016). In addition, advances in identifying theoretical relationships among variables, as well as advances in empirical research, are also a vital part of the process of intervention development (Stall et al., 2016).

There are many variables to address through public health interventions as part of *third phase/generation* research aiming to *reduce, eliminate, or resolve health disparities;* these variables range from the biological to the behavioral, interpersonal, community, and structural levels. The results of randomized trails for efficacy will identify effective interventions for dissemination (Stall et al., 2016). Others acknowledge the role of variables such as the larger environment, political economy, and health services factors, including patient-level, provider-level, and healthcare organizational-level factors, which collectively operate so that vulnerable populations receive a lower quality of care; the impact is reflected in healthcare processes and/or health outcomes (Kilbourne et al., 2006).

In addition, the *third phase/generation research task of reducing or eliminating health disparities or resolving them* includes widespread knowledge translation into service delivery (Kilbourne et al., 2006). Translation into routine care settings necessitates customizing and adapting interventions for vulnerable groups. This depends on adequate resources and technical assistance, including a role for collaborating with community members and their providers. Findings on interventions need to be translated to a variety of treatment settings, while knowledge translation includes making findings accessible to various communities, policymakers, and varied stakeholders. It may also be necessary to fundamentally change organizational financing, the organization of health systems, and relevant policy to ensure knowledge translation to service delivery across multiple settings (Kilbourne et al., 2006).

Finally, Stall et al.'s (2016) conceptualization of *three phases or generations* of health disparities research for LGBT populations also proceeds across generations, given the length of time needed for each phase of the proposed research agenda. It necessitates training the workforce needed to conduct the research. This means paying "increased attention to support and training of junior researchers interested in the health of LGBT populations" as an essential element of "resolving health disparities in sexual and gender minority populations" (p. 788).

Additional Recommendations for Advancing LGBT Health Disparities Research

Also essential to evolution in research on LGBT populations' health disparities is ongoing advocacy for the routine inclusion of questions on sexual identity and sexual behavior in future national surveys and registries (Schlittler, Grey, & Popanz, 2016; Stall et al., 2016). Indeed, there is widespread consensus that the health disparities research agenda will be advanced through the implementation of and adherence to consistent methods for both collecting and reporting health data, which will enable public health efforts to reduce disparities and advance health equity (Massetti, Ragan, Thomas, & Ryerson, 2016).

Also, toward the ultimate goal of achieving health equity for sexual minorities, the Centers for Disease Control and Prevention (CDC) strives to improve the health of sexual minorities by focusing on issues of healthcare access, supporting culturally appropriate and relevant interventions and science, and taking a public health approach to the promotion of health equity (Massetti et al., 2016). Also, the USDHHS seeks to promote health equity by working to identify the health needs of sexual minorities, ensuring equal treatment and access to care (e.g., health coverage), working for the provision of culturally tailored resources, and having population-based data surveys collect data on sexual and gender identities. Thus, there is a role for *surveillance research* activities in order to build the evidence base needed to guide public health programming, including for planning interventions and evaluating them. More specifically, the use of *behavioral surveillance via survey methods* depends on the collection of data from individual members of the target population, and necessitates inclusion of appropriate sexual orientation and gender identity in population-based data systems (Massetti et al., 2016).

Health disparities research is also needed to detect any gaps in the quality of care provided to vulnerable groups in comparison to less vulnerable groups (Kilbourne et al., 2006). Such research necessitates the measurement of disparities in the quality of healthcare between subpopulations as well as evidence-based performance measures that can detect gaps in the quality of care delivered (Kilbourne et al., 2006).

Others recommend that sexual orientation health disparities research also evolve by focusing on the society-wide impact of disparities, in terms of the health-related economic burden, which may motivate the development of interventions (Max, Stark, Sung, & Offen, 2016). For example, cigarette smoking has been identified as a potential causal factor in the high rates among sexual minorities of various diseases (e.g., asthma, cancer, cardiovascular disease, diabetes). Research may then proceed by specifying the health-related economic burden, healthcare, and other costs associated with tobacco. Findings may then spur action to reduce the impact of tobacco for the vulnerable population of sexual minorities (Max et al., 2016). Beyond this example, there are implications for other health conditions with a high health-related economic burden, the analysis of which may motivate development of a range of interventions to alleviate health disparities.

Other research has sought to identify the underlying mechanisms operating in health disparities toward the goal of alleviating them (Bränström, Hatzenbuehler, Pachankis, & Link, 2016). Sexual orientation minority health disparities have been largely explained using minority stress theory (i.e., Meyer, 1995, 2003), which emphasizes the excess stress experienced in comparison to heterosexuals; however, alternative and complementary theoretical analyses have been advanced (Bränström et al., 2016). For example, fundamental cause theory focuses on plausible mechanisms underlying health disparities that involve the "unequal distribution of health-protective resources such as knowledge, prestige, power, and supportive social connections" (p. 1114). More specifically, fundamental cause theory posits that "health inequalities persist even though health-relevant mechanisms and risk factors change over time and place"; this persistence occurs because societal members of "higher-status groups have access to more health-protective resources" (i.e., knowledge, prestige, power, and supportive social connections), in comparison to members of lower status groups (p. 1113). There are implications for a line of ongoing future research that may carry implications for interventions to reduce health disparities.

Finally, future ongoing research needs to continue to focus on those underlying determinants, including social inequities, that "result in differential treatment" (Kilbourne et al., 2006, p. 2114). Potential factors may include access to care and patient preferences with regard to healthcare. More comprehensively, potential factors operating in causing or exacerbating disparities are not only patient-level (e.g., beliefs, preferences, race/ethnicity, culture, familial context, education, resources, biology) but also provider-level (e.g., knowledge, attitudes, competing demands, bias), clinical encounter-level (e.g., provider communication, cultural competence), and healthcare-system level (e.g., health services organization, financing, service delivery, organizational culture, quality improvement efforts; Kilbourne et al., 2006).

TOWARD SOLUTIONS: CUTTING-EDGE ADVANCES TO IMPROVE LGBT SERVICE DELIVERY

In moving toward solutions, special attention has been given to the factors operating on the provider, clinical encounter, and healthcare-system levels. In support of this, Blosnich, Hanmer, Yu, Matthews, and Kavalieratos (2016) indicated that the task of reducing and eliminating health disparities will require cutting-edge strategies that combine individual-level, provider-level, and system-level approaches. It is vital to rectify disparities in accessing and receiving healthcare as well as disparities in the quality of care delivered—which may translate into health disparities—as a rationale for moving toward solutions (Hollenbach et al., 2014).

Focus on Cultural Competence and Practice Guidelines

As an individual-level and provider-level approach, a body of research has documented the need for significant improvements in the delivery of health care to LGBT people, including those aimed toward the delivery of *culturally competent healthcare*, as an approach for reducing health disparities (Butler et al., 2016). Recommendations advanced for the creation of culturally competent health care for sexual minorities include the following: providing practitioners and all personnel with education on those specific health disparities commonly experienced by LGBT populations; providing education regarding how to obtain sexual orientation, gender identity, and sexual history information; providing training on how to use gender-neutral language on all intake forms and medical forms, and during all interpersonal communication; ensuring education on how to refrain from making assumptions regarding a patient's sexual orientation and gender identity by routinely asking all patients questions to obtain this information; creating an LGBT-welcoming environment by displaying LGBT-friendly symbols in healthcare settings; including in the training of all providers and personnel in the process of self-examination regarding any strongly held beliefs and biases in order to facilitate creation of a welcoming environment for healthcare service delivery; and creating and displaying inclusive and nondiscriminatory policies (Butler et al., 2016).

Still, evaluations have indicated that the majority of contemporary providers have had little to no training in the area of LGBT health (Butler et al., 2016). Despite the publication of protocols and recommendation, many providers remain unaware of them or hold misconceptions and explicit and implicit bias toward sexual minorities. Some providers have indicated being uncomfortable when treating sexually transmitted infections among sexual minorities (Butler et al., 2016). Others have documented the reality of that exposure to training still leaves providers feeling ill-prepared to deliver LGBT healthcare (Fallin-Bennett et al., 2016).

Yet, other key practice guidelines include embracing the task of ensuring the confidentiality of patients' health records while also obtaining sexual orientation and gender identity information, including with the use of electronic records (Callahan, Henderson, Ton, & MacDonald, 2016). The benefits of collecting such data include accumulating knowledge of patterns of health disparities so that they can be reduced. These data can also be compared to epidemiological data on health issues and outcomes for sexual minority populations. Clients tend to then make requests for LGBT-welcoming primary care and specialty providers, necessitating the identification and listing of LGBT-welcoming providers to accommodate referrals. Ultimately, the benefits of collecting data on sexual orientation and gender identity include the potential to identify the effectiveness of interventions with sexual minority populations. These data can then lead to the provision of yet higher-quality LGBT healthcare (Callahan et al., 2016).

Other recommendations to improve healthcare service delivery include establishing a medical home with sexual minorities (Fallin-Bennett et al., 2016).

Focus on System-Level Approaches

The recommendations articulated previously partly reflect the solutions and cutting-edge advances put forth over a decade ago by the Gay & Lesbian Medical Association (GLMA, 2006) through their *Guidelines for Care of Lesbian, Gay, Bisexual, and Transgender Patients*. Important standards advanced by GLMA (2006) included: the importance of creating a welcoming clinical environment (e.g., posting a rainbow flag or pink triangle, having magazines, posters of diverse same-sex couples, brochures); ensuring that the intake forms utilized have appropriate/inclusive questions (e.g., partner option); recommending culturally sensitive patient-provider discussions (e.g., make no assumptions of heterosexuality, ask for clarification, admit inexperience); emphasizing the importance of confidentiality (e.g., written confidentiality statement); highlighting the vital need for providers to use appropriate language (i.e., the term used by the patient); and ensuring attention to issues of staff sensitivity (e.g., hire openly lesbian, gay, bisexual, and/or transgender staff). Their comprehensive approach extended to physical plant changes, such as universal gender-inclusive restrooms

(GLMA, 2006). This begins to suggest one dimension of the essential system-level changes that need to occur (Blosnich, Hanmer, et al., 2016). This is consistent with the call for health to be addressed in all policies, including those policies determining physical environments (IOM, 2012).

McNair and Hegarty (2010) also produced evidence-based clinical guidelines for primary care clinicians working with the LGB population, following standards for developing guidelines. McNair and Hegarty (2010) extracted from a review of documents on the primary care of LGB patients consensus guidelines on how to create inclusive settings for service delivery, standards for how to engage in appropriate clinician-patient communication, and standards for how to document the sexual orientation of patients. Collectively, the efforts of several organizations and researchers (e.g., Ard & Makadon, 2012; GLMA, 2006; Makadon et al., 2008; McNair & Hegarty, 2010) have contributed to major advances that are also beginning to have impacts on the larger system level.

In order to transform the entire system of healthcare service delivery, it is necessary but not sufficient to seek to educate primary care providers regarding guidelines and standards of care for sexual minorities (e.g., McNair & Hegarty, 2010). Such efforts must begin much earlier in the training of professionals.

For example, the education delivered to medical providers, starting with their undergraduate medical education, has been targeted as a factor operating, at least in part, in perpetuate health disparities for LGBT populations (Grubb, Hutcherson, Amiel, Bogart, & Laird, 2013). Data have shown that as little as five hours have been devoted to teaching LGBT-related content during the four-year premedical college education, while the quality of that education has been largely poorly rated. Meanwhile, other data have underscored that the majority of sexual minorities report discrimination during healthcare service delivery. Following from this recognition, there have been calls for infusing into undergraduate medical education sufficient LGBT-related curriculum content, including by the American Medical Association (AMA), IOM, and the Association of American Medical Colleges (AAMC; Grubb et al., 2013).

For example, toward a major system-level transformation, the AAMC launched a curriculum for the training of future physicians (Hollenbach et al., 2014). In doing so, according to Eckstrand and Sciolla (2014), the AAMC acknowledged and sought to rectify the historic medical education neglect of sexual minorities, healthcare service delivery disparities, and disproportionate harms that have been experienced by sexual minorities. The AAMC also sought to accelerate transformation using enhanced medical curricula and creation of positive and welcoming institutional climates, in order to improve healthcare service delivery to LGBT populations. A resultant curriculum for training future physicians covers topics such as the following: individual-level stigma experiences (self-stigma, disclosure); interpersonal-level stigma (abuse, rejection, discrimination); and structural stigma (societal conditions, cultural norms, state

policies, institutional policies). The framework taught in training future physicians views health disparities as stemming, in part, from broad societal stigmatization processes that effectively devalue sexual and gender minority identities.
The curriculum aspires to ensure the provision of high-quality, patient-
centered care to sexual minorities and seeks to inspire advocacy for the population (Eckstrand & Sciolla, 2014).

Also, individual colleges have taken up the challenge of training medical students for the task of delivering high-quality healthcare to sexual minorities by inau-
gurating medical education initiatives covering the care of LGBT populations
(Grubb et al., 2013). For example, the Columbia University College of Physicians
and Surgeons in New York City created and evaluated a new LGBT health curriculum. Key objectives included providing education on sexuality, gender, sexual orientation, gender identity, and sexual and gender expression; teaching appropriate
LGBT terminology; creating a safe and welcoming LGBT clinical environment,
using specific strategies; and engaging with clients in light of principles of cultural
humility. This curriculum focus reflects how, among the solutions to the health disparities impacting the LGBT populations in the United States, there are calls for
providers develop *cultural humility*—that is, a lifelong process of self-examination
for the personal biases and assumptions, with emphasis on providers engaging in a
self-critique and identifying the personal factors that may be playing a role in the
perpetuation of health disparities. Also, cultural humility includes respecting the
client as a source of expertise on their own life and capable of educating the provider. An evaluation of the curriculum using data with a small sample ($N = 29$)
matched for pre- versus post-test suggested a positive and significant impact on students' medical knowledge and attitudes with respect to LGBT populations (Grubb
et al., 2013). Yet, the small sample size underscores how these data are just
suggestive.

Seeking a much wider impact, the AAMC effectively provided in 2014, with
their new curriculum, a template for transformation across the training and
organizational systems for all healthcare professions—that is, nursing, dentistry,
physician assistants, psychology, social work—with a potential for wide system-
level change. Meanwhile, the AAMC intent is to not only implement but also
evaluate the curriculum and potential impact on institutional climate, with the
ultimate goal of improving outcomes for sexual minorities (Hollenbach
et al., 2014). Thus, there is hope for future institutional, organizational, and
system-level change.

Lack of an Evidence Base for Individual-, Provider-, and System-Level Interventions

Despite recent efforts to implement LGBT health curricular content,
published evaluations are rare, suggesting the lack of an evidence base

(Fallin-Bennett et al., 2016). This underscores the relevance of an essential and timely question posed by Butler et al. (2016), as follows: What is the evidence base with regard to "whether cultural competency interventions change the clinicians' behaviors (such as communication and clinical decision-making), the patient-provider relationship, and/or clinical systems to result in better outcomes for the patient" (p. 34)? There is a lack of an evidence base for the individual-, provider-, and system-level interventions implemented to date.

Further, unfortunately, research is lacking with regard to the long-term effects and patient health outcomes where cultural competence training was provided to those working in clinical settings with LGBT populations (Butler et al., 2016). Indeed, some studies have documented harm from provider training in cultural competence, revealing an increase in negative attitudes or stigma following exposure to the cultural competence training intervention. Research is compromised by the lack of consensus with regard to the definition of cultural competence when working with LGBT populations. Another challenge involves how the heterogeneity and diversity within the LGBT population are typically not acknowledged, and the intersectionality of the LGBT population with other populations (e.g., race/ethnicity) is not considered. Also, cultural competence for service delivery to transgender people has been sorely neglected in research. And, no studies to date actually "measured the effect" of cultural competence interventions on healthcare disparities (p. 47). Not surprisingly, the compelling conclusion to be drawn is that there is no evidence base regarding what constitutes culturally competent LGBT healthcare, while research evaluating the available interventions to reduce health disparities is even more rare (Butler et al., 2016).

As a sign of progress, there is a significant body of research that has sought to evaluate culturally competent approaches to delivering HIV prevention for MSM (Butler et al., 2016). However, this represents a "disparity within the disparity," as few studies have investigated culturally competent services for the other groups within the LGBT umbrella, including sexual minority women, sexual minority youth, transgender people, and MSM beyond a focus on HIV (p. 46). Yet, overall, there is a lack of an evidence base substantiating "what works."

System-Level Changes Require Policy Changes

Healthy People 2020 (USDHHS, 2010) recognized the key role of policies in order to impact system-level variables, whether the physical environment or the social environment, including cultural institutions as well as the overall healthcare delivery system. Given that laws and legislative policies may contribute to health disparities for marginalized and vulnerable populations, policy changes become a focus for change (Blosnich, Marsiglio, et al., 2016).

The policy implications of sexual orientation group disparities include the need for "greater allocation of resources by policymakers and funders and by society in general to understand and eliminate sexual orientation group disparities in abuse victimization," as just one example (Austin et al., 2008). Such policy actions are essential to make progress toward the goal of reducing the "psychological, physical, economic, and societal cost of child abuse" (p. 604). Sexual minorities have been found to have higher rates of histories of child and adolescent emotional, physical, and sexual abuse victimization, which place them at risk for revictimization later in life as well as engagement in risk behaviors such as alcohol/drug use, which are linked to serious health disparities (Austin et al., 2008).

Thus, policy changes are needed to improve the mental and physical health of LGBT populations, across the life span. Needed policy changes include a focus on state hate crime protection and employment discrimination protection (Blosnich, Marsiglio, et al., 2016). Consider how findings from a national sample of transgender veterans found a link between sociopolitical indicators of LGBT climate and medical outcomes. Those living in states with nondiscrimination in employment evidenced decreased odds of mood disorders and self-directed violence (Blosnich, Marsiglio, et al., 2016). Also, recall estimates from a meta-analysis that uncovered how up to 80 percent of sexual orientation minorities had experienced some form of harassment across their life span, while such stressful experiences have been linked to health disparities (Lick et al., 2013).

The 2015 Supreme Court decision that made same-sex marriage a right nationwide represents progress in system-level change in the United States, yet much more societal progress is needed. There is a vital need to overturn discriminatory policies, given empirical evidence that institutionalized forms of discrimination may serve as a risk factor for health disparities (Hatzenbuehler, McLaughlin, Keyes, & Hasin, 2010). System-level changes that are essential to improving health outcomes for LGBT populations must by necessity include wide-ranging changes in policy that impact sexual minorities across the life span.

CONCLUSION

This chapter covered the limitations and weaknesses as well as the advances and evolution in health disparities research for LGBT populations in the United States. The topics covered in this chapter spanned the following: (1) a review of weaknesses and advances in health disparities research for LGBT populations, including those dominant frameworks utilized to propel evolution in research and (2) strategies and recommendations for moving toward solutions and cutting-edge advances to improve healthcare service delivery to LGBT populations, including a focus on innovative curriculum and cultural competence training for providers, as well as other individual-level, provider-level, and system-level approaches, in order to reduce and eliminate health disparities.

What has emerged from this chapter is that LGBT populations' health disparities have been neglected in research (IOM, 2011). As a result, the field of sexual orientation health disparities research is largely still in its infancy (Cochran & Mays, 2016, p. e4). Without sufficient evolution and maturation in the field of sexual minority health disparities research, clinical practice has not been able to advance toward the desired standard where healthcare providers' practice with LGBT populations is evidence based (Makadon et al., 2008). To rectify this situation, compelling frameworks for advancing health disparities research have been proposed by researchers—for example, the framework of Stall et al. (2016). Pioneering research is emerging (e.g., Cochran et al., 2016).

Unfortunately, we must face the reality of the fundamental lack of an evidence base regarding "what works" with regard to designing cultural competency training; educating diverse healthcare providers during their professional training; improving healthcare service delivery systems; and, therefore, actually reducing and eliminating health disparities. If we value the goal of clinical practice truly being evidence based, then our society must make a substantial investment in research on LGBT populations' health disparities. This must include a focus on specific sexual minority populations, including, for example, transgender, adolescent, and older sexual minorities as well as those presenting the unique challenges of intersectionality as racial/ethnic sexual minorities.

REFERENCES

Ard, K. L., & Makadon, H. J. (2012). *Improving the health care of lesbian, gay, bisexual and transgender (LGBT) people: Understanding and eliminating health disparities.* Boston, MA: The Fenway Institute.

Austin, S. B., Jun, H. J., Jackson, B., Spiegelman, D., Rich-Edwards, J., Corliss, H. L., & Wright, R. J. (2008). Disparities in child abuse victimization in lesbian, bisexual, and heterosexual women in the Nurses' Health Study II. *Journal of Women's Health, 17*(4), 597–606.

Blosnich, J. R., Hanmer, J., Yu, L., Matthews, D. D., & Kavalieratos, D. (2016). Health care use, health behaviors, and medical conditions among individuals in same-sex and opposite-sex partnerships: A cross-sectional observational analysis of the Medical Expenditures Panel Survey (MEPS), 2003–2011. *Medical Care, 54*(6), 547–554.

Blosnich, J. R., Marsiglio, M. C., Gao, S., Gordon, A. J., Shipherd, J. C., Kauth, M., ... Fine, M. J. (2016). Mental health of transgender veterans in US states with and without discrimination and hate crime legal protection. *American Journal of Public Health, 106*(3), 534–540.

Bostwick, W. B., Boyd, C. J., Hughes, T. L., West, B. T., & McCabe, S. E. (2014). Discrimination and mental health among lesbian, gay and bisexual adults in the United States. *American Journal of Orthopsychiatry, 84*(1), 35–45.

Bränström, R., Hatzenbuehler, M. L., Pachankis, J. E., & Link, B. G. (2016). Sexual orientation disparities in preventable disease: A fundamental cause perspective. *American Journal of Public Health, 106*(6), 1109–1115.

Butler, M., McCreedy, E., Schwer, N., Burgess, D., Call, K., Przedworski, J., . . . Kane, R. L. (2016). *Improving cultural competence to reduce health disparities*. Rockville, MD: Agency for Healthcare Research and Quality.

Callahan, E. J., Henderson, C. A., Ton, H., & MacDonald, S. (2016). Utilizing the electronic health record as a tool for reducing LGBT health disparities: An institutional approach. In K. Eckstrand & J. M. Ehrenfeld (Eds.), *Lesbian, gay, bisexual, and transgender healthcare: A clinical guide to preventive, primary, and specialist care* (pp. 81–91). Switzerland: Springer International Publishing.

Cochran, S. D., Björkenstam, C., & Mays, V. M. (2016). Sexual orientation and all-cause mortality among US adults aged 18 to 59 years, 2001–2011. *American Journal of Public Health, 106*(5), 918–920.

Cochran, S. D., & Mays, V. M. (2016). A strategic approach to eliminating sexual orientation-related health disparities. *American Journal of Public Health, 106*(9), e4.

Eckstrand, K. L., & Sciolla, A. F. (2014). History of health disparities among individuals who are or maybe LGBT, gender nonconforming, and/or born with DSD. In A. D. Hollenbach, K. L. Eckstrand, & A. Dreger (Eds.), *Implementing curriculum and institutional climate changes to improve health care for individuals who are LGBT, gender nonconforming, or born with DSD: A resource for medical educators* (pp. 10–21). Washington, DC: Association of American Medical Colleges. Retrieved from https://members.aamc.org/eweb/upload/Executive%20LGBT%20FINAL.pdf

Fallin-Bennett, K., Henderson, S. L., Nguyen, G. T., & Hyderi, A. (2016). Primary care, prevention, and coordination of care. In K. L. Eckstrand & J. M. Ehrenfeld (Eds.). *Lesbian, gay, bisexual, and transgender healthcare: A clinical guide to preventive, primary, and specialist care* (pp. 95–114). Switzerland: Springer International Publishing.

Gamson, J., & Moon, D. (2004). The sociology of sexualities: Queer and beyond. *Annual Review of Sociology, 30*, 47–64.

Gay and Lesbian Medical Association (GLMA). (2006). *Guidelines for care of lesbian, gay, bisexual, and transgender patients*. San Francisco, CA: Gay and Lesbian Medical Association.

Grubb, H., Hutcherson, H., Amiel, J., Bogart, J., & Laird, J. (2013). Cultural humility with lesbian, gay, bisexual, and transgender populations: A novel curriculum in LGBT health for clinical medical students. *MedEdPORTAL Publications, 9*. Retrieved from http://doi.org/10.15766/mep_2374-8265.9542

Hatzenbuehler, M. L., McLaughlin, K. A., Keyes, K. M., & Hasin, D. S. (2010). The impact of institutional discrimination on psychiatric disorders in lesbian, gay, and bisexual populations: A prospective study. *American Journal of Public Health, 100* (3), 452–459.

Hatzenbuehler, M. L., Phelan, J. C., & Link, B. G. (2013). Stigma as a fundamental cause of population health inequalities. *American Journal of Public Health, 103*(5), 813–821.

Hollenbach, A. D., Eckstrand, K. L., & Dreger, A. (Eds.). (2014). *Implementing curricular and institutional climate changes to improve health care for individuals who are LGBT, gender nonconforming, or born with DSD: A resource for medical educators*. Washington, DC: Association of American Medical Colleges. Retrieved from https://members.aamc.org/eweb/upload/Executive%20LGBT%20FINAL.pdf

Institute of Medicine (IOM). (2011). *The health of lesbian, gay, bisexual, and transgender people: Building a foundation for better understanding*. Washington, DC: The National Academies Press.

Institute of Medicine (IOM). (2012). *How far have we come in reducing health disparities? Progress since 2000—Workshop summary*. Institute of Medicine of the National Academies. Washington, DC: The National Academies Press.

Kilbourne, A. M., Switzer, G., Hyman, K., Crowley-Matoka, M., & Fine, M. J. (2006). Advancing health disparities research within the health care system: A conceptual frame-work. *American Journal of Public Health, 96*(12), 2113–2121.

Lick, D. J., Durso, L. E., & Johnson, K. L. (2013). Minority stress and physical health among sexual Minorities. *Perspectives on Psychological Science, 8*(5), 521–548.

Makadon, H. J., Mayer, K., Potter, J., & Goldhammer, H. (2008). *The Fenway guide to lesbian, gay, bisexual, and transgender health*. Philadelphia, PA: ACP Press.

Marmot, M. (2005). Social determinants of health inequalities. *The Lancet, 365*(9464), 1099–1104.

Massetti, G. M., Ragan, K. R., Thomas, C. C., & Ryerson, A. B. (2016). Public health opportunities for promoting health equity in cancer prevention and control in LGBT populations. *LGBT Health, 3*(1), 11–14.

Max, W. B., Stark, B., Sung, H. Y., & Offen, N. (2016). Max et al. respond. *American Journal of Public Health, 106*(9), e4–e5.

McNair, R. P., & Hegarty, K. (2010). Guidelines for the primary care of lesbian, gay, and bisexual people: A systematic review. *Annals of Family Medicine, 8*(6), 533–541.

Meyer, I. H. (1995). Minority stress and mental health in gay men. *Journal of Health and Social Behavior, 36*(1), 38–56.

Meyer, I. H. (2003). Prejudice, social stress, and mental health in lesbian, gay, and bisexual populations: Conceptual issues and research evidence. *Psychological Bulletin, 129*(5), 674–607.

Schlittler, R. L., Grey, M. J., & Popanz, T. (2016). LGBT health and LGBT psychology: Emerging policy issues. In R. Ruth & E. Santacruz (Eds.), *LGBT mental health: Advances and emerging edges* (pp. 217–235). Santa Barbara, CA: Praeger Publishers.

Stall, R., Matthews, D. D., Friedman, M. R., Kinsky, S., Egan, J. E., Coulter, R. W., . . . Markovic, N. (2016). The continuing development of health disparities research on lesbian, gay, bisexual, and transgender individuals. *American Journal of Public Health, 106*(5), 787–789.

Thomas, S. B., Quinn, S. C., Butler, J., Fryer, C. S., & Garza, M. A. (2011). Toward a fourth generation of disparities research to achieve health equity. *Annual Review of Public Health, 32*, 399–416.

U.S. Department of Health and Human Services (USDHHS). (2010). *Healthy people 2020: Framework*. Washington, DC: U.S. Department of Health and Human Services, Office of Disease Prevention and Health Promotion. Retrieved from https://www.healthypeople.gov/sites/default/files/HP2020Framework.pdf

11

LGBT Health and LGBT Psychology: Emerging Policy Issues

Ronald L. Schlittler, Melissa J. Grey, and Timothy Popanz

Emerging directions in data gathering and research, and expansion of health-care access throughout much of the United States, have the potential to revolutionize how public policy affecting the health and mental health of lesbian, gay, bisexual, and transgender (LGBT) people is thought about, informed, and implemented. There is evidence that some policies intended to expand social equality for LGBT people and reduce stigma have the added benefit of improving mental health outcomes. Others that expressly aim to improve access to healthcare or to reduce harms are at the cutting edge of policy and practice.

As measurable progress is made, another policy front involves efforts to block or reduce the impact of policies favorably affecting LGBT legal status and health and mental health. This chapter attempts to survey this policy landscape that is the purview of elected bodies, government agencies, and the courts while also noting the historic role that LGBT people have played and continue to play in advocating on behalf of their healthcare needs. It concludes by considering what this potential new knowledge and expanded access to healthcare may imply for institutions and professions responsible for training providers and delivery of health and mental health services.

LGBT MENTAL HEALTH RESEARCH AND STATE-LEVEL EQUALITY POLICY

The cornerstone of a contemporary understanding of LGBT mental health is the minority stress model (Meyer, 1995), which describes how stigma operates at levels of self-stigma (e.g., internalized homophobia), interpersonal (i.e. discriminatory behavior and hate crimes), and structural levels (societal norms and policies). The model shows that, because of stigma, prejudice, and discrimination, sexual and gender minorities experience unique stressors that heterosexual and cisgender people do not, and this additional stress can lead to poorer physical and mental health outcomes. Minority stress comes from multiple social levels, including institutional and interpersonal heterosexism and homophobia (Herek, Gills, & Cogan, 2009). Research shows how cultural-level experiences "get under the skin" (Hatzenbuehler, 2009), resulting in stress and also resilience development during all stages of the LGBT life course (Rosenberg, 2000).

The minority stress model additionally suggests opportunities to inform interventions and resiliency enhancement strategies, including changes in public policy (Lick, Durso, & Johnson, 2013; Meyer, 2003; Meyer & Frost, 2013). Research has revealed an association between policy and health: LGB people living in states and cities with nondiscrimination policies inclusive of sexual orientation perceive a more positive environment and experience less minority stress (Riggle, Rostosky, & Horne, 2010), and, in states with same-sex marriage policies, there was a reduction in the proportion of high school students reporting suicide attempts (Raifman, Moscoe, Austin, & McConnell, 2017). Public policy that addresses discrimination against or equalizes basic civil rights for LGBT people *is*, therefore, also health policy.

Policy designed to achieve equal protection and equal rights under the law, when enacted, also has the effect of reducing minority stress, thereby resulting in more favorable health outcomes for people affected by it. One study by Hatzenbuehler and colleagues assessed the modifying effect of state-level policies related to protections against hate crimes and employment discrimination based on sexual orientation in states where they exist and states where they do not and the corresponding prevalence of psychiatric disorders. They found that "compared with living in states with policies extending protections, living in states without them predicted a significantly stronger association between lesbian, gay, and bisexual status and psychiatric disorders over a 12-month period, including generalized anxiety disorder, posttraumatic stress disorder, and dysthymia" (Hatzenbuehler, Keyes, & Hasin, 2009). In a second study, the authors "sought to determine whether healthcare use and expenditures among gay and bisexual men were reduced following the enactment of same-sex marriage laws in Massachusetts in 2003" (Hatzenbuehler et al., 2012, p. 285). They found that, over the year after the legalization of same-sex marriage, sexual minority men had a statistically significant decrease in medical and mental healthcare visits, and mental healthcare costs, compared with the year before the law change. The health effects of same-sex marriage laws were similar for partnered and nonpartnered men. A study by Raifman and colleagues found a seven percent relative reduction in the proportion of high school students attempting suicide owing to same-sex marriage implementation (Raifman et al., 2017). These findings demonstrate that policy addressing stigma and discrimination also serves as a form of LGBT health and mental health enhancement policy.

NEW DIRECTIONS FOR FEDERALLY FUNDED RESEARCH

Until 2011, the National Institutes of Health (NIH) had not considered including demographic questions about sexual orientation and gender identity in federally funded research. In the absence of such data, LGBT people are rendered invisible for a host of policy and funding considerations and any research that relies on the data gathered by NIH-funded research. The cornerstone of the future for understanding LGBT health broadly in ways not before possible are the recommendations in the 2011 report by the Institute of Medicine (IOM), *The Health of Lesbian, Gay, Bisexual, and Transgender People: Building a Foundation for Better Understanding*. NIH, an agency of the U.S. Department of Health and Human Services (HHS), commissioned the report in 2009 "to assess the state of knowledge about the health of LGBT [people], to identify research gaps and formulate a research agenda that could guide NIH in enhancing and focusing its research in this area" (IOM, 2011, p. ix). The IOM report concluded that "far too little is known about LGBT people in the United States." It provided seven recommendations for the implementation of a research agenda centered around five themes: (1) development and implementation of a research agenda to advance knowledge and understanding of LGBT health as well as research gaps and opportunities; (2) collection of data on sexual orientation and gender identity in federally funded surveys and in electronic health records; (3) development and standardization of sexual orientation and gender identity measures and methodological research that relates to LGBT health; (4) creation and implementation of a comprehensive research training approach to strengthen LGBT health research at NIH; and (5) policy on research participation that encourages grant applicants to explicitly address the inclusion or exclusion of sexual orientation and gender minorities in their samples.

The first recommendation about development of a research agenda was elaborated by highlighting the differences among LGBT populations and subpopulations. It recommended incorporating four conceptual perspectives as a research framework. They include (1) a minority stress perspective, (2) a life course perspective, (3) an intersectionality of dimensions of identity perspective, and (4) a social ecology perspective. Also noted are research areas for which this multiperspective approach is essential for building a solid evidence base for LGBT health, including demographic research and research on social influences on the lives of LGBT people, inequalities in healthcare, intervention research, and transgender-specific health needs.

In October, 2015, NIH issued a call for input from researchers in academia and industry, healthcare professionals, patient advocates and health advocacy organizations, scientific and professional organizations, public agencies, and the public about proposed goals and objectives for advancing research and other research-related activities with sexual and gender minority (SGM)[1] populations. These stakeholders were invited to offer comments on the *NIH FY 2016–2020, Strategic Plan to Advance Research on the Health and Well-Being of Sexual and Gender Minorities* (NIH, 2015). This plan essentially operationalizes implementation of the IOM report recommendations. It is the primary policy guidance document for federally funded research through 2020 and seeks to promote and support the advancement of basic, clinical, and behavioral and social sciences research to improve the health of SGM people.

Taking together the growing awareness of how minority stress affects mental health, how the presence of policy that fosters equality appears to reduce minority stress and to lead to improved mental health, and the frontiers opening up for far-reaching federally funded research into SGM health, the field of LGBT mental health appears to be entering a period of maturity not before possible to inform future research, health policy, the education and training of medical and mental healthcare providers, and practice. The first results of the new focus on SGM people by NIH are reflected in the 2013 National Health Interview Survey (NHIS), which "for the first time in its 57-year history, included a measure of sexual orientation." Findings will enable "researchers and data users to examine how the prevalence of a wide variety of health-related behaviors, health status indicators, and measures of healthcare service utilization and access vary across categories of sexual orientation in a representative sample of the civilian non-institutionalized U.S. adult population." The 2013 NHIS concluded that its "sexual orientation data can be used to track progress toward meeting the Healthy People 2020[2] goals and objectives related to the health of lesbian, gay, and bisexual persons, and to examine a wide range of health disparities among adults identifying as straight, gay or lesbian, or bisexual" (HHS, 2015). However, nearly two months into the Donald Trump presidential administration, HHS removed questions about sexual orientation and gender identity from surveys of older Americans and people with disabilities. By removing these questions from the National Survey of Older Americans Act Participants and the Annual Program Performance Reports for Centers for Independent Living, the government made a policy decision to ignore whether

---

[1]The NIH strategic plan explains use of the language "sexual and gender minority" as an umbrella uniform term to encompass lesbian, gay, bisexual, and transgender people as well as people who do not identify with those specific terms, yet who refer to themselves with often changing or evolving terminology, such as queer or gender variant, as well as those with specific medical conditions resulting in differences or disorders of sex development, sometimes called intersex people.
[2]Healthy People, an initiative of HHS, provides science-based, 10-year national objectives for improving the health of all Americans (http://www.healthypeople.gov/2020/About-Healthy-People).

key programs for seniors and people with disabilities are effectively serving LGBT Americans (Center for American Progress, 2017).

FEDERAL EQUALITY POLICY: PAST AND FORESEEABLE FUTURE

There has been a decades-long history of struggles in the U.S. Congress on a wide range of policy affecting LGBT people, which will likely continue into the foreseeable future. Three policies are noted here with attention to what broad health effects can, and likely cannot, be measured. The three policies are (1) the Matthew Shepard and James Byrd, Jr. Hate Crimes Prevention Act, enacted in 2009; (2) the Defense of Marriage Act (DOMA), enacted in 1994, and then overturned in two decisions by the U.S. Supreme Court in 2014 and 2015; and (3) the Employment Non-Discrimination Act (ENDA), first introduced in 1994.

After a contentious history outside of the LGBT community and within, the variously named federal hate crimes bill, initially introduced in 1992, was signed into law by President Barack Obama as the Matthew Shepard and James Byrd, Jr. Hate Crimes Prevention Act on October 28, 2009. The source of contention within the LGBT community was whether gender identity should be included as a protected category along with sexual orientation. It was not until 2007 that gender identity was added over objections that it would make the bill much harder, if not impossible, to pass. Later the same year, these concerns were tempered when it became the first piece of gender identity inclusive legislation to pass in both the House and the Senate, though it was later removed as an amendment to a defense reauthorization bill under threat of veto by President George W. Bush. Also, some within the LGBT community argued that hate crimes laws, like other criminal punishment legislation, are used unequally and improperly against communities that are already marginalized in our society (Sylvia Rivera Law Project, 2009).

Hate crimes are a very tangible and violent expression of discrimination. While often directed at individuals, they are widely regarded as "message" crimes. That is, they send a message to all other members of the victim's community that they also are not safe (Herek & Berrill, 1991). As noted previously, Hatzenbuehler's research, conducted before the federal hate crimes law was enacted, indicated that the presence of hate crimes laws at the state level appeared to contribute to a reduction in minority stress and improvements in health. Due to the absence of sexual orientation and gender identity data collection in federally funded population-based surveys in the years before and after adoption of the hate crimes law, it is unlikely that researchers can assess if there were any broad health improvements for LGBT people overall following its passage.

The second federal public policy issue considered here is DOMA and its eventual overturning by the Supreme Court of the United States (SCOTUS) through two rulings. The rulings underscore that the judicial system can also have a significant impact on policy linked with LGBT health. DOMA was signed into law by President Bill Clinton on September 21, 1996. The organization Freedom to Marry characterized the law as mandating "unequal treatment of legally married same-sex couples and selectively depriving them of the 1,138 protections and responsibilities that marriage triggers at the federal level" (Freedom to Marry, n.d.). In June, 2013, in *U.S. v. Windsor*, SCOTUS struck down parts of DOMA, finding that its purpose and effect were "to impose a disadvantage, a separate status, and so a stigma upon all who enter into same-sex marriages" in violation of the Fifth Amendment's guarantee of equal protection (*U.S. v. Windsor*, 2013, p. 21). In June, 2015, in *Obergefell v. Hodges*, the court settled the questions of marriage equality for same-sex couples and recognition of out-of-state marriages. In an example of the influence that professional associations can have in bringing a research-based perspective to bear on public policy matters, the court in *Obergefell* cited the amicus brief on which the American Psychological Association (APA) took the lead for a broad coalition of state and national health and mental health organizations (APA, 2015). Justice Kennedy's majority opinion cited 10 pages of APA's amicus brief (*Obergefell v. Hodges*, 2015, pp. 7–17) in discussing the evolution of the institution of marriage and the rights of gays and lesbians over time. With marriage equality for same-sex couples now law, it raises a question suggested by the work noted earlier by Hatzenbuehler and Raifman and their colleagues: if the SGM research initiatives at NIH made possible during the Obama administration had been in effect before the Supreme Court decisions, and were to continue, might it be possible for researchers to use such data to measure the effects of DOMA on SGM health nationally? Looking ahead, the data that may be gathered through the NIH capacities would be useful in assessing the health effects on SGM people who are married, and that of their families, as is done presently with heterosexual people and for informing policy.

There is pushback against the Supreme Court rulings, an effort to limit the scope of these decisions. Framed as an issue of religious rights, this was the intent of HR 2820, the First Amendment Defense Act (FADA), introduced in June, 2015, in the U.S. House of Representatives. FADA "prohibits the federal government from taking discriminatory action against a person on the basis that such person believes or acts in accordance with religious belief or moral conviction that: (1) marriage is or should be recognized as the union of one man and one woman, or (2) sexual relations are properly reserved to such a marriage" (FADA, Summary, 2015, p. 1). This effort is part of a wider effort to claim religious exemption from laws concerning sex, reproduction, and marriage on the grounds that such laws make the objector complicit in the presumed sinful conduct of others (NeJaime & Siegel, 2015). Arguably, such laws would contribute to stigmatization of SGM people and associated health disparities.

The third public policy issue considered here is ENDA. Versions of ENDA have been introduced into every Congress since 1994. Amid controversy among advocates for the bill, gender identity protections were added in 2007, removed, and then added again in 2009. Subsequent versions have retained gender identity provisions. The 2007 version of ENDA without gender identity protections passed in the Democratic-controlled House but died in the Senate. The 2013 gender identity–inclusive version passed in the Senate; President Obama was ready to sign it, but the Republican-controlled House did not take it up.

In 2015, ENDA's proponents undertook a new strategy. ENDA was rolled into a comprehensive bill to ban discrimination on the basis of sex, gender identity, and sexual orientation by amending Title II of the Civil Rights Act of 1964. The new bill, called the Equality Act (2015), would extend protections under federal civil rights law to credit, education, employment, federal funding, housing, jury service, and public services and spaces. There are no expectations that this approach has any better chance of becoming law than the stand-alone ENDA without a more favorable political climate (Eilperin, 2015), but a *The New York Times* editorial stated, "It is nonetheless a worthy piece of legislation that establishes what more is needed to ensure full equal rights" (Editorial Board, *New York Yimes*, 2015). Given that the Equality Act is not law, this may be an instance where data gathered under the NIH 2015–2020 strategy, if pursued, may in time be useful to researchers in determining if eventual passage of the law has measurable health effects for LGBT people. The long history of ENDA failing to become law nationally has not been without important impact. As a message bill leveraged by advocates to further a national discussion and raise awareness about discrimination faced by LGBT people in the workplace, ENDA arguably has a significant legacy at state and local levels and in the private sector, where employment nondiscrimination policies are fairly common.[3]

DIRECTIONS FOR FEDERAL AND STATE LGBT MENTAL HEALTH POLICY

There are and will likely continue to be emerging federal policy directions specific to addressing mental health care disparities that will affect all Americans. These are reflected in bills such as the 21st Century Cures Act, passed in

---

[3]Nineteen states and the District of Columbia have employment nondiscrimination laws inclusive of sexual orientation and gender identity, which means that 40 percent of the country's LGBT people are covered. Another three states have nondiscrimination laws covering sexual orientation only, meaning that 48 percent of the country's LGB people are covered. This still means more than 50 percent of LGBT people are not covered (Movement Advancement Project, n.d.). Also, there have been significant strides in the private sector and in organized labor. In its 2016 Corporate Equality Index, the Human Rights Campaign reported that two-thirds of the Fortune 500 and 89 percent of all businesses surveyed offered explicit sexual orientation and gender identity nondiscrimination protections (Human Rights Campaign, 2016). They report that, in 2002, 61 percent of Fortune 500 companies provided protection based on sexual orientation, with only 3 percent offering protections based on gender identity at that time. In 2015, 89 percent provided protections based on sexual orientation.

December, 2016. Then APA president, Dr. Susan H. McDaniel, said, "It will increase access to effective, evidence-based care, particularly for those with serious mental illness" (APA, 2016). In these and other mental healthcare initiatives, consumers and advocates will have to remain vigilant to ensure that, disparities unique to SGM people are not overlooked or swept aside.

Also significant are a wide range of legislative proposals generated at the state level that can have national ramifications. Equality California, for example, reported in 2015 that of the eight "pro-equality priority bills" sponsored, all were adopted by the state legislature and headed to the governor's desk (Equality California, e-mail communication from executive director, Rick Zbur, September 25, 2015). Bills included those directly related to reducing health disparities through collection of SGM demographic information, helping teachers combat bullying, and ensuring students receive accurate, comprehensive, age-appropriate, and SGM-inclusive sexual health education. Equality California reported that as of 2015, the organization successfully sponsored 110 pieces of pro-LGBT legislation, including one in 2012 banning sexual orientation change efforts with minors by licensed mental health providers.

SEXUAL ORIENTATION AND GENDER IDENTITY OR EXPRESSION (SOGIE) CHANGE EFFORTS

The United States has a long history of mental health workers attempting to ostensibly treat, cure, convert, or repair marginalized sexual orientations (APA Task Force on Appropriate Therapeutic Responses to Sexual Orientation, 2009) and gender identities (Substance Abuse and Mental Health Services Administration [SAMHSA], 2015). Multiple leading health authorities have taken a more definitive turn toward affirming diversity in SGM identities as normal variations of human sexuality and gender and to discourage or ban mental health interventions that pathologize or claim to change SGM identities (SAMHSA, 2015; UNHRC, 2015). Evolving public policy is one social force addressing concerns about SOGIE change efforts.[4]

Those advocating for banning SOGIE change efforts locate "the problem" for persons with SOGIE-related distress not necessarily in SGM identities but more commonly in cultural bias as is highlighted by the #BornPerfect campaign led by the National Center for Lesbian Rights (NCLR, 2014). At the same time, many mental health professionals are encouraging affirmative therapeutic approaches to distress over same-sex attractions or gender nonconformity, which are not

---

[4]These practices have been referred to by many names, including "conversion therapy," "reparative therapy," and "sexual orientation change efforts (SOCE)." "SOGIE change efforts" is the term used here to capture the collection of efforts professionals use to try to change an individual's sexual orientation, their gender identity, and/or their gender expression to be consistent with majority groups: heterosexual, cisgender, and gender conforming.

based on an expectation of SOGIE change to heterosexuality or achieving congruence of gender identity to sex assigned at birth (APA Task Force on Appropriate Therapeutic Responses to Sexual Orientation, 2009; Reconciliation and
Growth Project, n.d.). Professional health and mental health associations cau-
tion providers about the potential harms of and weak claims of evidence for
effectiveness of such practices (e.g., American Academy of Child and Adolescent Psychiatry, 2012; American Psychiatric Association, 2000; Anton, 2010;
Whitman, Glosoff, Kocet, & Tarvydas, 2013). As of 2016, five states and the
District of Columbia have translated these cautions into statutory restrictions
on licensed mental health providers' use of SOGIE change efforts, primarily with
minors.

Legislation to ban SOGIE change efforts has advanced in scope with each
iteration and demonstrates an interplay between judicial decisions and developments at the state and federal policy levels. California's Senate Bill 1172 (Sexual
Orientation Change Efforts, S.1172, CA Legislature, 2012) was the first to ban
mental health providers from use of sexual orientation change efforts with
minors and to withstand constitutionality challenges (*Pickup v. Brown*, 2015;
Welch v. Brown, 2013). In a challenge to a similar law in New Jersey, the court
ruled the law "restricts neither speech nor religious expression" (*King v. Christie*,
2013) and let it stand. The 2015 ban in Illinois expanded further, allowing survivors to cite consumer fraud protections.

The consumer fraud protections provisions in the Illinois legislation followed
an unprecedented lawsuit, *Michael Ferguson, et al., v. JONAH, et al.* (2015). A
jury found in favor of the plaintiffs, former clients of Jews Offering New Alternatives to Healing (JONAH), who argued that JONAH had violated New Jersey's
Consumer Fraud Act. At best there was no evidence that JONAH's remunerated
practices could produce the outcomes promised; at worst they were harming
their clients. A law introduced in the 114th Congress took the broadest
approach, with the Therapeutic Fraud Prevention Act (2015), which classifies
all so-called conversion therapy as fraudulent, making it illegal to advertise as
effective, offer, or conduct such practices under the Federal Trade Commission
Act for anyone of any age and regardless of licensure status of the provider.

At least 22 states introduced SOGIE change efforts bans in 2015 (Movement
Advancement Project, n.d.), and several jurisdictions have since introduced
legislative bans (e.g., Prevention of Emotional Neglect and Childhood Endan-
germent in Erie County, New York [Marans, 2016]). Although most of the bills
did not pass, they focused attention of the public and healthcare professionals
to the inappropriateness and potential harms of such change efforts. This type
of regulation initially raised concern among health professionals wary of legislators asserting a legal boundary between appropriate and inappropriate practice.
On the other hand, advocates highlight the needs for patient protection
(Southern Poverty Law Center, 2012) and to send the message that freedom

from scientifically unsupported and abusive practices like SOGIE change efforts is a protected right (UNHRC, 2015).

Despite developments in codifying the prohibition of SOGIE change efforts with minors, opponents frame the bans as individual rights violations. Similar to the approach used with the FADA (2015) noted earlier, Oklahoma proposed the first bill to restrict state intervention into health providers' behaviors for the purposes of SOGIE change practices. The Parental and Family Rights in Counseling Protection Act (2015) died without a vote in the Senate. Even as courts have dismissed claims that professionals' and parents' rights override professional standards and the public's rights, such judicial and legislative attempts highlight the ongoing conflict among various interests and social currents.

A POLICY AND PRACTICE FRONTIER: COMPREHENSIVE CARE FOR TRANSGENDER AND GENDER-NONCONFORMING PEOPLE

Transgender and gender-nonconforming (TGNC)[5] people in the United States experience patchy access to healthcare, disproportionately experience hostility from providers, and experience barriers to gender-affirming health interventions, including routine healthcare (Grant et al., 2011; Rachlin, Green, & Lombardi, 2008; Shires & Jaffee, 2015). In the largest survey of TGNC peoples' health and healthcare experiences in the United States, approximately 20 percent reported being refused healthcare services, half reported healthcare providers who did not understand TGNC people's needs, and 28 percent reported delaying medical care when sick or injured because of discrimination (Grant et al., 2011). This suggests an area where policy that impacts education and training warrants attention. Also, in a stark example of how intersecting minority identities can compound health disparities, TGNC people of color experience even higher rates of discrimination and exclusion in healthcare, including lower rates of health insurance coverage and increased rates of discrimination (e.g., healthcare providers refuse to touch their patient) and other forms of unfair or poor quality care (Lambda Legal, 2010). Moreover, many TGNC people, particularly TGNC people of color, who also face employment and educational discrimination, miss opportunities for healthcare coverage because of poverty and unemployment (Grant et al., 2011).

Access to comprehensive healthcare for TGNC people could markedly improve TGNC people's physical and mental health and quality of life. TGNC people who received gender-affirming healthcare services experienced better mental health, including lower rates of suicidal behavior, and utilized fewer

---

[5]Note that TGNC is an attempt to include all people whose gender identities and expressions are marginalized in mainstream U.S. culture and can include people who identify as transgender, transsexual, gender nonconforming, two-spirited, nonbinary, genderqueer, agender, and gender fluid.

medical services than those who had not received gender-affirming interventions (DeCuypere et al., 2006; Murad et al., 2010). Even though public discourse does not consistently reflect it (McHugh, 2014), scholarly reviews of decades of research have led every major health professional association to support access to gender-affirming health interventions (American Medical Association, 2008; American Psychiatric Association, 2012; Anton, 2009; Coleman et al., 2012). Mounting evidence also indicates that including gender-affirming services in healthcare coverage is affordable or even cost neutral (Baker & Cray, 2013; Department of Insurance, State of California, 2012; Herman & Cooper, 2013), in part because it reduces healthcare costs for those receiving it over time.

The Patient Protection and Affordable Care Act of 2010 (ACA), a significant health policy initiative, included several strategies to improve healthcare and healthcare access for most Americans. With prohibitions against preexisting conditions exclusions, transgender people and people with gender dysphoria could no longer be excluded from coverage because of these "preexisting conditions." Multiple marginalized social groups, including low-income, racially and ethnic minorities, as well as SGM people, were expected to benefit from expanded coverage, and there are some indications of improved healthcare coverage (Quealy & Sanger-Katz, 2014) as well as continued racial and income-based healthcare and access disparities (Alliance for a Just Society, 2015). Section 1557 of the ACA attempted to protect patients from access- and benefits-related discrimination, including discrimination on the basis of race, color, national origin, sex, age, and disability, and the rule's use of the sex category includes sex-stereotyped behavior, gender identity, and sexual orientation (HHS, 2016).

In 2015, the nondiscrimination rule provided guidance for the first time (Cornachione, Musumeci, & Artiga, 2015). Modifications to the initial rule in Section 1557 further clarified TGNC people's rights to healthcare coverage. Gender discrimination was prohibited in healthcare and coverage, and insurers could no longer require interventions be sex-specific, so that TGNC people with one gender marker should not be denied sex-specific interventions designated for another gender marker (e.g., prostate exams for transwomen; Gillespie, 2015; Office for Civil Rights [OCR], n.d.). However, in December, 2016, the U.S. Court for the Northern District of Texas issued an opinion enjoining Section 1557 prohibitions of discrimination on the basis of gender identity and termination of pregnancy. The HHS OCR may not enforce the provisions while the injunction remains in place (HHS, 2017).

Although the ACA appears to have effected some tenuous progress for TGNC people, denial of access to care has continued in a key way. Gender transition care (e.g., hormone therapies, hysterectomies) are not required components of coverage, even when they are covered for other medical reasons for cisgender people. Moreover, many states have adopted benchmark policies—the minimum standard or model for providers in the state—that include blanket exclusions on transition-related care or gender-affirming medical interventions, creating a standard of care refusal. These practices are becoming recognized as forms of discrimination (American Psychiatric Association, 2012; Anton, 2009). As of 2016, in 13 states and the District of Columbia, TGNC people are protected from discrimination in healthcare coverage by state law, and 18 states and the District of Columbia prohibit blanket exclusions (Movement Advancement Project, Healthcare Laws and Policies, n.d.). At the federal level, categorical exclusions for transition-related care were removed from the Federal Employee Health Benefits plans (FEHB) and Medicare. Healthcare advances achieved during the Obama administration will require vigilance as ACA regulations and their implementation policies provide opportunities for progress as well as efforts to return to a policy of exclusion.

COMMUNITY ACTION INFORMING POLICY

Although there is increasing awareness of LGBT health disparities and the need to address them, as is demonstrated with the NIH SGM initiatives, the LGBT community has been advocating to meet its own healthcare needs for decades. Born from contexts of health crisis—most notably HIV and AIDS disproportionately affecting gay and bisexual men and transgender women—LGBT communities have developed strategies and initiatives to meet basic healthcare needs, deliver services to specific populations, implement community-based prevention efforts, and demand that SGM identities and healthcare needs be recognized and addressed in policy. Significantly, these innovations have occurred in the context of the broader culture's stigmatization of SGM identities, a lack of knowledge and adequate training at all levels of service delivery to meet the needs of SGM people, and slow or inadequate policy responses from elected officials (IOM, 2011). This history of community-based interventions dramatically reached an apex during the AIDS crisis of the 1980–90s. Due to lack of government response and inadequate funding for basic needs, such as housing, in-home care services, and access to medicine and healthcare, LGBT community, particularly in urban areas, self-organized these services outside the traditional service delivery models. The effects were improved access to these basic services and improved health outcomes (HHS, 2010). A long-term legacy of this community-driven response is local healthcare systems today often recognizing that communities affected must have a voice in formulating solutions and recognizing that a "one-size-fits-all" healthcare delivery model is not effective. A key lesson from the AIDS crisis was that, for any healthcare system to effectively evolve and respond to emergent needs, it must engage the affected communities in the ongoing development of response system (HHS, 2010; IOM, 2011).

An example of a population where engagement to inform strategies and policies is critical is homeless LGBT youth. LGBT youth are overrepresented in homeless populations. In five studies of unaccompanied youth in midsize and large cities, between 20 and 40 percent of respondents identified as gay or lesbian (Ray, 2006), with homelessness commonly resulting from strained family relationships. LGBT homeless youth experience greater risk of violence, higher risk of sex-for-survival behavior, higher risk of substance abuse, and suicide (Ray, 2006). LGBT homeless youth, particularly transgender youth, often do not feel welcome or safe in traditional youth homeless facilities, and the admittance policies of these facilities, such as requiring prospective residents be clean and sober before placement or not allowing companion animals, may exacerbate continued homelessness. In November, 2015, Seattle was among several U.S. cities to declare homelessness a state of emergency (Beitsch, 2015). Just prior to the mayor's declaration, two staff and ten of the youths serving at the local organization, Peace for the Streets by Kids from the Streets (PSKS), went to City Hall to advocate for more resources for homeless youth, including an additional caseworker for a neighborhood particularly affected (PSKS, 2015b). They were back the next day when the mayor signed legislation for additional funding for services. Since it was founded in 1995, PSKS has operated from the belief that the youth themselves know their biggest needs in ending homelessness, and many of the agency's programs were created by PSKS participants, including the provision of case management, GED tutoring, paid internships, shelter, food, clothing, and basic survival supplies. PSKS staff report that engaging LGBT youth to educate service providers and develop and deliver services appropriate to their communities creates safer spaces where they can trust that their identities and orientations will be respected, and they are therefore more likely to utilize and benefit from those services (Popanz, 2015). PSKS interns who surveyed their peers in the SGM homeless community found that the majority had been diagnosed with mental health conditions and were struggling with drug and alcohol addictions and that utilizing their input to create safe, affirming spaces and services lowered the barriers to access.

CONCLUSION: NEW KNOWLEDGE, NEW ACCESS, AND NEW CHALLENGES

Inclusion of SGM populations and subpopulations in federally funded research can inform policy and practice in ways not previously possible or probably yet fully imagined. Informed by sophisticated research utilizing relatively limited data sources, there is already a strong foundation for understanding how a wide range of policies emanating from all levels and branches of government affect the health and mental health of SGM populations, but pushback is persistent. Other policy initiatives rely on well-established but newly accepted empirical understandings supportive of prohibitions on harmful treatment and of the value of healthcare for all. Expanding healthcare access could

soon more fully include many people with intersecting and historically marginalized identities, including those who are LGBT, with a particular attention to
the T. The tradition of LGBT communities organizing and advocating for action
to address urgent social and health disparities will continue to be an important
component of progress. An emerging area for attention is that of a rapidly aging
SGM population, which is expected to grow to over five million by 2030 (Choi
& Meyer, 2016). The health outcomes for this population are projected to have
unique and significant impacts on our healthcare delivery systems, which are unprepared to meet these needs and, importantly, will impact aging people themselves,
their families, and allies (HHS, 2015). This underscores the urgency for questions
on sexual orientation and gender identity to be returned to the previously noted
HHS survey to inform sound healthcare policy and training. Advocacy at all levels
provides constituent input as a source of important data to inform the development
of policies and their implementation. Engagement in such advocacy by individuals
could itself also be a key health-promotion strategy for advocates (Russell &
Richards, 2003) and communities.

This emerging context of new knowledge, new equality, new access, ongoing
pushback, and sustained advocacy suggests important challenges and directions
for the future of health and mental health training and delivery and the involvement of all stakeholders. Considerations include how to achieve the following:

- Local, state, and federal government bodies effectively including the perspectives of
  practitioners, advocates, and populations being served in the development and
  implementation of equality and other health policy.
- Professional associations (1) reviewing and improving curricular and other training
  standards and methods as well as mechanisms for best serving the social and healthcare needs of SGM people; (2) reviewing standards of ethical professional conduct
  to ensure alignment with increasing empirical understandings of SGM identity and
  care needs across the lifespan [or life-span, depending on publisher's style preference],
  and (3) offering training in evidence-based advocacy as part of health practice.
- Educational and training institutions developing, implementing, and regularly
  updating inclusive, comprehensive, and affirmative curricular standards related to
  SGM populations.
- Health and mental health professionals effectively translating and applying emerging knowledge to the health needs of SGM people.

The record of health and mental healthcare training and delivery that
adequately understands and addresses the needs and concerns of LGBT people
has historically proved hostile at worst and weak at best (Lambda Legal,
2010). With the new tools for how to officially recognize the existence and
diversity of LGBT people in federal research, and expanded healthcare access
for millions of Americans, LGBT health and mental healthcare have the
potential to enter a new era.

REFERENCES

Alliance for a Just Society. (2015). Breaking barriers: Improving health insurance enrollment and access to health care. Retrieved from http://allianceforajustsociety .org/wp-content/uploads/2015/04/BreakingBarriers_Natl_sm.pdf

American Academy of Child and Adolescent Psychiatry. (2012). Policy parameter on gay, lesbian, or bisexual sexual orientation, gender nonconformity, and gender discordance in children and adolescents. Retrieved June 27, 2017, from https://www .guideline.gov/summaries/summary/38417?#Section420

American Medical Association. (2008). Resolution 122. Removing financial barriers to care for transgender patients. Retrieved from http://www.tgender.net/taw/ ama_resolutions.pdf

American Psychiatric Association. (2000). Committee on Psychotherapy by Psychiatrists (COPP) position statement on therapies focused on attempts to change sexual orientation (reparative or conversion therapies). *American Journal of Psychiatry, 157,* 1719–1721.

American Psychiatric Association. (2012). Position statement on access to care for transgender and gender variant individuals. Retrieved from https://www.psychiatry .org/file%20library/about-apa/organization-documents-policies/policies/position-2012 -transgender-gender-variant-access-care.pdf

American Psychological Association. (2015). Guidelines for psychological practice with transgender and gender nonconforming people. Retrieved from http://www.apa.org/ practice/guidelines/transgender.pdf

American Psychological Association. (2016). APA applauds Senate passage of the mental health provisions in 21st Century Cures Act. Retrieved from http://www.apa.org/ news/press/releases/2016/12/cures-act.aspx

Anton, B. S. (2009). Proceedings of the American Psychological Association for the legislative year 2008: Minutes of the annual meeting of the Council of Representatives, February 22–24, 2008, Washington, DC, and August 13 and 17, 2008, Boston, MA, and minutes of the February, June, August, and December 2008 meetings of the Board of Directors. *American Psychologist, 64,* 372–453. doi:10.1037/a0015932

Anton, B. S. (2010). Proceedings of the American Psychological Association for the legislative year 2009: Minutes of the annual meeting of the Council of Representatives and minutes of the meetings of the Board of Directors. *American Psychologist, 65,* 385–475. doi:10.1037/a0019553

APA Task Force on Appropriate Therapeutic Responses to Sexual Orientation. (2009). *Report of the Task Force on Appropriate Therapeutic Responses to Sexual Orientation.* Washington, DC: American Psychological Association.

Baker, A. & Cray, A. (2013). *Why gender-identity nondiscrimination in insurance makes sense.* Center for American Progress. Retrieved from https://www.americanprogress. org/issues/lgbt/report/2013/05/02/62214/why-gender-identity-nondiscrimination-in-insurance-makes-sense/

Beitsch, R. (2015, November 11). Cities, states turn to emergency declarations to tackle homeless crisis. *Huffington Post.* Retrieved from http://www.huffingtonpost.com/ entry/state-of-emergency-homeless_564361dfe4b0603773472469

Choi, S. K. & Meyer, I. H. (2016). *LGBT aging: A review of research findings, needs, and policy implications.* Los Angeles, CA: The Williams Institute.

Coleman, E., Bockting, W., Botzer, M., Cohen-Kettenis, P., DeCuypere, G., Feldman, J., . . . Zucker, K. (2012). Standards of care for the health of transsexual, transgender, and gender nonconforming people, 7th version. *International Journal of Transgenderism*, *13*, 165–232. http:// dx.doi.org/10.1080/15532739.2011.700873

Cornachione, E., Musumeci, M., & Artiga, S. (2015, October 19). Summary of HHS's proposed rule on nondiscrimination in health programs and activities. The Henry J. Kaiser Family Foundation. Retrieved from http://kff.org/disparities-policy/issue-brief/summary-of-hhss-proposed-rule-on-nondiscrimination-in-health-programs-and-activities/

DeCuypere, G., Elaut, E., Heylens, G., Van Maele, G., Selvaggi, G., T'Sjoen, G., ... Monstrey, S. (2006). Long-term follow-up: psychosocial outcome of Belgian transsexuals after sex reassignment surgery. *Sexologies*, *15*, 126–133.

Department of Insurance, State of California. (2012). Economic impact assessment: Gender nondiscrimination in health insurance. Retrieved from http:// transgenderlawcenter.org/wp-content/uploads/2013/04/Economic-Impact-Assessment-Gender-Nondiscrimination-In-Health-Insurance.pdf

Editorial Board, *The New York Times*. (2015, July 29). The challenges that remain after marriage equality. *The New York Times*. Retrieved from http://www.nytimes.com/2015/07/29/opinion/the-challenges-that-remain-after-marriage-equality.html?_r=1

Eilperin, J. (2015, November 10). Obama supports altering Civil Rights Act to include LGBT discrimination. *The Washington Post*. Retrieved from https://www.washingtonpost.com/politics/obama-supports-altering-civil-rights-act-to-include-gender-discrimination/2015/11/10/3a05107e-87c8-11e5-9a07-453018f9a0ec_story.html

Equality Act, H.3185, 114th Cong. (2015). Retrieved from https://www.congress.gov/bill/114th-congress/house-bill/3185

First Amendment Defense Act (FADA), H.2802, 114th Cong. (2015). Retrieved from https://www.congress.gov/bill/114th-congress/house-bill/2802/text

First Amendment Defense Act (FADA), H.2802, Summary, 114th Cong. (2015). Retrieved from https://www.congress.gov/bill/114th-congress/house-bill/2802

Freedom to Marry. (n.d.). Frequently asked questions: What is DOMA? Retrieved from http://www.freedomtomarry.org/states/entry/c/doma

Gillespie, L. (2015, July 23). Transgender people still denied health services despite Affordable Care Act. *PBS Newshour: The Rundown*. Retrieved from http://www.pbs.org/newshour/rundown/transgender-people-still-denied-health-services-despite-affordable-care-act/

Grant, J. M., Mottet, L. A., Tanis, J., Harrison, J., Herman, J. L., & Keisling, M. (2011). *Injustice at every turn: A report of the National Transgender Discrimination Survey*. Washington, DC: National Center for Transgender Equality and National Gay and Lesbian Task Force.

Hatzenbuehler, M. L. (2009). How does sexual minority stigma "get under the skin"? A psychological mediation framework. *Psychological Bulletin*, *135*, 707–730.

Hatzenbuehler, M. L., Keyes, K. M., & Hasin, D. S. (2009). State-level policies and psychiatric morbidity in lesbian, gay, and bisexual populations. *American Journal of Public Health*, *99*, 2275–2281.

Hatzenbuehler, M. L., O'Cleirigh, C., Grasso, C., Mayer, K. Safren, S., & Bradford, J. (2012). Effect of same-sex marriage laws on health care use and expenditures in sexual minority men: A quasi-natural experiment. *American Journal of Public Health*, *102*, 285–291.

Herek, G. M., & Berrill, K. T. (1991). *Hate crimes: Confronting violence against lesbians and gay men.* Thousand Oaks, CA: Sage Publications.

Herek, G. M., Gillis J., & Cogan J. (2009). Internalized stigma among sexual minority adults: Insights from a social psychological perspective. *Journal of Counseling Psychology, 56,* 2–43.

Herman, J. L., & Cooper, P. J. (2013). Costs and benefits of providing transition-related health care coverage in employee health benefits plans: Findings from a survey of employers. The Williams Institute. Retrieved from http://williamsinstitute.law.ucla.edu/wp-content/uploads/Herman-Cost-Benefit-of-Trans-Health-Benefits-Sept-2013.pdf

Human Rights Campaign. (2016). *Corporate equality index: Rating American workplaces for lesbian, gay, bisexual, and transgender equality.* Washington DC: Author.

Institute of Medicine. (2011). *The health of lesbian, gay, bisexual, and transgender people: Building a foundation for better understanding.* Washington, DC: The National Academies Press.

King v. Christie, 981 F.2d 296 (U.S. District Court 2013).

Lambda Legal. (2010). When health care isn't caring: Lambda Legal's survey of discrimination against LGBT people and people with HIV New York, NY: Lambda Legal. Retrieved from www.lambdalegal.org/health-care-report

Lick, D. J., Durso, L. E., & Johnson, K. L. (2013). Minority stress and physical health among sexual minorities. *Perspectives on Psychological Science, 8,* 521–548.

Marans, D. (2016, November). New York lawmaker's "Pence" bill would ban abusive LGBTQ "conversion therapy." *Huffington Post.* Retrieved from http://www.huffingtonpost.com/entry/pence-bill-banning-lgbtq-conversion-therapy_us_5835bda8e4b09b6055ffc26a

Matthew Shepard and James Byrd, Jr., Hate Crimes Prevention Act of 2009, 18 U.S.C. § 249 (2009). Retrieved from https://www.congress.gov/amendment/111th-congress/senate-amendment/1511

McHugh, P. (2014, June 12). Transgender surgery isn't the solution: A drastic physical change doesn't address underlying psycho-social troubles. *The Wall Street Journal.* Retrieved from http://www.wsj.com/articles/paul-mchugh-transgender-surgery-isnt-the-solution-1402615120

Meyer, I. H. (1995). Minority stress and mental health in gay men. *Journal of Health and Social Behavior, 36,* 38–56.

Meyer, I. H. (2003). Prejudice, social stress, and mental health in lesbian, gay, and bisexual populations: Conceptual issue and research evidence. *Psychological Bulletin 129,* 674–697.

Meyer, I. H., & Frost, D. M. (2013). Minority stress and the health of sexual minorities. In C. J. Patterson & A. R. D'Augelli (Eds.), *Handbook of psychology and sexual orientation,* (pp. 253–266). New York, NY: Oxford University Press.

Michael Ferguson, et al., v. JONAH, et al., HUD-L-5473-12 (SC of New Jersey 2015).

Movement Advancement Project. (n.d.). Healthcare laws and policies. Retrieved from http://www.lgbtmap.org/equality-maps/healthcare_laws_and_policies

Murad, M. H., Elamin, M. B., Garcia, M. Z., Mullan, R. J., Murad, A., Erwin, P. J., & Montori, V. M. (2010). Hormonal therapy and sex reassignment: a systematic review and meta-analysis of quality of life and psychosocial outcomes. *Clinical Endocrinology, 72,* 214–231.

National Center for Lesbian Rights. (2014). #BornPerfect: The campaign to end conversion therapy. Retrieved from http://www.nclrights.org/our-work/bornperfect/

National Institutes of Health. (2015). *NIH FY 2016-2020: Strategic plan to advance research on the health and well-being of sexual and gender minorities (SGM)*. Washington DC: Author. Retrieved from http://edi.nih.gov/sites/default/files/EDI_Public_files/sgm-strategic-plan.pdf

NeJaime, D., & Siegel, R. (2015). Conscience wars: Complicity-based conscience claims in religion and politics. *The Yale Law Review, 124*, 2516–2591. Retrieved from http://papers.ssrn.com/sol3/papers.cfm?abstract_id=2560658

Obergefell v. Hodges, 576 U.S. ___ (2015).

Office for Civil Rights. (n.d.). Fact sheet: Nondiscrimination in health programs and activities proposed rule. Section 1557 of the Affordable Care Act. Retrieved from http://www.hhs.gov/ocr/civilrights/understanding/section1557/nprmsummary.html

The Parental and Family Rights in Counseling Protection Act, H1598, 55th Oklahoma Leg. (2015). Retrieved from http://www.oklegislature.gov/BillInfo.aspx?Bill=hb1598

Peace for the Streets by Kids from the Streets. (2015a, September 9). Happy Birthday PSKS! Retrieved from http://www.psks.org

Peace for the Streets by Kids from the Streets. (2015b, November 17). PSKS goes to City Hall. Retrieved from http://www.psks.org

Pickup v. Brown, 740 F.3d 1208, 1222 (9th Cir. 2015).

Popanz, T. (2015). Interview with Peace for the Streets by Kids from the Streets youth homeless advocate, Jessica Churchill, unpublished.

Quealy, K., & Sanger-Katz, M. (2014, October 29). "Obama's health law: Who was helped most." *The New York Times*. Retrieved from http://www.nytimes.com/interactive/2014/10/29/upshot/obamacare-who-was-helped-most.html

Rachlin, K., Green, J., & Lombardi, E. (2008). Utilization of health care among female-to-male transgender individuals in the United States. *Journal of Homosexuality, 54*, 243–258. doi:10.1080/00918360801982124

Raifman, J., Moscoe, E., Austin, S., & McConnell. (2017). Difference-in-differences analysis of the association between state same-sex marriage policies and adolescent suicide attempts. *Journal of the American Medical Association Pediatrics, 171*, 350–356. doi:10.1001/jamapediatrics.2016.4529

Ray, N. (2006). *Lesbian, gay, bisexual, and transgender youth: An epidemic of homelessness*. New York, NY: National Gay and Lesbian Task Force Policy Institute and the National Coalition for the Homeless.

Reconciliation and Growth Project. (n.d.). Principles and practices for mental-health professionals helping faith-based individuals respond to same-sex attractions. Retrieved June 17, 2017, from http://reconciliationandgrowth.org/guidelines/Riggle, E. D. B., Rostosky, S. S., & Horne, S. G. (2010). Does it matter where you live? State non-discrimination laws and the perceptions of LGB residents. *Sexuality Research and Social Policy, 7*, 168–172.

Rosenberg, L. G. (2000). Phase oriented psychotherapy for gay men recovering from trauma. *Journal of Gay & Lesbian Social Services, 12*, 37–73.

Russell, G. M., & Richards, J. A. (2003). Stressor and resilience factors for lesbians, gay men, and bisexuals confronting antigay politics. *American Journal of Community Psychology, 31*, 313–328.

Sexual Orientation Change Efforts, S.1172, CA Legislature. (2012). Retrieved from https://leginfo.legislature.ca.gov/faces/billNavClient.xhtml?bill_id=201120120SB1172

Shires, D. A., & Jaffee, K. (2015). Factors associated with health care discrimination experiences among a national sample of female-to-male transgender individuals. *Health & Social Work*, 40, 134–141. doi:10.1093/hsw/hlv025

Southern Poverty Law Center. (2012, October). SPLC files complaint against Illinois social worker offering "ex-gay" therapy. Retrieved from https://www.splcenter.org/news/2012/10/11/splc-files-complaint-against-illinois-social-worker-offering-%E2%80%98ex-gay%E2%80%99-therapy

Substance Abuse and Mental Health Services Administration. (2015). *Ending conversion therapy: Supporting and affirming LGBTQ youth.* HHS Publication No. (SMA) 15-4928. Rockville, MD: Substance Abuse and Mental Health Services Administration. Retrieved from http://store.samhsa.gov/product/SMA15-4928

Sylvia Rivera Law Project. (2009). SRLP on hate crimes laws. Retrieved from https://srlp.org/action/hate-crimes/

Therapeutic Fraud Prevention Act, H.2450, 114th Cong. (2015). Retrieved from https://www.congress.gov/bill/114th-congress/house-bill/2450

UN Human Rights Council (UNHRC). (2015, May). Annual report of the UN High Commissioner for Human Rights and reports of the Office of the High Commissioner and the Secretary-General (A/HRC/29/23). Retrieved from http://www.ohchr.org/EN/HRBodies/HRC/RegularSessions/Session29/Documents/A_HRC_29_23_en.doc

U.S. Department of Health and Human Services, Administration for Community Living. (2015). 2015 White House Conference on Aging: Final report. Retrieved from https://whitehouseconferenceonaging.gov/2015-WHCOA-Final-Report.pdf

U.S. Department of Health and Human Services, Civil Rights. (2016). Summary: Final rule implementing Section 1557 of the Affordable Care Act. Retrieved from https://www.hhs.gov/sites/default/files/2016-06-07-section-1557-final-rule-summary-508.pdf

U.S. Department of Health and Human Services, Civil Rights. (2017). Section 1557 of the Patient Protection and Affordable Care Act. Retrieved from https://www.hhs.gov/civil-rights/for-individuals/section-1557/

U.S. Department of Health and Human Services, Health Resources and Services Administration. (2010). Gay men and the history of the Ryan White HIV/AIDS program.

U.S. v. Windsor, 570 U. S. ____ (2013).

Welch v. Brown, No. 13-15023. D.C. No. 2:12-CV-02484-WBS-KJN (9th Cir. 2013).

Whitman, J. S., Glosoff, H. L., Kocet, M. M., & Tarvydas, V. (2013). Ethical issues related to conversion or reparative therapy. American Counseling Association. Retrieved from www.Counseling.org/news/updates/2013/01/16/Ethical-Issues-Related-to-Conversion-or-Reparative-Therapy

12

Quality and Equality: An Interdisciplinary Graduate Program to Develop Agents of Change in LGBT Health

Stephen L. Forssell, Nathaniel Swift-Erslev, Colin J. Davis, Richard Ruth, Alyssa N. Zucker, Sharon J. Glezen, Merle Cunningham, Blaine Parrish, Carl G. Streed Jr., and Ronald L. Schlittler

This book has the expressed aim of highlighting cutting-edge research and emerging approaches to improving the mental health of the LGBT population. Previous chapters have provided findings, observations, and theories on the topic that suggest future actions and policies that might be enacted to improve the health of LGBT people. This chapter presents the history of the evolution of one specific, concrete step in that direction. It documents the early development and initial implementation of the LGBT Health Policy and Practice (LGBTHP&P) Program, a graduate-level interdisciplinary certificate program in LGBT health that is by necessity innovative, unconventional, and "cutting edge." The following review of its progress to date is a collaborative effort from faculty, alumni, and administrators who participated in LGBTHP&P's early design and implementation. As of this writing, LGBTHP&P is recruiting its fifth cohort of students, set to matriculate in June, 2017.

In an effort to mitigate LGBT health disparities and the lack of adequately trained healthcare practitioners in LGBT health, a faculty group at The George Washington University (GWU) in Washington, DC, sought to develop a program that would be accessible to direct-care providers and other health professionals, including those working in underserved parts of the country and abroad. The result was an interdisciplinary graduate certificate program that uses a hybrid online and on-campus course model to train current and future healthcare professionals on how to improve healthcare for the diverse array of LGBT communities. The program teaches students to conduct, evaluate, and apply evidence-based best practice research to key health issues facing LGBT people. The scope of the program provides students with the skills and resources needed to advocate for the health needs of LGBT people and extends to current and future policy professionals. This chapter describes the creation, early evolution, goals, and initial outcomes of the graduate certificate program in LGBT Health Policy and Practice at GWU; discusses how the program affects its students and LGBT communities they serve; and concludes with the future directions the program is now undertaking.

BACKGROUND AND DEVELOPMENT

Contextual Origins

The United States has experienced a sea change in the social and legal acceptance of LGBT people. In the past several years, public opinion on same-sex marriage has swung from majority opposition to majority support (Gallup, 2016); the Supreme Court struck down key repressive sections of the Defense of Marriage Act (DOMA; Gonzales, Moltz, & King, 2014), and Congress has repealed the Department of Defense's Don't Ask Don't Tell (DADT) policy (Bumiller, 2011). Legal access to same-sex marriage has expanded from four jurisdictions in 2009 to 36 states plus the District of Columbia in early 2015, and now to the entire nation with the U.S. Supreme Court's *Obergefell v. Hodges* ruling on June 26, 2015 (Lambda Legal, 2015).

During this time, federal policymakers have increasingly realized that LGBT health is integral to LGBT equality. The specific health needs of LGBT people first became a topic of interest for the federal government in 2000, winning mention in the goals for *Healthy People 2010* (U.S. Department of Health and Human Services, 2000). However, it was not till *Healthy People 2020* that the federal government intimated a critically important commitment to LGBT health through specific, targeted goals to eliminate LGBT health disparities and configure emerging health systems toward positive outcomes for LGBT communities (U.S. Department of Health and Human Services, 2010). These goals have driven research initiatives, program and health-systems development, and funding streams never before available.

This federal trend of acknowledgment and attention to LGBT health needs has most recently culminated in the formal designation of sexual and gender minorities as a "health disparity population" for research purposes by the National Institutes of Health (NIH) as of October 2016 (Perez-Stable & National Institute on Minority Health and Health Disparities, 2016).

Prior to *Healthy People 2020*, healthcare professionals seeking information on LGBT health relied on reports, such as Health Professionals Advancing LGBT Equality's (Gay and Lesbian Medical Association [GLMA]) 2001 companion document to *Healthy People 2010*, (funded in part, though not produced, by the U.S. Department of Health and Human Services; Health Professionals Advancing LGBT Equality [GLMA] and LGBT Health Experts, 2001). While such reports made important contributions, it was not until 2011 that the Institute of Medicine (IOM) published its groundbreaking report, *The Health of Lesbian, Gay, Bisexual, and Transgender People: Building a Foundation for Better Understanding*, documenting health disparities related to sexual orientation and gender identity (IOM, 2011).

These milestone documents catalyzed the initial conceptualization and development of the GWU certificate program. Such reports and accompanying progressive legislation resonated with what many of the program faculty already knew: more providers, researchers, and policy professionals were needed who could develop and implement culturally competent, evidence-based best practices in order to create LGBT-affirmative health systems and promote LGBT health equity. Moreover, increased access to health services for LGBT patients and their families as a result of the Affordable Care Act (ACA) and expansion of same-sex marriage further supported our assertion that the program was needed; the sociopolitical climate was favorable, and the skill sets the program would offer were in demand (Baker & Cray, 2012; Durso, Baker, & Cray, 2013; Gonzales, 2014; Gonzales & Blewett, 2013; Hager, 2013).

Advisory Groups and Faculty Workgroup

In October, 2011, the program's inceptor and director, Stephen Forssell, PhD, assembled a provisional advisory committee to provide input on the program's early direction. As the scope of the program became apparent, Dr. Forssell assembled a formal advisory board that assisted in the drafting of the program's official mission statement:

> To train current and future leaders to develop and apply best practices and shape policy to eliminate disparities and improve health outcomes for lesbian, gay, bisexual, and transgender (LGBT) people.

The mission statement would ultimately guide the board and faculty in the creation of program goals and learning objectives, which in turn would inform the program's construction. The initial committee and formal advisory board drew their diverse professional composition from academic, healthcare, business, LGBT advocacy, and policy communities; from the beginning, the director and advisory group believed that an interdisciplinary approach would be necessary to address the multifaceted challenges facing the health of LGBT people. Interdisciplinary programs are increasingly understood to better prepare students to address real-world problems (Misra et al., 2009; O'Donnell & Derry, 2013).

However, designing and implementing programs across schools and departments of a university can pose logistical challenges because of the "siloed" nature of higher education and the flows of revenue through a university system

(Campbell, 2013). To counter expected early resistance related to control of the program curriculum and tuition revenues, the program's director secured buy-in by reaching out to as many potential stakeholders across schools and departments within the GWU as could be identified. He offered each the opportunity to provide input and to participate in the program's creation. He identified graduate faculty whose work in various fields (health care, mental health, health policy, women's studies, queer theory, and LGB history) within and outside of GWU might connect to the program's mission. These faculty were invited to become involved in the program's development, which would be housed administratively in the Professional Psychology Program.

The goal of this effort was twofold: to ensure that no potentially interested stakeholder was left out of the process and to identify and select those who would form the core faculty workgroup (see Table 12.1) directly responsible for the program's logistical development. While, for the most part, faculty self-selected into which role they would play, the director enlisted faculty members whose expert help he knew would be needed from relevant disciplines and departments (e.g., psychology, public health,, and public policy). GWU does not have graduate degree programs in certain other disciplines (e.g., social work), which were therefore unfortunately not represented in the board or faculty workgroups. To capture perspectives about the proposed curriculum from stakeholders outside GWU, the director sought input from health professionals in practice and in academia through direct contact with relevant professional organizations (e.g., the Gay and Lesbian Medical Association).

PROGRAM ORGANIZATION

The structure and curriculum of the program was crafted around core learning objectives designed to inform and prepare students for their real-world LGBT health endeavors postgraduation. These objectives have included learning to use an intersectional lens to analyze the ways diverse demographic factors come to bear on health realities, so that students become equipped to better evaluate health disparities of marginalized communities in general, and LGBT populations in specific. In line with this intersectional approach, students further learn to separate the unique health disparities of the different constituencies of the LGBT+ acronym and learn how these necessary distinctions impact research, policy, clinical, and public health strategies, for example, the distinct clinical concerns and approaches for a lesbian, a trans woman, or a straight-identifying man who has sex with men. Students are expected to demonstrate the ability to connect their own professional and personal experiences to LGBT health concerns, clinical practice, and policy issues. Ultimately, students translate these skills and connections into practice through the execution of a capstone project designed to reduce health disparities and improve access to culturally competent

Table 12.1
Core Faculty Workgroup, Years One and Two

Name	Role	Department or Affiliation	Program Courses Taught	Research or Professional Background
Stephen Forssell, PhD	Director	Psychology (GWU)	LGBT Mental Health	Male couples' relationships, parenting in same-sex couples, HIV risk behavior intervention and program evaluation
Blaine Parrish, PhD	Core Faculty	School of Public Health (GWU)	Capstone (Year One)	Community-based health program development, implementation, and evaluation; organization and management of community-based health service organizations
Merle Cunningham, MD		School of Public Health (GWU)	Capstone (Year Two)	Family practice physician. Healthcare management in safety net health organizations and public clinics
Alyssa Zucker, PhD		Psychology, Women's Studies (GWU)	Multidisciplinary LGBT Health	Discrimination and health; impact of sexism, racism, classism on health behaviors and outcomes
Elizabeth Rigby, PhD		School of Public Policy (GWU)	N/A	Interplay of politics, public policy, and social inequalities; health disparities, educational achievement gaps, and income inequality
Richard Ruth, PhD		Professional Psychology (GWU)	Transgender Health (Elective)	Clinical psychologist and psychoanalyst; research on cross-cultural psychological assessment and psychotherapy, psychological ethics, forensic psychology, intersectionality approaches to psychological assessment and treatment of LGBT persons
Roberta Downing, PhD	Adjunct Faculty	American Psychological Association (APA); Center on Budget and Policy Priorities (CBPP)	LGBT Health Policy	Senior legislative and federal affairs officer at APA; senior legislative associate at CBPP. Research on poverty, community-based participatory research, and health disparities
Michael Plankey, PhD		School of Medicine (Georgetown University)	HIV+ Men Who Have Sex with Men (Elective)	Infectious disease epidemiologist; expertise in longitudinal data in social, psychological, and behavioral risk factors for HIV

care for LGBT people. Throughout the program, faculty continually emphasize and connect these objectives to course assignments and materials.

Structure and Curriculum

The core faculty workgroup first met in July, 2012, to craft the structure of the program. Guided by the mission statement and core learning objectives, the workgroup made three decisions that shaped the development of the program:

1. To use the hybrid program model. It was felt that, by meeting mostly online, through Blackboard-mediated sessions, and with two brief in-person residencies each year, students from across the United States and abroad would be more capable of participating. This decision also helped win approval from university administrators and financial officials, as they saw a hybrid model as resource-efficient. Certain program development needs flowed from the decision to pursue a hybrid model. For instance, to support the mostly online program model, making the website the program's showcase and its primary source of information for applicants was critical. Given the program's intended expansive geographic and disciplinary reach, student recruitment efforts needed to be similarly broad. The faculty workgroup used existing personal networks and professional organizations to get the word out about the program through institutional listservs, newsletters, and other print media.
2. To orient the coursework around three core content areas: LGBT health and public policy, LGBT physical health, and LGBT mental health. Required courses in these three areas were supplemented by elective courses in relevant special topics (e.g., transgender health, sexual minority youth) offered within GWU or as transferred credits (see Table 12.2). The workgroup felt the breadth and flexibility of this curricular structure would equip students, regardless of their areas of current or future professional focus, with the knowledge and skill sets necessary for interdisciplinary work settings and collaborations.
3. To require students to complete a capstone project aligned with their academic and professional interests and aspirations. A capstone course was envisioned to provide students with specialized skill sets related to the design and implementation of a project that would define and address an LGBT health or health policy need, buttressed by evidence from relevant scientific and professional literatures. The capstone project is fundamental to the professional value of the certificate program, as it ensures that graduates will have demonstrated the ability to apply the knowledge and skills they have learned to real-world settings.

In line with these framing decisions, the final curriculum originally encompassed a 12-credit program that could be completed over three semesters (summer, fall, and spring) in one year. This remains the trajectory that most students prefer. An option to complete the program over two years was phased in starting with the second cohort, to meet the needs of students juggling home

Table 12.2
Elective Courses Accepted in First Cohort

Course Title and Department/Institution Where Applicable	Type
Transgender Health	elective offered through certificate program
HIV+ Men Who Have Sex with Men (MSM)	
Ethnic and Racial Diversity in Psychology (graduate psychology course)	approved GWU elective from external department
Women and Health (cross listed, graduate psychology and women's studies programs)	
Cross-Cultural Clinical Psychology (graduate Professional Psychology program)	
Designing and Evaluating HIV Prevention Programs (graduate course in school of Public Health)	
Sexuality and the Law (graduate women's studies program)	
Preventing Health Disparities (graduate course in school of Public Health)	
Medical Anthropology (graduate anthropology program)	
Health Science: Community Organization (San Jose State University)	approved non-GWU transfer credit
LGBTQ Clinical Psychology (Palo Alto University)	

and career demands and those for whom the cost of the program could be more readily met when spread out over two years. (See Table 12.3 for a depiction of the curriculum structure).

Classes meet on campus for a one-week summer residency and a four-day spring residency. Class meetings are augmented with expert panels, guest lectures, meetings with Washington policymakers, and social events in the local LGBT communities. The in-person residencies provide students with continuity and help strengthen networks among students, faculty, and guest presenters. Arrangements are made for out-of-town students to stay in one of the campus dormitories or the campus hotel; local students typically commute from home.

The residencies also impart valuable exposure to the policy process; students hear directly from legislators and executive branch personnel about their experiences and policy perspectives and priorities. Most residencies have provided students meetings with U.S. senators or members of Congress, officials from Health and Human Services and its bureaus, and the White House LGBT Affairs Liaison.

Table 12.3
Semester Structure and Course Layout

	One-Year Track	Two-Year Track
Summer—Year One	LGBT Health Policy (two credits)	LGBT Health Policy (two credits)
	Multidisciplinary LGBT Health (two credits)	
	On-Campus Residency (July)	*On-Campus Residency (July)*
Fall—Year 2	LGBT Mental Health (two credits)	LGBT Mental Health (two credits)
	Electives (two credits)	
Spring—Year One	Capstone (three credits)	
	Electives (one credit)	Electives (one to two credits)
	On-Campus Residency (January)	*On-Campus Residency (January)*
Summer—Year Two		Multidisciplinary LGBT Health (two credits)
		On-Campus Residency (July)
Fall—Year Two	N/A	Electives (one to two credits)
Spring—Year Two		Capstone (three credits)
		On-Campus Residency (January)

Online course components include asynchronous individual assignments, such as discussion boards, embedded short- and long-form videos, readings, recorded lectures, and Web-synchronized class meetings. These complement the in-person class sessions held during the residencies.

The summer semester is comprised of two hybrid core courses, punctuated in the fourth week by the required one-week residency. The fall semester is entirely online and consists of the third core course and a special topics elective course. The spring semester starts with the second, required in-person residency which includes meetings of the capstone project and course and additional special topics electives course meetings. Examples of summer residency activities from the first cohort can be found in Table 12.4.

Student Body

As informed by the mission statement, a chief objective of the certificate program was to produce graduates with a nuanced understanding of the clinical and anthropological manifestations of LGBT health disparities as well as the systemic

Table 12.4
Activities for the First Cohort's Summer Residency

Residency	Activity Type	Presenter/Event	Role, Title, or Affiliation	Topic
Summer 2013	Guest Presenter	Walter Dellinger	Former Solicitor General, President Bill Clinton, 1996–1997	The Affordable Healthcare Act Decision, the Gay Marriage Cases and the Future of LGBT Health
		Charlotte Patterson	Professor of Psychology; Director, Women, Gender & Sexuality Program, University of Virginia	Lesbian and Bisexual Women's Health
		Sylvia Fisher	Director of Research, Health Resources and Services Administration	Inside View of Federal Health and LGBT Initiatives
		Shane Snowdon	Health Policy Director, Human Rights Campaign	Advancing LGBT Issues in the Workplace
	Panel	Healthcare Consumer Panel	Various	Clinical experiences from the perspective of LGBT patients
		Healthcare Provider Panel	Various	Clinical experiences of providers in speech therapy, psychotherapy, medicine, psychiatry
	Field	U.S. Capitol Tour	Former Congressman Phil Sharp (D, IN)	Visit to the Capitol building, discussion of the history of LGBT rights legislation
		Senate Office Visit	Senator Tammy Baldwin (D, WI)	Discussion with the Senator of legislative priorities for health of LGBT population

forces that can perpetuate or mitigate those disparities. This objective—and the professional breadth of the student body—necessitated an interdisciplinary curriculum that could flexibly connect to each student's unique aspirations, be they clinical, academic, or policy related. The program was designed to recruit an occupationally diverse student body, to foster a working appreciation of the important, complementary linkages between health professions; clinicians van learn from insider perspectives on relevant policy dimensions, while students with policy expertise are exposed to the insights of clinicians with in-depth experience tackling ground-level LGBT health issues. For less experienced students, the program has aspired to offer exposure to the range of professional possibilities that can connect students' interest in the well-being of LGBT communities to their respective fields of interest.

Program applicants are required to have completed a bachelor's degree. Health-related backgrounds are preferred but not required. so long as students aspire to a future in health, mental health, or health policy careers. We prioritize applicants with a GPA of 3.2 or higher but do not use a strict cut-off, in recognition of the sometimes disadvantaged backgrounds of some of our applicants. GRE scores are not necessary, though Test of English as a Foreign Language (TOEFL) or International English Language testing System (IELTS) scores are required for international applicants. A statement of interest and recommendation letters are used to help assess whether applicants' interest and backgrounds are aligned with the program's focus. Applications are reviewed holistically for potential to succeed and contribute to the field.

The program's first cohort matriculated in June, 2013, and consisted of 16 students from ten states and the District of Columbia. They represented diverse academic and professional disciplines and a range of levels of educational achievement. Statistics and background data for the applicant pools and student cohorts of the program's first two years can be found in Table 12.5.

The Capstone Project

Students are asked to enter the program with an idea for a capstone project, the nature and parameters of which have evolved as the program has progressed and students have been exposed to innovative ideas. Students have used the summer residency session to conceptualize their projects, find project sites, and connect with mentors.

Aiming to enhance students' competencies in time and project management, course assignments have followed a timeline that reflects expected project benchmarks. Beyond this framing schedule, students have been given considerable freedom in designing and implementing their projects and have been responsible for developing and achieving their own project timelines and objectives.

Table 12.5
Certificate Program Application Statistics, Years One and Two

	Year #1	Year #2
Applications Started	18	60
Applications Submitted	18	32
Enrolled	16	20
Graduated	13	12
Education of Enrolled Class		
• Completed bachelor's	8	5
• In graduate school	4	4
• Completed master's	2	6
• Completed MD	1	3
• Completed PhD	1	2
Disciplinary Backgrounds	Clinical pharmacology, psychology, counseling, education, English, biology, international policy, medicine, nursing, public administration, public health, women's studies	clinical mental health counseling, education, international studies, medicine, nursing, public policy, psychology, public health, social work, sociology
Regional Representation	Northeast: New Jersey, New York, Pennsylvania South: District of Columbia, North Carolina, Virginia, West Virginia Midwest: Michigan, Ohio, Wisconsin West Coast: California	Northeast: Connecticut, Maryland, Massachusetts, New Jersey, New York South: District of Columbia, Florida, Georgia, TX, North Carolina, Texas Midwest: Ohio West Coast: Utah
Countries Represented	United States only	United States (including Puerto Rico), Colombia, Philippines

Capstone projects from the program's first two cohorts (see Table 12.6) reflect the diversity of students' professional foci. These projects have included the development of cultural competency training materials for care providers working with LGBT elders; a memorandum filed with District of Columbia Public Schools (DCPS) on recommended changes in DCPS health education standards, whose recommendations were ultimately adopted and implemented by DCPS; development of informational materials for transgender speech/language therapy patients in transition; HIV/AIDS patient-portal activities to advance

Table 12.6
Select Student Capstone, Years One and Two

Student Name, Year	Project Description
Policy	
Jeff Goodman, 2014	Developed a policy statement and recommendations on bullying and other disparities faced by LGBTQ youth. After being endorsed by the LGBT Caucus of Public Health Professionals, the statement was submitted to and ultimately *adopted by the American Public Health Association* as an official policy statement of the organization.
John Cullen, PhD, 2014	Project entailed the *successful lobbying of the University of Rochester* to provide transition-related coverage to treat gender dysphoria in student and employee health benefits plans. With approximately 22,000 faculty/staff and 9,000 students, the university is the largest employer in the Rochester region and sixth-largest private employer in New York State. Project addressed health insurance disparities for the transgender population at the university, ultimately promoting an environment where the human dignity of all employees and students is respected.
Education/Curriculum	
Sharon Glezen, MD, 2014	Conducted a review of existing LGBT health curricula and literature on LGBT education in leading medical schools in order to redesign the first-year medical-school curriculum in LGBT health at the University of Rochester Medical School. *The retooled curriculum was adopted by the medical school in the spring of 2014* following the curriculum's demonstrated success in improving the comfort and knowledge of medical students in regard to LGBT health issues in pilot trainings. The new curriculum incorporates components of a "flipped classroom" design and training in communication skills regarding sexual orientation and gender identity and comprehensive content addressing specific healthcare needs of LGBT patients.
Chris Obermeyer, 2015	Researched problems in the health curricula of secondary schools, specifically sexual education programs and education about LGBTQ issues, in the District of Columbia (DC). Produced recommendations regarding discussions of sex, gender, and sexual orientation in sexual education classes, methods of protection from pregnancy and STIs, healthy relationships, positive representations of different types of families, and the mandated use of nongendered terminology in classes. After being appointed by the DC Board of Education to review the Health and PE Standards for DC Public Schools for LGBT cultural competency, Chris employed the results of his capstone

Table 12.6 (Continued)

Student Name, Year	Project Description
	to help him author the March, 2016, "Public Comment on Proposed Health Education Standards," *which was approved by the school board in April 2016.*

Community Services

Damián Cabrera Candelaria, 2015	Developed an LGBT Health Services Directory in collaboration with the Puerto Rico Psychological Association—Committee for LGBT Issues. It is the first tool to provide Puerto Ricans access to a network of LGBT-friendly medical providers. The Web page, first published in April, 2015, with a listing of 25 psychologists, has since expanded to include (to date) 62 listings of 18 medical providers, including 12 different medical specialties (including internal medicine, urology, gynecology, family medicine, and pediatric endocrinology); 34 mental health providers, including psychology and pediatric psychiatry; and eight different locations of centers of care that provide services that range from sexually transmitted infections testing, mental health services, and community-building strategies.
Lore Espinoza Guerrero, 2015	Project responds to the climate for LGBTQ people in Colombia, where LGBTQ people experience high amounts of discrimination, health disparities, and lack of access to government services and health care. Lore formed Tacones Morados Research and Art Collective in Bogotá, a nonprofit organization for LGBTQ-identified Latin American people. Tacones Morados has three lines of action: art participation and workshops, well-Being actions, and research. Since August, 2014, Tacones Morados has delivered hygiene kits on a monthly basis to those in need and has organized clothing drives, art workshops, and leisure activities. Capstone identified the healthcare resources established under Colombian law and the health concerns of homeless transgender persons in Bogota and the barriers they face accessing care; analyzed the accessibility of services; and evaluated the quality of the resources and the quality of the services that are offered and their sustainability over time.

Research

Cramer McCullen, MD, 2014	Conducted a systematic literature review of data since 1987 regarding LGBT populations and smoking cessation. Project identified higher rates of smoking in LGBT populations compared to heterosexual peers due to minority stress, discrimination, tobacco marketing, acceptance, and social network structures. Resulted in a study *published in 2014 in the American Journal of Preventive Medicine.* The data review,

(continued)

Table 12.6   (Continued)

Student Name, Year	Project Description
	available nationwide and worldwide to providers and intervention programs for LGBT populations, will impact the standard of care guidelines for LGBT smoking cessation and direct future research endeavors.
Gregory Haskin, 2014	Researched different approaches to speech feminization and masculinization, including speech articulation, rate, intonation, pragmatics, and resonance. Developed a short presentation for patients explaining major concerns related to speech feminization and masculinization as part of the process of a transgender transition. The project aimed to limit psychological distress in patients, increase caregiver knowledge, and build more productive provider-patient relationships for transgender individuals. This research also focused on the cultural competence, general knowledge, and attitudes of speech-language pathologists working with the LGBTQ community, especially transgender populations, and was *published in 2015 in the American Journal of Speech-Language Pathology.*

the self-management of healthcare; an intervention with homeless and at-risk transgender women in Bogotá, Colombia; a successful policy initiative with the American Public Health Association (APHA) to acknowledge disparities in ways bullying is addressed when it affects LGBT youths; a curriculum revision for first-year medical students to equip them to provide culturally competent care for LGBT patients; and a successful lobbying campaign at the University of Rochester (UR) to expand its health insurance to include transition-related coverage for transgender students, staff, and faculty.

As these capstones each have had unique objectives and timelines, quantifying what constituted successful execution—the evaluation piece of the capstone—has varied from project to project. For some, success was captured by a specific *a priori* outcome or result, such as the adoption of a particular policy (transgender health coverage at UR and the APHA policy initiative). For others, "success" was completing the first step in a long process intended to be carried out beyond completion of the certificate program (the medical school and DCPS curriculum revisions). Thus, evaluation of the impact of capstones was necessarily completed on a project-by-project basis. Of the 16 students originally enrolled in the certificate

S first cohort, 13 successfully completed their capstone projects and graduated the program on schedule. Four of the 13 completed capstones required modification of the work plan and deliverables required to constitute successful completion, due to lack of financial or infrastructural resources, delays in Institutional Review Board approvals,, or unrealistic initially projected timetables. Overall, after the first cohort students completed their capstone work, the faculty agreed that more additional resources were required in the form of project management consultation as well as more rigorous evaluation of the impact of capstones to better capture not just process-oriented success but also outcome-oriented success.

PROGRAM EVALUATION

The certificate program's novel combination of structure, curriculum, and objectives means that evaluation is a necessary part of the program's ongoing evolution. As with any curriculum-based program, it was important to obtain evaluative feedback from students about the clarity and usefulness of the material and instructor effectiveness. Similarly, faculty perspectives were deemed essential in evaluating how well the program achieved its objectives in the inaugural year. As a program whose mission statement includes having a positive impact on the LGBT population, evaluation of the primary mechanism of that impact—students' capstone projects—was a third critical focus of evaluation.

Students provided feedback through completion of online quantitative and qualitative evaluations at the end of each semester and in-person residency. Following the completion of the program year, the director solicited direct open-ended feedback via e-mail from all teaching faculty in the program about components of the program they perceived went well or not so well, whether or not the program objectives had been met, and ideas for improvement. Follow-up feedback was also obtained from alumni several months following completion of the program. The views expressed in these anecdotal assessments and survey results weighed heavily and helped guide efforts to shape the evolving program.

Student Experiences and Feedback

At the 2014 LGBT Health Forum, Sharon Glezen, MD (LGBT Health Graduate Certificate, 2014), in reference to her experiences as a student in the program's first cohort, stated, "It's been a very exciting and empowering year ... I learned so much from each and every member of my class; and some of them were born a full generation after I was, long after a mysterious illness began to kill gay men in the 1980s ... [and There is still so much work to be done."

Indeed, the first cohort was driven by a united interest in reducing LGBT healthcare disparities—a concern that spans generations, localities, and professions. Qualitative responses from the first cohort reflect that the diverse generational, racial, gender, and socioeconomic perspectives of the cohort helped students deconstruct their own subjective experiences and knowledge and enhance their understanding of the numerous health disparities in LGBT communities as well as those in other marginalized populations (see Table 12.7).

Table 12.7:
Select Responses by Alumni to Follow-Up Feedback Request

Kudos to Dr. Forssell and the program—I really feel that it was the catalyst and springboard for my career development and people taking me seriously in my work! Since then I have worked with multiple organizations, both on campus and in the Rochester community, to help address many of the social injustice issues and healthcare disparities that are faced by the LGBT community.

The rich experiences I gained from the LGBTHPP Program, through both my capstone project and collaborating in the community, helped me achieve a very important goal, to gain admission to my choice of doctoral programs. I have since begun pursuing a Ph.D. in applied social and health psychology. I feel very fortunate to say that I was one of only two incoming students accepted this year, and that I am fully funded. The interdisciplinary nature of the LGBTHPP Program, drawing on both the psychology and public health departments, is what made me a truly competitive applicant. I look forward to honing the passions and skills I first developed during the LGBTHPP Program as I advance through the academy.

Participating in the LGBT Health Policy and Practice program while concurrently pursuing my Medical Doctorate, allowed me to not only substantiate my previous interest and involvement in LGBT healthcare, but also allowed me to connect with like-minded peers and to develop a network of resources which ultimately led to the publication of an innovative systematic review of the literature addressing the LGBT smoking cessation while highlighting the future goals and direction for providers of LGBT healthcare. It is my hope that such research will serve as a platform for future initiatives by community organizations and governmental agencies in addressing LGBT health needs, and will serve to underscore my commitment to LGBT health as my career in medicine advances.

As an advocate for LGBTQ youth for years I only knew the struggles LGBTQ youth faced within the school environment. I had heard of health disparities but hadn't considered how a school could be utilized to combat them and allow youth to prosper both in physical and mental health. After hearing from my students that they weren't receiving health information that was relevant for them I delved deep into the standards and curriculum to see what was really happening in the classroom. The LGBT Health Policy and Practice Certificate Program has given me the health background necessary to examine health curricula and standards to ensure they are relevant and taught appropriately to reduce the health disparities LGBTQ youth experience. My participation in the program and growing expertise in the field has given me the opportunity to now be a reviewer for the revised health standards to ensure LGBTQ inclusivity and relevance. This is a tangible success as I fight to ensure LGBTQ youth receive the health education they so desperately need and deserve.

After years of working within the LGBTQ community, I was shocked to learn how much I didn't know and the LGBT Health Policy& Practice program provided me new knowledge and perspectives to further build my career. This was most evidenced through my capstone project—a portion of which involved authoring a policy on addressing disparities faced by LGBT Youth with bullying. I did this for the benefit of the American Public Health Association's (APHA) LGBT Caucus of Public Health Professionals which had not submitted policy for over 15 years. The policy was grounded in theories I learned through the LGBT Health Policy & Practice program. After rigorous review by science and policy boards, the policy was adopted by APHA's Board of Governors.

Student opinions of the benefits of specific courses and coursework varied, though they were generally positive:

> I found the assignments, videos, and other coursework to be very relevant and practical. I appreciate the flexible approach that each professor took, so that each student would gain something unique to their goals and needs. I have learned a great deal already.

Students felt that, depending upon each individual student's knowledge entering the program, some courses were more enriching than others (i.e., medical caregivers derived more knowledge from the policy course than policy professionals):

> One other area to possibly consider—and I have no idea how this could work— but with the diversity that occurs within the student body it might be great to have different tracks. For example I found the policy class to be of little value to me, while I found the multidisciplinary health class to be enormously rich in content. I know others in the cohort felt the opposite—it all depended on our training.

In regard to structure, the flexibility of distance-learning coursework was particularly beneficial for students with professional commitments that would have conflicted with traditional in-person class schedules, though feedback also cited the untapped potential of real-time discussion opportunities:

> I would love to see some use of synchronous class lecture/discussion. The [online discussion] Boards became more lively after we met each in [the] summer residency—but there is no substitute for a lively real-time discussion. Our class has such a wide variety of experiences and expertise that can really be an important part of our overall learning.

Many students cited the in-person residencies as the most beneficial part of the program, offering them direct exposure to policymakers and researchers in the field and providing time to clarify goals while strengthening new and old connections:

> The residency presented so many cool opportunities I never could have gotten in any other way, and I really appreciate the chance to do so many things. I particularly enjoyed the healthcare consumer/provider panels because they were the most helpful in painting a picture of the healthcare in a clinical setting and not just from the policy standpoint. Shane Snowdon's lecture was probably my favorite because it was the most concrete in providing information useful for the workplace. The meeting with Senator Baldwin was exceptional both to get a realistic idea of the political process and also to see how effective individual (or group) advocacy can really be in connecting to legislators.

Critiques of the residencies centered around advocacy for increased racial and ethnic diversity of presenters—"though the patient panel was very good, the lack of racial/socioeconomic diversity was apparent"—as well as suggestions for new activities, potential for improvements in the timing of events and assignments, and planning for students to have more time to process and discuss their experiences.

The successes of the program's capstone course were balanced by critiques of its still emerging structure, which may be reasonably understood as the growing pains of an unprecedented academic program. Some students cited difficulties finding appropriate project mentors and requested more structure and guidance from both their mentors and faculty:

> I also recommend drafts of the project be submitted periodically to both the capstone course instructor and the capstone mentor. I believe that a more present and easier-to-reach instructor is needed for a large, time-consuming project such as the capstone. It would also be nice if mentors could be matched to those students who need a mentor (and do not already have someone in mind).

Overall evaluations of program components and the program as a whole were strongly positive. In particular, feedback surveys indicated that the selected texts, videos, and discussion board assignments for the various courses of the first cohort were all favorably received. For the residencies, the most highly regarded activities included the guest presenters, visits to the Capitol and with Senator Tammy Baldwin, and the annual LGBT Health Forum (a public awareness event held at GWU as a part of the summer residency). In general, students were highly pleased with the residencies, thought the in-person aspect was valuable, and were likely to recommend the program to other potential students. As a whole, students found the diversity of the student body's backgrounds and professional disciplines to be assets of the program.

Long-term follow-up with alumni was conducted with students in the first two cohorts between six and 18 months following graduation. The director contacted alumni directly via e-mail requesting informal,, open-ended updates on their professional progress and commentary on the impact of the program on their professional development and work since graduation.

The feedback received was overwhelmingly positive. Students benefited from translating academic learning to real-world initiatives and felt empowered to be advocates in both their personal and professional lives for the well-being and health of LGBT people.

Faculty Feedback

Comments from faculty were similar to those of students and followed a few key themes. The comments about what worked best noted that students and fellow faculty were engaged, enthusiastic, motivated, diverse in experience and discipline, and able to learn from each other, and that the residencies were highly positive, transformative experiences that energized students and faculty alike:

> How wonderful it was to work with so many engaged, insightful, and motivated students. It felt very rewarding as an instructor that students knew that an important need was being met by offering the certificate program, and they seemed motivated to make change with the education they received.

Faculty brought up areas for improvement and challenges, including obtaining a more racially and ethnically diverse selection of guest speakers and presenters; providing better structure, guidance, and mentoring for student capstones; insufficient financial resources; and financial and time constraint challenges observed for some students in completing the program successfully.

Changes Implemented

The feedback received from students and faculty suggested minor improvements that could be made to core and elective courses (readings, timing of assignments) and led to adjustments undertaken by the individual faculty members who taught those courses. Minor changes to residencies that were also made largely concerned the pace of the day's events, racial and ethnic diversity of speakers and topics chosen, and offering students daily opportunities to discuss residency events and take-home lessons. Lastly, efforts were undertaken to expand fundraising in order to underwrite curriculum-development initiatives and student scholarships.

The same feedback suggested more significant adjustments for the capstone course. Substantial changes were made following the first cohort. First, capstone project planning began earlier. Applicants were asked to discuss potential projects as part of the initial application process. Successful applicants were then asked to share specific potential project ideas at the initial summer residency. Second, a structured approach to project management (PM) was introduced during the initial residency, with a role-playing exercise that included the standard PM steps. Asynchronous discussion boards were made available to discuss progress on the standard PM steps. These supports are now supplemented with periodic synchronous Skype or conference calls with faculty to discuss progress and issues. Lastly, recognizing that more rigorous evaluative methods were needed to assess the impact of the projects, formal training in evaluation techniques was added to the capstone curriculum.

FUTURE DIRECTIONS

Learning from the program's first two years, the director and faculty members have identified four key priorities in the forward progress of the program. First is the centrality and financial sustainability of the capstone project component. As the capstone represents the single most important feature of the program's educational objectives and contribution to LGBT health, it is crucial to implement strategies that support (1) better and earlier planning of capstones; (2) better evaluation to document projects' impact properly; (3) the recruitment of ever-higher-quality students prepared to take on the challenges of a capstone project; and (4) the allocation of funding to help cover the expenses of students' capstones.

A second area identified as a priority has been to secure the financial sustainability of the program. Efforts to expand fundraising have been necessary to both support scholarships necessary to attract diverse, competitive applicants and help their high-quality capstone projects bring about community impact.

A third area of priority identified was maintaining the relevance and timeliness of the program's course curricula. The director now works to engage the advisory board and external stakeholders in adapting the certificate's existing courses to adjust to changes in the field.

The fourth and final areas of priority for forward progress identified regard managed growth of the program. Options for expanding, both horizontally in the number of credits available within the certificate, and vertically into a potential terminal degree program, are being considered.

A limitation of this program self-evaluation is that it is just that. The status of the authors as program faculty and alumni entails an inherent positive bias toward the certificate program and its participants" achievements that may affect the objectivity of our evaluation of the program's outcomes. However, this same perspective also has allowed us to provide a more nuanced subjective account from within of the program's execution and trajectory.

While our recommendations may serve as a blueprint for other institutions interested in developing similar programs, it is important to note that our particular, auspicious circumstances may not necessarily be easily applicable or replicable outside of our unique, specific context. For instance, the success of our situation was in part due to a receptive and progressive private university administration open to advancing of the concerns, needs, and visions of the LGBT community. The university in which our program has launched has many departments that have been crucial assets to the program's ability to build and unite a diverse faculty, drawing from a public health school ,a medical school, a policy school, a women's studies department, and two doctoral-level programs in mental health.

CONCLUSION

The creation of the LGBTHP&P graduate certificate program was undertaken by faculty at the GWU to meet the growing need for training healthcare professionals equipped to serve the LGBT community in efforts to improve access to culturally competent healthcare and to combat disparities in healthcare for the LGBT population. Program faculty, alumni, and students have reviewed the progress of the program after the first two cohorts of students now have completed the program to assess successes, challenges, ands areas for improvement, to map a plan forward, and to offer insight to others seeking to create similar programs at other institutions.

Multiple sources of data support an impression that the program has been largely successful, having graduated two consecutive classes of students whose experiences in the program have been predominantly positive. From student and faculty feedback, changes were made to program curriculum and residency programming. Additionally, efforts were made to improve fundraising to support program development and student scholarships. Substantial attention has been given to the capstone project, by providing increased support, structure, and training to students to help improve the quality of their projects and to better document their impact on the community—the program's ultimate goal, whose demonstrable impact this chapter has worked to document.

REFERENCES

Baker, K., & Cray, A. (2012). *Ensuring benefits parity and gender identity nondiscrimination in essential health benefits.* Washington, DC: Center for American Progress.

Bumiller, E. (2011, July 22). Obama ends "Don't Ask, Don't Tell" policy. *The New York Times.* Retrieved from http://www.nytimes.com/2011/07/23/us/23military.html

Campbell, D. (2013). Ethnocentrism of disciplines and the fish-scale model of omniscience. In S. J. Derry, C. D. Schunn, & M. A. Gernsbacher (Eds.), *Interdisciplinary collaboration: An emerging cognitive science* (pp. 3–22). New York, NY: Psychology Press.

Durso, L. E., Baker, K., & Cray, A. (2013). *LGBT communities and the Affordable Care Act: Findings from a national survey.* Washington, DC: Center for American Progress.

Gallup. (2016). *Marriage: Gallup historical trends.* Retrieved from http://www.gallup.com/poll/117328/marriage.aspx

Gonzales, G. (2014). Same-sex marriage—A prescription for better health. *New England Journal of Medicine, 370,* 1373–1376.

Gonzales, G., & Blewett, L. A. (2013). Disparities in health insurance among children with same-sex parents. *Pediatrics, 132,* 703–711.

Gonzales, G., Moltz, R., & King, M. (2014). Health insurance coverage for same-sex couples: Disparities and trends under DOMA. In V. L. Harvey & T. Heinz Housel (Eds.), *Health care disparities and the LGBT population,* (pp. 87–106). New York, NY: Lexington Books.

Hager, C. (2013). *Memorandum for secretaries of the military departments under secretary of defense for personnel and readiness: Extending benefits to the same-sex spouses of military members.* Washington, DC: Department of Defense.

Health Professionals Advancing LGBT Equality (GLMA) and LGBT Health Experts. (2001). *Healthy people 2010 companion document for lesbian, gay, bisexual, and transgender (LGBT) health.* San Francisco, CA: Gay and Lesbian Medical Association.

Institute of Medicine (IOM): Committee on Lesbian, Gay, Bisexual, and Transgender Health Issues and Research Gaps and Opportunities, Board on the Health of Select Populations, Institute of Medicine. (2011). *The health of lesbian, gay, bisexual, and transgender people: Building a foundation for better understanding.* Washington, DC: The National Academies Press.

Lambda Legal. (2015, June 26). Victory! In landmark ruling Supreme Court strikes down bans on marriage for same-sex couples. Retrieved from http://www.lambdalegal.org/blog/20150626_henry-victory

LGBT Health Graduate Certificate, Columbian College of Arts and Sciences. (2014). WEBCAST—"Global LGBT Health & Human Rights". Retrieved from http://lgbt.columbian.gwu.edu/webcast

Misra, S., Harvey, R. H., Stokols, D., Pine, K. H., Fuqua, J., Shokair, S. M., & Whiteley, J. M. (2009). Evaluating an interdisciplinary undergraduate training program in health promotion research. *American Journal of Preventative Medicine, 36,* 358–365.

O'Donnell, A., & Derry, S. (2013). Cognitive processes in interdisciplinary groups: Problems & possibilities. In S. J. Derry, C. D. Schunn, & M. A. Gernsbacher (Eds.), *Interdisciplinary collaboration: An emerging cognitive science* (pp. 51–84). New York, NY: Psychology Press.

Perez-Stable, E. J., & National Institute on Minority Health and Health Disparities. (2016, October 6). *Director's message: Sexual and gender minorities formally designated as a healthy disparity population for research purposes.* Bethesda, MD: National Institutes of Health. Retrieved from http://www.nimhd.nih.gov/about/directors-corner/message.html

U.S. Department of Health and Human Services. (2000). *A systematic approach to health improvement.* Washington, DC: U.S. Government Printing Office.

U.S. Department of Health and Human Services. (2010). *Healthy people 2020: Framework.* Washington, DC: U.S. Department of Health and Human Services, Office of Disease Prevention and Health Promotion. Retrieved from https://www.healthypeople.gov/sites/default/files/HP2020Framework.pdf

13

Going Forward: Summary and New Directions

Richard Ruth and Erik Santacruz

This book has evolved and morphed in the course of its development.

When we were first asked to bring together a book about new developments in LGBT psychology and mental health, we anticipated a collection of essays that would be primarily celebratory, a marking of the field's post–coming out coming of age. We knew there was much to be celebrated in the flowering of LGBT psychology. It seemed a simple-enough task to gather relevant strands together.

Reviewing the contributions to this volume, there is a part of our initial vision we take pride and pleasure in reaffirming. We hope you will share our sense that, in their diversity, richness, and vision, the chapters in this book are indeed to be celebrated.

However, as we have collaborated with the contributing writers in the process of giving shape to and sharpening the focus of their respective chapters, we found something unexpected—that is, taken together, this volume's offerings mark (and advance) less a coming-of-age and more a vital, generative, exciting maturation of LGBT psychology and mental health. In thinking about this unexpected unfolding—how it came to be and its implications for what the further development of LGBT psychology might bring—we have come to a few thoughts we would like to share.

We start by coming back to something we set out in this volume's introduction, but that we appreciate in a new way at the end of this book's journey—that it was our intention to identify psychologists, and professionals from related fields of endeavor, who we felt had something very important to say about LGBT psychology and mental health; and we wanted to create supportive, facilitative space for them to say what they had to say in the way they wanted to say it. We intentionally wanted our writers to write in their own voices and idioms. We, also, intentionally, wanted to bring together colleagues from different branches of psychology and related fields, and with different "takes" on psychology and mental health, and to include both emerging/early career and established/more senior colleagues. We wanted, and believe that with the help of our writer collaborators we have achieved, a book that is diverse, in multiple dimensions. The contributors to this volume are of diverse ethnicities, social-class backgrounds, sexual orientations, and gender identities/expressions, and are diverse as well in their work focus (clinical, research, policy), work settings, theoretical orientations and methodologies.

In important ways, this reflects an essential characteristic of LGBT communities and LGBT culture. Like LGBT venues, historically and today, this book is a kind of crossroads, not readily found in other spheres of society (Bérubé, 2010; Chauncey, 1994; Kennedy & Davis, 2014; Lewin & Leap, 2002; Lockard, 1986; Stryker, 2008; Walters, 2003). By logical extension, this imports into, and shapes, research, policy, and clinical spheres of professional life for those involved with LGBT mental health. And that is essential to understanding something intrinsic and important to the nature of LGBT psychology—that it makes space for, affirms, embraces, and learns from its own diversity. If you detect that unifying sensibility in the tone and between the lines of the chapters in this book, it is not inadvertent or tangential.

We find this crossroads quality not just among but within many, if not all, the contributions in this volume. The writers included here draw on a diversity of approaches to psychology in their thinking and their work, something not often seen in literature reviews in our field's journals or in edited volumes that come together with a shared, but too often overly narrow, perspective. Here, instead, we have clinicians drawing on diverse strands of psychological thinking that they find of use in their work with LGBT clients and communities. In closer proximity than is often the case in collections of psychological texts, you have encountered here quantitative and qualitative researchers; scientists and clinicians and policy professionals; and clinicians with depth of engagement with research and researchers with depth of engagement with clinical "real life," all in dialog with each other. You have also encountered a community of contributors that is explicitly and intentionally lesbian, gay, bisexual, and transgender. Not all the views and findings presented in this volume concur, but all are engaged in appreciative, respectful interchange.

We noted in this volume's introduction that LGBT psychology, over the course of its development, has shifted from a predominant focus on helping non-LGBT audiences understand LGBT experience to a focus on an LGBT psychology not just by but for, arising from, and grounded in the cultures of LGBT people. The writers in this volume exemplify, extend, and in places point to the emerging future directions of this essential shift. Our contributors are a group of highly capable professionals and talented emerging professionals, with masterful, sophisticated grasp of their fields' (and subfields') theories, methods, literatures, and findings; but they also are comfortable taking necessary freedom to challenge established views. A number of contributors here use innovative methodologies and theoretical frameworks. Several, for example, describe lines of research, clinical work, and policy development guided by LGBT community input and collaborations. Many writers here confront biases outside (and sometimes inside) LGBT psychology, contesting, for example, the tendency in some influential lines of research to ignore or minimize transgender particularities, and problematizing terminology that has been found constricting and oppressive, such as the assumption that "LGB" and "transgender" are necessarily mutually exclusive categories. While no one writing here pathologizes lesbianism, gayness, bisexuality, or being transgender or gender nonconforming—at times, reading these chapters, it is (thankfully) difficult to remember how prevalent and hegemonic these attitudes once were, not so long ago—this volume's contributors go beyond a nonpathologizing stance to describe specific characteristics and pathways of resilience, creativity, vision, and self-determination in LGBT people and communities. Ways LGBT experience continues to be affected by hatred, biases, discrimination, danger, and violence are given due weight here; but so are the ways LGBT communities resist and thrive. The language about LGBT *communities*, plural, is intentional—not just privileged and European American LGBT communities and experiences are represented here, but perspectives of African American, Latino/a, Asian American, and working-class LGBT people are given prominence as well. We feel we have succeeded in creating a diverse, and inclusive, collection of texts and that that reflects something vital, robust, essential, and visionary in LGBT psychology today.

That said, we are also well aware that not every topic we had originally hoped to include in this book is represented here. Missing, among other important and deserving topics, are a thorough treatments of the history of LGBT psychology; critical appraisal of the evolution of the minority stress model as applied to LGBT experience; research and clinical explorations of the particular experiences of LGBT immigrants; the range of contemporary developments in LGBT social and community psychology; what has been learned about the experiences of LGBT homeless youth and the services that are helping them; and more in-depth explorations of what has been learned about adapting specific approaches to clinical treatment (cognitive-behavioral therapy; family systems therapy; group therapies; psychoanalytic and psychodynamic therapies; newer approaches, such as harm reduction, mindfulness, acceptance and commitment therapy; and dialectical behavioral therapy) to the cultures and needs of LGBT communities. If the list seems long, the list of topics it did not occur to us to be curious about is probably even longer.

In some ways, our editorial regrets about what is not included here are prosaic and grounded in pragmatic realities—some people whose contributions we had hoped to include were not able to contribute; for other topics, it was difficult for us to identify potential contributors with relevant background and expertise. But something unexpected came up as chapters took shape and began to come together, and we think it is relevant and worthy of comment.

In looking over an early draft of the volume as a whole, our publisher commented that this was a book of "deep science." The comment caught us by surprise but engaged our imagination and helped us articulate an aspect of our experience working to bring this book together. What LGBT psychology is discovering, in its and ever-expanding range of branches, routinely reaches into transformative depths. So our original fantasy—that 20 or so smart people would quickly and happily write crisp, assured reviews of 20 or so well-understood sets of established wisdom in LGBT psychology—proved not to match the "map" of our field at this point in its evolution. So much new information is emerging (and at such a rapid pace!), and so much of it challenges previous assumptions and conventions, that our chapters are denser than we had originally contemplated. A corollary is that a number of potential contributors were so immersed in their consuming work of clinical and research discoveries that stopping to try to survey the state of their subfields was something they could not pull away from their offices, hospitals, and laboratories to contemplate producing.

But, to paraphrase Tina Turner as she once put it, "There's just one thing—that is, you see, somehow [we] never ever seem to do nothing completely nice and easy." (Take a break from reading, if you like, and listen for yourself: https://www.youtube.com/watch?v=UJGoNeM3WzY.) As we stated in the introduction, we did not set out to produce an encyclopedic volume. Rather, our hope was to capture some of the living fire of LGBT psychology and mental health—how leading contributors to our field think and work; a sampling of our field's methods and discoveries; and our emerging, widely shared beliefs, directions, and aspirations. Our notion of inclusivity is not that every important idea and finding will be represented and summarized here, but that what made its way into this book will give a sense of LGBT psychology's current range and possibilities. If we have succeeded in conveying something of that to our readers, and if it offers something of value to our readers' professional and activist work with LGBT populations and communities, we feel we, and our contributors, have succeeded in a shared, important goal.

* * * *

One final point, perhaps inevitable in a volume of this nature: By the time this book reaches you, some of its content will be out of date. New discoveries in LGBT psychology and mental health emerge in geometrically increasing profusion. Google cited almost 900,000 more entries on LGBT psychology two days before this manuscript was submitted than it had a year earlier—more than a doubling of the number of publications. Several of our contributors wanted to amend their chapters as we approached our deadline, not because they discovered they had been careless or overlooked something, but because key new findings had emerged, some of them challenging what seemed to be true just a year or so previously. We accommodated as many of these last-minute emendations as we could, but it was impossible to update chapters more thoroughly or systematically.

But the issue goes beyond that.

We have not surveyed our contributors, but it is a safe bet that few of them are happy with the result of the November, 2016, national (and state) elections. Many of the hard-won advances in LGBT well-being and LGBT legal rights and protections celebrated here—advances LGBT psychology has not just documented and studied but also contributed to bringing about—are being questioned, if not challenged, and in some cases assaulted, by the policy proposals, initiatives, and trial balloons of the national and state governments that have come to power in the most recent election cycle. Laws and government policies that constrict or threaten LGBT rights are emerging rapidly. Our communities are angry, worried, and hurt and have every right to be. This book emerges at a time of strategic mobilizations.

In this sense, drawing on the central, unifying findings from this volume—that psychological science and practice-based evidence (Barkham & Mellor-Clark, 2003; Fox, 2003) show definitively that pathologizing, denied rights, and prejudices damage LGBT people and that personal and communal self-determination and empowerment, and full rights and respect, unleash the generative potential in LGBT people and communities—is more important than ever. So we hope that this book will inspire not just continuing advances in LGBT psychological theory, research, and practice, but also the informed activism the current political and historical junctures demand. Surely this is a time when LGBT psychology and LGBT movements need to grow closer and stay united. We hope the contributions in this book will help make that happen.

But there is a still-farther shore. Policies and laws confront evolving LGBT facts on the ground. Yes, the numbers of LGBT people facing violent assault every day are large, enraging, and unacceptable (Berrill, 1990; Rothman, Exner, & Baughman, 2011; Stotzer, 2009). But it is equally the case that, in no small measure due to advances in LGBT psychological understanding, young LGBT people today are having experiences far different from those of generations past. There is robust evidence that LGBT adolescents now coming into awareness of their identities in most cases do not suffer the rejection and the depth and damaging intensity of oppression that shaped the trajectories of previous generations (Savin-Williams, 2016). Gay-straight alliances are now an established, and empowering, part of the school landscape, in many localities both urban and rural, and transform the experience of LGBT youth (Craig, Tucker, & Wagner,

2008; Russell, Muraco, Subramaniam, & Laub, 2009). The voices and contributions of resilient and self-determined transgender youth are being documented not just in our psychological literature (Singh, 2013) but also in prominent, and affirming, inclusion in mass media.

So our book will be somewhat outdated by the time it comes out for an additional good reason—the world is changing for the better, and both forces who question or oppose LGBT rights and freedoms and those, in and beyond psychology, who champion the blossoming of LGBT possibilities carry out agendas amid that grounding reality. From this vantage point, what we offer in this book is not a historical snapshot but perhaps a capturing-in-time of an LGBT psychology that is aware of where it comes from, both proud of and dissatisfied with where it is now, focused on meeting the demands of our full research and policy portfolios and our commitment to serve the diverse constituencies who seek our professional help and support, and looking, always, to a future beyond the wildest dreams we can imagine but that we steadily help to build.

REFERENCES

Barkham, M., & Mellor-Clark, J. (2003). Bridging evidence-based practice and practice-based evidence: Developing a rigorous and relevant knowledge for the psychological therapies. *Clinical Psychology & Psychotherapy*, 10, 319–327.

Berrill, K. T. (1990). Anti-gay violence and victimization in the United States: An overview. *Journal of Interpersonal Violence*, 5, 274–294.

Bérubé, A. (2010). *Coming out under fire: The history of gay men and women in World War II.* Raleigh, NC: University of North Carolina Press.

Chauncey, G. (1994). *Gay New York: Gender, urban culture, and the making of the gay male world, 1890–1940.* New York, NY: Basic Books.

Craig, S. L., Tucker, E. W., & Wagner, E. F. (2008). Empowering lesbian, gay, bisexual, and transgender youth: Lessons learned from a safe schools summit. *Journal of Gay & Lesbian Social Services*, 20, 237–252.

Fox, N. J. (2003). Practice-based evidence: Towards collaborative and transgressive research. *Sociology*, 37, 81–102.

Kennedy, E. L., & Davis, M. D. (2014). *Boots of leather, slippers of gold: The history of a lesbian community* (2nd ed.). New York, NY: Routledge.

Lewin, E., & Leap, W. L. (Eds.). (2002). *Out in theory: The emergence of lesbian and gay anthropology.* Chicago, IL: University of Illinois Press.

Lockard, D. (1986). The lesbian community: An anthropological approach. *Journal of Homosexuality*, 11, 83–95.

Rothman, E. F., Exner, D., & Baughman, A. L. (2011). The prevalence of sexual assault against people who identify as gay, lesbian, or bisexual in the United States: A systematic review. *Trauma, Violence, & Abuse*, 12, 55–66.

Russell, S. T., Muraco, A., Subramaniam, A., & Laub, C. (2009). Youth empowerment and high school gay-straight alliances. *Journal of Youth and Adolescence*, 38, 891–903.

Savin-Williams, R. C. (2016). Being who I am: Young men on being gay. *Becoming who I am.* Cambridge, MA: Harvard University Press.

Singh, A. A. (2013). Transgender youth of color and resilience: Negotiating oppression and finding support. *Sex Roles, 68,* 690–702.

Stotzer, R. L. (2009). Violence against transgender people: A review of United States data. *Aggression and Violent Behavior, 14,* 170–179.

Stryker, S. (2008). *Transgender history.* Berkeley, CA: Seal Press.

Walters, S. D. (2003). *All the rage: The story of gay visibility in America.* Chicago, IL: University of Chicago Press.

About the Editors

RICHARD RUTH, PhD, is associate professor of clinical psychology and former director of clinical training at The George Washington University PsyD program and founding/core faculty of the university's LGBT Health Policy and Practice graduate certificate program, where he has taught one of the first U.S. university courses in transgender health. A clinical psychologist, psychoanalyst, neuropsychologist, and family therapist, he is also on the faculty of the Washington School of Psychiatry and in private practice. Dr. Ruth's research and theoretical and clinical scholarship have been wide-ranging; he has published on cross-cultural psychotherapy and psychological assessment, forensic psychology, disability issues, trauma, mental health ethics, LGBT issues, deafness and AIDS, and the need for a transgender-affirmative psychoanalysis. He has published two previous books, *Sometimes You Just Want to Feel like a Human Being: Case Studies in Empowering Psychotherapy with People with Disabilities* (with Mary Ann Blotzer) and *Healing after Parent Loss in Childhood and Adolescence: Therapeutic Interventions and Theoretical Considerations* (with Phyllis Cohen and K. Mark Sossin). He has been on the board of directors of Division 39/Psychoanalysis of the American Psychological Association and has represented Division 39 on the APA Council of Representatives. Dr. Ruth has taught and lectured throughout the United States and in the Caribbean, Latin America, Europe, Africa, and Australia. Bilingual in Spanish and bicultural, he is especially proud to be among the first generation of legally married gay men.

ERIK SANTACRUZ, EdD, is a clinical psychologist in training at The George Washington University. His current work addresses intergenerational HIV-related trauma in families affected by the HIV virus and the unique challenges that arise to the efficacy of interventions aimed at addressing depression, medication adherence, and health promotion in this population. Dr. Santacruz is a graduate of Teachers College, Columbia University, where he earned a doctorate in health education with a focus in addressing the health needs of LGBT youth of color. In May, 2014, he was named a Distinguished Fellow at Columbia

University's Research Group on Disparities in Health (RGDH), where he maintains active participation in research pertaining to substance dependence
observed in the general population and research that utilizes integrated theory
to explore the extent to which young men who have sex with men perceive,
respond to, and cope with racism as active Internet participants accessing social
networking sites for meeting romantic and sexual partners. Dr. Santacruz has
trained with the renowned sex therapist and author Dr. Ruth Westheimer;
clinical psychologist, radio host, media commentator, and well known journalist
Dr. Judy Kuriansky; and renowned minority psychology and addictions expert
Dr. Barbara C. Wallace.

About the Contributors

CHRISTIAN D. CHAN, PhD, NCC, is an assistant professor of counseling at Idaho State University. His interests revolve around intersectionality of cultural and social identity; multiculturalism in counseling, supervision, and counselor education; social justice; career development; critical research methods; acculturative stress; intergenerational conflict; and cultural factors in identity development and socialization.

DEANNA N. COR, PhD, LPC, is an assistant professor of counseling at Portland State University. Her research focuses on facilitating multicultural counseling competencies in students, specifically for those who aspire to work with clients identifying as trans and gender nonconforming. Her clinical specialties include working with LGBTQ+ clients and exploring life transitions and relational concerns.

MERLE CUNNINGHAM, MD, was a family physician with over 35 years of experience in healthcare management. He was network medical director of the Sunset Park/Lutheran Family Health Centers in Brooklyn, New York, for almost 20 years and was on the faculty of The George Washington University Milken Institute School of Public Health.

COLIN J. DAVIS studied biology and English at the College of William & Mary and developed an interest in HIV, community health, and LGBT care through The George Washington University's graduate certificate program in LGBT Health Policy and Practice. He is currently working with the research department and STD clinic of Whitman-Walker Health in Washington, DC.

TAMARA DEUTSCH is a master's student in forensic mental health counseling at John Jay College of Criminal Justice, City University of New York.

TANYA ERAZO has two master's degrees and is completing her PhD in clinical psychology. She is also a certified alcohol and substance abuse counselor in training (CASAC-T) in New York state.

STEPHEN L. FORSSELL, PhD, is founding director of the graduate certificate in LGBT Health Policy & Practice and codirector of the Institute for Health Promotion in Underserved Populations at The George Washington University. His research investigates male couple partner relationship quality and parenting in adoptive same-sex-headed families.

SHARON J. GLEZEN, MD, FACP, is an internist and staff physician at the Center for Health and Wellbeing, University of Vermont. While a student in the first cohort of The George Washington University LGBT Health Policy and Practice certificate program, she was staff physician and medical chief at the University Health Service, University of Rochester.

MELISSA J. GREY, PhD, a licensed psychologist in Michigan, is passionate about psychology and social justice. She is an associate professor of psychology at Monroe County Community College and practices at the Integrative Empowerment Group. She has been active in local, state, and federal advocacy through community and professional associations.

HEATHER HAN is a master's student in forensic psychology at John Jay College of Criminal Justice, City University of New York.

SHANE HENISE is currently an EdM candidate in the psychological counseling program at Teachers College, Columbia University. His research interests include gender studies, experiences of diverse sexualities, transgender microaggressions, and the intersection of gender identity and sexual orientation.

KEVIN L. NADAL, PhD, is professor of psychology at the City University of New York (CUNY), the executive director of CUNY's Center for LGBTQ Studies, president of the Asian American Psychological Association, and a cofounder of LGBTQ Scholars of Color Network. He is a leading expert on understanding the impact of microaggressions.

BLAINE PARRISH, PhD, is an advocate for healthcare equality for sexual minorities. An expert in the fields of leadership, organization, and management, Dr. Parrish's interests focus on community-based organizations that provide public health services to vulnerable and underserved populations.

TIMOTHY POPANZ, PhD, practices clinical psychology and integrative healthcare in Seattle, Washington. He has advocated for programs and policies that improve health outcomes and access to care for the LGBTQ community for more than 25 years. Dr. Popanz is a former president of the Washington State Psychological Association.

SHARA SAND, PsyD, is a licensed clinical psychologist, an associate professor of psychology at LaGuardia Community College, and director of counseling at Manhattan School of Music, and she maintains a private practice in New York City.

RIDDHI SANDIL, PhD, is an assistant professor of practice and program coordinator of the EdM Program in Psychological Counseling at Teachers College, Columbia University. Sandil's research and clinical interests include minority stress, LGBTQ issues in counseling, counseling expectations of South Asian populations, and complex trauma and its impact on the well-being of gender minorities.

RONALD L. SCHLITTLER, MA, is program coordinator at the American Psychological Association's Office on Sexual Orientation and Gender Diversity in Washington, DC. He holds a master's in international policy and practice and was in the first cohort of The George Washington University's LGBT Health Policy & Practice graduate certificate program.

JULIA SCHULMAN is a master's student in forensic mental health counseling at John Jay College of Criminal Justice, City University of New York.

CARL G. STREED, JR., MD, is an advocate, researcher, and physician to lesbian, gay, bisexual, transgender, and queer communities, working always in concert, never solo, in moving forward the needs of those most vulnerable.

NATHANIEL SWIFT-ERSLEV, RN, holds a BA in sociology and a BSN from the University of Pittsburgh. In 2014, he completed The George Washington University's LGBT Health Policy and Practice graduate certificate program. He currently works at Sibley Memorial Hospital, in Washington, DC.

BARBARA C. WALLACE, PhD, is a tenured professor, Department of Health and Behavior Studies, Teachers College, Columbia University. She has been honored as a Fellow by Division 50 (Addictive Behaviors) and Division 45 (Society for the Psychological Study of Ethnic Minority Issues) of the American Psychological Association for outstanding contributions to psychology.

ALYSSA N. ZUCKER, PhD, is the Vada A. Yeomans chair of women's studies at the University of Florida Center for Gender, Sexualities, and Women's Studies Research. She pursues a social justice research and teaching program, centered on the role of structural and interpersonal discrimination in shaping health outcomes.

About the Practical and Applied Psychology Series and Series Editor

The books in this series address topics immediately relevant to issues in human psychology, behavior, and emotion. Topics include a wide range of subjects, from the psychology of Black boys and adolescents, to new strategies against terrorism, ecopsychology, and insights for living in an environmentally traumatized world.

Series editor **Judy Kuriansky**, PhD, is a licensed clinical psychologist and adjunct faculty in the Department of Clinical Psychology at Teachers College, Columbia University and also in the Department of Psychiatry at the Columbia University College of Physicians and Surgeons. Dr. Kuriansky is a UN representative for the International Association of Applied Psychology and for the World Council for Psychotherapy. She is also visiting professor at the Beijing University Health Sciences Center, a fellow of the American Psychological Association (APA), founder of the APA Media Psychology Division, a widely known journalist for CBS, CNBC, LIFETIME, and A&E, and a regular weekly columnist for the *New York Daily News*. She has also been a syndicated radio talk show host for more than 20 years. Authors may reach Dr. Kuriansky at DrJudyK@aol.com.

Index